THE LAW OF INTERVENING CAUSATION

This book is dedicated to my wife Chandra Kala Rai and to the memory of the late Right Honourable Bora Laskin who served as the Chief Justice of the Supreme Court of Canada between 1973 and 1984

The Law of Intervening Causation

DOUGLAS HODGSON
The University of Western Australia

ASHGATE

© Douglas Hodgson 2008

All rights reserved. No part of this publication may be reproduced, stored in a retrieval system or transmitted in any form or by any means, electronic, mechanical, photocopying, recording or otherwise without the prior permission of the publisher.

Douglas Hodgson has asserted his right under the Copyright, Designs and Patents Act, 1988, to be identified as the author of this work.

Published by
Ashgate Publishing Limited
Gower House
Croft Road
Aldershot
Hampshire GU11 3HR
England

Ashgate Publishing Company
Suite 420
101 Cherry Street
Burlington, VT 05401-4405
USA

Ashgate website: http://www.ashgate.com

British Library Cataloguing in Publication Data
Hodgson, Douglas
   The law of intervening causation
   1. Liability (Law) 2. Causation
   I. Title
   346'.03

Library of Congress Cataloging-in-Publication Data
Hodgson, Douglas.
   The law of intervening causation / by Douglas Hodgson.
      p. cm.
   Includes index.
   ISBN 978-0-7546-7366-8
   1. Liability (Law). 2. Causation. I. Title.

   K579.L5H63 2008
   346.02--dc22
                                                                                    2007049172

ISBN 978 0 7546 7366 8

Mixed Sources
Product group from well-managed forests and other controlled sources
www.fsc.org Cert no. SA-COC-1565
© 1996 Forest Stewardship Council

Printed and bound in Great Britain by
MPG Books Ltd, Bodmin, Cornwall.

Contents

List of Cases	*vii*
Acknowledgements	*xvii*

PART I Introduction

1	Introduction	3
2	Early Judicial Development of Intervening Causation Law	13

PART II The Legal Tests

3	Reasonable Foreseeability	31
4	Unreasonableness/Abnormality	51
5	Voluntary and Deliberate Human Action	69
6	Probability	91
7	Scope of Risk	101

PART III Operative Contexts

8	Intervening Negligent Acts and Omissions	121
9	Extraordinary Natural Phenomena, Coincidences and Animals	133
10	Maritime Incidents	147
11	The Suicide Cases	155
12	Professional Malpractice	169
13	Rescue of Persons and Property	189
14	Children	199
15	Escaping from Danger and Inconvenience	209
16	Negligence Causing Susceptibility to Later Harm	219
17	Miscellaneous Operative Contexts	227

PART IV Conclusion

18	The Influence of Contributory Negligence and Apportionment Legislation on Intervening Causation Issues	245
19	The Inter-relationship Between Remoteness of Damage and *Novus Actus Interveniens*	253
20	Conclusion	259

Index   *267*

List of Cases

England and Scotland

A.C. Billings & Sons Ltd *v* Riden (1958) 196 213
Adams *v* The Lancashire and Yorkshire Railway Company (1869) 15; 44; 193; 197; 222
.... 52–3, 56, 63, 214, 216, 245–6
Aldham *v* United Dairies (London) Ltd [1940] 125 142
Algol Maritime Limited *v* Acori [1997] 163 179
Alphacell Ltd *v* Woodward [1972] 120 137
Arneil *v* Paterson [1931] 125
Attorney General *v* Hartwell (British Virgin Islands) [2004] 84 95
Banque Bruxelles Lambert S.A. *v* Eagle Star Insurance Co. Ltd [1995] 30; 122 .... 38, 139
Barber *v* British Road Services (1964) 224
Barings plc (in liquidation) *v* Coopers & Lybrand (a firm) [2003] 111
Bird *v* Holbrook (1828) 12; 60; 61 .... 16, 70, 71
Blyth *v* The Birmingham Waterworks (1856) 117 134
Bower *v* Meggitt and Jones (1916) 155
Brandon *v* Osborne Garrett & Co. Ltd [1924] 81; 173; 195 .... 92–3, 191, 212
British Columbia Electric Railway Co. Ltd *v* Loach [1916] 4 7
Burrows *v* The March Gas and Coke Company (1870) (1872) 16 20–1
Butterfield *v* Forrester (1809) 222 245
Carmarthenshire County Council *v* Lewis [1955] 214 234
Carslogie Steamship Co. Ltd *v* Royal Norwegian Government [1952] 121; 132 138–7
Cavanagh *v* London Transport Executive (1956) 140 157
Church *v* Dugdale & Adams Ltd (1929) 139
Clark *v* Chambers (1878) 17; 80; 185; 209 .... 21–2, 23, 91–2, 202, 228
Clayards *v* Dethick (1848) 13; 44; 61; 195; 208 .... 18, 52, 71, 213, 227–8
Cobb *v* Great Western Railway [1894] 91 103
Collins *v* The Middle Level Commissioners (1869) 90 103
Collinson *v* Manvers Main Collieries Ltd (1937) 128 145
Colvilles *v* Devine [1969] 44
Corr *v* IBC Vehicles Ltd [2006] 141; 233 .... 158n16
Coulter *v* Coltness Iron Co. [1938] 139
Cox *v* Burbidge (1863) 124 141–2
Cutler *v* United Dairies (London), Ltd [1933] 62; 173; 175 .... 191–2, 191N22, 193
Davies *v* Mann (1842) 223 246
Davis *v* St Mary's Demolition Co. [1954] 188
Dixon *v* Bell (1816) 11; 90; 183 .... 15–16, 102, 116, 200, 237
Dominion Natural Gas Co. Ltd *v* Collins and Perkins [1909] 2; 59; 61; 217 .... 69, 237
Donoghue *v* Stevenson [1932] 213
Donovan *v* Union Cartage Co. [1933] 184
Doolan *v* Henry Hope & Sons Ltd (1918) 128

Dulieu v White & Sons [1901] 148
Dunham v Clare (1902) 20; 45; 127; 138 .... 24–5, 53, 155–6
D'Urso v Sanson [1939] 179.. 196
Emeh v Kensington and Chelsea and Westminster Area Health Authority [1984] 43; 49; 75; 167; 238... 57–8, 86n112, 184
Engelhart v Farrant & Co. [1897] 19 24
Environment Agency (Formerly National Rivers Authority) v Empress Car Co. (Abertillery) Ltd [1999] 6; 65; 89; 116; 118; 123 ....76, 101, 109, 134, 135–6, 140
Forbes v Merysyide Fire and Civil Defence Authority [2002] 94; 163.................... 106, 180–1
Froom v Butcher [1976] 228
Glanville v Sutton [1928] 125
Glasgow Corporation v Muir [1943] 58
Glasgow Corporation v Taylor [1922] 183
Grant v Sun Shipping Co. Ltd [1948] 213 233
Groom v Selby [2001] 167
Halestrap v Gregory (1895) 209
Harrison v The Great Northern Railway Company (1864) 119... 136
Harvey v Road Haulage Executive [1952] 224
Haynes v Harwood [1935] 5; 62; 82; 174; 184.. 8, 73, 93, 94, 97, 192
Herschtal v Stewart & Ardern Ltd [1940] 115; 213... 131, 232–3
Hobbs v London and South Western Ry Co. (1875) 4
Hoey v Felton (1861) 14; 230... 18–19, 254
Hogan v Bentinck West Hartley Collieries (Owners) Ltd [1949] 4; 5; 161; 207; 240...............
.... 178–9, 225, 264
Holgate v Lancashire Mental Hospitals Board [1937] 215
Home Office v Dorset Yacht Co. Ltd [1970] 27; 63; 80; 83; 214; 231 ....
.... 34–5, 36, 74, 91, 94, 97, 99, 255
Hughes v Lord Advocate [1963] 25
Hughes v Macfie (1863) 61; 184; 222... 71n24, 201–2, 245
Humber Oil Terminal Trustee Ltd v Owners of the Ship 'Sivand' [1998] 31; 50; 122.......... 38
Hyett v Great Western Railway Company [1947] 46; 82 .... 54, 93
Illidge v Goodwin (1831) 13.. 17–18
Imperial Chemical Industries Ltd v Shatwell [1965] 228
In Re Etherington and the Lancashire and Yorkshire Accident Insurance Company [1909] 7; 127.. 9, 143–4
Isitt v The Railway Passengers Assurance Company (1889) 126.. 143
Jebson v Ministry of Defence [2000] 228
Jones v Boyce (1816) 11; 44; 193... 16, 20, 52, 211, 214
Jones v Jones [1985] 210
Kimball v Butler Bros (1910) 171
Kirkham v Chief Constable of the Greater Manchester Police [1990] 141 158–9
Knight v Home Office [1990] 141
Knightley v Johns [1982] 29; 83; 109; 113; 176; 232............ 36–7, 57, 94, 125, 129, 194, 256
Lamb v Camden London Borough Council [1981] 2; 28; 64; 93; 232; 23...........................
.... 4, 35, 57, 75, 106, 256
Lathall v Joyce & Son [1939] 125
Latham v Johnson & Nephew, Ltd [1913] 25; 182... 33
Lynch v Knight (1861) 44... 52
Lynch v Nurdin (1841) 12; 90; 183; 225 .... 102, 200–1, 248
Malone v Cayzer Irvine & Co. (1908) 139 156

Manchester Corporation v Markland [1936] 117
Mangan v Atherton (1866)185 202
Marriott v Maltby Main Colliery Co. (1920) 139
Marshall v Caledonian Railway (1899) 63
Martin v Stanborough (1924) 188
McAuley v London Transport Executive [1958] 115 131
McDowall v Great Western Railway Company [1903] 13; 186 203
McFarlane v Tayside Health Board [1999] 167 184
McKew v Holland & Hannen & Cubitts (Scotland) Ltd [1970] 2; 26; 48; 77; 109; 204 ....
 .... 33–4, 56, 63, 88, 125, 185n80, 221, 222–3
Meah v McCreamer [1985] 65; 232 .... 75–6, 256–7
Meah v McCreamer (No. 2) [1986] 65; 233 76
Muirhead v Industrial Tank Specialities Ltd [1986] 113 129
Newton v Edgerley [1959] 82; 186 .... 93n14, 203–4
Nichols v Marsland (1876) 119 136
Northwestern Utilities Ltd v London Guarantee and Accident Co. Ltd [1936] 91 103
Overseas Tankship (UK) Ltd v Morts Dock & Engineering Co. Ltd (The Wagon Mound (No.
 1)) [1961] 8; 26; 229 .... 10, 33, 253
Overseas Tankship (UK) Ltd v The Miller Steamship Co. Pty Ltd (The Wagon Mound
 (No. 2)) [1967] 25; 28; 42; 239 36
Owners of Steamship Singleton Abbey v Owners of Steamship Paludina [1927] 62; 131 ....
 .... 148–9, 153
Perry v Kendricks Transport Co. Ltd [1970] 63
Philco Radio and Television Corporation Ltd v J. Spurling Ltd [1949] 2; 4; 60; 91; 108; 219
 .... 4, 70n17, 103–4, 124–5, 238–9
Pidgeon v Doncaster Health Authority [2002] 168 .... 185n80
Pigney v Pointer's Transport Services Ltd [1957] 140; 147; 231 ...... 157–8, 162, 165n46, 255
Polemis & Furness, Withy & Co. Ltd, Re [1921] 7; 26; 233 .... 10, 33, 78
Prendergast v Sam & Dee Ltd [1989] 164
Quinn v Burch Bros (Builders) Ltd [1966] 24 31
Rahman v Arearose Ltd [2001] 161 177
Reeves v Commissioner of Police of the Metropolis [2000] 6; 43; 66; 94; 109; 141; 151;
 215; 226 .... 51, 77, 106, 110, 115, 125, 159–60, 163, 234, 249
Rickards v Lothian [1913] 25; 60; 61 .... 32–3, 70, 71–2
Roberts v Bettany [2001] 2; 50 58–9
Robinson v The Post Office [1974] 163 180
Robson v North Eastern Railway Co. (1874–75) 196 213
Rocca v Stanley Jones & Co. (1914) 161 177–8
Rose v North Eastern Railway (1876) 198 214–15
Roswell v Prior (1701) 9 13–14
Rothwell v Caverswall Stone Co. Ltd [1944] 161 178
Rouse v Squires [1973] 93; 106; 110; 224 .... 105–6, 122–3, 126, 247
Rushton v Turner Bros Asbestos Co. Ltd [1959] 63 74
Sabri-Tabrizi v Lothian Health Board [1998] 168 .... 185n80
Sayers v Harlow Urban District Council [1958] 47; 181; 193; 199; 208; 227; 231 ....
 .... 55–6, 198, 216, 251, 255
Scaramanga & Co. v Stamp (1880) 171 189
Scott v Shepherd (1773) 9; 25; 43; 60; 61; 80; 193 .... 13–14, 32, 52, 70, 71, 91, 210
Scott's Trustees v Moss (1889) 81 92
Selvanayagam v University of West Indies (1983) 166 182–3

Sharp v Powell (1872) 117
Shawinigan v Vokins [1961] 110
Slipper v British Broadcasting Corporation [1991] 83; 216; 233 .... 94, 236–7, 257
Stansbie v Troman [1948] 38; 63; 92.. 73–4, 104, 114
Steele v Robert George & Co., (1937), Ltd [1942] 45; 165.. 181
Taylor v Rover Co. Ltd (1966) 219.. 239
Tennent v Earl of Glasgow (1864) 116
The Calliope [1970] 132 149
The City of Lincoln (1889) 18; 44; 81; 130; 231........... 22, 53, 92, 147–8, 149, 151, 153, 255
The Fritz Thyssen [1968] 131
The Guildford [1956] 131
The Metagama (1927) 2; 45; 132; 178 .... 53, 149–51, 196
The Oropesa [1943] 4; 46; 134; 230; 235; 241 .... 7, 54–5, 151–2, 153, 259
The Sisters (1876) 209
Vaughan v Menlove (1837) 57 66
Vicars v Wilcocks (1806) 10... 14–15
Videan v British Transport Commission [1963] 176 194
Ward v Cannock Chase District Council [1985] 30; 64....................................... 37–8, 75
Ward v T.E. Hopkins & Son Ltd [1959] 83; 174; 175 .... 94, 192, 193–4
Ward v Weeks (1830) 11; 61; 215 .... 15, 71, 235
Webb v Barclays Bank plc and Portsmouth Hospitals NHS Trust [2001] 162 .... 179n52
Weld-Blundell v Stephens [1920] 4; 59; 61; 209; 216 .... 69, 73, 228, 235
Wieland v Cyril Lord Carpets, Ltd [1969] 48; 93; 202.. 57, 105, 220–1
Wilkinson v Kinneil Cannel and Coking Coal Co. (1897) 81
Williams v Eady (1893) 185 202–3
Wilson v Coulson [2002] 211
Withers v London, Brighton & South Coast Railway Company [1916] 139 156–7
Woods v Duncan [1946] AC 401 140
Wright v Lodge [1993] 49; 110; 225... 57, 127–7
Yachuk v Oliver Blais Co. Ltd [1949] 92; 188; 219; 225 .... 104–5, 205–6, 238, 248

Canada

Abbott v Kasza [1975] 117; 199
Anderson v Northern Railway Company (1875) 171
Bishop v Sharrow (1975) 187
Blais v Yachuk [1946] 86... 97
Block v Martin (1951) 159; 202... 220
Bohlen v Perdue and City of Edmonton [1976] 227
Boss v Robert Simpson (Eastern) Ltd (1968) 202
Bradford v Kanellos (1973) 33; 99; 109 .... 40, 112, 125
Brain v Mador (1985) 166
Canphoto Ltd v Aetna Roofing (1965) Ltd [1971] 68 78–9
Cotic v Gray (1981) 147; 229 .... 165, 165n48, 253
C.P.R. v Calgary [1971] 119
Crotin v National Post [2003] 100
Dallaire v Paul-Emile Martel Inc. [1989] 111; 191; 225...................................... 127–8, 207–8
Davidson v Connaught Laboratories (1980) 160 177
Doughty v Township of Dungannon [1938] 109 125

List of Cases

Duce v Rourke (1951) 67; 86; 100; 233 .... 78, 97, 113, 257
Edwards v Smith [1941] 187
Engel v Kam-Ppelle Holdings Ltd [1993] 166
Fetherston v Neilson and King Edward Hotel [1944] 108 124
Fleming v Atkinson [1959] 125
Fujiwara v Osawa [1938] 106 122
Funk v Clapp (1986) 146 164
Geall v Dominion Creosoting Co. (1917) 186
Gray v Gill [1993] 166
H. (M.) v Bederman [1995] 100
Harris v Toronto Transit Commission [1967] 188; 227 .... 205, 250
Hayes Estate and Hayes v Green and Green (1983) 147
Hewson v Red Deer (1977) 33; 68 .... 41, 79
H.L. v Canada (Attorney General) (2005) 69; 237 80
Hobbs v Robertson (2004) 165
Hoffer v School Division of Assiniboine South [1973] 188
Holian v United Grain Growers (1980) 33; 68; 100; 189 .... 41, 79, 113, 206
Ingram v Lowe (1975) 187
Ippolito v Janiak (1981) 166 182
Ives v Clare Brothers Ltd [1971] 213
Jane Doe v Board of Police Commissioners for Metro Toronto [1998] 100
Jones v Shafer [1948] 31; 67 .... 39, 78
Katzman v Yaeck (1982) 160
Kirk v Trerise (1979) 125
Kolesar v Jeffries (1976) 159 176
Lamberty v Saskatchewan Power Corp. (1966) 32; 114 .... 40, 130–1
Lawson v Wellesley Hospital [1978] 215
Lepine v University Hospital (1964) 145
Martin v McNamara Construction Co. Ltd [1955] 32; 100 .... 39, 112–13
Menow v Honsberger and Jordan House Ltd [1974] 106 122
Mercer v Gray [1941] 158 175
Michaluk v Rolling River School [2001] 214
Mitchell v Rahman [2002] 2; 3; 159
Oke v Weide Transport Ltd (1963) 32 39–40
Ostash v Sonnenberg (1968) 214 233
Papp v Leclerc (1977) 159
Patten v Silberschein [1936] 67; 233 .... 77–8, 257
Price v Milawski (1977) 160 176
Priestley v Gilbert [1972] 205 223
Q v Minto Management Ltd (1985) 69 79
Rehak v McLennan [1992] 159 176
Roberge v Bolduc [1991] 56; 168 .... 65–6, 185
Robson v Ashworth (1985) 147 164–5
Ryan v Hickson (1975) 188
Schlink v Blackburn [1993] 100
Seymour v Winnipeg Electric Railway (1910) 172 190
Smith v Inglis (1978) 32; 108 124
Stadel v Albertson [1954] 145
Swami v Lo (No. 3) (1979) 34; 147 .... 41–2, 164
The Queen in right of British Columbia v Zastowny (2006) 69; 236; 237 80–1

Thompson v Toorenburgh (1975) 114; 160 .... 130, 177
Toronto Hydro-Electric Commission v Toronto Railway Co. (1919) 67............................. 77
Town of Prescott v Connell (1893) 18; 85; 178 .... 96, 196
Turner v Koren (1932) 7
Urbanski v Patel (1978) 68; 179 79
Villemure v L'Hopital Notre-Dame (1972) 146... 164
Walker v DeLuxe Cab Ltd [1944] 67... 78
Watson v Grant (1970) 159 175–6
Whelan v Parsons & Sons [2005] 187
Wickberg v Patterson (1997) 227
Williams v New Brunswick (1985) 34; 69; 100; 214 .... 41, 79–80, 113, 233–4
Winnipeg Electric Railway Co. v Canadian Northern Railway Co. and Bartlett (1920) 99; 192... 112
Wright Estate v Davidson (1992) 148
Wright v McCrea [1965] 33 41

Australia

Adelaide Chemical and Fertilizer Company Limited v Carlyle (1940) 53; 128; 165................ .... 62, 146, 182
Alford v Magee (1952) 223
Allianz Australia Insurance Ltd v GSF Australia Pty Ltd (2004–2005) 236 .... 260n11
AMP General Insurance Ltd v RTA (2001) 144... 161n29
Anderson v Corporation of the City of Enfield; Turco (Aust.) Pty Ltd (Third Party) (1983) 38; 220.. 45–6, 239
Aquilina v N.S.W. Insurance Ministerial Corporation (1994) 157 174
Australian Eagle Insurance Company Ltd v Federation Insurance Ltd (1976) 206; 207 224–5
Australian Shipbuilding Industries (WA) Pty Ltd v Packer (1993) 113
Beavis v Apthorpe (1962) 36; 156
Bennett v Minister of Community Welfare (1992) 77; 99; 114; 168 .... 88, 111–12, 130, 185–6
Bohdal v Streets [1984] 87
Boyd v SGIC [1978] 165 182
Cameron v Nottingham Insurance Co. Ltd [1958] 210
Canterbury Bankstown Rugby League Football Club Ltd v Rogers (1993) 124........... 140–1
Caterson v Commissioner for Railways (1973) 54; 73; 86; 198................ 62–3, 84, 97–8, 215
CES v Superclinics (Aust.) Pty Ltd (1995) 75; 166; 238.. 86, 183
Chapman v Hearse (1961) 4; 25; 36; 95; 106; 175; 224...... 44–5, 48, 107–8, 122, 123, 192, 247
Chappell v Hart (1998) 124
Charlton v Public Trustee for the Northern Territory (1967) 107; 228
Chomentowski v Red Garter Restaurant Pty Ltd (1970) 37; 74; 96 .... 45, 85, 108, 109
Club Italia (Geelong) Inc. v Ritchie (2001) 74; 97 .... 85n107, 109
Commonwealth Trading Bank of Australia v Sydney Wide Stores Pty Ltd (1981) 74
Commonwealth v McLean (1997) 210
Curmi v McLennan [1994] 73; 96; 187 .... 84n102, 109, 204
De Alba v Freehold Investment Co. (1895) 194
Evenden v Manning Shire Council (1929) 171; 173 191
Expokin Pty Ltd v Graham [2000] 203.. 221

List of Cases

Fishlock *v* Plummer [1950] 207
Forbes *v* Olympic General Products (Qld) Pty Ltd (1989) 220 240
Forrester *v* Torrensford Sand and Gravel Pty Ltd (1928) 36 44
Gardiner *v* Henderson & Lahey [1988] 114
GIO *v* Aboushadi (1999) 207
Goodsell *v* Murphy (2002) 212 231
Haber *v* Walker [1963] 7; 72; 122; 143; 240; 241 .... 83–4, 139, 160–1
Havenaar *v* Havenaar [1982] 42; 210 229
Hird *v* Gibson [1974] 38; 210
Hirst *v* Nominal Defendant [2004] 97; [2005] 56; 97; 226 109–10
Hogan *v* Gill (1992) 218 238
Holdlen Pty Ltd *v* Walsh [2000] 144 .... 162n29
Jacques *v* Matthews [1961] 107; 228
Joslyn *v* Berryman (2003) 223
Kavanagh *v* Akhtar (1998) 56; 75 86–7
Kenny & Good Pty Ltd *v* MGICA (1992) Ltd (1999) 122 139
Kessey *v* Golledge [1999] 55; 203 .... 64, 221
Krakowski *v* Trenorth (1996) 212 232
Lawrie *v* Meggitt (1974) 156
Lindeman Ltd *v* Colvin (1946) 154
Lisle *v* Brice [2002] 144 161
Liston *v* Liston (1981) 156 173
Lothian *v* Rickards (1911) 35; 95 .... 43–4, 47, 107, 114
Mahony *v* J Kruschich (Demolitions) Pty Ltd (1985) 4; 38; 54; 112; 156 ...... 46, 63, 173–4, 186
Malleys Ltd *v* Rogers (1955) 44; 194
March *v* E. & M. H. Stramare Pty Ltd (1990–91) 73; 98; 108; 223; 227 ....
.... 63, 84, 110–11, 124, 250
Martin *v* Isbard (1946) 156
McHale *v* Watson (1966) 191
Medlin *v* The State Government Insurance Commission (1994–95) 54; 76 .... 63–4, 110n55
Melchior *v* Cattanach [2000] 168 184–5
Migge *v* Wormald Bros Industries Ltd [1972] 154
Moore *v* A.G.C. (Insurances) Ltd [1968] 156
Mount Isa Mines *v* Bates (1972) 37; 96; 114; 226 .... 108–9, 130, 249
Muller *v* Lalic [2000] 218 238
Munce *v* Vinidex [1974] 166
Neall *v* Watson (1960) 126
Nicolson *v* Tucker (1984) 205 223–4
NSW Insurance Ministerial Corporation *v* Myers (1995) 144; 210
O'Brien *v* Thorpe (1987) 113; 169 186
Parkdale Custom Built Furniture Pty Ltd *v* Puxu Pty Ltd (1982) 212
Parramatta City Council *v* Lutz (1988) 96 109
Parry *v* Yates & Griffin (1963) 195 212
Pitt Son & Badgery Ltd *v* Proulefco SA (1984) 74; 96 .... 85, 108
Pyne *v* Wilkenfeld (1981) 49; 55; 202 .... 57n43, 64, 220
Re Armstrong and State Rivers and Water Supply Commission [1952] 119
Reg Glass *v* Rivers (1968) 74; 95 .... 84–5, 108
Richters *v* Motor Tyre Service Proprietary Ltd [1972] 144 161
Rigg *v* State of New South Wales (1993) 142
Rolfe *v* Katanga Lucerne Mill Pty Ltd [2005] 221 241

Sarkis v Summitt Broadway Pty Ltd [2006] 144 .... 162n29
Scout Association of Queensland v Central Regional Health Authority (1997) 152; 157 174
Skea v NRMA Insurance Ltd [2005] 38; 203
South Australian Stevedoring Company Limited v Holbertson [1939] 154 171–2
State Government Insurance Commission v Oakley [1990] 55; 203; 206............., 64, 222, 224
State Rail Authority of New South Wales v Wiegold (1991) 65; 74; 210; 237 .... 85–6, 229–30
Taco Co. of Australia Inc. v Taco Bell Pty Ltd (1982) 212
Telstra Corporation Ltd v Smith (1998) 144
The Commissioner of Railways (Western Australia) v Stewart (1936) 120 137
The Duke Group v Pilmer (1999) 213
Thompson v Bankstown Corporation (1953) 183
Thorpe Nominees v Henderson & Lahey [1988] 87
Travel Compensation Fund v Tambree (2005) 99; 169 186–7
Vieira v Water Board [1988] 157 .... 174n23
Walker-Flynn v Princeton Motors Pty Ltd (1960) 165 182
Watts v Turpin (1999) 91
Woolfe v Tasmania (Department of Health and Human Services) [2001] 129................... 145–6
Wyong Shire Council v Shirt (1980) 42
Yates v Jones (1990) 75; 211; 237 .... 86, 230–1, 261–2
Zavitsanos v Chippendale [1970] 143

USA

Aetna Insurance Co. v Boon (1877) 21; 84.. 26, 95
Albala v City of New York (1981) 167 .... 183n73
American Mutual Liability Insurance Co. v Buckley & Co. Inc. (1941) 6; 190 207
Anderson v Baltimore & Ohio Railroad Company (1937) 52; 226 .... 60–1, 249–50
Arsnow v Red Top Cab Co. (1930) 149
Baione v Heavey (1932) 70... 81
Brower v N.Y. Central Railway (1918) 70; 85.. 81, 95
Burrell Township v Uncapher (1887) 105.. 121–2
Chicago, Milwaukee, St Paul & Pacific Railroad Company v Goldhammer (1935) 51 60
Daniels v New York Railroad (1903) 149 166
Dominices v Monongahela Connecting R.R. Co. (1937) 35 42–3
Exxon v Sofec Inc. (1995) 112; 135 .... 128, 152–3
Fehrs v McKeesport (1935) 190 207
Ferroggiaro v Bowline (1957) 34.. 42
Jacobson v Suderman and Young Inc. ('The Mariner') (1927) 117..................................... 135
Johnson v Kosmos Portland Cement Co. (1933) 118 136
Kline v Moyer (1937) 106.. 122
Koelsch v Philadelphia Co. (1893) 16 21
Lane v Atlantic Works (1872) 34 42
Liberty National Life Insurance v Weldon (1958) 70
Lillie v Thompson (1947) 71; 102 .... 82–3, 115–16
Liming v Illinois Central Railway (1890) 172; 177... 195
Louisiana Mutual Insurance Co. v Tweed (1869) 22; 118 .... 26–7, 135
Lowden v Shoffner Mercantile Co. (1940) 52; 178 .... 61, 195
McKenna v Baessler (1892) 53
McLaughlin v Sullivan (1983) 150

Memphis and Charleston Railroad Company *v* Reeves (1870) 120 137–8
Milwaukee and St Paul Railway Company *v* Kellogg (1877) 9; 21; 84 .... 13, 25–6, 95
Molton *v* City of Cleveland (1988) 150
New York Central Railway Company *v* Brown (1933) 51 .... 59–60, 96
New York Eskimo Pie Corporation *v* Rataj (1934) 85; 189 206–7
O'Neill *v* City of Port Jervis (1930) 123 140
Railroad Co. *v* Stout (1873) 188 204–5
Sandri *v* Byram (1929) 194 211
Scheffer *v* Washington City Railroad Co. (1882) 149 166
Shuster *v* City of New York (1958) 71 81
Smith *v* Cohen (1935) 70 81
St Louis-San Francisco Railway Company *v* Mills (1924) 71; 85 .... 81–2, 96
Sudderth *v* White (1981) 150
Thompson *v* Fox (1937) 153 170
Troietto *v* G.H. Hammond Co. (1940) 108 124
Wagner *v* International Railroad Company (1921) 172; 175 .... 190, 193
Watters *v* T.S.R. Inc. (1990) 150

New Zealand

Burnett *v* Wairoa Co-operative Meat Company Ltd [1921] 128 145
Grant *v* Cooper, McDougall and Robertson Ltd (1940) 220 240
John Mill and Co. Ltd *v* Public Trustee [1945] 101 114
McCarthy *v* Wellington City [1966] 4; 25; 39; 77; 101; 189; 219 .... 32, 47–8, 114, 206
McFarland *v* Stewart (1900) 144 162
Murdoch *v* British Israel World Federation (New Zealand) Inc. [1942] 145 162
Pallister *v* Waikato Hospital Board [1975] 4; 102; 145; 215 .... 115, 163, 234
Reid *v* Friendly Societies' Hall Company (1880–81) 39; 101 .... 47, 113–14
Smith *v* Auckland Hospital Board [1965] 202
Taupo B.C. *v* Birnie [1978] 87 98

Ireland

Breslin *v* Corcoran [2003] 78; 88 .... 89, 99
Byrne *v* Wilson (1862) 14; 105 .... 19, 121
Conley *v* Strain [1988] 162
Cooke *v* Midland Great Western Railway of Ireland [1909] 187 204
Crowley *v* A.I.B. and O'Flynn, Green, Buchan and Partners [1988] 115 131
Cunningham *v* MacGrath Bros [1964] 87; 209 .... 98–9, 228
Dockery *v* O'Brien [1975] 78 89
Hogg *v* Keane [1956] 57; 194 66
Kingston *v* Kingston (1965) 57; 195 212
Martin *v* Moore [1946] 128 145
McKenna *v* Stephens and Hall [1923] 106 122
Sullivan *v* Creed [1904] 60; 103; 186 .... 70n17, 116, 203, 237

Other Jurisdictions

Moini v The Government of Papua New Guinea [1977] 40; 78.. 48
Sarl Les transports heandais v SA Les grands travaux du Forez (1977) (France) 40; 78
 ....48–9, 89

Acknowledgements

I wish to express my gratitude to my research assistant, Julia Ker, for her useful insights and diligent efforts in accumulating and collating materials and information in support of this undertaking. I am also indebted to Dianne Hollis for her tireless and conscientious efforts in typing, correcting and formatting successive drafts of the manuscript. I would also like to thank Professor William Ford, Dean of the School of Law of The University of Western Australia, for his help in providing financial assistance and teaching relief which facilitated a timelier completion of this monograph. Finally, I would like to acknowledge the assistance of Carol Hicks, Law Library Reference Librarian, in chasing down some rather obscure and venerable case citation references.

Douglas Hodgson
The University of Western Australia
2008

PART I
Introduction

Chapter 1

Introduction

Proving the causal connection between the defendant's negligence and the plaintiff's damage is often a straightforward matter. For example, a typical motor vehicle accident may be attributable to the negligent driving of one or both of the drivers. Proof of causation through the application of the traditional so-called 'but for' test yields a simple result that the accident would not have occurred but for the negligent driving which becomes a necessary condition of the plaintiff's loss. Proof of the causal connection may become more complicated, however, when subsequent events conspire with the situation generated by the defendant's negligence to produce the plaintiff's loss. What if the plaintiff's injuries are made worse by subsequent negligent medical treatment administered at a nearby hospital to which the plaintiff was taken? What if the pain and disability accompanying such injuries result in a state of depression which eventually drives the plaintiff to suicide? In other contexts, how is causation resolved when a merchant vessel which has been damaged through the negligent navigation of another vessel sinks while *en route* to port for repairs during an extraordinary and unseasonal storm? Or what is the situation where a person is injured while attempting to rescue another person who has been imperilled by the negligence of the tortfeasor? Application of the 'but for' test would yield the result that the defendant would be liable for everything which followed the negligent conduct – the negligent medical treatment, the suicide, the sinking of the vessel and the injury to the rescuer – because none of the events would have transpired without that negligence. But is that fair? In such cases, the defendant could plausibly argue that he or she should not be liable where an act or event has intervened between the defendant's negligence and the plaintiff's injury. The defendant may argue that his or her conduct no longer operates as the effective legal cause of the plaintiff's injury, having been replaced by the intervening act or event which is said to have broken the chain of causation. Such a chain-breaking event is referred to by English judges as a *novus actus interveniens* and by US commentators as a 'superseding cause'. If the intervening event breaks the chain of causation, such event rather than the defendant's negligence will be considered the effective cause of the plaintiff's injury in attributing legal causal responsibility. It has been a long-standing judicial technique to focus on certain intervening events which, in conjunction with the defendant's default, precipitate or aggravate the plaintiff's injury.[1] The crucial question becomes whether the defendant is to be held liable for loss caused by or contributed to by the

---

1 J. Fleming *The Laws of Torts* (Law Book Company Ltd, 9th edn, 1998) 246.

intervening event. As we shall see, the answer to this question depends on a variety of considerations and is subject to the application of varying legal tests.[2]

A *novus actus interveniens* may take three different forms. From the above-mentioned examples, it may consist of the conduct of the plaintiff (the suicide), the act (or omission) of a third party (the hospital and its employees), or some natural event or coincidence independent of any human agency (the extraordinary and unseasonal storm).[3] The legal effect of a successful *novus actus interveniens* plea is to absolve the defendant or original wrongdoer of legal liability or further legal liability.[4] As is the case with the duty of care and remoteness of damage ingredients of any cause of action in negligence, the *novus actus interveniens* doctrine is a judicially-developed liability limitation device. One US commentator has observed that what a court is really concerned with in determining whether intervening events constitute a superseding cause is some rule of law which restricts liability short of requiring the defendant to pay for all the harm caused by the breach of duty, and that such a restrictive rule is inevitably based on policy considerations.[5] In *Lamb* v *Camden London Borough Council*[6] Lord Denning M.R. stated:

> The truth is that all these three – duty, remoteness and causation – are all devices by which the courts limit the range of liability for negligence or nuisance. As I said recently '…it is not every consequence of a wrongful act which is the subject of compensation. The law has to draw a line somewhere'. Sometimes it is done by limiting the range of the persons to whom duty is owed. Sometimes it is done by saying that there is a break in the chain of causation. At other times it is done by saying that the consequence is too remote to be a head of damage. All these devices are useful in their way. But ultimately it is a question of policy for the judges to decide.

As a limitation of liability device, the onus rests on the defendant to persuade the court that the intervening event 'so overwhelms the original wrongdoing that the original wrongdoer [the defendant] avoids responsibility.'[7] Or, as Singleton L.J. put it in *Philco Radio and Television Corporation Ltd* v *J. Spurling Ltd*,[8] 'the onus is on the defendants to show that there was a new act intervening which relieves them from responsibility.'

---

[2] These tests include reasonable foreseeability, unreasonableness/abnormality, voluntary human action, probability/likelihood, and the content and scope of the duty of care. They will be analysed in detail in subsequent chapters.

[3] J. Murphy *Street on Torts* (LexisNexis, 11th edn, 2003) 294–5; A.M. Dugdale and M.A. Jones (eds) *Clerk & Lindsell on Torts* (Sweet & Maxwell, 19th edn, 2006) [101], para. 2–78.

[4] *McKew* v *Holland & Hannen & Cubitts (Scotland) Ltd* [1970] SC 20 (HL); *Mitchell* v *Rahman* [2002] MBCA 19 (Manitoba CA) para. 30.

[5] L.H. Eldredge *Modern Tort Problems* (George T. Bisel Company, 1941) 209.

[6] [1981] QB 625 (CA) at 636.

[7] *Mitchell* v *Rahman* [2002] MBCA 19 para. 31.

[8] [1949] 2 All ER 882 at 886 (CA) citing *Dominion Natural Gas Co. Ltd* v *Collins and Perkins* [1909] AC 640. See also the judgment of Viscount Haldane in *The 'Metagama'* (1927) 29 *Lloyd's List Law Reports* 253 (HL).

In cases where the defendant has raised a *novus actus*, commentators and some judges have found it useful to analyse the causation issues by subdividing them into 'factual causation' and 'legal causation'. As Buxton L.J. has recently reaffirmed in *Roberts v Bettany*,[9] resolving *novus actus* issues involves a determination of mixed questions of fact and law. The first step in the causal enquiry is to determine whether or not the defendant's negligence factually caused the plaintiff's loss. This is the factual causation stage. This is resolved by determining whether the defendant's negligence was a necessary condition in a set of conditions jointly sufficient to produce the plaintiff's injury, and cases involving intervening events are no exception.[10] Determining the question whether the defendant's negligent act or omission is a factual cause of the plaintiff's loss entails ascertaining whether the defendant's negligence was a *causa sine qua non* or *conditio sine qua non* (necessary condition) of the occurrence of that loss.[11] This is established through the application of the 'but for' test. The defendant's conduct satisfies the but for test in circumstances where without his or her wrongful conduct the plaintiff's loss would not have occurred. Factual causation is sometimes alternatively referred to as 'scientific causation' in the sense that physical laws or the laws of physics are relied on to determine whether there is an uninterrupted sequence of cause and effect stretching from the defendant's breach of duty to the sustaining of the plaintiff's injury.[12] Only if the defendant's negligence is shown to have factually caused the plaintiff's loss will the causal enquiry proceed to consider legal causation – that is, whether the defendant's conduct should be attributed with legal responsibility for that loss. Legal causation is sometimes alternatively referred to as 'attributive causation'. Legal causation does not involve the finding of the physical facts and their causal inter-relation but rather the separate and value-laden question of the extent to which the community should go in requiring the defendant to pay for damages which his or her conduct has in fact been a significant factor in producing along with the intervening agency. This is a question of substantive law.[13] As the answer to the legal causation enquiry involves intuitive and evaluative judgements[14] based on the judicial application of concepts of fairness and justice[15] and various public policy considerations,[16] predictability

---

9   [2001] EWCA Civ. 109, para. 12.

10   S. Yeo 'Making Sense of Liability for Intervening Acts' (1997) 5 *Torts Law Journal* 45, 49.

11   P.E. Nygh and P. Butt (eds) *Butterworths Australian Legal Dictionary* (Butterworths, 1997) 172.

12   Eldredge, *Modern Tort Problems*, 205.

13   Ibid., 207.

14   Ibid., 208; M. Jones 'Multiple Causation and Intervening Acts' (1994) 2 *Tort Law Review* 133.

15   W. van Gerven, J. Lever and J. Larouche *Cases, Materials and Texts on National, Supranational and International Tort Law* (Hart Publishing, 2000) 395; A. Linden and B. Feldthusen *Canadian Tort Law* (Butterworths, 8th edn, 2006) 402; Dugdale and Jones *Clerk & Lindsell on Torts* [101], para. 2–78.

16   J. Fleming *The Law of Torts* (Law Book Co. of Australasia Pty Ltd, 2nd edn, 1961) 193; Dugdale and Jones *Clerk & Lindsell on Torts* [101], para. 2–78. When deciding a case, judges need to consider whether their particular decision will be beneficial or harmful

and uniformity in the decided cases are unattainable. Nevertheless, courts in the common law world have evolved over the past two centuries certain legal rules and tests which have been applied in resolving legal causation issues in cases involving intervening forces and these will be examined in forthcoming chapters.

Causation issues arising in the civil law context do not admit of easy resolution in many instances. Professor John Fleming has remarked, '[c]ausation has plagued courts and scholars more than any other topic in the law of torts.'[17] It is submitted by this writer that this comment applies *a fortiori* in relation to *novus actus* cases. Judges and commentators alike have noted the challenging nature of these cases. One scholar has referred to 'the vexed question of *novus actus interveniens*'.[18] A Canadian judge has recently commented, '[w]hether or not the intervening conduct amounts to a *novus actus interveniens* is a question that has plagued the courts for centuries.'[19] Tucker L.J. of the English Court of Appeal once stated, 'these questions of causation and of *novus actus interveniens* are always difficult.'[20] Perhaps it may be said that tackling intervening causation issues may be likened to 'having to draw a line between night and day; there is a great duration of twilight.'[21]

Why, then, have intervening causation cases proven so difficult for judges and scholars? One significant factor is that such cases appear to be impervious to any universal test. It is not easy to work out from the cases what test is to be applied in deciding whether an intervening event has broken the chain of causation.[22] Lord Wright confessed 'I find it very difficult to formulate any precise and all-embracing rule.'[23] This has resulted in a situation in which not all cases can be reconciled.[24] That there is no such all-embracing formula to cover all intervening causation cases is due in part to the varying nature of intervening events and their surrounding circumstances.[25] These cases are very much fact- and circumstance-sensitive. In two *novus actus* cases, the High Court of Australia has stated that whether the chain of causation has been broken is 'a matter of circumstance and degree'[26] and 'a matter of fact and degree'[27] to be decided on the facts of each particular case. The judgment

---

for society generally. See C.R. Symmons 'The Function and Effect of Public Policy in Contemporary Common Law' (1977) 51 *Australian Law Journal* 185, 189 (the essential function of public policy 'is to bring into judicial consideration the broader social interest of the public at large').

17   J. Fleming *The Law of Torts* (Law Book Company Ltd, 9th edn, 1998) 218.
18   B. McMahon and W. Binchy *Irish Law of Torts* (Butterworths, 2nd edn, 1990) 53.
19   *Mitchell* v *Rahman* [2002] MBCA 19 (Manitoba CA) para. 30 *per* Philp J.A.
20   *Philco Radio and Television Corporation Ltd* v *J. Spurling Ltd* [1949] 2 All ER 882, 885 (CA).
21   *Hobbs* v *London and South Western Ry Co.* (1875) 10 LRQB 111, 121 *per* Blackburn J.
22   F. Trindade and P. Cane *The Law of Torts in Australia* (Oxford University Press, 3rd edn, 1999) 493.
23   *Lord* v *Pacific Steam Navigation Co. Ltd ('The Oropesa')* [1943] 1 All ER 211, 213 (CA).
24   McMahon and Binchy, *Irish Law of Torts*, 53.
25   C. Baker *Introduction to Tort* (Law Book Company, 2nd edn, 1996) 225.
26   *Chapman* v *Hearse* (1961) 106 CLR 112, 122.
27   *Mahony* v *J. Kruschich (Demolitions) Pty Ltd* (1985) 156 CLR 522, 528.

of Lord Wright in *The Oropesa*[28] is replete with references to the determinative influence of fact and circumstance in resolving intervening causation issues. The New Zealand Court of Appeal has also acknowledged the central role fact and circumstance perform in adjudicating upon *novus actus* pleas.[29] Such fact-sensitivity and the absence of an all-embracing legal test, combined with evaluative, intuitive and policy-driven judicial approaches, 'lend[s] a certain measure of imprecision and unpredictability to [*novus actus*] decisions'.[30]

A further concern in this field of causation law is an obscuring of legal analysis induced by what might be referred to as terminological multiplicity. Judges have resorted frequently to metaphor and descriptive terms suggestive of some mechanical process.[31] So, for example, it has been asked whether the 'chain of causation' has been broken. Did the intervening event 'isolate' or 'insulate' or 'eclipse' the defendant's conduct or was it a 'more conduit pipe' or 'transmission gear set in motion by the defendant'?[32] In delivering the judgment of the Board in *British Columbia Electric Railway Co. Ltd* v *Loach*,[33] Lord Sumner decried the use of the many epithets judges have relied on in addressing the causal enquiry:

'Efficient or effective cause,' 'real cause,' 'proximate cause,' 'direct cause,' 'decisive cause,' 'immediate cause,' '*causa causans*,' on the one hand, as against, on the other, '*causa sine qua non*,' 'occasional cause,' 'remote cause,' 'contributory cause,' 'inducing cause,' 'condition,' and so on. No doubt in the particular cases in which they occur they were thought to be useful or they would not have been used, but the repetition of terms without examination in other cases has often led to confusion…

Professor Fleming has argued that such epithets and metaphors 'spell the illusion of scientific and objective reasoning, but are in reality only a screen behind which judges have all too often in the past retreated to avoid the irksome task of articulating their real motivation'.[34]

Similarly, in intervening causation cases, judges have resorted to using Latin phrases such as *novus actus interveniens*, *causa sine qua non* (a cause without which the event could not have occurred)[35] and *causa causans* (an immediate or effective cause).[36] Lord Normand has argued that although '[i]t has often been said

---

28 Lord v *Pacific Steam Navigation Co. Ltd* ('*The Oropesa*') [1943] 1 All ER 211 (CA). See also the judgment of Lord Simonds in *Hogan* v *Bentinck West Hartley Collieries (Owners) Ltd* [1949] 1 All ER 588, 593 (the effect of a *novus actus* 'can only be answered on a consideration of all the circumstances…').

29 See the judgment of Woodhouse J. in *Pallister* v *Waikato Hospital Board* [1975] 2 NZLR 725, 745 and the judgments of North P. and Turner J. in *McCarthy* v *Wellington City* [1966] NZLR 481, 511 (North P.), 517 (Turner J.).

30 J. Fleming *The Law of Torts* (Law Book Company Ltd, 9th edn, 1998) 247.

31 M. Jones, 'Multiple Causation and Intervening Acts', 133; J. Fleming *The Law of Torts* (Law Book Company Ltd, 9th edn, 1998) 247.

32 *Weld-Blundell* v *Stephens* [1920] AC 956, 986 *per* Lord Sumner.

33 [1916] AC 719, 727–8 (JCPC).

34 J. Fleming *The Law of Torts* (Law Book Company Ltd, 9th edn, 1998) 247.

35 B. Garner (ed.) *Black's Law Dictionary* (West Group, 7th edn, 1999) 211.

36 Ibid.

that Latin phrases cannot help to solve problems of causation...they are sometimes so convenient a label that the careful avoidance of them becomes an inverted kind of pedantry.'[37] Other senior judges and eminent scholars disagree. Professor Goodhart has argued:

> To call a cause a *novus actus interveniens* is not to give a reason for the Court's decision, but to state a result that has been arrived at on other, perhaps intuitive, grounds...These decorative [Latin] phrases are harmless so long as we realise that they have no definite meaning, but they are dangerous when we accept them at their face value and therefore fail to seek the true reason for a rule.[38]

In the celebrated rescue case of *Haynes* v *Harwood*[39] Maugham L.J. remarked, '[t]he criticisms of jurists on the Latin terms used in a great number of reported cases may well be, and are, I think, well founded; the maxims "*novus actus interveniens*" and "*volenti non fit injuria*"...are vague and uncertain and may easily be misunderstood.'[40] In a similar vein, Lord Hobhouse of Woodborough laments, 'causation as discussed in the authorities has been complicated...by the use of metaphor and Latin terminology, e.g., *causa sine qua non*, *causa causans*, *novus actus* and *volenti*, which in themselves provide little enlightenment and are not consistently used.'[41] This judicial deprecation of the utility of the particular Latin term '*novus actus interveniens*' is, with respect, misplaced in this writer's view. As we shall see shortly, it does have a relatively precise meaning. In the context of legal or attributive causation, it signifies a break in the causal chain between the defendant's breach of duty and the plaintiff's injury thereby exonerating the defendant either from liability or further liability. This Latin phrase does have a 'definite meaning'. Any vagueness or uncertainty stems not from any imprecision in defining the term itself but rather from confusion over which legal tests will be applied and in which circumstances in order to determine whether, in the view of the court, a *novus actus* plea should succeed in exculpating the defendant. The balance of this monograph will be devoted to attempting to dispel some of this confusion.

It is necessary at this point to attempt to define a number of concepts which will be frequently used in subsequent chapters. These terms are 'intervening force', '*novus actus interveniens*' and 'superseding cause'. An intervening force is an event extraneous or additional to something else preceding it. It may be an act which is independent of the initial act starting the chain of events leading to the plaintiff's injury, and which has the potential to break the chain of causation between the defendant's

---

37 *Hogan* v *Bentinck West Hartley Collieries (Owners) Ltd* [1949] 1 All ER 588, 596 (HL).

38 A.L. Goodhart 'Rescue and Voluntary Assumption of Risk' (1934) 5 *Cambridge Law Journal* 192, 201.

39 [1935] 1 KB 146 (CA).

40 Ibid., 160–61.

41 *Reeves* v *Commissioner of Police of the Metropolis* [2000] 1 AC 360, 391 (HL). See also the judgment of Lord Hoffman in *Environment Agency (Formerly National Rivers Authority)* v *Empress Car Co. (Abertillery) Ltd* [1999] 2 AC 22, 29 (HL) where His Lordship refers to the phenomenon of judges being driven to take refuge in metaphor and Latin.

negligence and the plaintiff's injury.[42] Temporally speaking, an intervening force is an event that comes between the initial event (being the defendant's negligence) and the end result (being the sustaining of the plaintiff's injury). If the intervening force is considered by the court to be strong enough to relieve the defendant of liability, it becomes a superseding cause (in the US vernacular) or a *novus actus interveniens*.[43] 'Intervening force' is defined by the American Law Institute's *Restatement of the Law of Torts, Second* as 'one which actively operates in producing harm to another after the [defendant's] negligent act or omission has been committed'.[44] A distinction is sometimes drawn between dependent and independent intervening forces. A dependent, intervening force is one which operates in response to a stimulus arising out of a situation created by the defendant's negligence; an independent intervening force is one the operation of which is not stimulated by a situation created by the defendant's conduct.[45] The latter is one that operates on a condition produced by the antecedent cause but in no way results from that cause.[46] Dependent intervening forces usually take the form of human actions while independent intervening forces often comprise some natural event.[47] A '*novus actus interveniens*' is essentially an intervening force which has been adjudged by a court for the purposes of legal and attributive causation to be the effective cause of the plaintiff's loss. An early definition of a *novus actus* accepted by Vaughan Williams L.J. in *In re Etherington and the Lancashire and Yorkshire Accident Insurance Company*[48] was as follows:

> [*novus actus interveniens*] means some new and independent thing started, which together with the existing cause…ultimately causes a certain result; you must have something that may be called a new intervening cause, in order to prevent the existing cause…from being said to be the real effective cause of what has happened.[49]

For a later act or event to constitute a *novus actus* it must be 'a new act which gives a fresh origin to the after consequences'.[50] A concise and useful definition of '*novus actus interveniens*' is an independent, intervening event, for which the defendant is not legally responsible, which breaks the chain of causation between the defendant's

---

42   Nygh and Butt, *Butterworths Australian Legal Dictionary*, 629.
43   Garner, *Black's Law Dictionary*, 212.
44   (1965–79) s. 441. (1). This definition was accepted by the US Third Circuit Court of Appeals in *American Mutual Liability Insurance Co. v Buckley & Co. Inc.* 117 F. 2d 845 (1941).
45   *Restatement of the Law of Torts, Second* (American Law Institute, 1965–79) s. 441. (1) Comment 466.
46   Garner, *Black's Law Dictionary*, 212.
47   Trindade and Cane, *The Law of Torts in Australia*, 493. Professor Fleming argues that such dichotomy 'involves a somewhat artificial distinction between later events that act on a situation already created by the defendant and conditions existing at the time of the wrongdoer's conduct which are – so to speak – part of the stage set for his activity'. See J. Fleming *The Law of Torts* (Law Book Company Ltd, 9th edn, 1998) 246.
48   [1909] 1 KB 591 (CA).
49   Ibid., 598.
50   *Haber v Walker* [1963] VR 339, 349 *per* Lowe J. See also *Turner v Koren* (1932) 1 WWR 480 (Alberta CA) (the intervention should constitute a fresh independent cause).

negligence and the plaintiff's injury, thereby absolving the defendant from liability for that injury.[51] While English judges and scholars tend to use the term '*novus actus interveniens*', their US counterparts prefer the phrase 'superseding cause', which has been defined as '[a]n intervening act that the law considers sufficient to override the cause for which the original tortfeasor was responsible, thereby exonerating that tortfeasor from liability'.[52] Thus, the two terms are interchangeable. Superseding cause has alternatively been defined as 'an act of a third person or other force which by its intervention prevents the [defendant] from being liable for harm to another which his [or her] antecedent negligence is a substantial factor in bringing about'.[53]

Two developments have emerged which have impacted on defendants raising the *novus actus* plea. These are the statutory codification of the common law contributory negligence defence and the overruling of the decision of the English Court of Appeal in *Re Polemis & Furness, Withy & Co. Ltd*.[54] As mentioned earlier, one of the three forms a *novus actus* most commonly takes is the conduct of the plaintiff himself or herself. Now that contributory negligence and apportionment legislation has been enacted in most common law jurisdictions, it is possible for the defendant to plead the statutory contributory negligence defence to reduce the quantum of damages otherwise payable. As we have already seen, however, a successful *novus actus* plea is more advantageous to the defendant in that he or she will be absolved absolutely from having to pay damages. Under the common law, a successful contributory negligence plea also had the same effect. Thus, *novus actus* no longer has the same effect *vis-à-vis* contributory negligence but has an enhanced effect from the defendant's standpoint.[55] The second development mentioned concerned the overruling by the Judicial Committee of the Privy Council in *The Wagon Mound (No. 1)*[56] of *Re Polemis* in which the Court of Appeal overturned previous case-law by abolishing reasonable foreseeability as the test of remoteness of damage in negligence actions. As a consequence, this limitation of liability device was lost to defendants between 1921 and 1961 and they were forced to resort more often to the chain-breaking *novus actus* to exonerate themselves. In delivering the judgment of the Board, Viscount Simonds rued the substitution by the Court of Appeal of the 'direct consequence' test for that of reasonable foreseeability which, in His Lordship's view, 'leads to nowhere but the never-ending and insoluble problems of causation'.[57] No doubt Viscount Simonds had in mind the increasing resort to *novus actus* pleas by defendants over this period. Since the resurrection of reasonable foreseeability as the remoteness test by the Privy Council in 1961, defendants have had restored to their arsenal an additional limitation of liability device thus making resort to *novus actus*

---

51 Nygh and Butt, *Butterworths Australian Legal Dictionary*, 803.
52 Garner, *Black's Law Dictionary*, 213.
53 *Restatement of the Law of Torts, Second* (American Law Institute, 1965–79) s. 440.
54 [1921] 3 KB 560 (CA).
55 The relationship between *novus actus* and contributory negligence (under both the common law and statute) will be examined more closely in Chapter 18.
56 *Overseas Tankship (UK) Ltd v Morts Dock & Engineering Co. Ltd (The Wagon Mound (No.1))* [1961] AC 388 (JCPC).
57 Ibid., 422.

not as imperative as before that date. Nonetheless, as we shall see, defendants still continue to plead *novus actus* on a fairly consistent and regular basis.

It remains to set out the aims of this monograph and its structure. The remaining chapters will examine on a comparative basis how the courts in the leading common law jurisdictions of the United Kingdom, the United States of America, Canada, Australia and New Zealand have applied *novus actus interveniens* in actions in tort. The focus will be a civil, rather than criminal, law perspective. The historical evolution of the *novus actus* concept will be traced and a humble and modest attempt will be made to identify and examine the application of various *novus actus* tests, to distil general principles from the case-law, and monitor emerging trends. The judicial application of the *novus actus* doctrine will then be observed in specific contexts and types of cases such as maritime incidents, natural events, rescue and suicide cases, professional negligence, and children. The influence exerted by policy considerations upon *novus actus interveniens* and its relationship with remoteness of damage issues and contributory negligence and apportionment legislation will also be canvassed prior to the author's concluding thoughts and summary in the final chapter.

Chapter 2

Early Judicial Development of Intervening Causation Law

This chapter will present a representative sampling of eighteenth- and nineteenth-century decisions of English and US courts which involved judicial deliberation upon intervening causation issues. As we shall see, up until at least the mid-nineteenth century, the courts were wary of unduly restricting the defendant's liability which would otherwise occur were they to recognise too readily the severance of the causal chain by a *novus actus*. This the courts did by applying the *Polemis*-like 'direct consequence' test[1] in England and the 'proximate cause' formula in the United States. In *Milwaukee and St Paul Railway Company* v *Kellogg*[2] the United States Supreme Court stated that the proximate cause of a plaintiff's injury may still be attributable to the defendant's negligence even though such injury operated through successive agencies, so long as that injury was the 'natural and probable consequence' of that negligence.[3] Gradually, however, the courts of both countries relaxed the rigorous application of these tests such that *novus actus* pleas enjoyed more success as the nineteenth century ended.

Our first case is the early 1701 decision of *Roswell* v *Prior*[4] which held that if a tenant for years creates a nuisance for which damages are recovered and the nuisance is continued in the lands of his lessee, an action for the continuance of such nuisance lies against either. The Court stated that 'it is a fundamental principle in law…that he that does the first wrong shall answer for all consequential damages' so that 'if a wrong-doer conveys his wrong over to another, whereby he puts it out of his power to redress it, he ought to answer for it.'[5] This rudimentary direct consequence test was followed and developed in the celebrated 'Squib Case' of *Scott* v *Shepherd*.[6] In that case the defendant threw a lighted squib made of gunpowder from the street into a covered market-house filled with people. The squib fell on the stall of one Yates whereupon one Willis, instantly and to prevent injury to himself and the wares of Yates, picked up the squib and threw it across the market-house. It landed on the stall of one Ryal who likewise picked up the squib and threw it to another part of the market-house where it struck the plaintiff in the face, exploded and put out one of his eyes. The plaintiff's trespass action succeeded by a majority decision. Nares J.

---

1 J. Fleming *The Law of Torts* (Law Book Co. of Australasia Pty Ltd, 2nd edn, 1961) 193.
2 (1877) 94 US 469.
3 Ibid., 474–5.
4 (1701) 88 ER 1570.
5 Ibid., 1573.
6 (1773) 2 W Bl 892.

cited with approval *Roswell* v *Prior* in holding that he who does the first wrong is answerable for all the consequential damages. The intermediate acts of Willis and Ryal did not 'purge' or supersede the defendant's tort since the plaintiff's injury was the 'natural and probable consequence' of the defendant's act.[7] Gould J. considered that the terror created by the defendant's act deprived Willis and Ryal of the power of recollection or deliberation and prompted them of necessity to act in self-defence. What they did was therefore the 'natural' and 'inevitable' consequence of the defendant's unlawful act.[8] De Grey C.J. held that the plaintiff's injury was the 'direct and immediate' consequence of the defendant's trespass, reasoning as follows:

> I look upon all that was done subsequent to the original throwing as a continuation of the first force and first act, which will continue till the squib was spent by bursting. And I think that any innocent person removing the danger from himself to another is justifiable; the blame lights upon the first thrower. The new direction and new force flow out of the first force, and are not a new trespass [or *novus actus interveniens*]…It has been urged, that the intervention of a free agent will make a difference: but I do not consider Willis and Ryal as free agents in the present case, but acting under a compulsive necessity for their own safety and self-preservation.[9]

Thus, the intervening behaviour of Willis and Ryal was instinctive, involuntary, unpremeditated and lacking in independent volition[10] and, as such, could not reasonably be considered to have purged or superseded the defendant's tort. *Scott* v *Shepherd* also indirectly endorsed the principle that persons who are distracted by terror in a sudden emergency and choose the wrong one of several options should not be disentitled to recover damages, thereby paving the way for the eventual emergence of the doctrine of 'alternative danger'.[11]

At the beginning of the nineteenth century, intervening human action did not ordinarily amount to a superseding cause. At about that time, however, the 'last human wrongdoer' rule emerged. Text writers generally point to the Court of King's Bench decision in *Vicars* v *Wilcocks*,[12] a slander case, as the origin of this doctrine.[13] The rule posited that if there intervened after the defendant's negligence the culpable act of a third person, the latter relieved the defendant from liability and the 'last human wrongdoer' was solely responsible for the plaintiff's injury. In slander cases the rule effectively insulated defendants from liability. If A defamed B inducing C to do something injurious to B which was also culpable, such as a wrongful dismissal from a contract of employment, A was not liable for B's harm because it was not the natural consequence of the defamatory words uttered. B might have recourse

---

7   Ibid., 893–4.
8   Ibid., 898.
9   Ibid., 899–900. Blackstone J. dissented on the ground that no direct and immediate injury passed between the parties, being an essential ingredient for a successful trespass action.
10   *Town of Prescott* v *Connell* (1893) 22 SCR 147, 163 *per* Sedgewick J. (referring to *Scott* v *Shepherd*).
11   'Alternative danger' cases will be discussed in Chapter 15.
12   8 East 1 (KB 1806).
13   L.H. Eldredge *Modern Tort Problems* (George T. Bisel Co., 1941) 209.

against C for breach of contract but not against A for the defamation since one could not be held liable for another's unlawful act.[14] So, in *Vicars* v *Wilcocks* the plaintiff complained that he had been wrongfully dismissed from his employment shortly after the defendant had maliciously uttered a slander against him to his employer. In dismissing the action, Lord Ellenborough C.J., speaking for the Court, held that the special damage produced by the slander 'must be the legal and natural consequence of the words spoken' and that the defendant could not be held liable for the master's wrongful act.[15] This marked the beginning of the emergence of a judicially-developed *novus actus interveniens* doctrine. In *Ward* v *Weeks*,[16] another slander case, the plaintiff alleged that the defendant had said to one Edward Bryce that the plaintiff 'is a rogue and a swindler' and that Bryce subsequently (without the defendant's authority) repeated the defamatory words (as the statement of the defendant) to one John Bryer. It was further alleged that prior to hearing the defamatory words, Bryer was about to sell goods on credit to the plaintiff who was about to commence business as a shopkeeper but, upon hearing the words, lost trust in the plaintiff and in consequence refused to extend credit to him. Tindal C.J. held that the plaintiff had failed to prove special damage, stating, '[e]very man must be taken to be answerable for the necessary consequences of his own wrongful acts: but such a spontaneous and unauthorised communication cannot be considered as the necessary consequence of the original uttering of the words.'[17] The republication of the words by Bryce to Bryer was held to be 'the voluntary act of a free agent' over whom the defendant had no control and for whose acts the defendant was not answerable.[18] The unauthorised republication was the effective and immediate cause of the plaintiff's injury, effectively severing the causal link between the defendant's slander and the plaintiff's injury.

Dixon v *Bell*[19] is the progenitor of a long line of cases dealing with the liability of a firearms owner for accidental shootings allegedly caused by the owner's want of care. In that case, the defendant had left a loaded gun with another man and sent his young servant girl to collect it, with a message to this man to remove the priming. The latter, as he thought, did but, as it turned out, did not do this effectively. The servant returned home with the gun and, believing that the priming had been removed so that the gun could not be discharged, pointed it at the plaintiff's son, a child, and pulled the trigger. The gun went off and struck out the child's right eye. The defendant was held liable in an action upon the case. Lord Ellenborough C.J. considered that the defendant did not do enough to render the gun safe and harmless such as by ensuring that all of the priming had been removed.[20] Bayley J. said, '[t]he gun ought to have been so left as to be out of all reach of doing harm.'[21] Thus, the intentional act of the

---

14 J. Fleming *The Law of Torts* (Law Book Co. Ltd, 9th edn, 1998) 609.
15 *Vicars* v *Wilcocks* 8 East 1, 3 (KB 1806).
16 (1830) 7 Bing 211.
17 Ibid., 215.
18 Ibid.
19 (1816) 5 M & S 198.
20 Ibid., 199.
21 Ibid., 200.

servant in firing the gun did not break the chain of causation in the sense that what actually transpired fell squarely within the scope of what the defendant should have anticipated and guarded against. *Jones v Boyce*[22] was decided in the same year as *Dixon v Bell* and, like the latter, is a forerunner of long line of 'alternative danger' cases.[23] *Jones v Boyce* was an action on the case against the defendant, a coach proprietor, for allegedly failing to provide a safe and proper means of conveyance such that the plaintiff, an outside passenger, felt obliged in order to avoid imminent danger to jump off a coach, thereby sustaining a broken leg. The coach was not overturned, however. The jury found a verdict for the plaintiff. In his address to the jury, Lord Ellenborough C.J. set out the principle that if A negligently places B in such a situation that B is forced of necessity to adopt a 'perilous alternative' and B's adoption of that alternative is not unreasonable in the circumstances, A remains responsible for the consequences of B's choice. However, Lord Ellenborough added the significant qualification that 'if the plaintiff's act resulted from a rash apprehension of danger, which did not exist, and the injury which he sustained is to be attributed to rashness and imprudence, he is not entitled to recover.'[24] Thus, a prudent precaution adopted for the purpose of self-preservation would not sever the causal chain; a rash and imprudent act not justified by the circumstances would amount to *novus actus* absolving the defendant of liability.

The next notable decision of *Bird v Holbrook*[25] concerned the issue of whether the plaintiff's trespass on the defendant's land could exculpate the latter from liability for his negligent conduct. The defendant was the owner of a walled garden which was located at some distance from his dwelling-house. Because the garden had been subject to depredations, he set within it without notice a loaded spring-gun for its better protection. Several wires were attached to the gun by the treading upon which the gun would be discharged. The plaintiff, who was not aware of the gun's existence, climbed over the wall and entered the defendant's garden in order to retrieve a stray fowl which had escaped into the garden. The plaintiff trod upon one of the wires attached to the gun causing its discharge and the maiming of one of his legs. In an action upon the case the defendant was held liable for having failed in his duty to give notice or warning of the gun's existence, even though the plaintiff's act of trespass had been the immediate cause of the gun's discharge. Both Best C.J.[26] and Park J.[27] based their decision on the ground that the defendant's failure to warn disclosed an intent on his part to injure the plaintiff or someone in his class for the purpose of apprehension. As we shall later see,[28] subsequent cases have established the proposition that an intent on the defendant's part to injure neutralises *novus actus* and remoteness of damage as limitation of liability devices.

---

22   (1816) 1 Stark 493.
23   The 'alternative danger' cases will be examined in Chapter 15.
24   (1816) 1 Stark 493, 495.
25   (1828) 4 Bing 628.
26   Ibid., 641–2.
27   Ibid., 643.
28   Chapter 5.

The case of *Lynch v Nurdin*[29] is one of the first of many cases to consider children's propensity for mischief and their lack of experience and judgement and the extent to which these qualities impact on *novus actus* and contributory negligence pleas. In that case the defendant's cart was parked in a London street. The driver left the horse and cart without any supervision and went into a house for about half an hour. The plaintiff, a six-year-old boy, and several other children began playing about the cart. During the driver's absence, the plaintiff climbed upon the cart and another boy proceeded to lead the horse on which caused the plaintiff to fall off. He was then run over by the cart and sustained a broken leg. The plaintiff, by his next friend, his mother, sued the owner of the cart, alleging that his servant had been negligent in leaving the horse-drawn cart in an open street unsupervised for half an hour. The defendant argued that the negligence of his servant could not be considered the legal cause of the plaintiff's injury; rather, the effective and immediate cause of such injury was the plaintiff's trespass on the defendant's chattel. This argument was rejected. According to Lord Denman C.J. the plaintiff's unlawful act of trespass constituted 'a co-operating cause of his own misfortune'[30] but that that should not disentitle him to a remedy. Although the causal potency of the boy's conduct in relation to his injury was significant, the degree of self-care to be expected of a normal six-year-old boy was 'very small indeed'.[31] In the words of Lord Denman:

> [The plaintiff] merely indulged the natural instinct of a child in amusing himself with the empty cart and deserted horse...The most blameable carelessness of [the defendant's] servant having tempted the child, he ought not to reproach the child with yielding to that temptation. He has been the real and only cause of the mischief. He has been deficient in ordinary care: the child, acting without prudence or thought, has, however, shewn these qualities in as great a degree as he could be expected to possess them. His misconduct bears no proportion to that of the defendant which produced it.[32]

As in *Bird v Holbrook*, then, the plaintiff's trespass was not held to be a claim-defeating *novus actus interveniens* or act of contributory negligence. The cart driver had, in effect, a duty to guard against the very risk of injury which eventuated. The vulnerability of the class of potential victims of such neglect – young children – no doubt weighed heavily in the reasoning of Lord Denman. The same decision was reached in *Illidge v Goodwin*[33] and is important for the *dictum* of Tindal C.J. expressed therein. While the defendant's cart and horse were left standing unattended in the street, the horse backed the cart against the plaintiff's window. Two defence witnesses swore they had seen a passer-by strike the horse and the defendant argued that the passer-by was instead liable. However, their evidence was disbelieved by the jury. Tindal CJ stated that even if such evidence was to be believed, it would not

---

29   (1841) 1 QB 29.
30   Ibid., 36.
31   Ibid.
32   Ibid., 38. For a case where an *obiter* view was expressed that an act of trespass by boys would amount to a *novus actus interveniens*, see the English Court of Appeal decision in *McDowall v Great Western Railway Company* [1903] 2 KB 331 (CA).
33   (1831) 5 Car & P 192; 172 ER 934.

exculpate the defendant, reasoning that if a person chooses to leave a conveyance standing unattended in a street, that person must anticipate and guard against any mischief that may be perpetrated.

Clayards v *Dethick*[34] raised the issue of what effect the plaintiff's knowledge of a dangerous situation and the incurring of risks inherent therein should have on the defendant's liability in negligence. There the plaintiff was a cab proprietor with stables in a particular mews which was linked to a nearby street only by a narrow passage. The defendants, acting under directions from the commissioner of sewers, were deepening a sewer in the street and for this purpose made an open trench which was left unfenced. Although warned of the danger by the defendants, the plaintiff proceeded in the exercise of his calling to bring one of his horses out of the mews along a narrow passage next to the trench. Rubbish which had been left by the defendant gave way and the horse fell into the trench and died during a rescue attempt. The plaintiff claimed damages for the horse. It was held that the defendant's negligence in failing to fence off the trench was not excused merely because the plaintiff knew that some danger existed through the defendant's neglect and assumed the risk posed by such danger in order to pursue his calling. Thus, the defendant was not relieved from liability on the basis of contributing negligence, voluntary assumption of risk or *novus actus*. According to Patteson J. the critical question was whether the danger was so obvious and great that no sensible prudent person could have assumed the inherent risks.[35] Coleridge J. stated that the plaintiff was not obliged to abstain from pursuing his livelihood because there was some danger and formulated the appropriate jury question to be whether the plaintiff acted as a person 'of ordinary prudence would have done, or rashly and in defiance of warning'.[36] Underlying their judgments is the notion that whether or not the causal link between the defendant's negligence and the plaintiff's injury is severed depends on the extent to which the conduct of the author of the intervening event – in this case the plaintiff – is judicially deemed to be reasonable or normal in the circumstances.[37]

Hoey v *Felton*,[38] a false imprisonment case, is one of the earlier cases where a *novus actus* was held to have broken the chain of causation, although the court's reasoning also included a remoteness of damage analysis. The plaintiff, a cigar-maker, went to the defendant's shop for refreshment, in payment for which he tendered money which was found to be bad. Thereupon the defendant uttered a slander against the plaintiff and detained him in custody for half an hour. The special damage allegedly sustained by the plaintiff was that he lost an employment opportunity with a cigar manufacturer. He claimed that he felt so unwell in consequence of the slander and detention that he was obliged to go home thereby missing a job interview. The court found that although the plaintiff was unwell as a result of his treatment at the hands of the defendant, it was not suggested that he was so unwell as to be unable to go to the interview. In delivering the judgment of the court, Erle C.J. held that the type of

---

34   (1848) 12 QB 439.
35   Ibid., 446.
36   Ibid., 447.
37   This notion will be fully explored in Chapter 4.
38   (1861) 11 CB (NS) 142.

damage sustained by the plaintiff was too remote in the circumstances. According to His Lordship:

> The damage does not immediately and according to the common course of events follow from the defendant's wrong...The wrong would not have been followed by the damage, *if some facts had not intervened for which the defendant was not responsible*. Thus, there was the act of the plaintiff, who returned home instead of going to the factory and explaining...[39]

Thus, the decision of the plaintiff to return home rather than attend the scheduled interview was deemed sufficient to constitute a superseding cause of his own loss.

Byrne v *Wilson*,[40] an Irish case, involved an action under *Lord Campbell's Act 1843*[41] brought by the plaintiff on account of the death of his relative. It was alleged that the defendant undertook to safely carry one Mary Byrne in an omnibus but by reason of the defendant's negligence the omnibus was precipitated into a canal lock causing her death by drowning. The defendant conceded that the deceased had been cast into the canal lock through its negligence but that such negligence had not caused her death. It was contended that her death was caused instead by the act of a third person – the lock-keeper – (who was neither employed nor authorised by the defendant or otherwise under his control) who allowed water into the canal after the omnibus had landed therein. The Court of Queen's Bench held, however, that although the death had not been caused immediately by the defendant's act, it was such a consequential result of that act that it should be regarded as the cause of the death for legal purposes. Le Froy C.J. stated, '[i]t was not the negligence of the defendant that was the immediate occasion of her death; but it was the negligence of the defendant that put her into a position by which she lost her life, as a consequential injury resulting from that negligence...'[42] O'Brien J. considered that although the death would not have occurred but for the lock-keeper's subsequent act which was its more immediate and 'proximate' cause, the defendant's negligence in precipitating the omnibus into the lock remained 'the primary cause of her death'.[43] This was so even though the lock-keeper's subsequent act was not the necessary consequence of the defendant's negligence.[44]

Adams v *The Lancashire and Yorkshire Railway Company*[45] concerned an action to recover damages for personal injuries sustained by the plaintiff through the alleged negligence of the defendant railway company. The plaintiff was a passenger

---

39 Ibid., 146 (emphasis supplied).
40 (1862) 15 Ir CLR 332.
41 At common law a civil action for the accident-related death by negligence of a relative could not be maintained by a personal representative as the right of action died with the death of the accident victim.
42 (1862) 15 Ir CLR 332, 340.
43 Ibid., 342.
44 There appears to have been no factual finding as to the degree of culpability or negligence inherent in the lock-keeper's act which makes it difficult to assess the correctness of the Court's decision.
45 (1869) LR 4 CP 739.

on one of the defendant's trains. He sat next to the carriage door but could have sat further away from the door had he chosen to do so as there were only two or three passengers in the carriage at the time. Shortly after the journey began, the carriage door flew open due to a defective door lock attributable to the defendant's negligence. The plaintiff shut and fastened the door but shortly afterwards it again flew open and he shut and fastened it again. This occurred three times and on the fourth occasion the plaintiff fell out of the train while holding the door shut and trying to fasten it. The Court of Common Pleas overturned a jury verdict in favour of the plaintiff and held that the defendant was not liable. The plaintiff's injury was not considered to be the necessary or natural result of the company's negligence since the inconvenience the plaintiff would have suffered if he had not attempted to shut the door was slight compared with the considerable peril incurred in his attempt to shut it. The inconvenience was not so great as to make it reasonable for the plaintiff to place himself in such a perilous situation since the train would have arrived at the station in three minutes and the plaintiff might have changed his seat to a safer one. Ryles J. held that although the accident would not have happened but for the defendant's negligence, '[such] negligence, however, was neither the immediate nor the efficient cause of the accident; that cause was the act of the plaintiff, in trying to shut the door...'[46] Brett J. attempted to formulate a general principle that 'if the inconvenience is so great that it is reasonable to get rid of it by an act not obviously dangerous, and executed without carelessness, the person causing the inconvenience by his negligence would be liable for any injury that might result from an attempt to avoid such inconvenience.'[47] Such principle was not satisfied on the instant facts, however, and Brett J. denied the plaintiff a remedy on the ground of his contributory negligence. Montague Smith J. distinguished *Jones* v *Boyce*[48] on the basis that the doctrine of alternative danger had no application to the facts of the instant case. By 'voluntarily' undertaking to shut the door, the plaintiff exposed himself to significant danger when he was not suffering any tangible inconvenience. Thus the repeated attempts of the plaintiff to shut the door were unreasonable in the circumstances and constituted a superseding cause of his own injury.[49] As we shall see in Chapter 4, unreasonable intervening conduct has since been held on many occasions to sever the chain of causation.

In *Burrows* v *The March Gas and Coke Company*,[50] a rather serious case of intervening negligence failed to exculpate the defendant from liability. The plaintiff desired to have gas in his shop and engaged a gasfitter to liaise with the defendant gas company for that purpose. The defendant contracted to supply pipes from the gas main to a meter inside the plaintiff's shop but one of the pipes was supplied with a hole in it. Gas escaped from this pipe into the plaintiff's shop. A servant of the gasfitter happened to be at work in another room at the time of the gas escape and entered the plaintiff's shop to find the source of the leakage. He was carrying a

---

46 Ibid., 741.
47 Ibid., 744.
48 (1816) 1 Stark 493.
49 (1869) LR 4 CP 739, 742–3.
50 (1870) LR 5 Exch 67.

lighted candle and an explosion caused extensive damage to the plaintiff's stock and premises. The jury made factual findings that the gas leak was caused by a defect in the pipe which had been supplied by the defendant and that the gasfitter's servant had also been negligent in entering the room with a lighted candle. Kelly C.B. held that these were concurrent negligent acts and that the plaintiff could, accordingly, maintain an action in negligence against both or either of the tortfeasors.[51] Pigott B. was of the view that 'the escape of the gas and its ignition [were] the proximate cause of the injury, but the defective condition of the pipe was the main or efficient cause, and for that defect the defendants are responsible...'[52] On appeal, the Court of Exchequer Chamber likewise held that the intervening negligence of the gasfitter's servant did not relieve the defendant from liability.[53] In *Koelsch* v *Philadelphia Co.*[54] a Pennsylvania appellate court reached the same result on similar facts in refusing to hold that the intervening negligence amounted in law to a superseding cause or *novus actus*. There the defendant was negligent in permitting its gas main to fall into disrepair thereby causing a gas leakage into the plaintiff's cellar. With knowledge of the presence of the gas, a third person entered the cellar and negligently lit a match causing an explosion and injury to the plaintiff. The defendant argued that the intervening negligence of this third person was a superseding cause of the plaintiff's injury but the court stated:

> The concurrence of the presence of the gas and the lighting of the match, the negligence of the defendant with that of Walters, was necessary to and did cause the explosion. In such cases the injured party has his redress against either of the wrongdoers, or both...[55]

In the nineteenth century courts were reluctant to uphold a *novus actus* plea even in cases where the intervening event was the product of a voluntary and intentional or deliberate act of a third person. In *Clark* v *Chambers*[56] the defendant occupied certain premises used for sports activities. These premises abutted on a private road which consisted of a carriageway and footway. The defendant had unlawfully erected a barrier across the road to prevent persons driving vehicles gaining access to his premises. In the middle of this barrier was a gap which was usually open for the passage of vehicles but which was closed when the sports were in progress by means of a pole let down across it. Some person, acting without the defendant's authority, removed a part of the barrier armed with spikes from the carriageway where the defendant had placed it and put it in an upright position across the footpath. On a dark night the plaintiff lawfully passed along the footpath and lost an eye when it came in contact with one of the spikes. The defendant argued that he could not be held liable for the plaintiff's injury where its immediate cause was the act of an unknown third person over whom he had no control. The plaintiff contended that the defendant had caused his injury for legal purposes by placing a dangerous object on the roadway

---

51 Ibid., 71.
52 Ibid., 74.
53 (1872) LR 7 Exch 96.
54 (1893) 152 Pa. 355.
55 Ibid., 364.
56 (1878) LR 3 QBD 327.

thereby affording the occasion for its relocation on the footpath. The Court of Queen's Bench held that the defendant, having unlawfully placed a dangerous object across a roadway, was liable for the injury occasioned by it to the plaintiff, notwithstanding that the immediate cause of the accident was the intervening act of a third party in repositioning that object across the footpath. In delivering the judgment of the court Cockburn C.J. stated:

> For a man who unlawfully places an obstruction across [a road] may anticipate the removal of the obstruction, by some one entitled to use the way, *as a thing likely to happen*; and if this should be done, the *probability* is that the obstruction so removed will…be placed somewhere near; it will *very likely* be placed, as was the case here, on the footpath. If the obstruction be a dangerous one, wheresoever placed, it may, as was the case here, become a source of damage, from which, should injury to an innocent party occur, the original author of the mischief should be held responsible.[57]

This appears to be the first English decision to rely on the concepts of 'probability' or 'likelihood' as an aid to determining whether or not the intervening agency amounts in law to a chain-breaking *novus actus*. That is to say, the greater the probability or likelihood of the intervening event occurring as a result of the defendant's negligence, the less likely will a court be inclined to find *novus actus*. Chapter 6 will be devoted to an examination of the extensive case-law which has subsequently applied this legal test.

By the latter part of the nineteenth century, *novus actus* issues had entered the realm of maritime collisions. In *The City of Lincoln*[58] the barque *Albatross* was run into by the steamer *City of Lincoln* in the North Sea. The steamer was solely to blame for the accident. As a result of the collision the barque was damaged and essential components of its navigational equipment were lost. The captain of the barque immediately made for a port of safety, navigating it as best he could in the difficult circumstances. Nevertheless, the barque was grounded and subsequently necessarily abandoned, without any negligence having been found on the part of the barque's captain or crew. The Court of Appeal held that the owners of the steamer were liable for the loss of the barque. In the view of Lord Esher M.R. 'the ultimate loss of the ship was caused by the captain being deprived of the means of finding out where his ship was, which deprivation was the direct result of the wrongful act of the defendants.'[59] Lindley L.J. held that the loss of the barque was 'the natural and reasonable result' of the negligent navigation of the steamer and that the attempt by the captain of the barque to avoid further loss could not be considered unreasonable conduct severing the causal link between breach of duty and injury.[60] Lopes L.J. held that the defendants were responsible for all of the 'natural consequences' of their negligence; His Lordship could not identify 'any intervening independent moving cause' which might have otherwise exonerated the defendants.[61]

---

57 Ibid., 338 (emphasis supplied).
58 (1889) 15 PD 15 (CA).
59 Ibid., 17.
60 Ibid., 18.
61 Ibid., 19.

Towards the end of the nineteenth century, the Supreme Court of Canada was called on to consider cases involving intervening causation issues. One of the earliest cases involved a plaintiff's attempt to rescue property imperilled by the defendant's negligence. In *Town of Prescott* v *Connell*[62] the servants of the defendant municipality were constructing a drain in one of the streets. For that purpose it was necessary to blast rock by means of gunpowder. The plaintiff had driven his horses into a lumber yard adjoining the street in which blasting operations were being conducted and left them in charge of the owner of another team of horses while he attended to business with the lumber yard proprietor. Shortly afterwards a blast went off and stones thrown up by the explosion fell on the roof of a shed in which the plaintiff was standing. The jury found that care had not been taken by the defendant's servants to confine the broken rock to the trenches. These events frightened the plaintiff's horses which began to run away. The plaintiff immediately ran out in front of the horses and endeavoured to stop them but he failed and was injured in attempting to get out of harm's way. The defendant argued that it should not be made liable since the immediate or proximate cause of the accident was the plaintiff's act in voluntarily rushing from a place of safety to a place of danger that caused the accident. In delivering the majority judgment, Sedgewick J.[63] adopted the statement of the law as expressed by one of the leading contemporary text writers as follows:

> The general rule of law is that whoever does an illegal or wrongful act is answerable for all the consequences that ensue in the ordinary and natural course of events, though those consequences be immediately and directly brought about by the intervening agency of others, provided the intervening agents were set in motion by the primary wrong-doer, or provided their acts causing the damage were the...natural consequence of the original wrongful act.[64]

Accordingly, in the view of Sedgewick J., the fright caused to the horses and the plaintiff's attempt to regain control of them were, in the ordinary course of events, 'the natural or probable result' of the negligence of the defendant's employees.[65] Reminiscent of the language adopted by the Court of Queen's Bench in *Clark* v *Chambers*,[66] what actually transpired was 'likely to happen, probable to happen, natural to happen, as the direct and immediate result of [the negligence of the defendant's servants]'.[67] The plaintiff's actions were not unreasonable in the circumstances[68] and so the chain of causation linking the defendant's negligence with the plaintiff's injury remained intact. Nor was Sedgewick J. prepared to accept the defendant's contention that the plaintiff's act was 'voluntary' and instead preferred to characterise the plaintiff as acting 'instinctively' in response to the emergency situation created by the defendant's negligence.[69]

---

62 (1893) 22 SCR 147.
63 Ibid., 160.
64 *Addison on Torts* (6th edn) 40.
65 (1893) 22 SCR 147, 161.
66 (1878) LR 3 QBD 327.
67 (1893) 22 SCR 147, 162 *per* Sedgewick J.
68 Ibid., 162–3 *per* Sedgewick J.
69 Ibid.

The next significant English decision involving an intervening causation issue was the Court of Appeal decision in *Engelhart* v *Farrant & Co.*[70] which involved an action to recover damages for damage to the plaintiff's carriage allegedly caused by the negligence of the defendant's servant. The defendant had employed one Mears to drive a cart for the purpose of making deliveries of goods to the defendant's customers. Mears had been instructed not to leave the cart and horse unattended. One Tucker had also been employed by the defendant to accompany Mears on his delivery rounds but Tucker had been prohibited from driving. On the occasion in question, Mears left the cart to enter a house and during his absence Tucker drove on some distance, intending to turn the cart and return to the house. While driving the cart Tucker collided with the plaintiff's carriage. The defendant argued that the negligent driving of Tucker intervened between the negligence of Mears in leaving the cart unattended (for which the employer would be liable under the common law doctrine of vicarious liability) and the collision with the plaintiff's carriage and that, accordingly, Tucker's driving was its sole legal cause.[71] The Court of Appeal, however, held the defendant liable on the ground that the negligence of Mears was the effective legal cause of the plaintiff's damage.[72] Mears was aware that he had been prohibited from leaving the cart and that Tucker had been prohibited from driving. Lopes L.J. incorporated into his reasoning the concept of foreseeability in determining that the causal link between the negligence of Mears and the plaintiff's damage had not been severed. The conduct of Mears in the circumstances constituted 'the real and effective cause' as Mears 'ought...to have anticipated that some casualty might happen...'[73] As we shall see in the next chapter, the concept of reasonable foreseeability has since emerged as one of the leading *novus actus* tests.

The next English decision, *Dunham* v *Clare*,[74] is particularly noteworthy as it would appear to be the first English case to refer specifically to the terms 'chain of causation' and '*novus actus interveniens*'. This case involved a claim for compensation by a dependant of a deceased workman under the *Workmen's Compensation Act 1897*. The worker had been a labourer in the defendant's employment. While at work a heavy iron tube fell on his left foot and injured his little toe. He was taken to hospital where he continued to attend daily as an out-patient for the next two weeks. He seemed to be recovering when he complained of feeling unwell and was diagnosed as having an unhealthy wound on the ball of his toe with symptoms of phlegmonous erysipelas. The worker died 25 days after the workplace accident of blood-poisoning caused by the erysipelas. His widow claimed compensation and was required to prove under the legislation that her husband's death resulted from the workplace accident. The medical evidence established that this very rare form of infection was

---

70 [1897] 1 QB 240 (CA).

71 The defendant employer would also be liable under the doctrine of vicarious liability for the negligence of Tucker as well since Tucker was also in the defendant's employ. Although the case report is not clear on the point, it would appear that the employer was contending that Tucker breached an absolute prohibition against driving the cart, thereby taking himself outside the scope of his employment and breaking the chain of causation.

72 [1897] 1 QB 240, 243 (Lord Esher M.R.), 245 (Lopes L.J.).

73 Ibid., 246.

74 (1902) 71 LJKB 683 (CA).

not due to the workplace injury itself but rather from a re-opening of the wound and the introduction of germs through damp or dirt penetrating the dressings. The County Court Judge held that the widow was not entitled to an award of compensation on the ground that her husband's death was not the natural or probable consequence of the accident. The Court of Appeal unanimously held that the Judge had misdirected himself, as the correct legal test under the legislation was whether the death resulted, not as a natural or probable consequence, but as a consequence in fact of the injury. Thus, the widow was held on appeal to be entitled to compensation as the death of her husband resulted in fact from his workplace injury, even though at the time of the injury the death through this rare infection could not be reasonably expected as the probable consequence of the accident. Both Collins M.R. and Mathew L.J. rejected the defendant's contention that the death resulted from the superseding cause of the infection. Collins M.R. stated:

> There must be no break in the chain [of causation]. If there is a break, then the final event is not the result of the initial event. But the break must be an actual effective break, a *novus actus interveniens*…To constitute an actual effective break in the chain, the predominant and really effective cause of the final event must be the new act intervening.[75]

Mathew L.J. also rejected the defendant's further contention that the deceased worker acted unreasonably and so aggravated his condition thereby severing the causal link.[76]

The Supreme Court of the United States had occasion to articulate and apply the doctrine of 'superseding cause' in a number of cases brought before it in the 1870s. A detailed exposition of principle is to be found in the Supreme Court's decision in *Milwaukee and St Paul Railway Co.* v *Kellogg*.[77] There the plaintiff brought an action to recover damages for the destruction of his saw-mill by fire. The plaintiff alleged that fire had been negligently allowed to spread from the defendant's steamboat to a wooden elevator also owned by the defendant and from there to the plaintiff's saw-mill which was located approximately 500 feet away. The Supreme Court refused to disturb the jury's finding that there was 'no intervening and independent cause' between the burning of the plaintiff's saw-mill and the negligent spread of fire from the defendant's steamboat as it was a result 'naturally and reasonably to be expected'.[78] This was so even though the immediate cause of the plaintiff's loss was the burning of the defendant's elevator. In delivering the Court's judgment, Strong J. stated:

> The primary cause [of the plaintiff's injury] may be the proximate cause of a disaster, though it may operate through successive instruments, as an article at the end of chain may be moved by a force applied to the other end, that force being the proximate cause of the movement, or as in the oft-cited case of the squib thrown in the market place: *Scott* v *Shepherd* (Squib Case) 2 W.B1. 892. The question always is: was there an unbroken

---

75 Ibid., 685.
76 Ibid., 686.
77 (1877) 94 US 469.
78 Ibid., 476.

connection between the wrongful act and the injury, a continuous operation? Did the facts constitute a continuous succession of events, so linked together as to make a natural whole, or was there some new and independent cause intervening between the wrong and the injury?...But it is generally held that in order to warrant a finding that negligence... is the proximate cause of an injury, it must appear that the injury was the natural and probable consequence of the negligence...and that it ought to have been foreseen in the light of the attending circumstances...We do not say that even the natural and probable consequences of a wrongful act or omission are in all cases chargeable to the [defendant]. They are not when there is a sufficient and independent cause operating between the wrong and the injury. In such a case the resort of the sufferer must be to the originator of the immediate cause. But when there is no immediate efficient cause, the original wrong must be considered as reaching to the effect, and proximate to it. The inquiry must, therefore, always be whether there was any intermediate cause disconnected from the primary fault, and self-operating, which produced the injury.[79]

On the facts, the burning of the defendant's elevator, in the absence of any fault on the part of its occupants, was not 'self-operating' but rather part of a 'continuous succession of events'. The superseding cause doctrine therefore had no application.

The other important intervening causation case also decided in 1877 by the United States Supreme Court was *Aetna Insurance Co. v Boon*.[80] The plaintiff's store had been destroyed by fire and the plaintiff claimed for such loss under a policy of fire insurance he had taken out with the defendant company in 1864. At that time the country was gripped by civil war and the defendant had introduced into its fire insurance policy an exception clause in order to guard against more extended liability arising from the consequences of the armed conflict. The main issue before the Court was whether the fire which destroyed the plaintiff's store 'happened or took place by means of any invasion, insurrection, riot, or civil commotion, or any military or usurped power'. If it did, the plaintiff's loss was excepted from the risk undertaken by the defendant insurer. The plaintiff's store was located in a Union-held town which was besieged by Confederate forces superior in numbers. Fearing that a significant quantity of military stores would fall into the hands of the rebel forces, the Union commander ordered the torching of the building in which they were held when it became apparent that the town would be over-run and occupied by the Confederate troops. Without further interference or agency, the blaze spread to, and consumed, the plaintiff's store. The court of first instance had held that the order of the Union commander to destroy the military stores constituted a sufficient superseding cause to break the causal link between the Confederate attack and the destruction of the plaintiff's store and, as such, the plaintiff was held entitled to recover under the policy. The Supreme Court did not agree, however, that the deliberate and intentional act of the commander amounted to a superseding cause. In reaching this conclusion, it relied on the Latin maxim *causa proxima non remota spectator*[81] and one of its earlier decisions, *Louisiana Mutual Insurance Co. v*

---

79 Ibid., 474–5.
80 (1877) 95 US 117.
81 An efficient cause must be considered the true cause unless some other independent cause is shown to have intervened between it and the result: H. Black *Black's Law Dictionary* (West Publishing Co., Revised 4th edn, 1968) 278.

Tweed,[82] in which it was held that the efficient or proximate cause is the one that sets others in motion and is the cause to which the loss is to be attributed, even though other causes may follow it and operate more immediately in producing the loss.[83] It is only when causes are independent of each other that the nearest cause is to be considered the legal and proximate cause of the plaintiff's injury.[84] In applying these legal principles to the facts, the burning of the military stores and the subsequent spread of fire to the plaintiff's store did not constitute 'a new and independent cause' but rather a 'probable and reasonable consequence' of the Confederate attack and one of a continuous chain of events.[85] According to Strong J., who delivered the Court's judgment, the attack created the military necessity for the destruction of the military stores and set in motion every agency that contributed to the destruction of the plaintiff's property.[86] In the result, the plaintiff's loss was excepted in the circumstances from the risk undertaken by the defendant insurer.

The collection of nineteenth-century English, US and Canadian cases discussed in this chapter comprises a representative sampling of the early judicial approaches to, and operative contexts of, intervening causation cases. As we have seen, judges contented themselves for the most part with adopting what might be termed assertive reasoning by drawing on and applying such phrases as the primary cause, the proximate cause, the efficient cause, the superseding cause, *novus actus interveniens*, new and independent cause, real and effective cause and so forth without disclosing in a detailed and systematic manner why they were prepared to attach these labels to particular causes. This is not without significance as whether or not a particular cause is judicially labelled with one of these phrases will be determinative of the legal causation issue itself. Nevertheless, as we have also observed, a few cases did indeed make incipient attempts to articulate an underlying legal test to determine why a particular event should or should not be judicially deemed a chain-breaking *novus actus*. While *Scott* v *Shepherd*[87] and *Engelhart* v *Farrant & Co.*[88] foreshadowed the adoption of the concept of reasonable foreseeability as the relevant legal test, *Jones* v *Boyce*[89] and *Clayards* v *Dethick*[90] could be considered the progenitors of the reasonableness test. Likewise it could be said that judges drew inspiration from *Clark* v *Chambers*[91] and *Town of Prescott* v *Connell*[92] in developing the concepts of probability and likelihood to help them resolve *novus actus* issues in a more reasoned and rational manner. It is the reasonable foreseeability test to which we shall first turn.

---

82 (1869) 7 Wall. 44; 19 L. ed. 65 (USSC).
83 (1877) 95 US 117, 131.
84 Ibid., 130.
85 Ibid., 132–3.
86 Ibid.
87 (1773) 2 W Bl 892.
88 [1897] 1 QB 240 (CA).
89 (1816) 1 Stark 493.
90 (1848) 12 QB 439.
91 (1878) LR 3 QBD 327.
92 (1893) 22 SCR 147.

PART II
The Legal Tests

Chapter 3

Reasonable Foreseeability

In the case of *Quinn v Burch Bros (Builders) Ltd*[1] Salmon L.J. remarked:

> Although the foreseeability test is a handmaiden of the law, it is by no means a maid-of-all-work. To my mind, it cannot serve as the true criterion when the question is, how was the damage *caused*? It may be a useful guide, but it is by no means the true criterion.[2]

Although this observation was expressed in the context of the application of the *novus actus* doctrine to a breach of contract case, it is submitted that it nevertheless accurately reflects the current status of the concept of reasonable foreseeability as a *novus actus* test in the contemporary common law world in relation to tort actions.

As we shall see later in this chapter, reasonable foreseeability has assisted judges of most common law jurisdictions from early times to determine whether or not the causal link between the defendant's negligence and the plaintiff's injury has been severed by some intervening event. Early text writers also emphasised the central role to be played by the defendant's 'knowledge or notice' or anticipation of the intervening agency.[3] Oliver Wendell Holmes has expressed the principle that 'if the intervening events are of such a kind that no foresight could have been expected to look out for them, the defendant is not to blame for having failed to do so.'[4] This foresight test postulates that a defendant's liability is superseded by any intervening agency which could not reasonably have been foreseen; conversely it extends to any harm produced or aggravated by an intervening event which the defendant could reasonably have been expected to anticipate.[5] Or, in more prosaic terms, the more foreseeable the intervening event, the more likely it is that the court will not regard it as breaking the chain of causation.[6] The foresight test 'takes stock of the mental processes linking the defendant's conduct with the consequences of such conduct'[7] and recognises the need to focus on the conduct of the author of the intervening event (whether the plaintiff or a third party) through the eyes of a reasonable person in the defendant's position. This requires an evaluation of what the defendant could

---

1 [1966] 2 QB 370 (CA).
2 Ibid., 394 (emphasis supplied).
3 M. Bigelow *The Law of Torts* (Cambridge University Press, 2nd edn, 1903) 376.
4 O.W. Holmes *Common Law* (1881) 92.
5 J. Fleming *The Law of Torts* (The Law Book Co. of Australasia Pty Ltd, 2nd edn, 1961) 194.
6 J. Murphy *Street on Torts* (LexisNexis, 11th edn, 2003) 295; A.M. Dugdale and M.A. Jones (eds) *Clerk & Lindsell on Torts* (Sweet & Maxwell, 19th edn, 2006) [106], para. 2–89.
7 S. Yeo 'Making Sense of Liability for Intervening Acts' (1997) 5 *Torts Law Journal* 45, 47.

reasonably have anticipated the plaintiff or a third person might do as a consequence of, or in response to, the defendant's negligence.[8] What precisely is the defendant required to foresee in intervening causation cases? He or she is not required to foresee 'the precise concatenation of circumstances'[9] leading up to the sustaining of the plaintiff's injuries.[10] In *Chapman* v *Hearse*,[11] an intervening causation case which will be examined in more detail later in this chapter, the High Court of Australia held that the plaintiff does not have to prove that the defendant should have reasonably foreseen 'the precise sequence of events'; rather, it is sufficient 'to ask whether a consequence of the same general character as that which followed was reasonably foreseeable'.[12] In another intervening causation case from New Zealand, Tompkins J. stated in *McCarthy* v *Wellington City*,[13] '[t]he defendant is not absolved because the precise chain of circumstances which led up to the accident may not have been foreseeable.'[14]

What follows is a discussion of some of the leading cases decided by English, Canadian, US, Australian and New Zealand courts which have applied, or at least discussed the suitability of, the foresight test in resolving intervening causation issues. The latter portion of the chapter will briefly discuss the concerns scholars and commentators have expressed concerning the use of the foresight test as well as the effect the decision of the Judicial Committee of the Privy Council in *Overseas Tankship (UK) Ltd* v *The Miller Steamship Co. Pty Ltd (The Wagon Mound (No. 2))*[15] appears to have had on the application of the foresight test.

The United Kingdom

The foresight test can perhaps be traced as far back as the venerable authority of *Scott* v *Shepherd*[16] where it was quite foreseeable that intervening stallholders would react in the way they did when presented with the lighted squib. Indeed, Gould J. referred to 'the obvious and natural consequences'[17] of the throwing of the squib by the defendant. Well over a century later, the Judicial Committee of the Privy Council appeared to endorse the foresight test (albeit by way of an *obiter dictum*) in a case where it was alleged that an intervening criminal act had severed the chain of causation. In *Rickards* v *Lothian*[18] Lord Moulton, in delivering the

---

8   Ibid.
9   A.M. Dugdale (ed.) *Clerk & Lindsell on Torts* (Sweet & Maxwell, 18th edn, 2000) [72], para. 2–48.
10 *Hughes* v *Lord Advocate* [1963] AC 837.
11 (1961) 106 CLR 112.
12 Ibid., 120.
13 [1966] NZLR 481.
14 Ibid., 497.
15 [1967] 1 AC 617.
16 (1773) 2 W Bl 892. The facts of this case appear in Chapter 2.
17 Ibid., 898.
18 [1913] AC 263 (JCPC). The facts of this case will be cited later in this chapter when the decision of the High Court of Australia therein is examined.

opinion of the Board, stated that to succeed in his action 'the plaintiff must [show] that the defendant ought to have reasonably anticipated [the intervening criminal act] so that it became his duty to take precautions to prevent such an act causing damage to others.'[19] A clearer judicial endorsement of the foresight test was made contemporaneously by the English Court of Appeal in *Latham v Johnson & Nephew, Ltd*[20] where Hamilton L.J. said, '[n]o doubt each intervener is a *causa sine qua non*, but unless the intervention is a fresh, independent cause, the person guilty of the original negligence will still be the effective cause, if he ought reasonably to have anticipated such interventions and to have foreseen that if they occurred the result would be that his negligence would lead to mischief.'[21]

In 1961 the Judicial Committee of the Privy Council again endorsed the foresight test by way of an *obiter dictum*. *Overseas Tankship (UK) Ltd v Morts Dock & Engineering Co. Ltd (The Wagon Mound (No. 1))*[22] was primarily concerned with the issue whether the English Court of Appeal decision in *Re Polemis & Furness, Withy & Co. Ltd*[23] should be overruled and reasonable foreseeability resurrected as the test for remoteness of damage. In the course of delivering the opinion of the Board, Viscount Simonds lamented that the *Polemis* rule had had the unfortunate side-effect of encouraging defendants to plead *novus actus interveniens* in order to exculpate themselves from liability.[24] His Lordship then said:

> But if it would be wrong that a man should be held liable for damage unpredictable by a reasonable man because it was 'direct' or 'natural', equally it would be wrong that he should escape liability, however 'indirect' the damage, if he foresaw or could reasonably foresee the intervening events which led to its being done...Thus foreseeability becomes the effective test.[25]

Thus, the Board appeared to accept the proposition that the defendant would remain liable for the plaintiff's injury where the former should have reasonably foreseen that his or her negligence would trigger the intervening agency. The year 1970, however, marked a watershed in England for the foresight test, not so much for its endorsement but its rejection, particularly by Lord Reid in two important cases. In *McKew v Holland & Hannen & Cubitts (Scotland) Ltd*[26] the plaintiff workman sustained an injury in a workplace accident admittedly due to his employer's fault. His left leg was consequently weakened and on several occasions it became numb and he lost control of it for a short period. Some three weeks after the accident he went to inspect a house of which he had been offered the tenancy, accompanied by his wife and a relative. On leaving the premises and in the course of descending a steep staircase which lacked a handrail, his left leg went numb. Fearing that he might

---

19 Ibid., 274.
20 [1913] 1 KB 398 (CA).
21 Ibid., 413.
22 [1961] AC 388 (JCPC).
23 [1921] 3 KB 560 (CA).
24 [1961] AC 388, 423 (JCPC).
25 Ibid., 426.
26 [1970] SC 20 (HL).

fall, the plaintiff jumped to the bottom of the staircase, sustaining further injury. In an action brought by the plaintiff against the employer for damages in relation to both accidents, the House of Lords held that the defendant employer was not liable for the injury sustained in the second accident, on the ground that the plaintiff had acted unreasonably in descending the staircase as he did, thus amounting to a *novus actus interveniens*. In the course of his judgment, Lord Reid had occasion to consider the appropriateness of applying the foresight test to a case such as the present where it was alleged that it was the plaintiff himself who was the author of the intervening event. His Lordship stated:

> I do not think that foreseeability comes into this. A defender is not liable for a consequence of a kind which is not foreseeable. But it does not follow that he is liable for every consequence which a reasonable man could foresee. What can be foreseen depends almost entirely on the facts of the case, and it is often easy to foresee unreasonable conduct or some other *novus actus interveniens* as being quite likely. But that does not mean that the defender must pay for damage caused by the *novus actus*...For it is not at all unlikely or unforeseeable that an active man who has suffered such a disability will take some quite unreasonable risk. But if he does, he cannot hold the defender liable for the consequences.[27]

Thus, for Lord Reid, a reasonably foreseeable intervening event involving the plaintiff may still amount to a *novus actus*, unless it can also be said to be 'the natural and probable result'[28] of the defendant's negligence.[29]

In *Home Office* v *Dorset Yacht Co. Ltd*,[30] also decided in 1970, Lord Reid applied the same approach to a case involving not the intervening act of the plaintiff but that of a third person. There the plaintiff sued the Home Office in negligence for the damage done to its yacht by Borstal trainees who had been working on an island under the control and supervision of officers in the defendant's employ. Having escaped from the island at night, the trainees boarded, cast adrift and damaged the plaintiff's yacht which had been moored offshore. The plaintiff alleged that the defendant had breached its duty of care in failing to exercise effective supervision and control over the trainees.[31] The Home Office, in turn, denied that it or its employees owed any duty of care to the plaintiff. The House of Lords held that such a duty of care was indeed owed in law. Although the main issue before the House concerned the existence or otherwise of the duty of care, Lord Reid went on to consider the legal implications of the conduct of the escaped trainees. In considering which legal test should govern the determination of intervening causation issues, His Lordship posed this question:

---

27 Ibid., 25.
28 Ibid.
29 M.A. Millner '*Novus Actus Interveniens*: The Present Effect of Wagon Mound' (1971) 22 *Northern Ireland Legal Quarterly* 168, 183–4.
30 [1970] AC 1004 (HL).
31 It was alleged that the officers knew of the trainees' criminal records and previous escapes and also knew that craft were moored offshore in the immediate vicinity.

Is it foreseeability or is it such a degree of probability as warrants the conclusion that the intervening human conduct was the natural and probable result of what preceded it? There is a world of difference between the two. If I buy a ticket in a lottery or enter a football pool it is foreseeable that I may win a very large prize – some competitor must win it. But, whatever hopes gamblers may entertain, no one could say that winning such a prize is a natural and probable result of entering such a competition.[32]

Lord Reid then proceeded to answer the question thus posed, stating:

...where human action forms one of the links between the original wrongdoing of the defendant and the loss suffered by the plaintiff, that action must at least have been something *very likely to happen* if it is not to be regarded as *novus actus interveniens* breaking the chain of causation. I do not think that a mere foreseeable possibility is or should be sufficient, for then the intervening human action can more properly be regarded as a new cause than as a consequence of the original wrongdoing.[33]

For Lord Reid, at least, the hallmark of a *novus actus* is its low probability or likelihood of its occurring subsequent to the defendant's negligence.[34] The defendant would be required merely to argue or lead evidence that the intervening event was not the natural and probable consequence of his or her negligence, in order for the *novus actus* plea to succeed. Lord Reid's approach would effectively thus make it easier for such pleas to succeed as a device limiting the defendant's liability, given that the application of the foresight and probability/likelihood tests are not always coterminous in terms of result.

The approach of Lord Reid and the suitability of the foresight test in resolving intervening causation issues were considered by the English Court of Appeal in *Lamb v Camden London Borough Council*.[35] In that case the plaintiffs were the owners of a house which had been leased to a tenant. One year later, while the defendants, the local council and their contractors, were replacing a sewer in the adjoining road, a water main was broken. This undermined the house's foundations which caused the house to subside and the walls to crack. The tenant moved out and the house was left unoccupied for significant periods of time, thereby facilitating the invasion of the house by two successive sets of squatters. The plaintiffs alleged that the squatters had done damage to the house amounting to some £30,000 and claimed damages in negligence against the defendants. The central issue concerned whether the damage caused by the squatters was too remote to form part of the damages payable by the defendants. This issue was decided against the plaintiffs at first instance and this result was affirmed on appeal. Although the reasoning of the Court of Appeal was not directly concerned with intervening causation issues, the intentional and criminal acts of the squatters were interposed between the defendant's negligence and the plaintiffs' injury. Lord Denning M.R. considered the suitability of both the foresight test and the probability/likelihood test in determining whether the squatters' conduct severed the chain of causation. The Master of the Rolls rejected the reasonable

---

32 [1970] AC 1004, 1028.
33 Ibid., 1030 (emphasis supplied).
34 Millner, '*Novus Actus Interveniens*', 182.
35 [1981] 1 QB 625 (CA).

foresight test on the ground that '[i]t would extend the range of compensation far too widely.'[36] This is an apparent allusion to the undemanding nature of the meaning of the concept of reasonable foreseeability attributed to it by the Judicial Committee of the Privy Council in *The Wagon Mound (No. 2)*,[37] Oliver L.J. concurred with Lord Denning M.R. in regarding the foresight test 'at least in cases where the acts of independent third parties are concerned, as one which can...produce results which extend the ambit of liability beyond all reason'.[38] As for the probability/likelihood test favoured by Lord Reid in his speech in *Dorset Yacht*,[39] Lord Denning M.R. observed that Lord Reid's remarks were a mere *obiter dictum* since the case involved only a decision on a preliminary issue of whether a duty of care was owed by the defendant. Causation issues had not been raised for decision. Lord Denning M.R. also found it difficult to reconcile Lord Reid's test with the Privy Council's emphasis on reasonable foreseeability in the *Wagon Mound* cases.[40] By contrast, Oliver L.J. regarded Lord Reid's *obiter* views 'at least of the very highest persuasive authority'[41] and as providing 'a workable and sensible'[42] test. In light of the official referee's finding at first instance that the squatters' incursions were unlikely, they amounted to a *novus actus* and so defeated the plaintiffs' claim under Lord Reid's test. Watkins L.J. did not believe that words and phrases such as 'likely' and 'quite likely' assist in applying the foresight test which His Lordship preferred in its unqualified *Wagon Mound* form.[43] Such a judicial divergence of opinion over the appropriateness of applying the foresight and probability/likelihood tests does not inspire confidence in the pursuit of predictability and uniformity of decision-making in intervening causation cases.

Knightley v *Johns*[44] was another Court of Appeal decision handed down in the same year as the *Lamb* case. In that case the first defendant was involved in a serious motor vehicle accident near the exit of a tunnel at a particularly hazardous point. Realising that he had forgotten to close the tunnel to oncoming traffic, a police inspector ordered two police officers on motorcycles, one of whom was the plaintiff, to go back and close the tunnel. The officers then rode back through the tunnel against the oncoming traffic. Near the tunnel's entrance the plaintiff collided with an oncoming vehicle and was injured. Both the inspector and the plaintiff in so doing breached the police force's standing orders for such accidents. The plaintiff claimed damages from the first defendant and the police inspector. The first defendant conceded negligence but alleged that the negligence of the inspector and the plaintiff's contributory negligence had caused the accident. At first instance it was held that neither the inspector nor the plaintiff had been negligent and that, accordingly, the causation chain had not been broken. On the first defendant's

---

36   Ibid., 636.
37   [1967] 1 AC 617 (JCPC). This point will be examined in detail later in this chapter.
38   Ibid., 644.
39   [1970] AC 1004, 1030.
40   [1961] AC 388 (JCPC); [1967] 1 AC 617 (JCPC).
41   [1981] 1QB 625, 642 (CA).
42   Ibid., 644.
43   Ibid., 646.
44   [1982] 1 All ER 851 (CA).

appeal, it was affirmed that the plaintiff had not been contributorily negligent but that the inspector had been negligent in not closing the tunnel earlier and in issuing the order to the plaintiff in breach of police standing orders. In overturning the first instance decision, the Court of Appeal held that the inspector's negligence was a new cause which interrupted the sequence of events between the first defendant's negligence and the plaintiff's injuries. The first defendant was accordingly held not liable. That the first defendant would not have readily contemplated such a sequence of police errors was significant in the Court of Appeal concluding that the inspector's negligence amounted to a *novus actus*. According to Stephenson L.J., who delivered the main judgment, 'too much happened here, too much went wrong, the chapter of accidents and mistakes was too long and varied, to impose on [the first defendant] liability…'[45] In terms of which legal test should be applied in resolving the *novus actus* issue, Stephenson L.J. had this to say:

> I conclude from these rescue cases that the original tortfeasor, whose negligence created the danger which invites rescuers, will be responsible for injury and damage which are *the natural and probable results* of the wrongful act…There is no difference between what is natural and probable and what is *reasonably foreseeable*…If it is natural and probable that someone will come to the rescue it is also foreseeable; if it is foreseeable that in doing so he may take a particular kind of risk…his acts will be natural and probable consequences of the wrongful act which created the emergency.[46]

His Lordship then posed the question 'whether that whole sequence of events is a natural and probable consequence of the…defendant's negligence and a reasonably foreseeable result of it'.[47] With respect to Stephenson L.J., he appears to be confusing the two separate tests of foresight and probability/likelihood and incorporating them into a single test. Although it is true that a 'natural and probable' consequence will always include a foreseeable consequence, the converse is not always true and this point was clearly made by Lord Reid in his speech in *Dorset Yacht*.[48] The two tests are not coterminous since foreseeability has, as Lord Reid correctly points out, a much lower threshold than probability/likelihood.

The Court of Appeal decision in the *Lamb* case was distinguished in *Ward* v *Cannock Chase District Council*.[49] There, on similar facts, it was held that the criminal acts of vandals in damaging the plaintiff's house did not sever the chain of causation between the defendant council's negligence and the plaintiff's injury. Scott J. referred to the foresight and probability/likelihood tests and was of the view that whichever test was used the result would *generally* be the same. Applying these two tests to the facts of the case, His Honour held that the intervening acts of the independent third party – the vandals – did not sever the causal chain in either case. Scott J. appeared to rely specifically on the test of reasonable foreseeability in assessing the effect of the third party intervention on the council's breach of duty. Accordingly, it was held that

---

45 Ibid., 866.
46 Ibid., 860 (emphasis supplied).
47 Ibid., 865.
48 [1970] AC 1004, 1028.
49 [1985] 3 All ER 537 (Ch.D.).

it was foreseeable that if the house adjoining the plaintiff's house were to collapse, serious damage might be caused to the plaintiff's house, that if such damage were caused it might have to be vacated pending repairs, that if such repairs were not carried out expeditiously due to the council's inaction, the house would become unoccupied, and that if the house were to remain unoccupied for any length of time it was foreseeable that the vandals would damage the plaintiff's house.

The foresight test continues to find favour with the English Court of Appeal. The case of *Banque Bruxelles Lambert S.A.* v *Eagle Star Insurance Co. Ltd*[50] involved a *novus actus* issue similar to that raised in the *McKew*[51] case. That is whether the defendant was liable for also having caused the additional loss to the plaintiff which arose as a result of the alleged *novus actus* and where the original damage would have been sustained in the absence of the *novus actus*. In *Banque Bruxelles* the plaintiff loaned £800,000 on property worth £500,000 and negligently valued by the defendants at £1,000,000. The plaintiff claimed damages when the borrower defaulted in repayment and included in the amount claimed for damages the additional loss suffered on the sale of the secured property at the fallen market value of £300,000. The defendants contended that such fall in market value amounted to a *novus actus interveniens* and that, accordingly, they had not caused the additional loss of £200,000. Sir Thomas Bingham held, however, that the fall in market value was not to be considered as having 'broken the link between the valuer's negligence and the damage which the lender has suffered'.[52] It was quite foreseeable by the defendants, according to the Court of Appeal, that if the borrower failed to repay the loan, as happened, the plaintiffs would be forced to sell the secured property at an additional loss due to the fall in market value. The Court of Appeal has more recently applied the foresight test in *Humber Oil Terminal Trustee Ltd* v *Owners of the Ship 'Sivand', The Sivand*,[53] although it was there held that the fact that an intervening event was unforeseeable does not necessarily lead to the conclusion that it constitutes a *novus actus*. *The Sivand* negligently damaged the plaintiff's harbour installations. The plaintiff engaged contractors to carry out the required repairs on standard terms, which provided for additional payment to the contractor if physical conditions were encountered which could not have been reasonably foreseen and which added to the cost of carrying out repairs. The contractors lost a barge when the sea bed under one of the barge's legs collapsed. The contractors recovered this additional cost from the plaintiffs under the terms of the contract and the plaintiffs then sought to recover that cost from the owners of *The Sivand*. The defendants contended that the unforeseen condition of the sea bed constituted an intervening event which broke the chain of causation between their conceded negligence and the additional loss suffered by the plaintiffs. As in *Banque Bruxelles* the Court of Appeal held the defendants liable for the additional loss. Although the collapse of the sea bed was unforeseeable, it did not amount to a *novus actus* as the plaintiff was considered to have acted reasonably in engaging the contractors on standard terms.

---

50   [1995] 2 WLR 607 (CA).
51   [1970] SC 20 (HL).
52   [1995] 2 WLR 607, 636.
53   [1998] 2 Lloyd's Rep 97 (CA).

Although the foresight test has been applied in England on a fairly regular, and sometimes confusing, basis, other *novus actus* tests, including Lord Reid's probability/likelihood test and the duty of care approach, which will be examined respectively in Chapters 6 and 7, have also been applied from time to time.

Canada

For the past half-century or so, Canadian courts have applied the foresight test but such test has received majority endorsement in the Supreme Court of Canada on only one occasion during that period. In *Jones v Shafer*,[54] decided by the Supreme Court of Canada in 1948, the defendant was driving his lorry along a highway when it suffered a mechanical breakdown. He decided to leave the lorry in order to procure replacement parts and put out two safety flares, as required under the relevant provincial motor vehicle legislation, to provide adequate warning to oncoming traffic. During the night these flares were removed by some unknown person and, before sunrise on the following morning in very foggy weather when visibility was poor, the deceased (in relation to whom the action was brought) collided with the truck and was killed. The main issue before the Court was whether the deliberate removal of the flares by an unknown third party amounted to a *novus actus*. In a joint judgment, Rinfret C.J. and Estey J., after reviewing the case authorities, stated, '[t]he foregoing authorities emphasize...the principle that the intervening conscious act of a third party will break the line of causation and relieve the party who may be otherwise negligent of liability, unless to a reasonable man in the same circumstances that conscious act would have been foreseeable.'[55] Locke J., with whom Taschereau J. agreed, considered '[t]hat anyone would jeopardize the lives of people upon the highway by stealing articles of such slight intrinsic value is a contingency which, in my opinion, the [defendant] could not reasonably have foreseen.'[56] Accordingly, the defendant was not held liable.

Provincial courts have subsequently followed *Jones v Shafer* in applying the foresight test. For example, in *Martin v McNamara Construction Co. Ltd*[57] the Ontario Court of Appeal adhered to the 'established principle that damage is recoverable if, despite the intervening negligence of a third party, the person guilty of the original negligence ought reasonably to have anticipated such subsequent intervening negligence...'[58] In *Oke v Weide Transport Ltd*[59] the Manitoba Court of Appeal, by a majority, dismissed the action against the defendant on the basis of a successful *novus actus* plea. There the defendant knocked over a metal post on a strip

---

54 [1948] SCR 166.
55 Ibid., 170–71.
56 Ibid., 176.
57 [1955] OR 523.
58 Ibid., 527. See also the decision of the Nova Scotia Court of Appeal in *Smith v Inglis* (1978) 83 DLR (3d) 215 (negligent manufacturer of a refrigerator is not exculpated from liability where a delivery man subsequently and negligently deactivated a safety device where such an intervention should reasonably have been foreseen).
59 (1963) 41 DLR (2d) 53.

of gravel between two highway lanes and left it bent over. The deceased, who was improperly using the strip for passing, was killed when the post came up through the floor boards of his car and impaled him. In the majority's view, the defendant could not reasonably anticipate that someone would try to pass a motor vehicle at a point where it was unlawful and unsafe to do so. As one commentator[60] has observed, this is a curious result in that the defendant himself had earlier been in the same position. As was pointed out earlier in this chapter, the defendant is not required to foresee the precise manner in which an accident occurs. As a source of danger to the motoring public, the defendant is merely required to anticipate the post causing an accident of some kind, including one involving a breach of the highway traffic laws.

Lamberty v *Saskatchewan Power Corp.*[61] involved an intervening omission rather than act. In that case a plant operator negligently exposed a gas line in the course of some surface excavation (for which his employer was vicariously liable). It was alleged that the operator's employer was also independently negligent in directing where the excavation work was to be done. Having exposed the gas line, the operator notified an employee of the defendant gas company but neither the company nor any of its employees carried out any effective action to repair or isolate any gas leak. The plaintiff, a nearby resident, was injured when he lit a cigarette and his house exploded as a result of the damage caused to the gas line. Despite the negligence of the plant operator and his employer, the intervening negligence by omission of the gas company was held to constitute a *novus actus interveniens* on the ground that such omission was not a reasonably foreseeable consequence of the original negligence. The 1973 decision of *Bradford* v *Kanellos*[62] is the other major decision of the Supreme Court of Canada in which the foresight test has been applied. In that case, the plaintiffs, husband and wife, were customers in the defendant's restaurant. While seated at the counter, a negligently-started flash fire occurred in the cooking grill. Shortly after the start of the fire, an automatic fire extinguisher system was activated which quickly extinguished the fire without any damage having been caused. However, the fire extinguisher made a hissing noise when activated and this caused a restaurant customer to shout that gas was escaping and that it was about to explode. In the ensuing panic, the wife was pushed from her counter seat and sustained injury. The trial Judge awarded damages against the defendant restaurateur on the ground that the intervening panic could have reasonably been foreseen. By unanimous decision, the Ontario Court of Appeal overturned this judgment on the ground that such panic was not foreseeable.[63] On further appeal to the Supreme Court, it was held, by majority, that the intervening panic constituted a *novus actus* because it did not fall within the risk created by the defendant's negligence in permitting an undue quantity of grease to accumulate on the grill. Spence J. (with whom Laskin J. concurred) dissented, however, in preferring to apply the foresight test and finding, as the trial Judge had, that the panic was reasonably foreseeable.[64]

---

60 A. Linden and B. Feldthusen *Canadian Tort Law* (Butterworths, 8th edn, 2006) 413.
61 (1966) 59 DLR (2d) 246.
62 (1973) 40 DLR (3d) 578.
63 [1971] 2 OR 393.
64 (1973) 40 DLR (3d) 578, 581–2.

Canadian courts have more recently applied the foresight test to cases involving intervening acts of vandalism. In *Hewson v City of Red Deer*[65] the plaintiff sued the defendant for damage caused to their dwelling-house after one of its tractors had collided with it. One of the defendant's employees had parked the tractor and turned the ignition off but failed to remove the ignition key or lock the cab door. While it was left unattended, an unknown person had set the tractor in motion which was later found by the employee running against the plaintiff's house. It was held at first instance that it was reasonably foreseeable that if basic safety precautions were not taken by the tractor operator, persons in the nearby vicinity might be tempted to set the tractor in motion. Somewhat surprisingly, the Alberta Supreme Court (Appellate Division) overturned this decision on the ground that there was no evidence to support the conclusion that the tractor operator could reasonably have foreseen this criminal act. In so deciding, the Court purported to follow the Ontario Court of Appeal decision in *Wright v McCrea*[66] which on very similar facts held that the act of unauthorised strangers which was the immediate cause of the plaintiff's injury was not reasonably foreseeable and therefore amounted to a *novus actus interveniens*. Not all acts of intervening mischief have been held by Canadian courts to amount to a *novus actus*. *Holian v United Grain Growers*[67] involved some mischievous boys who took from the defendant's shed some fumigant tablets used to kill insects and placed them in the plaintiff's car as a 'stink bomb' thereby causing illness to the plaintiff. Morse J. held the defendant liable as it 'need not have been able to foresee the precise way in which the plaintiff...came to be injured. It is sufficient if the type of accident was reasonably foreseeable.'[68]

Canadian courts have also applied the foresight test to arson and suicide cases. In *Williams v New Brunswick*[69] a prisoner set fire to a lockup causing the death of 21 inmates. An action by families of some of the deceased against the defendant for negligently allowing the prisoners to obtain matches succeeded. Stratton C.J. considered that the consequence of the defendant's negligence was neither 'freakish, fantastic [n]or highly improbable but rather was foreseeable and proximate and constituted a substantial factor in the loss that occurred.'[70] While arson has been held to be a reasonably foreseeable intervening event rendering the tortfeasor liable, suicide has not. In *Swami v Lo (No. 3)*[71] the plaintiff's husband took his own life after being injured by the defendant's negligence. The injury had caused severe pain which led to a state of depression, culminating in suicide. The deceased was found to be sane when he took his own life. Gould J. held that the defendant was not liable on the ground that the suicide was not the type of injury which could have been foreseen. Gould J. concluded:

---

65 (1977) 146 DLR (3d) 32.
66 [1965] 1 OR 300.
67 (1980) 11 CCLT 184 (Manitoba Queen's Bench).
68 Ibid., 191.
69 (1985) 34 CCLT 299 (New Brunswick Court of Appeal).
70 Ibid., 319.
71 (1979) 11 CCLT 210 (British Columbia).

[The death] resulted from something which was not a reasonably foreseeable consequence of the motor vehicle accident, but rather resulted from suicide, which may be characterized as a *novus actus interveniens*. Death was brought about by an act of the plaintiff himself, for which the defendant cannot be held liable.[72]

It can thus be seen, then, that although the Canadian courts have applied the foresight test to a wide variety of intervening causation cases, the results of such application have not always been consistent, either within the judgments of the same case (as in *Bradford* v *Kanellos*) or between judgments involving similar facts and issues (as in *Hewson* v *City of Red Deer* and *Holian* v *United Grain Growers*).

The United States of America

Although the foresight test has been applied by US courts in intervening causation cases for well over a century, it has not featured prominently in the case-law compared with the doctrine of proximate cause. In the early leading case of *Lane* v *Atlantic Works*[73] the court held that intervening negligent human conduct did not relieve the defendant from liability where such intervention ought to have been foreseen. The foresight test has also been endorsed in *Ferroggiaro* v *Bowline*[74] where it was held that a negligent intervening act of a third person will not amount to a superseding cause of the plaintiff's injury which the original tortfeasor helped to bring about if that tortfeasor at the time of his or her negligent conduct should have realised that a third person might so act. The application of the foresight test is illustrated in the 1937 decision of a Pennsylvanian court in *Dominices* v *Monongahela Connecting R.R.Co.*[75] There the plaintiff's employer delivered to the defendant a car of sulphuric acid to be hauled a short distance to another plant of the employer. The employer (through an employee) had constructive knowledge that the cap on the car was defective. After the delivery of the car by the defendant, the employer's foreman ordered the plaintiff to empty it and he was severely burned when he removed the defective cap. Stern J. stated that when the foreman 'ordered plaintiff to go upon the car and unload it, any prior negligence on the part of the defendant was thereby superseded, because the consignee was an intervening human agency which, with full knowledge of the situation, by its act transformed a potential danger into an accident, and thus interrupted the chain of causation.'[76] His Honour then added:

> If the test as to whether one act of...negligence supersedes another is whether it was foreseeable by the first tort-feasor, it is clear that while a railroad company might be expected to foresee the failure of a consignee to inspect a car delivered for unloading, it could not reasonably be held to foresee that a consignee which itself owned the car and therefore presumably had full knowledge of its condition, would, in violation of the duty

---

72   Ibid., 216.
73   111 Mass. 136 (1872).
74   (1957) 64 Am LR (2d) 1355.
75   328 Pa 203 (1937).
76   Ibid., 209.

owed to an employee, order him to unload it if defective, and especially if the defect had actually been within the cognizance of the consignee.[77]

It should be noted that the foresight test is codified in Section 442A. of the American Law Institute's *Restatement of the Law of Torts, Second*[78] which provides that '[w]here the negligent conduct of the actor creates or increases the foreseeable risk of harm through the intervention of another force, and is a substantial factor in causing the harm, such intervention is not a superseding cause.'

Australia

Although the foresight test has been applied from time to time by the High Court of Australia in intervening causation cases, it has lain dormant in the High Court's jurisprudence since 1985. The first High Court decision to apply the foresight test in the *novus actus* context is that of *Lothian* v *Rickards*.[79] The plaintiff was a lessee from the defendant of business premises located on the second floor of a building. On the fourth floor of the same building was a lavatory in the defendant's possession and control. During the night a basin in the lavatory overflowed and the plaintiff's goods were damaged when the water percolated through to the second floor. The next morning the tap was found turned full on and the basin's plug-hole clogged with pieces of soap and other debris. The plaintiff sued the defendant in negligence, alleging that the latter breached his duty of care in failing to provide a lead-safe to carry away the overflow water. Although the jury found that the defendant had been negligent in failing to provide such a lead-safe and that such omission had caused the plaintiff's loss, they added the significant rider: 'We are of opinion that [the immediate cause] was the malicious act of some person.'[80] The causation issue was a finely balanced one which troubled the judges who sat on the case. The first instance decision in the plaintiff's favour was overturned on appeal to the Victorian Supreme Court by a majority decision.[81] The main issue to be decided by the High Court of Australia was whether the deliberate and criminal act of mischief of an unknown third party should be considered to have severed the causal link in these circumstances. Once again, judicial opinion was divided. In deciding in the plaintiff's favour, Griffith C.J. stated that the relevant test 'is whether the act is "of a kind that might have been reasonably foreseen"'.[82] In the Chief Justice's opinion, the word 'kind' refers to the physical nature of the act rather than the intervening actor's motives.[83] O'Connor J. held that it was open to the jury to find on the evidence that 'the occurrence of occasional overflows of the basin from wilful and mischievous acts of that kind might reasonably have been anticipated and provided for by the

---

77 Ibid., 209–10.
78 (1965–79) 468.
79 (1911) 12 CLR 165.
80 Ibid., 170–71.
81 (1910) VLR 425.
82 (1911) 12 CLR 165, 176–7.
83 Ibid., 177.

defendant.'[84] Isaacs J., dissenting, also applied the foresight test but reached the opposite conclusion, stating, 'I do not think that, without very special circumstances, a landlord can be expected to anticipate such a gross misuse of a lavatory...'[85] The High Court's decision was, in turn, overturned by the Judicial Committee of the Privy Council in the absence of a specific finding that the defendant ought to have foreseen the malicious act of the unknown third party.[86]

State courts in Australia followed the High Court's lead in *Lothian*. In *Forrester* v *Torrensford Sand and Gravel Pty Ltd*[87] a South Australian court applied the foresight test to a case where the intervening cause involved the plaintiff's conduct. There the plaintiff sustained injury as a result of his employer's negligence and subsequently developed a mental condition in the form of a compensation neurosis. It was held that the plaintiff's mental condition was not a reasonably foreseeable consequence of the employer's negligence; rather it had more to do with brooding over his imaginary pains. As such, it amounted in law to a *novus actus interveniens*.[88] In 1963 the High Court of Australia held that negligent, as opposed to malicious or criminal, human intervening conduct does not break the chain of causation if it should have been foreseen by the original tortfeasor. In *Chapman* v *Hearse*[89] a car overturned in the road as a result of the negligence of its driver, Chapman. A doctor named Cherry went to the assistance of Chapman who had been thrown free from his car and was lying unconscious in the roadway. While Dr Cherry was tending to Chapman's injuries, he was run over and killed by another vehicle driven by an aptly-named Hearse. Dr Cherry's estate sued Hearse, alleging that Dr Cherry's death had been caused by Hearse's negligent driving in adverse weather and light conditions. Hearse joined Chapman in third party proceedings, alleging that Chapman's negligent driving had caused, or at least contributed to, Dr Cherry's death. The primary issue was whether Hearse's negligent driving was a *novus actus interveniens* which severed the causal link between Chapman's prior negligent driving and Dr Cherry's death. At trial it was held that although Hearse had been negligent, Chapman was found liable to make a contribution to Hearse of one-fourth of the damages awarded against him. The High Court of Australia refused to disturb this determination. In a joint judgment of the full bench, the High Court stated, '[w]hen the question is whether damage ought to be attributed to one of several "causes" there is no occasion to consider reasonable foreseeability on the part of the particular wrongdoer unless and until it appears that the negligent act or omission has, *in fact*, caused the damage complained of.'[90] In establishing factual causation through the application of the 'but for' test, it was clear that but for the negligence of each of the two tortfeasors, Dr Cherry's death would not have occurred. The High Court then proceeded to determine legal or attributive causation through the application of the foresight test. In the Court's view, it was

---

84 Ibid., 179.
85 Ibid., 191.
86 *Rickards* v *Lothian* [1913] AC 263.
87 (1928) SASR 427.
88 See also *Beavis* v *Apthorpe* (1962) 80 WN (NSW) 852, 860.
89 (1961) 106 CLR 112.
90 Ibid., 122 (emphasis supplied).

reasonably foreseeable by someone in Chapman's position that subsequent injury by passing traffic could be sustained by those rendering aid after a highway accident, even when the intervening act was also a negligent act.[91]

The foresight test has also been applied by Australian lower courts in intervening causation cases in a variety of different contexts, including negligent intervening omissions by the plaintiff himself. In *Mount Isa Mines* v *Bates*[92] the plaintiff miner suffered injury when he struck a metal drill with a hammer in order to release it. A piece of metal flew into his eye and blinded him. As a safeguard against this type of injury, safety goggles had been provided to the plaintiff but he had failed to wear them. It was held that the plaintiff's negligent omission to wear the goggles should have been foreseen by the defendant employer and it was therefore negligent on its part to fail to adopt a simple, inexpensive modification of machinery which would have avoided the risk of flying metal particles. Hence, the plaintiff's negligence did not amount to a *novus actus* but did constitute contributory negligence under apportionment legislation. In 1970 the New South Wales Court of Appeal applied the foresight test to determine whether a serious criminal offence broke the chain of causation between the defendant employer's negligence and the plaintiff's injury. In *Chomentowski* v *Red Garter Restaurant Pty Ltd*[93] the plaintiff was employed by the defendant company as its manager. One of his duties included depositing each night's takings in the night safe of a nearby bank. Early one morning while the plaintiff was attempting to access the safe, he was attacked and robbed and suffered severe injuries. The plaintiff sued the defendant employer for an alleged breach of duty to take reasonable care for his safety and recovered damages at first instance. On appeal the defendant pleaded *novus actus interveniens*, arguing that although it may have provided the occasion, the plaintiff's injury was not caused by its negligence but by the independent conscious act of third persons whom it could not control. The New South Wales Court of Appeal rejected the *novus actus* plea. Sugarman P. cited with approval *Chapman* v *Hearse* and held that the risk of third party criminal intervention was reasonably foreseeable in the circumstances.[94] Asprey J.A. said, '[s]ome act by a third party effecting injuries to the plaintiff would be the very thing which the defendants ought reasonably to have foreseen as a result of their breach of the duty which they owed to the plaintiff…'[95] Mason J.A. also cited with approval *Chapman* v *Hearse* and held that '[t]he injury which the plaintiff sustained, although occasioned by deliberate human intervention, was the outcome of the very risk against which it was the duty of the defendants to safeguard the plaintiff as their employee.'[96] In 1983 the Supreme Court of South Australia applied the foresight test in an inherently dangerous product case. In *Anderson* v *Corporation*

---

91 Ibid., 121.
92 (1972) 46 ALJR 408; [1972–73] ALR 635.
93 (1970) 92 WN (NSW) 1070.
94 Ibid., 1075–6.
95 Ibid., 1083.
96 Ibid., 1086. See also *Hird* v *Gibson* [1974] Qd R 14; *Stansbie* v *Troman* [1948] 2 KB 48 (foreseeable intervening intentional acts do not sever the chain of causation).

of the City of Enfield; Turco (Aust.) Pty Ltd (Third Party)[97] King C.J. held that the intervening negligence of a municipal corporation in failing to take proper safety precautions concerning an inherently dangerous product did not break the chain of causation between the plaintiff's injury and the manufacturer's negligence in failing to adequately label the product. That was because, in the words of King C.J., 'it was reasonably foreseeable by [the defendant manufacturer] that if the labels on the... drums did not contain a sufficiently striking warning, an employer [the defendant municipal corporation] might not appreciate, as he should, the significance of the warning which did appear on the labels and might fail to take adequate precautions to protect his employees.'[98]

The most recent occasion on which the full bench of the High Court of Australia has approved and applied the foresight test in an intervening causation case occurred in 1985 when it decided *Mahony* v *J. Kruschich (Demolitions) Pty Ltd*.[99] In that case the plaintiff sued his employer for damages for personal injuries alleged to have been suffered by him in the course of his employment. The employer in turn brought a cross-claim against one of the medical practitioners who had treated the plaintiff and claimed that the former had been negligent in treating the latter and that such negligence had caused, or at least contributed to, the plaintiff's employment-related incapacities. In a joint judgment, the full bench of the High Court said:

> A negligent tortfeasor does not always avoid liability for the consequences of a plaintiff's subsequent injury, even if the subsequent injury is tortiously inflicted. It depends on whether or not the subsequent tort and its consequences are themselves properly to be regarded as foreseeable consequences of the first tortfeasor's negligence.[100]

In the circumstances of the case, the High Court held that although the original workplace injury carried some risk that medical treatment might be negligently given, the exacerbation of the plaintiff's condition resulting solely from 'grossly negligent medical treatment' would not be reasonably foreseeable and, as such, could amount to a *novus actus*.[101] Since its decision in *Mahony* in 1985, the High Court has from time to time applied other *novus actus* tests including unreasonableness, voluntariness, and the duty of care approach, all of which will be examined in subsequent chapters.

---

97 (1983) 34 SASR 472.
98 Ibid., 480.
99 (1985) 156 CLR 522.
100 Ibid., 528. This passage and the reasonable foreseeability test have recently been endorsed by the Supreme Court of the Australian Capital Territory (Court of Appeal) in *Skea* v *NRMA Insurance Ltd* [2005] ACTCA 9. This case dealt with the issue whether the plaintiff's stress in caring for injured family members severed the chain of causation between the defendant's negligence in causing the accident and the plaintiff's subsequent psychiatric illness. The Court of Appeal unanimously rejected the *novus actus* plea on the ground that it was reasonably foreseeable on the defendant's part that the plaintiff's initial psychiatric injury would be aggravated by the stresses of caring for the injured family members. See Crispin P. (at paragraphs 3, 4 and 6) and Lander J. (with whom Gray J. agreed) (at paragraphs 122 and 123).
101 Ibid., 530.

New Zealand and Other Jurisdictions

The New Zealand Court of Appeal has also had occasion to apply the foresight test in cases involving the intervening negligent conduct of third parties. The early case of *Reid v Friendly Societies' Hall Company*[102] was very similar on its facts to the *Lothian* case discussed previously in this chapter. However, unlike *Lothian*, there was insufficient evidence to establish whether the overflow of water from the basin had been caused by the wilful or merely careless act of an unknown third person. The Court of Appeal held that the defendant was liable for damage caused to its tenant, the plaintiff, when the water percolated from the upper floor to the ground floor and damaged his goods. Prendergast C.J. framed the relevant question as 'whether such an act [of an unknown third person] and the consequences of it ought to have been anticipated and guarded against...'[103] by the defendant. The Chief Justice held that intervening negligence would not break the causal chain but left open the possibility that a wilful intervention by the third party might amount to a *novus actus interveniens*.[104] Williams J. went further, however, in holding that even an intentional intervention would not sever the causal connection, as 'the defendants must be taken to have known that if the tap were accidentally or intentionally left turned on the water must of necessity have flooded the premises of the plaintiff, as no provision had been made for carrying off the overflow...'[105] Many years later, in a case involving children, the Court of Appeal again applied the foresight test and found the defendant liable in damages. In *McCarthy v Wellington City*[106] the defendant operated a quarry on which it kept detonators. Two boys broke into a safe in which the detonators were kept with a crowbar they had found. One of the boys took the detonators home and gave them to a younger brother who subsequently gave them to the nine-year-old plaintiff whose right hand was severely injured when one of the detonators exploded while he was playing with them. The Court of Appeal held that the defendant had been negligent in not adequately securing the detonators and that it was a reasonably foreseeable consequence of such negligence that the detonators could end up in the hands of children who had not entered the quarry. According to Turner J.:

> The [defendant], as the result of the jury's findings, must be taken as bound to foresee that if due precaution [*sic*] were not taken the detonators might come into the hands of boys such as Wood and Askew, and that they might pass them on as they did. Their acts in passing on the detonators are therefore foreseeable consequences of the original act of negligence, and not 'acts of conscious volition' such as will give rise to a plea of *novus actus*.[107]

---

102 (1880–81) 3 NZLR 238.
103 Ibid., 248.
104 Ibid.
105 Ibid., 251–2.
106 [1966] NZLR 481.
107 Ibid., 517.

McCarthy J. likewise held that the deliberate acts of the two boys in breaking open the safe and later distributing the detonators to other children were 'reasonably foreseeable' and were required to be guarded against.[108]

The National Court of Justice of Papua New Guinea has also applied the foresight test to a case involving serious intervening criminal offences committed by third parties. In *Moini v The Government of Papua New Guinea*[109] the plaintiff's husband was travelling as a passenger in a motor vehicle owned by the Government of Papua New Guinea when the vehicle became involved in an accident in which a child pedestrian was killed. Immediately after the accident, the plaintiff's husband and the driver of the motor vehicle were murdered in a 'payback' killing by irate villagers. In an action for damages brought by the plaintiff's widow pursuant to fatal accidents legislation,[110] Williams J. followed the decision of the High Court of Australia in *Chapman v Hearse*[111] (which, as it will be recalled, dealt with a case of an intervening negligent act) and applied the foresight test to determine whether the double murder by the villagers severed the causal link between the negligence of the driver (for whom the defendant was vicariously liable) and the plaintiff's loss. His Honour considered the question whether or not a reasonable person should have foreseen that failure to maintain proper control of the vehicle resulting in death or injury to another road user could bring about violent retaliatory action against the occupants of the vehicle at the hands of the relatives of the person killed or injured. Upon the evidence and in view of the considerable notoriety of violent retaliation at the scene of a motor vehicle accident to anyone familiar with Highlands customs, the type of violent reaction which occurred was a reasonably foreseeable consequence of negligent driving and, therefore, did not constitute a *novus actus interveniens*.

Some European civil law systems have also found it useful to rely on the foresight test to determine intervening causation issues. The French Cour de cassation has held that the causal link between the tortfeasor's negligence and the plaintiff's injury is broken when the intervention of a third party introduces a new risk which was not 'normally foreseeable'. In *Sarl Les transports heandais v SA Les grands travaux du Forez*[112] the defendant was the owner of an excavator which was left overnight in an open yard with the keys in the ignition. A vandal took the excavator and used it to damage vehicles which the plaintiff had left in the yard. The plaintiff sued the defendant for damages and succeeded at first instance. The Court of Appeal reversed and dismissed the claim and the Cour de cassation, in upholding the judgment of the Court of Appeal, stated:

> The Court of Appeal is criticized for having rejected the [plaintiff's] claim, despite its finding that the [defendant] was negligent in leaving the key in the ignition of a particularly dangerous vehicle which was parked in an open yard. According to the plaintiff, such negligence stands in a direct causal relationship with the harm that resulted when the thief

---

108 Ibid., 522.
109 [1977] PNGLR 39.
110 *Law Reform (Miscellaneous Provisions) Act 1962*.
111 (1961) 106 CLR 112.
112 Cass. Civ. 2e, 17 March 1977, D 1977. Jur. 631.

used that vehicle; the behaviour of the thief was more or less foreseeable and could not thus break the direct causal relationship...

However, the Court of Appeal found that, following the wrongful appropriations, the thief rammed the vehicle – in succession – against two of the [plaintiff's] cars, against other vehicles as well as against buildings used as a garage. The damage sustained by the [plaintiff] was therefore due to acts of vandalism. Furthermore, the Court of Appeal added that the exceptional and peculiar behaviour of the thief hence introduced a new and unnecessary risk, which was not normally foreseeable for the [defendant]. Given these findings and statements, the Court of Appeal could rightly hold that, since the driver of the vehicle entered into a course of voluntary wrongful conduct which was independent of the conduct of the owner, the favourable conditions under which the [driver] could take control of the excavator were without causal relationship with the alleged harm.[113]

Thus, it was not 'normally foreseeable' from the defendant's standpoint that a third party would engage in such a rampage and, accordingly, the chain of causation was held to have been broken. However, in certain cases, French courts have regarded the fault of the owner so gross that the causal link between that fault and the plaintiff's injury brought about by the thief remains intact.[114]

Post-Wagon Mound Concerns with the Foresight Test

The foresight test has not been embraced in recent times by scholars and academic lawyers as an intervening causation test. Speaking in the intervening causation context, Professor Fleming has claimed, 'whatever its attractions in point of apparent simplicity, fairness and consistency with central notions of fault liability... foreseeability is not a test of precision and that individual estimates may to some extent vary, depending on one's degree of experience...'[115] Professor Davies has also queried the appropriateness of reasonable foreseeability as a test of intervening causation:

> Reasonable foreseeability is concerned with possibilities; causation is concerned with proof on the balance of probabilities...an event that is very unlikely may nevertheless be reasonably foreseeable. If it is very unlikely, but reasonably foreseeable, that a subsequent event will arise as a result of the defendant's negligence, can it be said, on the balance of probabilities, that that subsequent event was...caused by the defendant's negligence?[116]

Others have expressed misgivings with the foresight test in this context.[117] The main problem is that over the years, the courts have undoubtedly developed the capacity,

---

113 Ibid.
114 Cass. civ., 20 November 1951, D 1952. Jur. 258, where the owner left his van parked at night in a bad neighbourhood, facing downhill, so that a mere push enabled the van to be put in motion, so that it rolled downhill and caused damage.
115 J. Fleming *The Law of Torts* (The Law Book Co. of Australasia Pty Ltd, 2nd edn, 1961) 194.
116 M. Davies and I. Malkin *Torts* (LexisNexis Butterworths Australia, 4th edn, 2003) 88.
117 A. Palmer 'Causation in the High Court' (1993) 1 *Torts Law Journal* 9, 17; B. McMahon and W. Binchy *Irish Law of Torts* (Butterworths, 2nd edn, 1990) 46, 48, 50.

as one judge has observed,[118] to foresee even quite bizarre consequences of accidents. This is due in no small measure to the lowering of the reasonable foreseeability threshold by the Judicial Committee of the Privy Council in its decision in *Wagon Mound No. 2*.[119] In rejecting the proposition that a real, albeit remote, risk is not reasonably foreseeable, Lord Reid, in delivering the judgment of the Board, included as a reasonably foreseeable risk any real risk which would occur to the mind of a reasonable person and which he or she 'would not brush aside as far-fetched'.[120] This judicial initiative to dilute the concept of reasonable foreseeability as a device to limit the defendant's liability has been taken up by other Commonwealth courts including the High Court of Australia.[121] As the application of this redefined concept of foreseeability in the intervening causation context would, as Lord Reid pointed out in *Dorset Yacht*, result in a *novus actus* plea succeeding much less often, it is submitted that it should remain, in the words of Salmon L.J. set out at the beginning of this chapter, a mere handmaiden of the law rather than a maid-of-all-work.

---

118 *Havenaar* v *Havenaar* [1982] 1 NSWLR 626, 627 *per* Hutley J.A.
119 *Overseas Tankship (UK) Ltd* v *The Miller Steamship Co. Pty Ltd (The Wagon Mound (No. 2))* [1967] 1 AC 617.
120 Ibid., 643.
121 See *Wyong Shire Council* v *Shirt* (1980) 146 CLR 40 where Mason J. stated that a risk of injury which is remote in the sense that it is extremely unlikely to occur may nevertheless constitute a foreseeable risk so long as it is not 'far-fetched or fanciful' (at 48).

Chapter 4

Unreasonableness/Abnormality

In *Reeves* v *Commissioner of Police of the Metropolis*[1] Lord Hobhouse observed that '[r]easonable human responses to situations [created by the defendant's negligence] are not treated as causative; they are a normal consequence of the antecedent event and it is that event which is described as the cause.'[2] The operation of an intervening agency will not ordinarily relieve the defendant from liability if it is considered by the court to be a not abnormal incident of the risk created by the defendant or if the response of the plaintiff or third person to the situation created by the defendant's negligence is considered not unreasonable in the circumstances.[3] Generally speaking, the more unreasonable the conduct of the intervening human agent or the more abnormal the intervening event, the more prone a court will be to uphold a defendant's *novus actus* plea.[4] Courts have assessed how normal or reasonable the reaction of the plaintiff or a third party has been to the situation in which the defendant's negligence has placed them. This assessment is typically made in cases involving imminent fear of injury to oneself or the desire to avoid significant inconvenience.

The hallmark of the reasonableness/normality test of intervening causation is that its application involves assessing the acceptability or propriety of the response to the defendant's negligence rather than calibrating its degree of likelihood of occurrence. As such, it differs from the foresight and probability/likelihood tests of intervening causation.[5] As we shall see later in this chapter, assessing the propriety of the response will not always be straightforward or uncontentious. In some cases courts have classified human behaviour in value-laden ways[6] and in contexts which involve a significant moral dimension.[7]

The reasonableness test enjoys a long tradition of application by English courts in intervening causation cases and the majority of the cases discussed in this chapter emanate from that jurisdiction. However, Australian and US courts have also applied the reasonableness test in this context and their case-law will also be examined.

---

1 [2000] 1 AC 360 (HL).
2 Ibid., 391.
3 J. Fleming *The Law of Torts* (The Law Book Co. Ltd, 9th edn, 1998) 247.
4 A.M. Dugdale and M.A. Jones (eds) *Clerk and Lindsell on Torts* (Sweet & Maxwell, 19th edn, 2006) [104], para. 2–86.
5 S. Yeo 'Making Sense of Liability for Intervening Acts' (1997) 5 *Torts Law Journal* 45, 52–3; R. Balkin and J. Davis *Law of Torts* (LexisNexis Butterworths, 3rd edn, 2004) 336, para. [9.14].
6 F. Trindade and P. Cane *The Law of Torts in Australia* (Oxford University Press, 3rd edn, 1999) 497.
7 *Emeh* v *Kensington and Chelsea and Westminster Area Health Authority* [1984] 3 All ER 1044 (CA).

The United Kingdom

The reasonableness test has venerable roots in the well-known case of *Scott* v *Shepherd*[8] where it was held to be no defence to the person who first threw the squib that the plaintiff would not have been injured had not a third party picked it up and given it fresh impetus. This was because in throwing the squib again, the third party was acting in self-preservation. Thus, where the defendant's negligent act has placed the plaintiff or a third party in a situation of so-called 'alternative danger', if that person behaves reasonably in the agony of the moment, that subsequent conduct will not sever the chain of causation.[9] Thus, in *Jones* v *Boyce*[10] the defendant was still held liable for the injuries sustained by the plaintiff who was obliged to jump off a runaway coach, on the ground that the defendant's negligence had placed the plaintiff in a situation that required him to not unreasonably adopt a perilous alternative for the purpose of self-preservation.[11] In *Clayards* v *Dethick*[12] Coleridge J. effectively applied the reasonableness test in holding that the plaintiff cabman was not bound to abstain from pursuing his livelihood because there was some danger in bringing his horse along a narrow passage overlooking an open trench. In incurring a significant risk of injury to his property, the plaintiff 'acted as a man of ordinary prudence would have done'.[13] Accordingly, a plea that the plaintiff's risk-taking amounted to a *novus actus* was rejected. Another early English case to apply the reasonableness test in a slander action was *Lynch* v *Knight*.[14] In that case the defendant warned the plaintiff's husband that the plaintiff was a 'notorious liar' and that she took 'delight in causing disturbances' wherever she went. Reference was also made to her laxity of manners prior to marriage. The plaintiff's husband reacted to these statements by divorcing the plaintiff. The House of Lords dismissed the plaintiff's action in slander against the defendant on the ground that the defendant's slander had not been the legal cause of the marriage breakdown; rather, that event was attributable to the judicial assessment that it had not been reasonable for the plaintiff's husband to have reacted to the defendant's words in the way he did. As the husband's response was more drastic than could have been expected in the ordinary course of events, it effectively severed the causal link between the defendant's slanderous statements and the plaintiff's injury. Another 'unreasonable' response to the defendant's negligence, this time on the part of the plaintiff, was held to be a *novus actus interveniens* in *Adams* v *The Lancashire and Yorkshire Railway Company*.[15] The Court of Common Pleas effectively engaged in a cost-benefit analysis in holding that the insignificant inconvenience suffered by the plaintiff was far outweighed by the dangers he ran

---

8 (1773) 2 Wm Bl 892. The facts of this case are presented in Chapter 2.
9 Balkin and Davis, *Law of Torts*, 335, para. [9.14].
10 (1816) 1 Stark 493. The facts of this case appear in Chapter 2.
11 For more contemporary applications of this principle, see *Colvilles* v *Devine* [1969] 1 WLR 475 (HL (Sc)); *Malleys Ltd* v *Rogers* (1955) 55 SR (NSW) 390.
12 (1848) 12 QB 439. The facts of this case appear in Chapter 2.
13 Ibid., 447.
14 (1861) 9 HLC 577.
15 (1869) LR 4 CP 739. The facts of this case appear in Chapter 2.

in endeavouring to close the carriage door. Accordingly, it was not considered reasonable for the plaintiff to attempt what he did in the prevailing circumstances.[16]

The reasonableness test was also applied early on by English courts in the fields of maritime collisions and worker's compensation. In *The City of Lincoln*[17] the plaintiff ship lost its compass and charts when the defendant's ship negligently collided with it. The plaintiff's ship consequently ran aground while trying to make for port. The Court of Appeal held the defendant liable for this further harm. Lindley L.J. stated, 'reasonable human conduct is part of the ordinary course of things' which 'includes at least the reasonable conduct of those who have sustained the damage, and are seeking to save further loss'.[18] Thus, the prudent attempt on the part of the crew of the plaintiff's ship to mitigate the initial loss was not a sufficiently abnormal response to the situation created by the defendant's negligence to sever the chain of causation. And in *Dunham* v *Clare*[19] Mathew J. rejected the defendant employer's argument that the deceased worker behaved unreasonably and so aggravated the consequences of his workplace accident-related injury, asking whether it can truly be said that a man behaves unreasonably 'when he uses the means within his reach and the information at his disposal?'[20] In 1927, the House of Lords applied the reasonableness test in another maritime collision case with facts similar to those in *The City of Lincoln*. *The Metagama*[21] involved a collision between the *Baron Vernon* and the *Metagama*. Although liability for the collision and the initial collision damage was admitted by the owners of the *Metagama*, they maintained that a large proportion of the damages claimed was caused by the negligence of those in charge of the *Baron Vernon* subsequent to the collision which broke the chain of causation. As such, the owners claimed, they were not liable for the additional damages flowing from the ultimate long-term stranding of the *Baron Vernon*. Viscount Haldane was of the view that even if those in charge of the *Baron Vernon* had been negligent subsequent to the collision, their attempts to navigate the ship to safety did not amount to a *novus actus interveniens*:

> When a collision takes place by the fault of the defending ship in an action for damages the damage is recoverable if it is the natural and reasonable result of the negligent act, and it will assume this character if it can be shown to be such a consequence as in the ordinary course of things would flow from the situation which the offending ship had created. Further, what those in charge of the injured ship do to save it may be mistaken, but if they

---

16 Ibid., 742 *per* Montague Smith J.; 744 *per* Brett J.
17 (1889) 15 PD 15 (CA).
18 Ibid., 18.
19 (1902) 71 LJKB 683 (CA). The facts of this case appear in Chapter 2. The *Dunham* case belongs to a series of cases in which the defendant employer has contended that the payment of worker's compensation should be terminated because the plaintiff worker's incapacity is due to an unreasonable refusal or unwillingness to accept necessary medical treatment. The House of Lords has held that in such cases where the worker's refusal has been unreasonable in the circumstances, the worker is not entitled to compensation: *Steele* v *Robert George & Co., (1937), Ltd* [1942] AC 497.
20 Ibid., 686.
21 (1927) 29 Lloyd's List Law Reports 253 (HL).

do whatever they do reasonably, although unsuccessfully, their mistaken judgment may be a natural consequence for which the offending ship is responsible...[22]

Viscount Haldane explicitly referred to and accepted the proposition laid down by Lindley L.J. in *The City of Lincoln* that reasonable human conduct 'extends to the reasonable conduct of those who have sustained the damage and who are seeking to save further loss'.[23] Thus, although those in charge of the *Baron Vernon* were under a duty of take steps to mitigate the loss post-collision, they would still discharge this duty if they only commit an error of judgement in deciding what to do in difficult circumstances. An instance of a more serious or gross case of negligence may have severed the causal link, however.

The reasonableness test has also been applied in the so-called rescue cases. *Hyett v Great Western Railway Company*[24] involved an attempt to rescue property. A fire broke out in a rail wagon which had been left by the defendants (the wagon's owner) in a railway siding. The cause of the fire was the defendants' negligence in leaving a number of leaking paraffin drums in the wagon. The plaintiff was employed to work on the wagons in the siding. Upon discovering the fire and while his friend went for assistance, the plaintiff attempted to remove a number of paraffin drums from the wagon. While he was doing so one of the drums exploded, injuring the plaintiff. Although the court considered that the plaintiff had voluntarily chosen to try to remove some of the drums, it was also considered reasonable for the plaintiff to do this. Thus, the chain of causation between the defendants' negligence and the plaintiff's injury had not been severed.

Perhaps *The Oropesa*[25] has come to be regarded as the leading English case to apply the reasonableness test to determine intervening causation issues. This decision of the Court of Appeal has been widely cited with approval by judges and scholars alike. There a collision occurred in the mid-Atlantic between the *Oropesa* and the *Manchester Regiment* during a gale. The *Manchester Regiment* was so seriously damaged that its captain ordered the majority of its crew to take to the lifeboats. Captain Raper then decided to set out in another lifeboat with 16 of its crew and row to the *Oropesa* in order to persuade its captain to take the *Manchester Regiment* in tow or to arrange for salvage assistance and, in any event, to arrange for messages for help to be sent out. Shortly after setting out, their lifeboat capsized and nine of the crew drowned. A collision action was brought in the Admiralty Court which apportioned the blame four-fifths to the *Manchester Regiment* and one-fifth to the *Oropesa*. The plaintiffs, the parents of one of the deceased seamen, sued the owners of the *Oropesa* in negligence, claiming that their son's drowning was the direct consequence of the negligent act of those in charge of the *Oropesa* in running down the *Manchester Regiment*. The defendants contended that the chain of causation had been broken by the act of Captain Raper in ordering members of his crew to row to the *Oropesa*. The Court of Appeal did not uphold the *novus actus* plea on the

---

22 Ibid., 254 (emphasis supplied).
23 Ibid.
24 [1947] 2 All ER 264.
25 [1943] 1 All ER 211.

ground that Captain Raper's action and the seaman's drowning were the natural and direct consequences of the negligent navigation of the *Oropesa* and the resultant emergency in which the former had been placed. Scott L.J. ruled that there was no break in the chain of causation as 'the action of the captain was taken in order to save the lives of those for whom he was responsible and was reasonable...'[26] Lord Wright delivered the main judgment. After having cited with approval the previous decision of the Court of Appeal in *The City of Lincoln*,[27] in which it was held that the decision of the captain to make for a port of safety was a reasonable response to the defendant's negligence and so did not sever the causal chain, Lord Wright stated:

> It must always be shown that there is something which I will call ultroneous, something unwarrantable, a new cause coming in disturbing the sequence of events, something that can be described as either unreasonable or extraneous or extrinsic. I doubt very much whether the law can be stated more precisely than that.[28]

Lord Wright held that there was an unbroken sequence of cause and effect between the negligent navigation of the *Oropesa* and the capsizing of the lifeboat and the drownings. Applying the test of reasonableness, it could not be said, in Lord Wright's view, that Captain Raper had acted unreasonably in the prevailing circumstances of being stranded in mid-Atlantic without any means of propulsion in heavy seas. According to Lord Wright, '[i]f the plaintiffs do whatever they do reasonably, though unsuccessfully, then their mistaken judgement may be a natural consequence for which the offending ship can be responsible.'[29] It would be otherwise, however, if Captain Raper 'did something which was outside the exigencies of the emergency'.[30] Thus, provided that the actions of a third party in response to the perilous situation created by the defendant's negligence are held to be reasonable – in the sense of being understandable in the circumstances – the third party's intervention will not be held to have severed the causal chain.[31] Although Captain Raper's decision to set out in the lifeboat may at one level be considered to have been an intentional or deliberate encountering of the risks involved, it was not a truly voluntary one in light of the peril thrust upon him by the defendant's negligence.

The English Court of Appeal has also applied the reasonableness test in a case involving a plaintiff's self-rescue attempt. In *Sayers* v *Harlow Urban District Council*[32] the plaintiff visited a public lavatory owned by the defendant and faced the ultimate nightmare when the lock on the toilet door jammed and she was unable to get out. For the next ten minutes or so she tried unsuccessfully to attract attention. She then decided to try to climb out by standing on the revolving toilet roll holder

---

26   Ibid., 216.
27   (1889) 15 PD 15.
28   [1943] 1 All ER 211, 215. This passage was cited with approval by Lord Guest in *McKew* v *Holland & Hannen & Cubitts (Scotland) Ltd* [1970] SC 20, 27 (HL).
29   Ibid., 216.
30   Ibid., 215.
31   P. Kaye *An Explanatory Guide to the English Law of Torts* (Barry Rose Law Publishers Ltd, 1996) 278.
32   [1958] 1 WLR 623 (CA).

which rotated, causing her to slip and fall and sustain injury. Although the Court of Appeal held the plaintiff to have been contributorily negligent, her self-rescue attempt was not adjudged to be a *novus actus interveniens* in these particular circumstances. In conducting herself as she did, 'the plaintiff...was behaving in a way which was reasonable'.[33] Morris L.J. considered that the 'most natural and reasonable action'[34] on the part of someone in such a predicament is to seek means of escape, and that the plaintiff 'acted carefully and prudently' rather than 'unreasonably or rashly or stupidly'.[35] In applying the reasonableness test, Lord Evershed M.R. concluded that the plaintiff 'was doing something...not at all unreasonable'.[36] The Master of the Rolls distinguished the early decision of the Court of Common Pleas in *Adams* v *Lancashire and Yorkshire Railway Co.*[37] on the ground that the degree of inconvenience suffered by Mrs Sayers far exceeded that experienced by the unsuccessful Mr Adams.

English courts have also applied the reasonableness test to cases where the plaintiff suffers further injury sustained as a result of being in a weakened or more vulnerable state as a result of the defendant's negligence. The question becomes whether the defendant is also liable to pay damages for the plaintiff's further injury. As we have seen in the previous chapter, the House of Lords held in *McKew* v *Holland & Hannen & Cubitts (Scotland) Ltd*[38] that the plaintiff's decision to descend a steep staircase alone and without a handrail some two weeks after suffering a workplace injury due to the defendant employer's negligence did not amount to a *novus actus interveniens*. This was because such decision was not reasonable in the circumstances.[39] Lord Reid stated:

> In my view the law is clear. If a man is injured in such a way that his leg may give way at any moment, he must act reasonably and carefully. It is quite possible that in spite of all reasonable care his leg may give way in circumstances such that as a result he sustains further injury. Then that second injury was caused by his disability, which in turn was caused by the defender's fault. But if the injured man acts unreasonably, he cannot hold the defender liable for injury caused by his own unreasonable conduct. His unreasonable conduct is *novus actus interveniens*. The chain of causation has been broken and what follows must be regarded as caused by his own conduct and not by the defender's fault or the disability caused by it.[40]

Curiously, unlike the *Sayers* case, the House of Lords refused to view the case as one of contributory negligence on the plaintiff's part necessitating an apportionment of damages between the plaintiff and defendant for the later injury.[41] Some six months

---

33 Ibid., 633 *per* Ormerod L.J.
34 Ibid., 630.
35 Ibid., 631.
36 Ibid., 629.
37 (1869) LR 4 CP 739. The *Adams* case is discussed fully in Chapter 2.
38 [1970] SC 20 (HL).
39 Ibid., 25–6 (*per* Lord Reid); 28 (*per* Lord Guest).
40 Ibid., 25.
41 Various commentators have criticised the House of Lords on this point, arguing that it would have been fairer to apportion damages rather than to deny them altogether since the

prior to the House of Lords handing down its decision in *McKew*'s case, a similar issue was presented for decision before Eveleigh J. in *Wieland* v *Cyril Lord Carpets, Ltd*.[42] There, the plaintiff, a bus passenger, received a jarring neck injury as a result of an accident admittedly caused by the defendant's negligence. An attending specialist prescribed a collar for her neck which was then fitted. She wore bi-focal glasses and the position of her neck in the collar deprived her of her usual ability to adjust herself automatically to the bi-focals. This produced some unsteadiness. While descending a flight of stairs with the assistance of her adult son, she fell and injured her ankles. Eveleigh J. held that there was no break in the chain of causation between the defendant's negligence and the plaintiff fracturing her ankles in the fall on the ground and that (unlike the *McKew* case) it had not been unreasonable for her in these circumstances to descend the stairs with the assistance of her son.[43]

There are some recent English decisions which have applied other *novus actus* tests to resolve the intervening causation issue but which could just as easily have been resolved through applying the reasonableness test. So, for instance, in *Lamb* v *Camden London Borough Council*[44] Watkins L.J. considered long-term squatting in the plaintiff's house as a 'kind of anti-social and criminal behaviour' which amounted to 'unreasonable conduct of an outrageous kind'.[45] Similarly, in *Knightley* v *Johns*,[46] the police inspector's order to the plaintiff to engage in a dangerous manoeuvre could equally have been viewed as unreasonable conduct amounting to *novus actus*.[47] And, in the Court of Appeal decision in *Wright* v *Lodge*,[48] Parker L.J. held that the reckless driving of an articulated container lorry in conditions of poor visibility constituted a *novus actus interveniens* as such driving was (to borrow from the terminology used by Lord Wright in *The Oropesa*[49]) 'unwarranted and unreasonable'.[50]

The reasonableness test has also been applied by the English courts in a case involving an unwanted pregnancy. In *Emeh* v *Kensington and Chelsea and Westminster Area Health Authority*[51] the plaintiff, the mother of three children, had

---

plaintiff's weakened condition attributable to the defendant's negligence did contribute, in part, to the second accident. See A. Palmer 'Causation in the High Court' (1993) 1 *Torts Law Journal* 9, 14; F. Trindade and P. Cane *The Law of Torts in Australia*, 494, n. 81; M.A. Millner '*Novus Actus Interveniens*: The Present Effect of Wagon Mound' (1971) 22 *Northern Ireland Legal Quarterly* 168, 178–9.

42   [1969] 3 All ER 1006 (QBD).
43   Ibid., 1008. See also *Pyne* v *Wilkenfeld* (1981) 26 SASR 441. There the defendants negligently inflicted neck injuries on the plaintiff so that her neck had to be placed in a collar. Due to the collar, her vision was restricted such that she could not see immediately in front of her. This caused her to fall over on a footpath and she also recovered for that later injury.
44   [1981] 1 QB 625 (CA).
45   Ibid., 647. See Chapter 3 for a detailed discussion of the *Lamb* case.
46   [1982] 1 All ER 851 (CA). See Chapter 3 for a detailed discussion of the *Knightley* case.
47   N.J. McBride and R. Bagshaw *Tort Law* (Pearson Education Ltd, 2001) 477.
48   [1993] 4 All ER 299 (CA).
49   [1943] 1 All ER 211, 215.
50   [1993] 4 All ER 299, 307.
51   [1984] 3 All ER 1044 (CA).

an abortion to terminate a fourth pregnancy and simultaneously had a sterilisation operation to prevent further pregnancies. The operation was performed negligently by two doctors employed by the defendant health authority and several months later the plaintiff became pregnant again, although she did not discover this until 20 weeks into the pregnancy. She then decided that because she did not want any more operations, she would not undergo another abortion. The plaintiff later gave birth to a congenitally abnormal child and an action was brought against the defendant health authority claiming damages for the maintenance of this child. The trial Judge held that the plaintiff's refusal to have an abortion was so unreasonable as to amount to a *novus actus interveniens* or a failure to mitigate damage. This was overturned on appeal to the Court of Appeal. Waller L.J. considered the 'conduct on the part of the plaintiff was not so unreasonable as to eclipse the [doctors'] wrongdoing.'[52] Slade L.J. referred in his judgment to the fact that an operation to terminate her pregnancy would have involved three days in hospital, the operation carried some risks due to the size of the foetus, and that such operation would have involved considerable pain and discomfort.[53] The plaintiff's decision not to have an abortion was not a *novus actus* or a failure to mitigate damage because the doctors' negligence (for which the defendant was liable) had confronted the plaintiff with the very dilemma of whether to have the child or an abortion which she had sought to avoid by having herself sterilised.[54] The Court of Appeal has more recently continued its application of the reasonableness test in a case involving intervening remedial work by a local government authority. *Roberts* v *Bettany*[55] involved a dispute between two neighbours. The plaintiffs occupied a property known as 'Sea Haze'. Their neighbour, the defendants, owned and occupied a property called 'Grove House'. At the back of Grove House existed an embankment which formed part of a colliery soil heap, upon which the plaintiffs' property, Sea Haze, was built. In September 1991 the defendants employed a gardener to clear part of the embankment on their property, in the course of which several small fires were lit. Several months later underground fires were detected and in May 1992 the Delyn Borough Council intervened in order to undertake works to excavate the embankment and fill the area from which the burning matter had been removed with inert material. Although the underground fires were eventually extinguished, cracking of the plaintiffs' garden walls and other property damage by ground movement were discovered beginning in September 1992. The plaintiffs contended that although the immediate cause of their property damage was the local authority's excavation works, the legal cause of such damage was nevertheless attributable to the underground fires lit by someone for whom the defendants were responsible. The defendants in turn pleaded *novus actus interveniens*, arguing that the manner in which the local authority had conducted its excavation works was sufficient in law to break the chain of causation. In reversing

---

52   Ibid., 1049.
53   Ibid., 1053.
54   Ibid. See also *Humber Oil Terminal Trustee Ltd* v *Owners of the Ship 'Sivand', The Sivand* [1998] 2 Lloyd's Rep. 97 (CA) (since the plaintiff had acted reasonably, it had not failed to mitigate its loss).
55   [2001] EWCA Civ 109 (CA).

the trial Judge, Buxton L.J., who delivered the main judgment in the case, applied the reasonableness test in holding that the local authority had acted neither negligently nor unreasonably in taking the steps it had done to avoid a potentially hazardous situation:

> What was done was in direct response to a hazardous situation created by the defendants. It was at their peril that an intervener might not act with full competence and might cause some further or different injury. That is apparently…what happened in this case, but it does not exculpate in law, in the circumstances of this case, the defendants from the consequences of their original act of negligence.[56]

Thus, the above survey of the English case-law demonstrates that both the House of Lords and the Court of Appeal have had a long tradition in applying the reasonableness test to determine intervening causation issues in a variety of contexts.

The United States of America

While English judges tend to apply the concept of reasonableness in resolving *novus actus* issues, their US counterparts have resorted to the notion of 'normality'. In many, but not all cases these two concepts will be coterminous and produce identical results on their application. Two provisions of the American Law Institute's *Restatement of the Law of Torts, Second*[57] are pertinent here. Section 442 (c) states that the fact that an intervening force is or is not a 'normal result' of a situation created by the defendant's negligence is an important consideration in determining whether such intervening force is a superseding cause of the plaintiff's injury. Similarly, Section 443 provides that '[t]he intervention of a force which is a normal consequence of a situation created by the [defendant's] negligent conduct is not a superseding cause of [the plaintiff's] harm…' According to the commentary accompanying Section 443, the term 'normal' denotes the antithesis of 'abnormal' and 'extraordinary' and that it is not necessary that the conduct of the plaintiff or third party be 'reasonable'.[58] Thus, a normal consequence of a situation created by the defendant's negligence can extend beyond a reasonable response to such negligence to include an unreasonable, but normal, response.

A series of decisions handed down by US intermediate appellate courts in the 1930s and 1940s draws on the *American Restatement*'s 'normality' approach in resolving intervening causation issues. *New York Central Railway Company v Brown*[59] involved a determination of the legal cause of an injury to a railway brakeman following the failure of a safety appliance. The plaintiff was a yard brakeman in the defendant's employ. While engaged with other members of a switching crew in an attempt to couple a switch engine to a refrigerator car, an automatic coupler on the latter failed to engage. The impact caused the refrigerator car to move along a down-

---

56   Ibid., para. 23.
57   (1965–79).
58   *Restatement of the Law of Torts, Second* (AL1, 1965–79) 472–3.
59   63 F 2d 657 (6 Cir 1933).

grade towards the defendant's tunnel. Fearing that the car could cause injury and damage, the plaintiff sprang to the car's ladder for the purpose of applying the brake wheel. In so doing, his head brushed an overhead electric third rail, from which he received a shock which caused him to fall to the ground and sustain serious injuries. The defendant employer's plea that the plaintiff's rescue attempt constituted a new and independent superseding cause of his injuries was rejected by the Sixth Circuit Court of Appeals. Simons, Circuit Judge, formulated the relevant test to be whether the plaintiff's act was a 'normal response' to the stimulus of a dangerous situation created by the defendant's fault. The defendant's *novus actus* plea was rejected on the basis that 'it has long been settled that the chain of causation is not broken by an intervening act which is a normal reaction to the stimulus of a situation created by the negligence, and such normal reaction has been held to include the instinct toward self-preservation...and the equally natural impulse to rush to others' assistance in emergency...'[60] *Chicago, Milwaukee, St Paul & Pacific Railroad Company v Goldhammer*[61] also involved an action for damages for personal injury following the failure of a safety appliance. The plaintiff, an experienced switchman, was in the defendant's employ at the time of the accident. While attempting to open a defective knuckle of a coupler, the plaintiff sustained a back injury. Although the defendant conceded negligence in using a railway car with a defective knuckle, it contended that its negligence was superseded by the plaintiff's negligence in attempting to lift the heavy knuckle back into place. The Circuit Court of Appeals, Eighth Circuit, expressly relied on an earlier version of Section 443 of the American Law Institute's *Restatement of the Law of Torts* to the effect that an intervening act of a human being which is a normal response to the stimulus of a situation created by the defendant's negligence is not a superseding cause of the plaintiff's injury. In the Court's view, the plaintiff's conduct was no more than a 'normal response' to the situation created by the defective knuckle and, thus, did not amount to a superseding cause or *novus actus*.[62] Yet another case which applied the normality test to a railway accident is the 1937 decision of the Second Circuit Court of Appeals in *Anderson v Baltimore & Ohio Railroad Company*.[63] This was an action for wrongful death brought under the *Employers' Liability Act 1908* for an alleged violation of a statutory duty by the defendant resulting in the death of one of its employees. The action was brought by the executrix and personal representative of the estate of the deceased railroad worker. The deceased met his death while employed by the defendant as a fireman on a pusher engine which was equipped with a sanding apparatus consisting of two sandboxes located above the boiler. On the fateful day in question, a grade was reached during the engine's journey when it became necessary to activate the sanders. However, the sanders failed to deliver sand to the rails causing the train to stall. Before the train had come to a complete stop, the deceased disembarked from the engine and, while examining the sanders, was struck and killed by a train coming from the opposite direction. The plaintiff alleged that a breach of Rule 120

---

60 Ibid., 658.
61 79 F 2d 272 (8 Cir 1935).
62 Ibid., 274.
63 89 F 2d 629 (2 Cir 1937).

Unreasonableness/Abnormality

promulgated under the *Boiler Inspection Act 1924* (which required locomotives to be equipped with a proper and safe sanding apparatus) had caused the deceased's death. The defendant employer's argument that the deceased's 'own act in placing himself in a position of danger where he would be struck by the Erie engine was the proximate cause of his death...'[64] was rejected by the appellate court. Although the deceased was deemed to have been contributorily negligent in failing to observe the approaching engine, 'his conduct was a normal reaction to the stimulus of a situation created by the defendant's violation of its statutory duty.'[65] Thus, the deceased's lack of awareness or vigilance did not go so far as amounting to a superseding cause or *novus actus* so as to preclude recovery of any damages.

Some US appellate courts, however, have applied the reasonableness test in resolving intervening causation issues. *Lowden* v *Shoffner Mercantile Co.*[66] involved an action against the trustees of the Chicago, Rock Island & Pacific Railway Company for damages for the destruction of the plaintiff's warehouse by fire. The warehouse was located near a side track of the defendant's railway. It was found at trial that in the course of carrying out their duties, the defendant's employees negligently commenced a fire near the plaintiff's warehouse and left the fire burning without care or attention. Anticipating that such fire might consume the plaintiff's warehouse, several of the plaintiff's employees commenced 'backburning' operations which ultimately proved unsuccessful. The Eighth Circuit Court of Appeals rejected the defendant's contention that the lighting of the backfires by the plaintiff's employees constituted a superseding cause of the plaintiff's loss, absolving them of all liability. In so holding, the Court stated:

> The use of back fires was reasonable and proper under the circumstances. To have refrained from using such means would have left the town at the mercy of the fires set by the [defendant's employees]. Under such circumstances, the original fires became the direct, efficient and proximate cause of all the fire that burned in and around Shoffner, and if any such fire caused the burning of the warehouse, the predominant cause of the damage was the original fire.[67]

Other cases have similarly held that it is 'reasonable and proper' for persons to defend their property from negligently-lit fires by backburning and that such attempts to mitigate their losses do not amount to a superseding cause of any subsequent loss.[68] One could also say, in the language of the *American Restatement of the Law of Torts, Second*, that the use of backburning techniques is a normal consequence of, or response to, the situation generated by the defendant's negligence.

---

64   Ibid., 631.
65   Ibid.
66   109 F 2d 956 (8 Cir 1940).
67   Ibid., 958–9.
68   See, for example, *McKenna* v *Baessler* (1892) 86 Iowa 197; 53 NW 103 (Supreme Court of Iowa).

Australia

The High Court of Australia has had occasion from time to time to apply the reasonableness test to determine intervening causation issues. However, such application has usually occurred in any one case by single judges rather than the full bench thereof. *Adelaide Chemical and Fertilizer Company Limited* v *Carlyle*[69] provides an early example. There the defendant company manufactured and supplied sulphuric acid in earthenware jars. The corrosive nature of sulphuric acid made it highly dangerous to persons handling the jars if they were broken and the acid escaped. While the plaintiff was picking up a supply of the acid on his employer's behalf, one of the jars broke spilling its contents over him. The plaintiff immediately began to wash the acid from his legs and was later treated at hospital and advised to see a doctor the following day. The plaintiff failed to do so. His wife instead treated him with tannemol, a preparation which a chemist advised her was a proper treatment for burns (as in fact it was). The plaintiff subsequently took a turn for the worse and a doctor was immediately summoned. Streptococcal septicaemia developed and the plaintiff died. The plaintiff's widow brought an action against the defendant company under wrongful death legislation.[70] Starke J. rejected a plea by the defendant that 'the disobedience of medical orders and the want of proper treatment of the injuries by the deceased and his wife'[71] amounted to a *novus actus interveniens*. His Honour stated:

> The cause of death was streptococcal septicaemia following, according to medical opinion, upon the infection of a wound or burn upon the body of the deceased brought about by the operation of sulphuric acid upon his skin. But the evidence does not establish any fault on the part of the deceased or his wife. After treatment at the Adelaide Hospital, the deceased did not report to the nearest doctor next day, as advised, but his wife treated him to the best of her ability with tannemol, which a chemist advised her was a proper treatment for burns, as in fact it was, and she called in a doctor so soon as unexpected conditions developed.[72]

It is clear that Starke J. considered the conduct of the deceased and his wife to be reasonable in the circumstances and, accordingly, the defendant was held liable not only for the original burning injury but for the death as well.

The reasonableness test was also applied as an intervening causation test by the High Court of Australia in *Caterson* v *Commissioner for Railways*.[73] The case involved an action against the defendant for damages for personal injuries. Accompanied by his 14-year-old son, the plaintiff had driven a friend some 40 miles to a railway station so that the friend might catch an express train. The plaintiff carried the friend's luggage into the carriage, and as he was leaving the carriage he noticed that the train had started to move. No warning had been given that the train

---

69 (1940) 64 CLR 514.
70 Part II of the *Wrongs Act 1936* (S.A.) (*Lord Campbell's Act*).
71 (1940) 64 CLR 514, 528.
72 Ibid.
73 (1973) 128 CLR 99.

was about to depart. The next scheduled train stop was some eighty miles away. The train was not travelling very fast when the plaintiff, thinking of his son on the platform 40 miles from home, jumped from the train on to the platform and was injured. Gibbs J. rejected the defendant's submission that the plaintiff's 'voluntary' act in jumping from the train broke the chain of causation. Distinguishing *McKew v Holland & Hannen & Cubitts (Scotland) Ltd*,[74] Gibbs J. described the plaintiff's conduct as 'not unreasonable'[75] in the circumstances and considered that 'a person who wished to avoid being carried on to a distant station might not unreasonably jump out from a train which was travelling very slowly.'[76] In contrast to *Adams v The Lancashire and Yorkshire Railway Company*,[77] the degree of inconvenience generated by the defendant's negligence far outweighed the danger posed, such that it was reasonable for the plaintiff to act as he did. In its 1985 decision in *Mahony v J. Kruschich (Demolitions) Pty Ltd*[78] the full bench of the High Court of Australia, in holding that only gross medical negligence would amount to *novus actus*, appeared to endorse the decision of the House of Lords in the *McKew* case which, it will be recalled, approved and applied the reasonableness test.[79] It would also appear that *McKew* has received the imprimatur of Mason C.J. in the decision of the High Court of Australia in *March v E. & M.H. Stramare Pty Ltd*.[80]

The reasonableness test has been applied more recently by McHugh J. of the High Court of Australia in *Medlin v The State Government Insurance Commission*.[81] The plaintiff was involved in a motor vehicle accident and sustained serious injuries. At the time of the accident the plaintiff was aged 56 and worked as a university professor. Three months after the accident the plaintiff resumed his university duties but continued to experience pain and discomfort. Some four-and-a-half years after the accident, the plaintiff retired four-and-a-half years before he would have been obliged to retire in accordance with his employer's early retirement scheme. The plaintiff complained that the pain, sleeplessness and associated loss of 'intellectual energy' made him no longer able to discharge his teaching and research duties at a sufficiently high level to satisfy himself (as opposed to his employer). The main issue in the appeal was whether the plaintiff was entitled to recover the equivalent of four and one-half years of salary as compensation for an alleged loss of earning capacity. McHugh J. rejected the contention that the plaintiff's 'voluntary' act in taking early retirement amounted to a *novus actus interveniens*, holding that 'it was not unreasonable for the plaintiff to retire early.'[82] Because the decision to retire early was not unreasonable in the circumstances and the reasons underlying it were the result of his accident-related injuries, the plaintiff's loss of earning capacity was caused for legal purposes by the

---

[74] [1970] SC 20 (HL).
[75] (1973) 128 CLR 99, 110.
[76] Ibid., 112.
[77] (1869) LR 4 CP 739.
[78] (1985) 156 CLR 522.
[79] Ibid., 528.
[80] (1990–91) 171 CLR 506, 517.
[81] (1994–95) 182 CLR 1.
[82] Ibid., 22.

defendant's negligence.[83] Australian lower courts have taken up the High Court's lead in applying the reasonableness test. For example, in *Pyne* v *Wilkenfeld*[84] the plaintiff received a neck injury in a motor vehicle accident caused by the defendant's negligence. Her neck had to be put in a surgical collar as a result thereof. The plaintiff later suffered further injuries when she stumbled on uneven ground because, due to the collar, her vision was restricted so that she could not see immediately in front of her. The Supreme Court of South Australia held that the plaintiff was entitled to recover for that further injury since these post-motor vehicle accident events were not sufficiently abnormal or unreasonable responses to the situation created by the defendant's negligence so as to amount to a *novus actus interveniens*.[85] In *State Government Insurance Commission* v *Oakley*[86] the plaintiff, a nurse, had received an injury to her right arm and shoulder in a motor vehicle accident caused by the defendant's negligence. This left her with a residual disability causing her to rely only on her left arm in lifting patients. While lifting a patient she suffered further injury when she slipped and fell. The defendant motorist responsible for the first injury was held liable for 50 per cent of the later injury since the first injury contributed to the second injury and the *McKew* case did not apply where the plaintiff is compelled to take the risk of further injury as part of her employment. A similar result obtained in the case of *Kessey* v *Golledge*[87] before the New South Wales Court of Appeal. The plaintiff was involved in a motor vehicle accident in July 1992 as a result of the defendant's conceded negligence. This aggravated an existing condition of spondylolisthesis which necessitated a lumbar fusion in late 1992. In July 1996 she fell in the course of her employment and further aggravated her back injury. The defendant contended that the plaintiff's fall at her place of work and consequent twisting of her back constituted a *novus actus interveniens* thereby terminating the defendant's liability for any injuries produced by the workplace accident. The defendant's *novus actus* plea was rejected at first instance as the defendant had not discharged the onus of proving that the plaintiff had acted so unreasonably and without regard to her own safety in the *McKew* sense prior to her workplace accident as to break the chain of causation. The New South Wales Court of Appeal agreed with the trial Judge's conclusion on the intervening causation issue on the ground that there was no evidence to suggest that the plaintiff was not acting 'reasonably and carefully' when she tripped over some books which had been left on the floor in her workplace.[88] In another intervening causation case, the New South Wales Court of Appeal has considered the plaintiff's family and cultural background in assessing the reasonableness of the plaintiff's response to the situation created by the defendant's negligence.[89]

---

83 Ibid., 23.
84 (1981) 26 SASR 441.
85 See to the same effect the English decision *Wieland* v *Cyril Lord Carpets, Ltd* [1969] 3 All ER 1006 (QBD) discussed earlier in this chapter.
86 [1990] Australian Torts Reports 81-003.
87 [1999] NSWCA 424.
88 Ibid., para. 66.
89 See *Kavanagh* v *Akhtar* (1998) 45 NSWLR 588, 601. See also the decision of the Queensland Court of Appeal in *Hirst* v *Nominal Defendant* [2005] 2 Qd R 133 (police officer's decision to engage in a high-speed chase on a highway not deemed unreasonable).

Other Jurisdictions

The instances are rare of the Supreme Court of Canada applying the reasonableness test to resolve an intervening causation issue but one such instance is its decision in *Roberge v Bolduc*.[90] This case emanated from the Province of Quebec, a civil law jurisdiction, and involved breach of contract and professional negligence issues. In 1987, upon acceptance of their offer to purchase the immoveable property of one Bolduc, the plaintiffs instructed the defendant notary to examine the vendor's title to assure them that he held good and valid title to the property and, if so, to prepare the deed of sale. In examining the chain of title, the defendant notary discovered that in 1977 one P.L. had obtained a loan from a lending institution secured by a mortgage (hypothec). The mortgage was registered against the subject property even though P.L. was not the owner, the property being registered at the time in the name of P.L. Inc. Both P.L. and P.L. Inc. later made assignments in bankruptcy and the same trustee was appointed for both bankrupt estates. The trustee registered a notice of bankruptcy of P.L. against the property but did not register a notice on behalf of P.L. Inc. Upon the default of P.L. on his loan, the lending institution took proceedings against the trustee and obtained a default judgment granting it title to the property. This judgment was duly registered against the property. In 1981, the lending institution sold the property to the wife of the prospective vendor who, in 1984, purchased the property from his wife. Following the title search, the defendant notary informed the plaintiffs that, in his opinion, the default judgment did not cure the defect in the vendor's title. As the mortgage had been granted by a person other than the registered owner, it was null and void and the judgment could not give more than the mortgage was worth. The vendor's attorney replied that the registration of the default judgment had perfected the title and had acquired the authority of *res judicata*. Faced with these opposing views, the plaintiffs consulted a second notary who confirmed the defendant's opinion. The plaintiffs then notified the vendor that they would not proceed with the purchase of the property and instructed their solicitor to take action against him. The vendor counterclaimed for damage allegedly suffered from the plaintiffs' refusal to purchase the property. In answer to this counterclaim, the plaintiffs exercised a recourse in warranty against the defendant on the basis that it was on his advice that they refused to purchase the property.

One of the issues before the Supreme Court of Canada was whether the defendant notary's error of law caused the plaintiffs' injury (liability in damages to the prospective vendor) or whether the legal opinion given by the second notary confirming the defendant's notary's opinion constituted a *novus actus interveniens* absolving the latter of liability to the plaintiffs. The Supreme Court of Canada rejected the defendant's notary's *novus actus* plea on the ground that the plaintiffs' decision to seek the second notary's opinion was in no way independent of the defendant's advice but, in fact, was completely dependent upon it. The only reason the second opinion was sought was due to the defendant's fault in erroneously concluding that the title was defective. The Supreme Court pointed to the irony that the plaintiffs were being reproached for taking an appropriate and cautious course of conduct in

---

90 [1991] 1 SCR 374.

the face of opposing legal opinions. Such a reasonable approach by the plaintiffs in such circumstances preserved the integrity of the causal link between the defendant notary's negligent advice and the plaintiffs' damage.[91]

The Irish courts have also applied the reasonableness test in the so-called 'alternative danger' cases[92] where the defendant's negligence has forced the intervening actor into pursuing a particular course of conduct, as where the plaintiff, fearing injury if she remains a passenger in the defendant's runaway car, jumps out hoping to avoid greater injury. The critical question for the Irish courts has been whether a reasonable person in the plaintiff's position would have acted in the same way. *Hogg* v *Keane*[93] is an example of the application of the objective reasonable person test where the court stated that 'if the plaintiff can connect her injuries to the accident by showing that her fright was reasonable, she is entitled to recover damages against the defendant.'[94]

Critique of the Reasonableness/Normality Test

The application of the reasonableness test, unlike other intervening causation tests, involves the judicial assessment of the propriety of the plaintiff's or third party's response to the situation created by the defendant's negligence. As such, it calls for a consideration of what would 'normally' transpire in such a situation or how a reasonable person in the position of the plaintiff or third party would conduct himself or herself. One significant advantage of the reasonableness test is that English judges have had considerable experience over nearly the past two centuries in applying the objective reasonable person test in the standard of care context. As Tindal C.J. said in *Vaughan* v *Menlove*,[95] the defendant's conduct is to be judged by the standard of care which a person 'of ordinary prudence'[96] would have exercised in the circumstances. Yet such an objective test is susceptible to subjectivity of application. Although the reasonable person test is theoretically objective, Lord Macmillan reminds us that different judges may take different views of what a reasonable person would do in the circumstances:

> The standard of foresight of the reasonable man is in one sense an impersonal test. It eliminates the personal equation and is independent of the idiosyncrasies of the particular person whose conduct is in question...But there is a sense in which the standard of care of the reasonable man involves in its application a subjective element. It is still left to the judge to decide what in the circumstances of the particular case the reasonable man would have had in contemplation...Here there is room for diversity of view...What to one judge may seem far-fetched may seem to another both natural and probable.[97]

---

91   For a similar case and holding, see the decision of the High Court of Australia in *Bennett* v *Minister of Community Welfare* (1992) 176 CLR 408.
92   The 'alternative danger' cases will be examined in Chapter 15.
93   [1956] IR 155.
94   Ibid., 158. See also *Kingston* v *Kingston* 102 ILTR 65 (Sup Ct, 1965).
95   (1837) 3 Bing NC 468.
96   Ibid., 475.
97   *Glasgow Corp.* v *Muir* [1943] AC 448, 457 (HL).

Lord Macmillan's observations are equally apt in the intervening causation context. Moreover, judging the unreasonableness or abnormality of the intervening conduct involves the idea of a departure from a particular norm and this may vary from case to case and across different contexts.[98] Because intervening causation cases are generally quite fact-sensitive, it is difficult to identify and apply a sufficiently objective test to measure the facts of a particular case against a presumed norm. The question of whether the degree of deviation from the norm is sufficiently great to warrant extinguishing a defendant's liability may, in truth, be no more than a judicial policy choice.[99] Yet another concern raised in relation to the reasonableness test is the unwelcome prospect of permitting a defendant to escape liability when it was the defendant's negligence itself which created the occasion for the unreasonable intervening conduct. Depending on the degree of peril to which the plaintiff or a third party is exposed as a result of the defendant's negligence, the fact that the intervening actor's conduct is quite unreasonable or irrational might be so precisely because of the pressure he or she was thereby placed under.[100]

---

98 A. Palmer, 'Causation in the High Court', 18.

99 D. Rosenberg *The Hidden Holmes: His Theory of Torts in History* (Harvard University Press, 1995) 72.

100 Yeo, 'Making Sense of Liability for Intervening Acts', 53, 60.

Chapter 5

Voluntary and Deliberate Human Action

Introduction

Historically it has generally been easier to successfully plead *novus actus interveniens* when the intervention of the third party is deliberate in the sense that the third party's act was intended to produce the consequences the intervention did in fact produce. It has been said that deliberate interventions are more likely to sever the causal chain than negligent interventions[1] and that 'the more flagrant and overwhelming the intervention the more likely it is to amount to a *novus actus*.'[2] For long the principle held sway that if, subsequent to the defendant's negligence, there intervened prior to the plaintiff's injury the culpable act of a third person, the 'last human wrongdoer' was alone liable.[3] This principle acknowledged 'the fact that the wilful wrongdoing of others cannot ordinarily be accounted a normal risk of the dangerous situation created by the defendant.'[4] In *Dominion Natural Gas Ltd* v *Collins and Perkins*[5] Lord Dunedin was not prepared to hold a defendant liable 'if the proximate cause of the accident is not the negligence of the defendant but the conscious act of another volition'.[6] And in *Weld-Blundell* v *Stephens*[7] Lord Sumner stated:

> In general even though A is in fault, he is not responsible for injury to C which B, a stranger to him, deliberately chooses to do. Though A may have given the occasion for B's mischievous activity, B then becomes a new and independent cause…he insulates A from C.[8]

Thus, where the third person's intervening deliberate act was actually intended to cause injury to the plaintiff, the defendant was generally exculpated from liability.

The common law evolved during the course of the twentieth century such that not all intervening deliberate acts had the automatic effect of breaking the chain of causation. The common law is now prepared to impose civil liability on a defendant

---

1 *Knightley* v *Johns* [1982] 1 All ER 851, 865 (*per* Stephenson L.J.) (CA).
2 A.M. Dugdale and M.A. Jones (eds) *Clerk & Lindsell on Torts* (Sweet & Maxwell, 19th edn, 2006) [104], para. 2–86.
3 J. Fleming *The Law of Torts* (The Law Book Company Ltd, 9th edn, 1998) 250. This principle was partly attributable to the refusal of the common law to allow contribution among tortfeasors.
4 Ibid., 253.
5 [1909] AC 640.
6 Ibid., 646.
7 [1920] AC 956.
8 Ibid., 986.

for negligently providing an opportunity for third parties to cause deliberate harm, as where the scope of the defendant's duty of care extends to taking precautions to guard against that very eventuality.[9] Even a criminal act by a third party will not necessarily constitute a *novus actus interveniens*, depending on how widely the court construes the scope of the duty of care owed by the defendant. In cases of deliberately inflicted harm, if the duty of care which has been breached was aimed at preventing deliberate third party conduct, then any loss caused by that third party's act was caused by that breach of duty for legal purposes. On the other hand, if the duty of care was designed to address some other risk or risks, and the breach of duty merely set the scene for the intervention, then the third party's act will amount to a *novus actus*.[10] As Section 442B. of the American Law Institute's *Restatement of the Law of Torts, Second* states, the chain of causation between the defendant's negligence and the plaintiff's injury will be severed 'where the harm is intentionally caused by a third person and is not within the scope of the risk created by the actor's conduct'.[11]

The existence of intent or deliberation is relevant not only from the third party's standpoint but from that of the defendant's as well. Early English cases recognised that, as a matter of principle, it would be unfair for a defendant who has intended to cause harm to benefit from limitation of liability rules such as *novus actus interveniens* or remoteness of damage. As De Grey C.J. said in *Scott* v *Shepherd*[12] '[e]very one who does an unlawful act is considered as the doer of all that follows; if done with a deliberate intent...'[13] Similarly in *Bird* v *Holbrook*[14] the plaintiff's trespass into the defendant's garden was held not to constitute a *novus actus* on the ground that the setting of spring guns by the defendant without giving notice exhibited an intention on his part to injure trespassers.[15] By the same token, and as discussed in the previous paragraph, intentional or deliberate conduct on the part of the intervening party will sever the causal chain, particularly where such conduct does not fall within the scope of the risk created by the defendant's negligence. This is the basis of the decision of the Judicial Committee of the Privy Council in *Rickards* v *Lothian*[16] where it was held that the deliberate and malicious act of a third person in clogging a lavatory basin amounted to a *novus actus interveniens*.[17]

---

9   Fleming, *The Law of Torts* (The Law Book Company Ltd, 9th edn, 1998) 253.
10 S. Todd (ed.) *The Law of Torts in New Zealand* (Brookers Ltd, 3rd edn, 2001) 1008.
11 (1965–79) 469.
12 (1773) 2 W Bl 892.
13 Ibid., 899.
14 (1828) 4 Bing 628.
15 Ibid., 641 (*per* Best C.J.).
16 [1913] AC 263 (JCPC).
17 *Obiter dicta* comments to the same effect may be found in various cases. For example, in *Sullivan* v *Creed* [1904] 2 IR 317, Holmes L.J. (at 356) observed that although a person who negligently lays aside a loaded gun ought to foresee that it may be taken up and negligently used by a third person, 'it would not be within reasonable contemplation that the finder of it would wilfully discharge it at another.' Similarly, in *Philco Radio and Television Corporation of Great Britain, Ltd* v *J. Spurling, Ltd* [1949] 2 All ER 882 (CA), Singleton L.J. opined that 'if it was shown that Mrs. Brady intentionally or deliberately and knowingly

The principle that the intervening conduct of a third person which is intentionally tortious or criminal, and is not within the scope of the risk created by the defendant's negligence, severs the chain of causation is based on the rationale that in such a case the third person has deliberately assumed control of the situation, and that all responsibility for the consequences should be shifted to him or her.[18]

The United Kingdom

Once again, the starting-point is the early leading case of *Scott* v *Shepherd*.[19] There the ground of the decision was that the causal chain was not broken as the acts of the intermediate persons in throwing the celebrated squib were instinctive, involuntary and unpremeditated in nature rather than being truly independent and conscious acts of volition. But, as we have just seen, *Bird* v *Holbrook*[20] established that even an intentional trespass to land (albeit for a good rescue of property motive) will not sever the causal chain where the defendant occupier is bent on harming trespassers by laying traps. In the early slander case of *Ward* v *Weeks*[21] the plaintiff's action failed on the ground that '[i]t was the repetition of [the slander] by Bryce to Bryer, which was the voluntary act of a free agent, over whom the Defendant had no control, and for whose acts he is not answerable, that was the immediate cause of the Plaintiff's damage.'[22] But in *Clayards* v *Dethick*[23] the plaintiff's voluntary decision to incur a significant risk in defiance of a warning did not sever the chain of causation as the plaintiff 'was not bound to abstain from pursuing his livelihood because there was some danger'.[24]

That the third person's act must be fully 'volitional' (in the sense in which Lord Dunedin used that term in *Dominion Natural Gas Ltd* v *Collins and Perkins*[25]) and that that person must understand and appreciate the consequences of such an act were reaffirmed by the Judicial Committee of the Privy Council in *Rickards*

---

put her cigarette to this material, intending to make only a little fire, and this damage resulted from that act, there was a new cause intervening, and that the damage flowed not from any negligence on the part of the defendants, but from the act of Mrs. Brady' (at 886) See to the same effect Jenkins L.J. (at 888).

18   American Law Institute *Restatement of the Law of Torts, Second* (1965–79) Commentary on Section 442B. 471.
19   (1773) 2 W Bl 892.
20   (1828) 4 Bing 628. This case is discussed in more detail in Chapter 2.
21   (1830) 7 Bing 211. This case is discussed in more detail in Chapter 2.
22   Ibid., 215 *per* Tindal C.J.
23   (1848) 12 QB 439.
24   Ibid., 447 *per* Coleridge J. This case is discussed in more detail in Chapter 2. By contrast, in *Hughes* v *Macfie* (1863) 2 H & C 744 it was held that the 'voluntary' act of the plaintiff (a seven-year-old child) in meddling with the defendant's property for no lawful purpose either amounted to contributory negligence (a complete bar at that time) or a *novus actus interveniens* (at 749). It is questionable whether the same holding would be reached today (see Chapter 14).
25   [1909] AC 640, 646.

v *Lothian*.[26] There, it was held that the vandal's deliberate and malicious act in clogging a lavatory basin constituted a *novus actus interveniens* on the basis of the satisfaction of these two criteria. In *Weld-Blundell* v *Stephens*[27] an agent had allowed documents potentially damaging to his principal to fall out of his possession. These documents were found by a third person who handed them to the persons who were defamed and who successfully sued the agent's principal for damages. A majority of their Lordships held that the plaintiff's liability for damages for libel did not result from the defendant's breach of duty but rather from the action of the third person. Lord Sumner stated:

> Again, between the negligence of a defendant and the infliction of hurt or loss on a plaintiff, the action of human beings may intervene in a great variety of ways…Darling J. thought that this case might be treated as if the letter was an 'explosive' dangerous in itself…the analogy was a false one. The letter could not 'go off' of itself. If let alone, it was quite harmless, and Mr Hurst's only motive for meddling with it must have been either its patent utility for mischief-making or his moral disapproval of Mr Weld-Blundell's own wrong-doing.[28]

Lord Sumner then proceeded to observe that in general even though A is negligent, A is not liable for injury to C which B, a third person, deliberately chooses to do.[29] As we shall see later in this section, Lord Sumner's principle has been subsequently judicially criticised for being too sweeping and unqualified.

The voluntariness/deliberateness test has also been applied by the House of Lords in the maritime collision sphere. In *Owners of Steamship Singleton Abbey* v *Owners of Steamship Paludina*[30] Lord Sumner characterised the conduct of one of the ship captains involved in the collision as 'wilful' and 'deliberate' and of such a quality as to amount to a *novus actus interveniens*.[31] In another context, a plea for assistance situation, the English Court of Appeal has applied the voluntariness test to deny recovery to the plaintiff. In *Cutler* v *United Dairies (London), Ltd*[32] the plaintiff saw from his house a horse and cart belonging to the defendants galloping past without a driver. Fearing for his children he went into the garden where they were playing. By this time the horse had come to rest in an adjoining field and the driver was trying to pacify it. He shouted for assistance and the plaintiff was knocked down and injured after the horse had reared from the plaintiff's attempt to hold the horse's head. In allowing the defendants' appeal, Scrutton L.J. held that the plaintiff had voluntarily assumed the risk of injury (*volenti non fit injuria*)[33] or, alternatively, assuming a breach of duty by the defendants, his voluntary act of assistance 'in a matter in which

---

26   [1913] AC 263.
27   [1920] AC 956 (HL).
28   Ibid., 984–5.
29   Ibid., 986.
30   [1927] AC 16 (HL).
31   Ibid., 28–9.
32   [1933] 2 KB 297 (CA).
33   Ibid., 303.

he has no duty to act' amounted to a *novus actus interveniens*.[34] It should be noted that *Cutler* was not a rescue case as no person or property was in imminent danger and the plaintiff was, in effect, a volunteer acting at the request of the defendants' servant.[35] The plaintiff in *Haynes* v *G. Harwood & Son*,[36] a rescue case, fared better. There the defendants' deliveryman left his horse-drawn van unattended in the street while he obtained a receipt for goods that he had delivered. A boy mischievously threw a stone at the horses which ran away. The plaintiff, a policeman on duty in the charge-room of a police station, saw what was happening and came outside where he saw that a woman and some children were in great danger. At considerable risk to himself he seized one of the horses and succeeded in pulling them up, but one horse fell on him and he was seriously injured. The English Court of Appeal held that the boy's mischievous act of throwing the stone did not amount to a *novus actus* on the ground that although the act itself was intentional and volitional, he did not fully understand and appreciate the consequences of his act. As juvenile mischief was one of the risks which the deliveryman should have anticipated if he carelessly left the van unattended, the defendant employers were held vicariously liable for his negligence.

The Court of Appeal decision in *Stansbie* v *Troman*[37] consolidated the proposition that liability may be exacted from tortfeasors for negligently providing an opportunity for wrongdoers to engage in intervening criminal conduct where the defendant is under a duty of care to guard against that very risk. In that case a contractor carrying out decorations in a house was left alone on the premises by the householder's wife. During her absence, he left the house for several hours to obtain wall-paper, but did not securely lock it up. During the decorator's absence, a thief entered the house and stole a diamond bracelet and clothes. In an action to recover damages for the value of these losses, the Court of Appeal held the decorator liable on the ground that he had breached his contractually-based duty to take reasonable care for the security of the premises if he left them during the performance of his work. On the causation issue, it was argued on behalf of the defendant decorator, relying on the above-mentioned dictum of Lord Sumner in *Weld-Blundell* v *Stephens*,[38] that the deliberate criminal act of the thief severed the causal chain between the decorator's negligence and the theft of the articles. In rejecting the defendant's *novus actus* plea, Tucker L.J., delivering the main judgment in the case, stated, 'I do not think that Lord Sumner would have intended *that very general statement* to apply to the facts of a case such as the present where…the act of negligence itself consisted in the failure to take reasonable care to guard against the very thing that in fact happened.'[39] This

---

34   Ibid., 305. See to the same effect the judgment of Slesser L.J. (at 305–6).
35   A.L. Goodhart 'Rescue and Voluntary Assumption of Risk' (1934) 5 *The Cambridge Law Journal* 192, 201–2.
36   [1935] 1 KB 146 (CA).
37   [1948] 2 KB 48 (CA).
38   [1920] AC 956, 986 (HL).
39   [1948] 2 KB 48, 51–2 (emphasis supplied). Compare *Perry* v *Kendricks Transport Co. Ltd* [1956] 1 WLR 85 (CA) (if the defendant accumulates non-natural substances on his property so as to fall within the rule in *Rylands* v *Fletcher* (1866) LR 1 Ex 265, aff'd

reaffirmed the court's holding in *Marshall* v *Caledonian Railway*[40] that intervening criminal conduct did not relieve the defendant from liability where such conduct could have been foreseen and the defendant's action created the opportunity for the criminal to enter and steal the goods.

The voluntariness/deliberateness test was once again applied to defeat the plaintiff's claim in *Rushton* v *Turner Bros. Asbestos Co. Ltd.*[41] A crusher had not been properly fenced in breach of statutory regulations. The plaintiff worker, who put his hand into the crusher while it was operating, was denied recovery. Ashworth L.J. considered that the breach of the statutory regulations was more accurately described as the circumstance in which the accident happened rather than its legally operative cause:

> I find that he did it quite deliberately, and that the cause of the accident, in the sense of the operative act and effective cause, is wholly to be attributed to him...looked at fairly, the plaintiff is the sole author of his own misfortune.[42]

In the 1970 decision of the House of Lords in *Home Office* v *Dorset Yacht Co. Ltd*[43] Lord Reid had occasion to make some significant *obiter dicta* comments concerning the effect on the chain of causation of intervening criminal acts of a third party. His Lordship said:

> Yet it has never been the law that the intervention of human action always prevents the ultimate damage from being regarded as having been caused by the original carelessness... But every day there are many cases where, although one of the connecting links is deliberate human action, the law has no difficulty in holding that the defendant's conduct caused the plaintiff loss.[44]

And Lord Reid concluded:

> Unfortunately...criminal action by a third party is often the 'very kind of thing' which is likely to happen as a result of the wrongful or careless act of the defendant. And in the present case...I think that the taking of a boat by the escaping trainees and their unskilful navigation leading to damage to another vessel were the very kind of thing that the Borstal officers ought to have seen to be likely.[45]

Thus, in Lord Reid's view, intentional intervening criminal conduct by a third party will not affect the defendant's liability where such conduct fell squarely within the risk the defendant ought to have anticipated at the duty of care stage.

(1868) LR 3 HL 330, he will not be liable if a complete stranger breaks into his property and engineers the escape of those substances).

    40   (1899) 1 Sess. Cas. (5th Ser.) 1060.
    41   [1959] 3 All ER 517.
    42   Ibid., 521.
    43   [1970] AC 1004 (HL). The facts and case are examined in Chapter 3.
    44   Ibid., 1027–8.
    45   Ibid., 1030.

The 1981 decision of the Court of Appeal in *Lamb* v *Camden London Borough Council*[46] is one of the most oft-cited cases denying liability where the plaintiff's damage has been caused by the deliberate criminal acts of a third party where such acts are committed in exploitation of a situation created by the defendant's negligence.[47] Reluctance to extend civil responsibility to the deliberate criminal wrongdoing of others is greatest where such wrongdoing was not the risk addressed by the rule which the defendant violated.[48] So, when, as in *Lamb*, a broken sewer caused damage to the plaintiff's house so that it had to be evacuated, subsequent acts of vandalism over the next three years were effectively held to constitute a *novus actus interveniens*. The defendant's duty of care encompassed the risk of water damage but did not extend to acts of vandalism. Thus, criminal wrongdoing will sever the causal chain where it is not considered by the court to constitute a primary or supplementary risk to be guarded against under the defendant's duty of care.

That even in the case of serious intervening criminal conduct, breach of the causal chain does not inevitably follow is illustrated in *Ward* v *Cannock Chase District Council*.[49] The plaintiff and his family lived in a house in a row of terraced houses. The other houses were owned by the defendant council and let to tenants. As a result of council policy to redevelop the area for industrial purposes, the houses were not re-let or maintained as they fell vacant. Many of the houses sustained damage as a result of the criminal activities of vandals and thieves. As a consequence of vandalism, the rear wall of the house which adjoined the plaintiff's house collapsed, causing damage to the roof of the plaintiff's house. The defendant council failed to carry out repairs to the plaintiff's house but forced the plaintiff and his family to relocate elsewhere. Shortly thereafter, vandals broke into the plaintiff's house and removed parts of the building. As a result, the house deteriorated over the next year until it was beyond repair. In an action against the council (in which negligence was conceded), the defendant council relied on the *Lamb* case and argued that the acts of vandals and thieves which damaged the plaintiff's unoccupied house were unforeseeable intervening criminal acts of independent third parties for which the council could not be held liable. Applying the test of reasonable foreseeability and distinguishing the *Lamb* case, Scott J. held that if the plaintiff's house were to remain unoccupied for any length of time due to the defendant council's negligence, there was a sufficiently high risk that vandals and thieves would break in and cause damage.

In a series of decisions in the mid-1980s, English courts were confronted with the intervening causation issue of the extent to which the defendant should be held liable for causing injury to the plaintiff where such injury caused a marked personality change leading to the commission of serious criminal offences. In *Meah* v *McCreamer*[50] the plaintiff was a passenger in a car driven by the defendant who was drunk at the time. Due to the defendant's negligence, the car was involved in

---

46 [1981] 1 QB 625 (CA). The facts and case are examined in Chapter 3.
47 H.L.A. Hart and T. Honore *Causation in the Law* (2nd edn, 1985) 136.
48 J. Fleming *The Law of Torts* (The Law Book Company Ltd, 9th edn, 1998) 254.
49 [1985] 3 All ER 537 (Ch D).
50 [1985] 1 All ER 367 (QBD).

an accident and the plaintiff sustained serious head injuries and brain damage. The plaintiff consequently experienced a significant change of personality. Prior to the accident the plaintiff had been convicted of theft and burglary but had no record of violence towards women. Some four years after the accident, the plaintiff sexually assaulted and maliciously wounded two women and raped and maliciously wounded a third woman, for which he was sentenced to life imprisonment. The plaintiff claimed damages against the defendant on the ground that but for the brain damage caused in the accident and the resulting personality change, he would not have committed the criminal offences for which he was imprisoned. Woolf J. held in the plaintiff's favour and awarded damages to compensate him for being imprisoned, as the commission of the crimes against the women and the plaintiff's incarceration were a direct consequence of the defendant's negligence.[51] The plaintiff's crimes evidently did not amount to a *novus actus* in view of his state of mind. However, a *novus actus* plea did succeed in *Meah* v *McCreamer (No. 2)*[52] when the court refused to hold the defendant liable to indemnify the plaintiff for the financial consequences of being held civilly liable for the rape committed by the plaintiff subsequent to the accident and personality change. The underlying tenor of the decision is that it would be going too far to hold the defendant liable for the consequences of a rational and voluntary decision to engage in criminal activity.

Environment Agency v *Empress Car Co. (Abertillery) Ltd*[53] was a case concerning criminal, as opposed to civil, liability for 'causing' polluting matter to enter controlled waters contrary to Section 85(1) of the *Water Resources Act 1991*, where it was the act of an unknown person who had opened the tap of a diesel oil tank. Although the case concerned a criminal prosecution, Lord Hoffman made some observations which are equally apposite in the civil intervening causation context:

> In answering questions of causation for the purposes of holding someone responsible, both the law and common sense normally attach great significance to deliberate human acts…[O]ne cannot give a common sense answer to a question of causation for the purpose of attributing responsibility under some rule without knowing the purpose and scope of the rule. Does the rule impose a duty which requires one to guard against…the deliberate acts of third persons? If so, it will be correct to say, when loss is caused by the act of such a third person, that it was caused by the breach of duty…In *Stansbie* v *Troman* the law imposed a duty which included having to take precautions against burglars. Therefore breach of that duty caused the loss of the property stolen.[54]

In linking the intervening criminal act with the content and scope of the duty of care owed by the defendant, Lord Hoffman is effectively endorsing the principle contained in Section 442B. of the American Law Institute's *Restatement of the Law of Torts*,

---

51 The plaintiff's damages were reduced by 25 per cent on account of the plaintiff's contributory negligence in travelling as a passenger in a car with a driver whom he knew to be drunk. The decision of Woolf J. was disapproved by the New South Wales Court of Appeal in *State Rail Authority of New South Wales* v *Wiegold* (1991) 25 NSWLR 500.

52 [1986] 1 All ER 943.

53 [1999] 2 AC 22 (HL).

54 Ibid., 30–32.

Second which was discussed at the beginning of this chapter. Such an approach was relied on by the House of Lords in *Reeves* v *Commissioner of Police of the Metropolis*[55] in determining the intervening causation issue whether the deliberate suicide of a prisoner of sound mind amounted to a *novus actus interveniens*. There the deceased was held in a police cell in the custody of the defendant's officers, who had been alerted to the risk that he might commit suicide. Taking advantage of the officers' inadvertence, the deceased hanged himself. In an action for negligence commenced by the plaintiff as administratrix of the deceased's estate, the defendant pleaded *novus actus*. The House of Lords (Lord Hobhouse dissenting) held that a deliberate and informed act intended to exploit a situation created by the defendant's negligence did not sever the causal link where the defendant breached a specific duty imposed by law to guard against that very act. The officers entrusted with the custody of prisoners had a duty to take reasonable care of their safety while in custody, regardless of their state of mind. Since the defendant was in breach of the duty of care owed, the deceased's deliberate act in committing suicide did not therefore amount to a *novus actus interveniens*.

It is apparent from the foregoing review of the English case-law that, unlike former times, some deliberate and voluntary intervening acts of the plaintiff or a third party will sever the chain of causation while others will not. Perhaps the most that can be said is that, as a general rule, the more wilful the intent, and the greater the difficulty in classifying the intervening event as a risk against which it was the defendant's duty to take care, the easier it will be for a court to sustain the defendant's *novus actus* plea.

Canada

By comparison with England, Canadian courts have had a much shorter tradition of applying the voluntariness/deliberateness test to resolve intervening causation issues. Such tradition has generally been confined to the lower courts with only rare instances of Canada's highest appellate court, the Supreme Court of Canada, setting its imprimatur on this particular *novus actus* test. Most of the Canadian cases have applied this test in the context of intervening criminal conduct.

One of the earlier cases was *Toronto Hydro-Electric Commission* v *Toronto Railway Co.*[56] which involved the setting in motion by some unknown person of a street car left by the defendant's servants standing upon a track. Middleton J., with whom Riddell J. agreed, held that 'the action of the trespasser who entered the car and set it in motion was "a fresh and independent cause", which, under the circumstances, the defendants had no reason to contemplate.'[57] Conversely in *Patten* v *Silberschein*[58] the plaintiff, a pedestrian, was run down and knocked unconscious by the defendant's negligent driving. During the period he lay unconscious on the street, he lost a sum of money which was in his pocket (presumably by theft by

---

55 [2000] 1 AC 360 (HL).
56 (1919) 45 OLR 470.
57 Ibid., 472.
58 [1936] 3 WWR 169 (BCSC).

an unknown person). The British Columbia Supreme Court held that the plaintiff was entitled to recover not only his general and special damages flowing from the accident but also for the subsequent loss attributable to the theft of money. Although McDonald J. considered that the loss of the money 'was not the natural and probable consequence of the defendant's act of negligence',[59] His Honour felt constrained to apply the now discredited *In re Polemis*[60] 'direct causal link' test to find in the plaintiff's favour. A decision more in line with the current common law is *Duce v Rourke*[61] in which the Alberta court disagreed with the decision in *Patten v Silberschein* and exonerated the negligent defendant from liability for the loss of some tools which had been stolen from the injured plaintiff's car after he was taken to hospital. The court refused to apply the *Polemis* test to the theft which amounted to a conscious, intervening and independent act for which the defendant could not be held civilly responsible. However, in *Walker v DeLuxe Cab Ltd*[62] the defendant was held liable when the plaintiff's baggage was stolen along with the taxi cab which had been left at the curb with the ignition key in it. The *Duce* and *Walker* cases may be reconcilable, however, on the basis of the differentiated levels of negligence and risks encompassed within the respective duties of care.

In its 1948 decision in *Jones v Shafer*[63] the Supreme Court of Canada relied on the voluntariness/deliberateness test to conclude that the criminal act of an unknown third person in stealing highway warning flares amounted to a superseding cause for which the defendant could not be held liable. Estey J., with whom Rinfret C.J. agreed, said that, even assuming that the defendant had been negligent in not taking sufficient precautions (which did not appear to be the case on the evidence), the deliberate and 'contemptible' removal of the flares 'by some person who had no regard whatsoever for the safety of the public' could not fall within the range of risks which someone in the defendant's position would have to anticipate.[64] And Locke J., with whom Taschereau J. agreed, stated, '[i]t was not the failure of the [defendant] to take reasonable care which was the direct or proximate cause of the accident, rather was it…the act of the thief, "the conscious act of another volition" of the nature referred to by Lord Dunedin in *Dominion Natural Gas Ltd v Collins and Perkins* [1909] AC 640, 646.'[65]

The operation of the *novus actus* plea was restricted, however, by a Manitoba court in *Canphoto Ltd v Aetna Roofing (1965) Ltd*.[66] There the employees of the defendant company left three propane gas tanks in a public laneway over a weekend. In doing so, they breached a provincial regulation concerning the safe storage of such tanks. During the night someone apparently meddled with the tanks causing a serious fire which damaged the plaintiff's premises. In finding in the plaintiff's

---

59 Ibid.
60 [1921] 3 KB 560 (CA).
61 (1951) 1 WWR (NS) 305 (Alta).
62 [1944] 3 DLR 175 (Ont.).
63 [1948] SCR 166 (SCC). The facts and case are examined in Chapter 3.
64 Ibid., 171.
65 Ibid., 176.
66 [1971] 3 WWR 116 (Man.).

favour, Wilson J. rejected the defendant's submission that the meddling with the tanks constituted a *novus actus interveniens*. Such meddling did not amount to a 'fresh independent cause' of the plaintiff's damage but rather fell squarely within the range of risks which the defendant's servants should have anticipated. By contrast, the Alberta Supreme Court (Appellate Division) held, somewhat surprisingly, in *Hewson* v *City of Red Deer*[67] that the theft and setting in motion of the defendant's tractor by an unknown third person which caused damage to the plaintiff's house was not reasonably foreseeable, thus amounting to a *novus actus interveniens*. It is submitted with respect that the approach of the court at first instance, that such criminal conduct did not constitute a *novus actus* on the ground that it was a reasonably foreseeable risk from the standpoint of the defendant's servant, is to be preferred.[68] A similar approach was indeed used by the court in *Holian* v *United Grain Growers*[69] where some mischievous boys took some fumigant tablets used to kill insects from the defendant's shed and placed them in the plaintiff's car as a 'stink bomb' causing the plaintiff to fall ill. The court imposed liability on the defendant since the theft and injury were 'within the risk created by the negligence of the defendant in leaving the shed unlocked and unattended'.[70] The defendant was not required to foresee the precise manner in which the plaintiff came to be injured; it was sufficient if the kind of injury was reasonably foreseeable.

The traditional application of the voluntariness/deliberateness test will be softened in its application, it would seem, where the plaintiff's conduct is particularly meritorious. A good illustrative case is that of *Urbanski* v *Patel*.[71] In that case a young woman underwent a sterilisation procedure during which the doctor negligently removed her only kidney (believing he was removing an ovarian cyst). Her father donated one of his kidneys to his daughter but the transplanted kidney was rejected and the daughter had to continue on dialysis. The father successfully sued the doctor for the damage associated with the donation of his kidney he had sustained. The Manitoba Queen's Bench held that the father's act of attempted rescue did not break the chain of causation as it was not truly volitional. The father's moral compulsion negated the traditional arguments that he had voluntarily incurred the risk of such loss or that he had acted following due deliberation.[72]

Canadian courts have regarded the serious crimes of rape and arson as something to be anticipated and guarded against. So, in *Q* v *Minto Management Ltd*[73] an apartment manager was held liable to a tenant who had been raped by the janitor because the failure to provide proper locks and supervise the keys to the apartments increased the likelihood of criminal activity. And in *Williams* v *New Brunswick*[74] an action by the families of deceased prisoners who had perished in a lockup fire deliberately lit

---

67   (1977) 146 DLR (3d) 32. The facts and case are examined in Chapter 3.
68   (1975) 63 DLR (3d) 168, 174 (Alta).
69   (1980) 11 CCLT 184 (Man. Q.B.).
70   Ibid., 191.
71   (1978) 84 DLR (3d) 650 (Man. Q.B.).
72   J. Fleming *The Law of Torts* (The Law Book Company Ltd, 9th edn, 1998) 248.
73   (1985) 31 CCLT 158 (Ont. H.C.); (1985) 15 DLR (4th) 581.
74   (1985) 34 CCLT 299 (New Brunswick C.A.).

by a prisoner succeeded against the Province of New Brunswick. Stratton C.J. held that the tragic aftermath involving the death of 21 inmates may 'fairly be regarded as within the ambit of the risk created by [the defendant's] negligence'.[75]

The Canadian courts have recently dealt with the issue whether the plaintiff's intervening criminal conduct has severed the causal chain between the defendant's tort (assault and battery) and the plaintiff's loss of past employment income. In *H.L. v Canada (Attorney General)*[76] the plaintiff was a former resident of a First Nations Reserve. At the age of 14 years he was sexually assaulted by a resident administrator on the reserve. The plaintiff alleged that he became addicted to alcohol, had emotional difficulties, and engaged in criminal conduct. He claimed damages, including loss of past income over a 22-year period, consequent on the sexual assaults. The claim included loss during periods of time for which he was incarcerated. Although successful at trial, the awards of loss of past income were overturned by the Saskatchewan Court of Appeal. On further appeal to the Supreme Court of Canada, the majority allowed the appeal to the extent of restoring the award for past wage loss in part, but excluded recovery for the periods during which the plaintiff was incarcerated. In delivering the majority judgment, Fish J. said:

>...[T]he chain of causation linking [the plaintiff's] sexual abuse to his loss of income while incarcerated was interrupted by his intervening criminal conduct. During these periods, his lack of gainful employment was caused by his imprisonment, not by his alcoholism; and his imprisonment resulted from his criminal conduct, not from his abuse by [the resident administrator] nor from the alcoholism which it was found to have induced.[77]

The upholding of the *novus actus* plea was not only supported by the evidence but justified on the public policy ground that to hold otherwise would undermine the very purpose of the criminal justice system.[78]

These same issues were subsequently considered by the British Columbia Court of Appeal in *The Queen in right of British Columbia v Zastowny*.[79] There the plaintiff was sexually assaulted by a correctional officer while he was incarcerated. Fifteen years later he brought an action for damages against the Crown. Of the 15 years following the sexual assaults, the plaintiff spent 12 years in prison. The trial Judge found that the sexual assaults were causally related to the plaintiff's subsequent drug addiction and his criminal lifestyle that supported the addiction, but the award of damages for past wage loss during periods of incarceration was overturned by a majority on appeal. Saunders J.A. held that the plaintiff's 'wage loss during the [periods of incarceration] is not compensable because the criminal law has said that he is responsible for his actions and must bear the consequences of them, looking at his criminal behaviour as the substantial cause of the loss, and considering public policy that eschews a clash between the civil and criminal law.'[80] Smith J.A., the

---

75 Ibid., 319.
76 (2005) 251 DLR (4th) 604; [2005] 1 SCR 401.
77 Ibid., para. 142.
78 Ibid., para. 137.
79 (2006) 269 DLR (4th) 510.
80 Ibid., 538.

other majority judge, applied notions of freedom, intention and deliberateness to determine whether the causal chain had been severed:

> [T]he trial judge's awards of damages for employment income lost while he was...in prison are contrary to judicial policy and cannot stand. The chain of causation was interrupted by the respondent's intervening criminal conduct. At the time of his criminal acts, the respondent was in control of the situation and was free to act or not act. He chose to act in a criminal way and thereby insulated the Crown from liability...[81]

The United States of America

By contrast to their Canadian counterparts, US courts have been more consistent in refusing to find a *novus actus interveniens* in cases involving serious intervening criminal conduct. In former times, criminal conduct was rarely anticipated but in contemporary times it has become much more commonplace, leading to a judicial extension of civil liability.[82] In one of the earlier cases, the court imposed liability for the loss of some barrels which were stolen when the driver of a wagon was stunned in an accident due to the defendant's negligence. This was considered in *Brower* v *N.Y. Central Railway*[83] to be a 'natural and probable' result of depriving the plaintiff of his driver's protection of the property in the setting of a street in a large city. The Pennsylvania courts have held that an intervening criminal act does not necessarily constitute a superseding cause. In *Baione* v *Heavey*[84] and *Smith* v *Cohen*[85] the Superior Court held that the intervening criminal act of stealing an automobile did not relieve the proprietor of the parking lot or garage from liability. In the latter case the court held that '[i]f an intervening act which ought to have been foreseen, contributes to the original negligence, the original wrongdoer will not be excused; his negligence remains the direct cause of the loss.'[86]

There is also a line of US authority holding defendants civilly liable for the criminal act of murder by third persons. So when someone creates an unreasonable risk of homicide by issuing a large life insurance policy in favour of a person who has no insurable interest in the life of the person insured, liability will ensue if the beneficiary murders the person insured to collect the insurance proceeds.[87] In *Shuster* v *City of New York*[88] the defendant was held liable when an informer was murdered because he had not been adequately protected by its police force. The case of *St Louis-San Francisco Railway Company* v *Mills*[89] involved an action under the federal

---

81   Ibid., 550.
82   A. Linden and B. Feldthusen *Canadian Tort Law* (Butterworths, 8th edn, 2006) 413.
83   (1918) 103 Alt. 166 (N.J.).
84   (1932) 103 Pa. Super. 529.
85   (1935) 116 Pa. Super. 395.
86   Ibid., 398.
87   *Liberty National Life Insurance* v *Weldon* (1958) 267 Ala. 171. A magazine publisher has been held liable for a shooting that was arranged through an advertisement offering a 'gun for hire': *Braun* v *Soldier of Fortune Magazine* (1992) 968 F. 2d 1110.
88   (1958) 5 N.Y. 2d 75.
89   (1924) 3 F 2d 882 (5 Cir.).

Employers' Liability Act 1908 to recover damages for the death of an employee of the defendant railway company. The deceased worked as a train inspector at the defendant employer's yards. Prior to and during his period of service, a bitter strike of the employer's former employees was in progress. During that period the employer provided guards to protect the employees who replaced the strikers while they were at work and during their journey to and from work. One evening while on his way home from work and while accompanied by a guard, the deceased was shot and killed by one of the strikers. The plaintiff, the personal representative of the deceased, alleged negligence on the defendant employer's part in failing to provide adequate protection on the fateful journey home, and this was borne out by the evidence at trial. The defendant employer argued, however, that its 'negligence was not a proximate cause of the employee's death, because his death would not have occurred, but for the supervening of an independent and disconnected agency.'[90] In rejecting the defendant's *novus actus* plea, the Fifth Circuit Court of Appeals stated, '[n]egligence properly may be regarded as the proximate cause of an injury, if it appears that the injury was the natural and probable consequence of the negligence, and that in the light of the attending circumstances it ought to have been foreseen by the wrongdoer.'[91] Thus, the defendant was held liable on the basis that the violent act of one of the strikers fell within the scope of the risk created by the defendant's failure to provide adequate protection.

The United States Supreme Court has also considered intervening causation issues in the context of the employer's duty to protect employees against a third person's criminal act. *Lillie* v *Thompson*[92] also involved an action for damages under the federal *Employers' Liability Act 1908*. The plaintiff alleged that she was injured as a result of the defendant's negligence in sending her to work in a place the defendant knew to be unsafe without taking reasonable measures to protect her. The plaintiff, a 22-year-old telegraph operator, was required by her employer, the defendant, to work alone between 11.30 p.m. and 7.30 a.m. in a one-room building situated in an isolated part of the defendant's railroad yards. Although the employer had reason to know the yards were frequented by dangerous characters, it failed to provide lighting for the building or to patrol it in any way. One of the plaintiff's duties was to receive and deliver messages to other employees operating trains in the yard. In order for these employees to receive the messages it was necessary for them to come to the building at irregular intervals throughout the night. It was the plaintiff's duty to admit them when they knocked. Because of a lack of windows the plaintiff could identify persons seeking entry to the building only by unlocking and opening the door. On the occasion in question the plaintiff responded to a knock by opening the door and before she could close it a man entered and beat her with a large piece of iron, seriously and permanently injuring her. The defendant pleaded *novus actus* on the basis that the assailant was not its employee and that the criminal act broke the chain of causation. The district court's dismissal of the plaintiff's action on the ground that the law does not permit civil recovery of damages for the intentional or

---

90   Ibid., 884.
91   Ibid.
92   (1947) 332 US 459 (USSC).

criminal acts of an independent third party was overturned by the Supreme Court. The Court stated, *per curiam*, that the fact that 'the foreseeable danger was from intentional or criminal misconduct is irrelevant; [the defendant] nonetheless had a duty to make reasonable provision against it.'[93]

The foregoing brief survey of US case-law is illustrative of the general trend of US courts to significantly restrict the operation of *novus actus interveniens* in the realm of intervening criminal conduct perpetrated by an independent third party, through the liberal application of the 'scope of the risk' doctrine against the defendant.

Australia

The 1963 decision of the Full Court of the Supreme Court of Victoria in *Haber v Walker*[94] is often cited as a leading Australian authority for the proposition that intervening causation issues should be resolved by applying the test of voluntariness/ deliberateness to the facts of the case. The plaintiff's husband sustained horrific injuries in a motor vehicle accident. He suffered some physical brain damage and also became profoundly depressed as a result of the condition in which his injuries had left him. His psychiatric condition and sense of hopelessness worsened and he committed suicide. The plaintiff, his widow, sued the defendant who had been the driver of the other vehicle involved in the collision. She alleged that her husband's death had been caused by the defendant's negligent driving. At first instance, the defendant had been adjudged negligent and that such negligence had caused the death of the plaintiff's husband. This was affirmed on appeal by a majority of the Supreme Court of Victoria. During the course of his judgment, Smith J. stated:

> [T]he intervening occurrence, if it is to be sufficient to sever the [causal] connection, must ordinarily be either –
>
> (a) human action that is properly to be regarded as voluntary, or
> (b) a causally independent event the conjunction of which with the wrongful act or omission is by ordinary standards so extremely unlikely as to be termed a coincidence …[95]

In addressing the critical causation issue of whether the deceased's conduct which led to his death was properly to be regarded as a voluntary act, Smith J. observed:

> [F]or an act to be regarded as voluntary it is necessary that the actor should have exercised a free choice…But if his choice has been made under substantial pressure created by the wrongful act, his conduct should not ordinarily be regarded as voluntary…[96]

Applying these principles, Smith J. held that, for legal causation purposes, the deceased's act in hanging himself was not a 'voluntary' act if the deceased, as a result

---

93 Ibid., 462. In so holding, the Supreme Court drew upon the American Law Institute's *Restatement of the Law of Torts, Second* and accompanying commentary.
94 [1963] VR 339.
95 Ibid., 358.
96 Ibid., 359.

of the defendant's negligence, was acting under the pressure of a mental disorder and was thereby prevented from exercising a free choice.[97] As the deceased was acting under the influence of a severe depression caused by his accident-related injuries, and without the necessary volition, the deceased's suicide was not a *novus actus interveniens* and the plaintiff therefore succeeded.

The volition test appears to have been endorsed and applied by Gibbs J. in the decision of the High Court of Australia in *Caterson v Commissioner for Railways*.[98] In that case the plaintiff leaped from a train which had started to move slowly out of the station without warning. The defendant's argument that the voluntary act of the plaintiff in jumping from the train broke the causal chain was rejected on several grounds, one of which was to the effect that the act was not truly voluntary, having been brought about by the pressure of circumstances created by the defendant's omission to warn persons in the railway carriage that the train was about to depart. Gibbs J. described the plaintiff's behaviour in the circumstances as having 'jumped instinctively' 'in the stress of the moment'.[99] In any case, His Honour was of the view that the intervention of a voluntary act of a plaintiff does not necessarily in itself have the result that the plaintiff's injuries were not caused by the defendant's negligence.[100]

In a series of decisions the High Court of Australia and some Australian state appellate courts have held that a duty to prevent deliberate criminal conduct by a stranger arises out of the particular relationship between the parties. Liability arises out of the failure to guard against the third party's intervention. As Mason C.J. observed in *March v E. & M. H. Stramare Pty Ltd*:[101]

> The fact that the intervening action is deliberate or voluntary does not necessarily mean that the plaintiff's injuries are not a consequence of the defendant's negligent conduct. In some situations a defendant may come under a duty of care not to expose the plaintiff to a risk of injury arising from deliberate or voluntary conduct or even to guard against that risk…To deny recovery in these situations because the intervening action is deliberate or voluntary would be to deprive the duty of any content.[102]

On the basis of these principles the High Court of Australia has held the manufacturer of a defective alarm system liable for a burglary loss. In *Reg Glass v Rivers*[103] the plaintiff purchased and installed a negligently manufactured burglar alarm and was subsequently burgled. The intervening volitional and criminal conduct of the third party thief was not held to be a *novus actus interveniens* relieving the defendant

---

97 Ibid.
98 (1973) 128 CLR 99.
99 Ibid., 112.
100 Ibid., 110.
101 (1990–91) 171 CLR 506 (HCA).
102 Ibid., 517–18. It was on this basis that the Supreme Court of Victoria (Appeal Division) held in *Curmi v McLennan* [1994] 1 VR 513 (FC) that the intentional shooting of one adolescent male with an air gun pellet by another adolescent male did not break the chain of causation between the defendant's failure to properly supervise and instruct the group of boys in the use of firearms and the plaintiff losing his eye.
103 (1968) 120 CLR 516 (HCA).

manufacturer of liability. The theft of goods was the very risk that was to be guarded against in so far as the manufacturer's duty of care extends to preventing that harm from occurring.

In *Chomentowski* v *Red Garter Restaurant Pty Ltd*[104] the New South Wales Court of Appeal held that the scope of an employer's duty to an employee may extend to protecting the employee from being bashed and robbed while attempting to deposit money from the employer's business in a bank's night-safe. Mason J.A. (as he then was) stated:

> The injury which the plaintiff sustained, although occasioned by deliberate human intervention, was the outcome of the very risk against which it was the duty of the defendants to safeguard the plaintiff as their employee. If, as was the case, it was the existence of that risk of injury which called for the exercise of care and the taking of precautions by the defendants, then the defendants' failure to take care may properly be regarded as the cause of the injury which occurred when the risk became an actuality.[105]

Pitt Son & Badgery Ltd v *Proulefco SA*[106] is another High Court of Australia decision in which the defendant was held to have caused the plaintiff's damage resulting from intervening criminal conduct on the ground that the defendant had a legal duty to safeguard the plaintiff against the risk of the intervening event occurring. The defendant was a wool broking company which had stored in its wool store wool that had been purchased but not yet delivered to the plaintiff. The wool store was constructed of weatherboard and enclosed by a paling fence from which several palings were missing. An intruder entered through a gap in the fence and set the wool store on fire. The High Court held the defendant liable to the plaintiff for the damaged wool on the ground that the defendant had not discharged its legal duty to keep the wool secure by providing an adequate fence. The intruder's entry and act of arson '[were] the very kind which [the defendant] was obliged to take reasonable care to prevent'.[107] Nevertheless, limits have been placed on the extent to which defendants can be made civilly liable for the plaintiff's injuries which flow directly from intervening criminal conduct. In *State Rail Authority of New South Wales* v *Wiegold*[108] the New South Wales Court of Appeal held that where the victim of a tort took to a life of drug-related crime committed by voluntary design because of

---

104 (1970) 92 WN (NSW) 1070 (NSWCA).
105 Ibid., 1086.
106 (1984) 153 CLR 644 (HCA).
107 Ibid., 648. See also *Commonwealth Trading Bank of Australia* v *Sydney Wide Stores Pty Ltd* (1981) 148 CLR 304 (HCA). In *Club Italia (Geelong) Inc.* v *Ritchie* (2001) 3 VR 447 the Victorian Court of Appeal held that the organisers of a social function that got out of control owed a duty of care to police who attended the scene to restore order. The defendant club had failed to eject a potential trouble-maker and did not warn police of the increasingly raucous criminal behaviour at the function. The responding police officer, who was beaten severely by some of the patrons, successfully sued the club. The Court of Appeal did not regard the beating as a *novus actus* as it was the very thing it was required under its duty of care to guard against.
108 (1991) 25 NSWLR 500 (NSWCA).

financial difficulties imposed on him by reason of his injury, the defendants were not liable for the loss of his job which resulted from his conviction.

Australian courts have also applied the voluntariness/deliberateness test to cases involving causation issues in a non-criminal context. In *Yates v Jones*[109] a 17-year-old was injured in a motor vehicle accident caused by the defendant's negligence. She suffered chest pains and lacerations and was hospitalised. She alleged that she had been given insufficient pain relief medication to alleviate her discomfort. A casual acquaintance visited her in hospital and suggested she try some heroin as pain relief. Although she initially resisted, she agreed to his suggestion on his third visit and he injected her with the drug. She subsequently developed a heroin addiction which she supported by criminal activity, including theft and prostitution. The New South Wales Court of Appeal by a majority rejected that part of her claim for damages which related to her subsequent heroin addiction. Meagher J.A. characterised the drug dealer's conduct and the plaintiff's own conduct of injecting heroin as new intervening acts which relieved the defendant of liability.[110] The volition test was also applied in *CES v Superclinics (Aust.) Pty Ltd*[111] to defeat the plaintiff's claim for damages. In that case doctors negligently failed to detect a young woman's pregnancy. When her pregnancy was finally diagnosed, she was too far along in her pregnancy to have an abortion. She claimed damages against the doctors for the cost of raising her healthy child. The New South Wales Court of Appeal held against her 'wrongful birth' claim for a number of different reasons, one of which included Priestley J.A.'s characterisation of the plaintiff's own conduct of not giving up her newborn child for adoption as a new intervening act. As Priestley J.A. stated:

> The point in the present case is that the plaintiff chose to keep her child. The anguish of having to make the choice is part of the damage caused by the negligent breach of duty, but the fact remains, however compelling the psychological pressure on the plaintiff may have been to keep the child, the opportunity of choice was in my opinion real and the choice made was voluntary. It was this choice which was the cause, in my opinion, of the subsequent cost of rearing the child.[112]

When a plaintiff has abandoned cultural and religious norms as a result of the defendant's negligence, such conduct has been held not to break the chain of causation. In *Kavanagh v Akhtar*[113] the plaintiff, a married Indian Muslim woman, received a severe shoulder injury while shopping at the defendant's premises. Her accident-related disabilities meant that she was no longer able to care for and maintain her

---

109 (1990) Australian Torts Reports 81-009.

110 The majority (which included Samuels J.A.) was influenced by public policy considerations. Kirby P. dissented, concluding that the plaintiff's own conduct was not truly volitional but the product of her vulnerability and pain.

111 (1995) 38 NSWLR 47 (NSWCA).

112 Ibid., 84–5. Compare the English Court of Appeal decision in *Emeh v Kensington and Chelsea and Westminster Area Health Authority* [1984] 3 All ER 1044 where a *novus actus* was not found because the court was satisfied that the plaintiff had not acted unreasonably in refusing to have an abortion.

113 (1998) 45 NSWLR 588 (NSWCA).

extremely long hair and she decided, accordingly, to cut it. The plaintiff's husband took objection to conduct which he had not authorised and which greatly upset him. The source of this displeasure is what he perceived as defiance of his scripturally-based right of control over his wife as well as her defiance of religious injunctions about women cutting their hair without permission of their husband. The husband's hostile reaction to the plaintiff cutting her hair eventually led to the breakdown of their marriage and the plaintiff suffering severe depression leading to psychiatric illness. The plaintiff failed to recover damages for her psychiatric illness at first instance on the ground that the trial Judge was not satisfied that the stress resulting from the marital breakdown resulting from the haircut was a reasonably foreseeable consequence of the negligence of the defendant's servants. However, the New South Wales Court of Appeal allowed the plaintiff's claim for psychiatric damages on the ground that the plaintiff's decision to cut her hair, though voluntary and conscious in the sense that she had a choice, was nevertheless the product of her tortiously-created pain and discomfort. Although the plaintiff knew that her husband had told her not to cut her hair, she believed he would not object because she cut it to help relieve her ongoing pain and discomfort. There was also evidence of the Imam that medical reasons might justify a married woman cutting her hair and that one might reasonably expect that an Islamic husband would grant his permission in such circumstances. In this sense, the plaintiff could not be said to be acting so unreasonably in the circumstances as to warrant a judicial *novus actus* determination.

The High Court of Australia has recently held that the plaintiff's free, informed and voluntary decision will amount to a *novus actus interveniens* unless the decision is directly or indirectly precipitated by, or attributable to, the defendant's breach of duty. In *Medlin* v *The State Government Insurance Commission*[114] the plaintiff was working as a professor when he was injured in a motor vehicle accident caused by the defendant's negligent driving. The plaintiff resumed his university duties but eventually decided to retire in accordance with the university's early retirement scheme. He took early retirement due to his continuing to suffer accident-related chronic pain which left him physically tired and lacking in sufficient intellectual energy as to enable him to discharge his employment duties to his own satisfaction. The plaintiff claimed damages for loss of earning capacity for the remaining four and one-half years that he would otherwise have worked as a university professor. The High Court unanimously held that the plaintiff's 'voluntary' decision to retire early did not constitute a *novus actus interveniens*. However, the legal reasoning relied on to reach that determination diverged. In a separate judgment, McHugh J. considered that the plaintiff's decision to retire early was not unreasonable in the circumstances.[115] In a joint judgment, Deane, Toohey and Gaudron JJ. held that the determination of legal causation issues, including intervening causation issues, is essentially a question of fact to be resolved 'as a matter of commonsense and experience'.[116] Their Honours concluded:

---

114   (1994–95) 182 CLR 1 (HCA).
115   Ibid., 22–3.
116   Ibid., 6.

> The necessary causation between a defendant's negligence and the termination of a plaintiff's employment...can exist notwithstanding the fact that the immediate trigger of the termination of the employment was the plaintiff's own decision to retire prematurely. If, for example, it appears that a plaintiff's decision to retire prematurely would not have been made were it not for the fact that the effect of accident-caused injuries is that the continuation in employment would subject him or her to constant pain and serious risk of further injury, it may well be that commonsense dictates the conclusion that the plaintiff's decision to retire prematurely was a natural step in [the] chain of causation...[117]

Thus, the plaintiff's decision was too closely linked to the pain and other disabilities brought about by the accident-related injuries, for which the defendant was liable, for it to amount to a *novus actus interveniens*.

The voluntariness/deliberateness test was endorsed in somewhat unqualified terms by McHugh J. in the decision of the High Court of Australia in *Bennett* v *Minister of Community Welfare*.[118] In citing from Hart and Honore's treatise on *Causation in the Law*[119] His Honour stated, '[t]he causal connection between a defendant's negligence and the plaintiff's damage is negatived by the subsequent conduct of another person *only* when that conduct is "the free, deliberate and informed act or omission of a human being, intended to exploit the situation created by the defendant"'.[120] This formulation of the test has been criticised[121] for being too narrow because it implies that the negligent conduct of a person not intending to exploit the situation created by the defendant's negligence can never constitute a *novus actus* but this is to ignore such cases as the House of Lords decision in *McKew* v *Holland & Hannen & Cubitts (Scotland) Ltd*[122] where the plaintiff's unreasonable intervening negligent act in descending the staircase without taking due precautions was adjudged to have broken the chain of causation. It has also been criticised for being too widely stated because, as we have seen, in many cases the defendant's liability has arisen when the author of the intervening event had deliberately exploited the situation created by the defendant's negligence *because* the latter was under a duty to guard against that very risk.[123]

Other Jurisdictions

The New Zealand Court of Appeal has held that the deliberate acts of young boys in breaking open a safe and subsequently distributing detonators to other children did not amount to a *novus actus interveniens* on the ground that such acts of conscious volition were reasonably foreseeable and ones which the defendant should have

---

117 Ibid., 10.
118 (1992) 176 CLR 408 (HCA).
119 H.L.A. Hart and T. Honore *Causation in the Law*, 136.
120 (1992) 176 CLR 408, 429–30 (emphasis supplied).
121 A. Palmer 'Causation in the High Court' (1993) 1 *Torts Law Journal* 9, 15.
122 [1970] SC 20 (HL). See Chapter 4 for a discussion of the case.
123 See, for example, *Home Office* v *Dorset Yacht Co. Ltd* [1970] AC 1004 (HL) and *Chomentowski* v *Red Garter Restaurant Pty Ltd* (1970) 92 WN (NSW) 1070 (NSWCA).

guarded against.[124] The National Court of Justice of Papua New Guinea has similarly held that even an intervening act of murder will not sever the chain of causation where such a violent retaliatory reaction to the defendant's negligent running down and killing of a pedestrian should have reasonably been foreseen by those familiar with the customs of the region.[125]

The Irish courts have also considered the effect of intervening criminal acts committed by third parties on the chain of causation. This has occurred in the context of cases involving the theft of motor vehicles where the thief has caused physical injury or property damage. In *Dockery v O'Brien*,[126] a Circuit Court decision, the defendant left his car on the street with the keys in the ignition. An intoxicated person took the car and crashed it into the plaintiff's parked car. McWilliam J. held the defendant liable as this was the very kind of intervening event which a reasonable person should have foreseen. On the other hand, the Supreme Court of Ireland has upheld in another case having similar facts the defendant's *novus actus* plea. In *Breslin v Corcoran*[127] the defendant left his car parked outside a coffee shop unlocked and with the keys in the ignition. As he came out of the shop he witnessed an unknown person jump into his car and drive off with it at speed. Shortly thereafter the stolen car ran into the plaintiff, a pedestrian, and seriously injured him. At first instance the High Court held that the thief's act amounted to a *novus actus interveniens* on the ground that the intervening event was an independent and illegal act of a third party over whom the defendant had no control. The High Court's decision was affirmed on appeal to the Supreme Court where Fennelly J., delivering the Court's joint judgment, held that there was nothing in the evidence presented in the instant case to suggest that the defendant should have anticipated 'as a reasonable probability' that his car, if stolen, would be driven so carelessly as to cause injury to another road user. The approach of the Irish courts in *Breslin* reflects the recent approach of the French Cour de cassation which has ruled in a series of cases that, in the absence of special circumstances, the thief's intervening conduct must be regarded as the legally operative cause of the plaintiff's injury in situations where the owner of a vehicle negligently leaves it in a vulnerable position to be stolen. So, in *Sarl Les transports heandais v SA Les grands travaux du Forez*[128] the Cour de cassation held that the thief's 'voluntary wrongful conduct' which was independent of the vehicle owner's conduct interfered with the causal relationship between the owner's carelessness and the plaintiff's injury.

---

124 *McCarthy v Wellington City* [1966] NZLR 481. This case is examined in more detail in Chapter 3.

125 *Moini v The State* [1977] PNGLR 39. This case is examined in more detail in Chapter 3. See also *Government of Papua New Guinea v Moini* [1978] PNGLR 184 (FC) (the immediate reaction of the villagers to the running down of the child pedestrian was described (at 192) as 'instinctive…not the subject of deliberation').

126 [1975] ILTR 127.

127 [2003] IESC 23.

128 Cass. civ. 2e, 17 March 1977 D1977. Jur. 631.

Conclusion

The voluntariness/deliberateness test as a test of intervening causation is no longer as influential as it once was. It can be said with confidence that deliberate interventions are more likely to sever the causal connection than negligent interventions. However, as we have seen during the course of this chapter, many cases from numerous common law jurisdictions have severely restricted the application of this test in cases involving criminal conduct. The 'international' common law, as it were, is now prepared to impose civil liability on a defendant for negligently providing an opportunity for third parties to cause deliberate harm when the scope of the defendant's duty of care extends to taking precautions to guard against that very eventuality. The point has been reached today that even in cases involving intervening non-criminal conduct, there is no automatic rule that intervening deliberate acts will sever the causal chain.[129] Thus, the current volition test (if it may be called that) may provide some guidance to a court in addressing intervening causation issues but it falls short of supplying an exclusive and conclusive determinant.

---

129 Consider, for example, *Medlin* v *The State Government Insurance Commission* (1994–95) 182 CLR 1 (HCA); *Haynes* v *G. Harwood & Son* [1935] 1 KB 146 (CA); *Reeves* v *Commissioner of Police of the Metropolis* [2000] 1 AC 360 (HL).

Chapter 6

Probability

Introduction

The probability test of intervening causation postulates that the more likely the intervention the less likely it is to break the chain of causation. The leading contemporary proponent of this test is Lord Reid who stated in *Home Office* v *Dorset Yacht Co. Ltd*[1] that the true *novus actus* test was not whether the intervention was 'a mere foreseeable possibility' but rather was it 'very likely'. Judicial expressions such as 'abnormal' or 'coincidental' on the one hand and 'in the ordinary course of things' and 'natural and probable consequence' on the other may be plotted on a continuum which calibrates the probability or likelihood (or lack thereof) of the intervening event happening as a result of the defendant's negligence. The probability test has been most widely accepted and applied in England and the United States of America but it has already enjoyed its heyday and is now in a state of decline, perhaps because of its potential to allow reasonably foreseeable acts to break the causation in an era of ever-increasing imposition of civil liability on defendants and their insurers.

The United Kingdom

The probability test can trace its lineage from the oft-cited decision of the Court of Common Pleas in *Scott* v *Shepherd*[2] where Nares J. considered whether the sequelae of the defendant's act of throwing the lighted squib were 'the natural and probable consequence[s]' of that act.[3] Various decisions handed down by English and Scottish courts during the course of the nineteenth century applied this probability test to determine the outcome of *novus actus* pleas. A good illustration appears in the judgment of Cockburn C.J. in *Clark* v *Chambers*[4] where the issue was whether the intervention of a third party in removing an obstruction placed across a roadway by the defendant severed the causal link:

> For a man who unlawfully places an obstruction across either a public or private way may anticipate the removal of the obstruction, by some one entitled to use the way, as a thing likely to happen; and if this should be done, the probability is that the obstruction so removed will…be placed somewhere near; thus, if the obstruction be to the carriageway,

---

1 [1970] AC 1004, 1030 (HL).
2 (1773) 2 Black. W. 892.
3 See also the judgment of Gould J. who considered that what the intermediaries did was the 'inevitable', 'obvious' and 'natural' consequence of the defendant's act: ibid., 898.
4 (1878) 3 QBD 327. This case is examined in Chapter 2.

it will very likely be placed, as was the case here, on the footpath. If the obstruction be a dangerous one, wheresoever placed, it may, as was the case here, become a source of damage, from which, should injury to an innocent party occur, the original author of the mischief should be held responsible.[5]

Judicial preoccupation with the degree of probability or likelihood of the intervening event occurring as a result of the defendant's negligence was also evident in the decision of the English Court of Appeal in *The City of Lincoln*,[6] a maritime collision case. There Lindley L.J. quoted with approval a leading text writer[7] to the effect that the relevant inquiry is whether the damage complained of is the 'natural and reasonable' result of the defendant's negligence in the sense that it flows from that negligence 'in the ordinary course of things'.[8] Lopes L.J. also asked whether the intervening events could be considered 'the natural consequences occasioned by [the defendants'] original misconduct'.[9]

The Scottish courts have also applied the probability test to determine intervening causation issues. In *Scott's Trustees* v *Moss*[10] the pursuers (plaintiffs) occupied land near a place where the defender (defendant), an entertainment promoter, had advertised that a balloon would descend. It descended in the pursuers' field and a crowd who had gathered burst into the field and caused considerable damage. The defender argued unsuccessfully that he could not be held liable for the damage done by a crowd of outsiders. Lord President Inglis held that the defender 'ought to have foreseen that the descent would be made in some field adjoining the recreation grounds, and that the natural and almost inevitable consequence of that would be that the crowd would break into the field and destroy the crops.'[11] Lord Shand added, 'the principle which ought to receive effect is that if the collection of the crowd, and the actings of the crowd, are the natural and probable consequence of the action of the defender – a consequence which the defender ought to have foreseen – then [the pursuers should be entitled to a verdict]...'[12]

The probability test continued to be applied by the English Court of Appeal and the lower courts in the twentieth century. In *Brandon* v *Osborne Garrett & Co. Ltd*[13] the plaintiffs, husband and wife, were in a shop occupied by the first defendants when a skylight in the roof of the shop was broken due to the negligence of the second defendants engaged to repair the roof. A piece of glass fell and struck the husband, causing severe shock. His wife, who was standing close to him at the time, was not

---

5   Ibid., 338.
6   (1889) 15 PD 15.
7   *Mayne on Damages* (4th edn) 45.
8   (1889) 15 PD 15, 18.
9   Ibid., 19.
10 (1889) 17 R. (Ct of Sess.) 32.
11 Ibid., 36.
12 Ibid., 37. See also the Scottish case of *Wilkinson* v *Kinneil Cannel and Coking Coal Co.* (1897) SLT 347; 24 R. 1001 (the very kind of intervening event which ought to have been anticipated as a natural and probable consequence of the wrongful act of the defendants' servant).
13 [1924] 1 KB 548.

hit by the falling glass but, reasonably believing her husband to be in danger, she immediately and instinctively put out her hand and clutched her husband's arm and tried to pull him away from the spot. In so doing, she strained her leg in such a way as to bring about a recurrence of thrombosis. The second defendants argued that the wife's own 'voluntary' act in trying to assist her husband constituted a *novus actus interveniens*. In finding for the plaintiffs, Swift J. held that the wife's conduct and injury were the 'natural and probable' consequences of the defendants' negligence having regard to the frightening and instantaneous nature of the accident.[14] The English Court of Appeal has applied the probability test on a fairly regular basis over the course of the twentieth century. In *Haynes* v *Harwood*[15] the Court of Appeal found in favour of a policeman who was injured while attempting to stop a runaway horse which had negligently been left unattended and which had been frightened by a mischievous boy. According to Greer L.J., the decided cases supported the proposition that an intervening act will not relieve the defendant of liability 'if the accident was the natural and probable consequence of the [defendant's] wrongful act'.[16] His Lordship further stated:

> If what is relied upon as *novus actus interveniens* is the very kind of thing which is likely to happen if the want of care which is alleged takes place, the principle embodied in the maxim is no defence. The whole question is whether or not…the accident can be said to be 'the natural and probable result' of the breach of duty. If it is the very thing which ought to be anticipated by a man leaving his horses, or one of the things likely to arise as a consequence of his wrongful act, it is no defence…There can be no doubt in this case that the damage was the result of the wrongful act in the sense of being one of the natural and probable consequences of the wrongful act.[17]

What was said by Greer L.J. has been approved in subsequent decisions of the English Court of Appeal. In *Hyett* v *Great Western Railway Co.*[18] Tucker L.J. stated that the approach of Greer L.J. concisely summarises the position under the English common law with regard to *novus actus interveniens*. At the end of his judgment Tucker L.J. concluded:

> …[I]f a man is going to act at all, in a case of fire he must act swiftly, and…the conclusion I have reached is that the act of the plaintiff was not *novus actus interveniens* breaking the chain of causation, but was the kind of act which the defendants might reasonably have anticipated as likely to follow from their act of negligence in leaving the leaking paraffin on this siding.[19]

---

14 Ibid., 555. See also *Newton* v *Edgerley* [1959] 3 All ER 337 (the intervention of a young boy in trying to grab a gun from another boy did not amount to a *novus actus interveniens* because this was just the sort of thing that was likely to happen if the defendant failed to take adequate precautions).
15 [1935] 1 KB 146.
16 Ibid., 153.
17 Ibid., 156.
18 [1948] 1 KB 345, 347 (CA).
19 Ibid., 348.

The statement of the law as laid down by Greer L.J. in *Haynes* v *Harwood* was similarly accepted as authoritative by Willmer L.J. in *Ward* v *T.E. Hopkins & Son Ltd*, *Baker* v *T.E. Hopkins & Son Ltd*.[20] There His Lordship rejected the defendant's plea that a physician's rescue attempt constituted a *novus actus interveniens*, considering that 'it was a natural and probable result of the wrongdoing of Mr Hopkins that, in the likely event of someone being overcome by the carbon monoxide poisoning, a doctor would be called in, and that such doctor, having regard to the traditions of his profession, would, even at the risk of his own safety, descend the well for the purpose of attempting a rescue.'[21]

The probability test again found favour in the Court of Appeal in its 1981 decision in *Knightley* v *Johns*.[22] In delivering the main judgment in the case, Stephenson L.J. reviewed the above-mentioned English 'rescue' cases and concluded from them that 'the original tortfeasor, whose negligence created the danger which invites rescuers, will be responsible for injury and damage which are the natural and probable results of the wrongful act…'[23] His Lordship later added that in his view the Court of Appeal is 'still bound to follow Greer L.J.'s approach in *Haynes* v *Harwood*...'[24] More recently the Court of Appeal has applied the probability test in *Slipper* v *British Broadcasting Corporation*[25] which involved an action in libel for damages. There it was decided that there were no special rules concerning republication peculiar to defamation, and whether the causal chain between the original defamation and the plaintiff's injury had been broken fell to be decided in accordance with the normal rules governing *novus actus interveniens*.[26] Slade L.J. was prepared to accept 'that prima facie the unauthorised repetition of a libel will be treated as a *novus actus interveniens*…[and that] prima facie repetition will not be treated as the natural and probable consequence of the original publication.'[27]

In recent times the House of Lords has not endorsed or applied the probability test to resolve intervening causation issues. However, in 1970 Lord Reid had occasion to formulate his own views by way of *obiter dicta* on this matter in *Home Office* v *Dorset Yacht Co. Ltd*[28] and these views have been the frequent subject of judicial and academic attention. Concerning the question of which test should be applied to determine intervening causation issues, Lord Reid pondered, '[i]s it foreseeability or is it such a degree of probability as warrants the conclusion that the intervening human conduct was the natural and probable result of what preceded it?'[29] Lord Reid answered:

---

20 [1959] 3 All ER 225 (CA).
21 Ibid., 242–3.
22 [1982] 1 All ER 851 (CA). This case is examined in more detail in Chapter 3.
23 Ibid., 860.
24 Ibid., 864.
25 [1991] 1 QB 283 (CA).
26 Ibid., 296 (*per* Stocker L.J.).
27 Ibid., 302 (*per* Slade L.J.). See also 296 (*per* Stocker L.J.).
28 [1970] AC 1004 (HL).
29 Ibid., 1028.

[W]here human action forms one of the links between the original wrongdoing of the defendant and the loss suffered by the plaintiff, that action must at least have been something *very likely* to happen if it is not to be regarded as *novus actus interveniens* breaking the chain of causation. I do not think that a mere foreseeable possibility is or should be sufficient, for then the intervening human action can more properly be regarded as a new cause than as a consequence of the original wrongdoing.[30]

In light of the recent judicial trend towards lowering the threshold of reasonable foreseeability, Lord Reid's 'very likely' approach would effectively result in *novus actus* pleas succeeding more often as there can exist a significant gulf between a mere foreseeable risk and a probable or likely one.[31] Lord Reid's approach would provide greater scope for foreseeable risks to sever the causal chain, thereby reinvigorating *novus actus interveniens* as a judicial device for limiting the defendant's liability. However, Lord Reid's probability test has not been endorsed by the House of Lords and has been approached with caution by the Judicial Committee of the Privy Council in its recent decision in *Attorney General* v *Hartwell (British Virgin Islands)*.[32]

The United States of America and Canada

The probability or 'natural and probable consequence' test of intervening causation has been applied by the United States Supreme Court and various Circuit Courts of Appeals and is codified by the American Law Institute's *Restatement of the Law of Torts, Second*. Section 449 thereof recites, '[i]f the likelihood that a third person may act in a particular manner is the hazard…which makes the actor negligent, such an act whether innocent, negligent, intentionally tortious, or criminal does not prevent the actor from being liable for harm caused thereby.'[33] In *Aetna Insurance Co.* v *Boon*[34] Strong J., in delivering the opinion of the Supreme Court, relied on the 'probable and reasonable consequence' test[35] to assess whether intervening acts severed the chain of causation. In *Milwaukee and St Paul Railway Co.* v *Kellogg*[36] Strong J., once again delivering the opinion of the Supreme Court, stated that in the civil intervening causation context, 'in order to warrant a finding that negligence…is the proximate cause of an injury, it must appear that the injury was the natural and probable consequence of the negligence…'[37] Similarly in *Brower* v *N.Y. Central Railway*[38] liability was imposed on the defendant for some barrels which had been stolen when the driver of a wagon was stunned in an accident. The court considered the theft to be a 'natural and probable' result of depriving the plaintiff of his driver's protection of the property in such circumstances. In the context of the intervening

---

30 Ibid., 1030 (emphasis supplied).
31 Ibid., 1028 ('There is a world of difference between the two' *per* Lord Reid).
32 [2004] UKPC 12 (23 February 2004) paragraphs 23–5.
33 (1965–79) 482.
34 (1877) 95 US 117 (USSC). This case is examined in more detail in Chapter 2.
35 Ibid., 132.
36 (1877) 94 US 469 (USSC). This case is examined in more detail in Chapter 2.
37 Ibid., 475.
38 (1918) 103 Alt. 166 (NJ).

criminal act of murder, the Fifth Circuit Court of Appeals in *St Louis-San Francisco Railway Co. v Mills*[39] expressly relied on the 'natural and probable consequence' test applied by the Supreme Court in the *Kellogg* case. Speaking for the majority, Walker, Circuit Judge stated that the defendant's negligence may be regarded as the legally operative cause of the plaintiff's loss 'if it appears that the injury was the natural and probable consequence of the negligence...'[40] The 'natural and probable consequence' test was also applied by the Third Circuit Court of Appeals in *New York Eskimo Pie Corporation v Rataj*.[41] In that case, the plaintiff, a 15-year-old girl, was seriously and permanently injured when a bottle containing dry ice exploded in her hands. The defendant's employee (for whose negligence the defendant was vicariously liable) had negligently thrown a paper bag containing the dry ice into the street where other children, attracted by the vapour emanating from the bag, subsequently began to play with it. The plaintiff was injured after warning the other children of the danger involved in playing with the dry ice. The Fifth Circuit Court rejected the defendant's argument that the children's meddling with the dry ice amounted to a superseding cause of the plaintiff's injuries. In light of the expansive and explosive qualities of dry ice, the defendant was not relieved of liability on the ground that the type of injury sustained by the plaintiff should have been anticipated 'as the natural and probable consequence of its conduct'.[42] In all of these cases the defendant was held liable on the basis that the intervening agency was considered to be the natural and probable consequence of the defendant's negligence. However, the clear implication of these decisions is that any intervening events falling short of the probability notch on the calibrated scale of probabilities would have been held to be a chain-breaking superseding cause relieving the defendant of liability. The US approach largely mirrors that of Lord Reid in *Home Office v Dorset Yacht Co. Ltd*.[43]

The Supreme Court of Canada and lower Canadian courts have also had experience, albeit rather limited, in applying the probability test to intervening causation issues. In the early rescue of property case of *Town of Prescott v Connell*[44] Sedgewick J., delivering the majority judgment, formulated the relevant test as whether the accident may be considered 'the natural or probable result' of the original wrongful act and whether it occurred 'in the ordinary course of events'.[45] His Honour applied this test to the facts of the instant case and concluded:

> The accident followed upon the negligent act in a natural order of sequence. It was an event likely to happen, probable to happen, natural to happen, as the direct and immediate result of [the defendant's] negligent act.[46]

---

39 (1924) 3 F 2d 882. This case is examined in more detail in Chapter 5.
40 Ibid., 884.
41 (1934) 73 F 2d 184.
42 Ibid., 186.
43 [1970] AC 1004, 1030.
44 (1893) 22 SCR 147 (SCC). This case is examined in more detail in Chapter 2.
45 Ibid., 161.
46 Ibid., 162.

In the later case of *Blais* v *Yachuk*[47] the Supreme Court of Canada relied on the approach of Greer L.J. in *Haynes* v *Harwood*.[48] Hudson and Estey JJ. held that the defendant could not successfully plead *novus actus interveniens* if the intervening event 'is the very kind of thing which is likely to happen if the want of care which is alleged takes place...'

The lower Canadian courts have also applied the probability test from time to time. In *Duce* v *Rourke*,[49] a case involving intervening criminal conduct, Egbert J. stated that an intervening event will not, generally speaking, relieve a tortfeasor of liability if the intervening event is the 'natural and probable result' of the defendant's negligence. And, in another case[50] involving intervening criminal conduct, Wilson J. relied on Greer L.J.'s statement of the law contained in *Haynes* v *Harwood*[51] to reject the defendant's contention that meddling with propane gas tanks broke the chain of causation.

Other Jurisdictions

The probability test has been applied rather sparingly by Australian courts to determine intervening causation issues. The high-water mark of its application occurred in the decision of the High Court of Australia in *Caterson* v *Commissioner for Railways*.[52] There the Court held that the plaintiff's act in jumping from a slowly moving passenger train did not sever the causal chain linking the defendant's failure to warn that the train would soon be departing from the station and the plaintiff's physical injuries. Gibbs J., who delivered the main judgment in the case, referred to the *obiter* observations of Lord Reid in *Home Office* v *Dorset Yacht Co. Ltd*[53] concerning His Lordship's preference for the application of the probability test to resolve intervening causation issues.[54] Gibbs J. also cited the following passage which appears in the judgment of Greer L.J. in *Haynes* v *Harwood*:[55]

> If what is relied upon as *novus actus interveniens* is the very kind of thing which is likely to happen if the want of care which is alleged takes place, the principle embodied in the maxim is no defence. The whole question is whether or not...the accident can be said to be 'the natural and probable result' of the breach of duty.

---

47   [1946] SCR 1, 15–16 (*per* Hudson and Estey JJ.).
48   [1935] 1 KB 146, 156 (CA).
49   (1951) 1 WWR (NS) 305 (Alta).
50   *Canphoto Ltd* v *Aetna Roofing (1965) Ltd* [1971] 3 WWR 116 (Man.) This case is examined in more detail in Chapter 5.
51   [1935] 1 KB 146, 156 (CA) ('If what is relied upon as *novus actus interveniens* is the very kind of thing which is likely to happen if the want of care which is alleged takes place, the principle embodied in the maxim is no defence.')
52   (1973) 128 CLR 99. This case is examined in more detail in Chapter 4.
53   [1970] AC 1004, 1030 (HL).
54   (1973) 128 CLR 99, 110.
55   [1935] 1 KB 146, 156 (CA).

In applying these principles to the instant case, Gibbs J. concluded that in the particular circumstances the plaintiff's action of jumping from the carriage was 'in the ordinary course of things' and 'the very kind of thing likely to happen as a result of the [defendant's] negligence'.[56] In *Taupo B.C.* v *Birnie*[57] the New Zealand Court of Appeal held that default to a secured creditor and ultimately a forced sale were 'the very kind of things which were likely to happen' as a consequence of negligently- inflicted damage to a profit-earning business. The National Court of Justice of Papua New Guinea has also applied the probability test in a case involving an intervening criminal act of murder. In *Moini* v *The State*[58] Williams J. quoted with approval the judgment of Greer L.J. in *Haynes* v *Harwood*[59] as well as that of Lord Reid in *Home Office* v *Dorset Yacht Co. Ltd*[60] in reaching the conclusion that a payback killing of a motor vehicle passenger after the fatal running down of a child pedestrian did not sever the chain of causation between the driver's negligent driving and the passenger's death if it can be shown that such a deliberate unlawful act is such as would be known to a reasonable person to be a 'likely consequence' of such driving.

The probability test of intervening causation has also found favour with the Supreme Court of Ireland. In *Cunningham* v *MacGrath Bros*[61] the plaintiff left her employer's premises to go for lunch. The defendant had been doing work on the employer's premises which had necessitated the use of double ladders. After removal of a blind, it was taken away for repairs but the ladders were left in position and unattended outside the employer's premises, causing a partial obstruction of the footpath. Some unknown person moved one of the ladders round a corner of the employer's premises into a small side street. As the plaintiff was passing the ladder on her way to lunch, it fell and injured her. She sued the defendant seeking damages in public nuisance for her personal injuries. The defendant argued that the intervention of the unknown person in moving one of the ladders from a position of relative safety to a position of danger amounted to a *novus actus interveniens*. Both the High Court at first instance and the Supreme Court on appeal rejected the defendant's *novus actus* plea. In delivering the judgment of the Supreme Court, Kingsmill Moore J. cited with approval the judgment of Greer L.J. in *Haynes* v *Harwood*[62] and stated:

---

56 (1973) 128 CLR 99, 110. See also McHugh J. in *March* v *E. & M.H. Stramare Pty Ltd* (1990–91) 171 CLR 506, 537 (The plaintiff's damage was 'a natural and probable consequence' of the defendant's breach of duty) and Mason C.J. (at 518).

57 [1978] 2 NZLR 397 (CA). See also *Bohdal* v *Streets* [1984] Tas R 82; *Thorpe Nominees* v *Henderson & Lahey* [1988] 2 Qd R 216 (the 'very likely' test applies only to the chance that a third party would intervene in the situation in such a way as to affect the plaintiff rather than to the precise part the third party in fact played).

58 [1977] PNGLR 39.
59 [1935] 1 KB 146, 156 (CA).
60 [1970] AC 1004, 1030 (HL).
61 [1964] IR 209.
62 [1935] 1 KB 146, 156 (CA).

I am of opinion that the test to be applied is whether the person responsible for creating the nuisance should anticipate as a reasonable and probable consequence that some person in pursuance of his rights would attempt to abate the nuisance and in so doing would create a danger. Applying this test it seems to me that [the defendant] should have anticipated as reasonable and probable that someone…would remove the ladder and put it somewhere near in a position where it would be less of an obstruction but might constitute more of a danger.[63]

The Supreme Court of Ireland has recently endorsed the probability test of intervening causation in *Breslin* v *Corcoran*.[64] In the context of a case involving an intervening criminal act of the theft of a motor vehicle, Fennelly J., delivering the judgment of the Court, expressly endorsed Lord Reid's 'probability' test in *Home Office* v *Dorset Yacht Co. Ltd*[65] and pointed out that the Supreme Court of Ireland had already adopted such test in *Cunningham* v *MacGrath Bros*.[66] Accordingly, the defendant would not be relieved from civil liability where the damage caused by the intervening actor was 'the very kind of thing which he was bound to expect and guard against and the resulting damage was likely to happen, if he did not.'[67]

Conclusion

Apart from the English Court of Appeal, Commonwealth courts have not regularly and systematically applied the probability test to resolve issues of intervening causation. This is due perhaps to the rather malleable and open-ended nature of phrases and terms like 'natural and probable consequence' and 'very likely' and difficulties associated with where to draw the line. Whether a court chooses to apply the probability test is basically a judicial policy choice. If a judge wishes to give full effect to the *novus actus* doctrine as a device limiting the liability of the defendant, he or she will find a friend in the probability test when even a foreseeable event may break the causal chain. If, on the other hand, a judge wishes to expand the incidence of the defendant's liability (or at least not restrict it on causal grounds) he or she will fall back on the reasonable foreseeability test of intervening causation for the reasons indicated in Chapter 3. It would appear that, absent legislative intervention to resolve concerns of the liability insurance industry, the common law application of the probability test will become increasingly rare.

---

63 [1964] IR 209, 215.
64 [2003] IESC 23. This case is examined in more detail in Chapter 5.
65 [1970] AC 1004, 1030 (HL).
66 [1964] IR 209.
67 [2003] lESC 23, 7.

Chapter 7

Scope of Risk

Introduction

In recent times a duty-based approach to intervening causation issues has emerged. Lord Hoffman has referred to this approach in the following passage from his judgment in *Environment Agency (formerly National Rivers Authority)* v *Empress Car Co. (Abertillery) Ltd*:[1]

> [O]ne cannot give a common sense answer to a question of causation for the purpose of attributing responsibility under some rule without knowing the purpose and scope of the rule. Does the rule impose a duty which requires one to guard against…the deliberate acts of third persons? If so, it will be correct to say, when loss is caused by the act of such third person, that it was caused by the breach of duty…Before answering questions about causation, it is therefore first necessary to identify the scope of the relevant rule.

And as noted by Hart and Honore, '[w]here a legal rule has been violated and harm has occurred which may be regarded as "within the risk" in the sense that the harm is of a kind which the rule was designed to prevent, the courts may consider it enough that the defendant, by his breach of the rule, has done something without which the harm would not have occurred and so provided an occasion for it.'[2] This duty-based approach is not unique to the common law world. German scholars have developed the theory of the *Schutzzweck der Norm* (translated as the 'scope of rule theory'). According to this theory, damage can be recovered only when it is within the scope of protection of the norm which has been infringed.[3]

It has only been comparatively recently that courts in common law jurisdictions have come to recognise that a negligent, and even an intentional or criminal, intervention may constitute a risk against which there is a duty to adopt precautions. Before then, the principle prevailed that if, after the defendant's negligence, there intervened the wrongful act of a third person, the 'last wrongdoer' was solely responsible for the plaintiff's injury.[4] The duty-based or 'scope of risk' approach is an alternative and increasingly preferred intervening causation test which inquires whether the consequences suffered by the plaintiff may fairly be regarded as within the risk created by the defendant's negligence.[5] This approach, as we have seen

---

1 [1999] 2 AC 22, 31 (HL).
2 H.L.A. Hart and T. Honore *Causation in the Law* (2nd edn, 1985) 6.
3 W. van Gerven, J. Lever and J. Larouche *Cases, Materials and Texts on National, Supranational and International Tort Law* (Hart Publishing, 2000) 398.
4 J. Fleming *The Law of Torts* (The Law Book Co. Ltd, 9th edn, 1998) 250.
5 Ibid., 245.

in Chapter 5, has been recently and consistently used in numerous common law jurisdictions in the context of intervening criminal and deliberately inflicted harm by third persons. As Lord Hoffman has observed, the 'scope of the risk' approach focuses attention on the purpose of the rule or norm breached by the defendant as an indication of the risks which should have been anticipated and avoided. The purpose of the rule that one should drive carefully is to protect other road users from injury, not to protect them from robbery. Thus a motorist who negligently injures another motorist will not be liable for additional loss when a third party steals tools from the latter's car while he is being taken to hospital.[6] It has been claimed that the 'scope of the risk' approach or the linking of intervening causation issues with the scope of the duty of care can better accommodate general community notions concerning the allocation of blame and judicial policy considerations relating to accident prevention, loss distribution and insurance.[7]

The United Kingdom

Early English cases recognised that persons having in their custody dangerous instruments such as firearms must exercise the utmost care in terms of their maintenance and control. So, in *Dixon v Bell*[8] the defendant was held liable in damages for injuries caused to the plaintiff's son in an accidental shooting where the defendant had not discharged his duty of care to keep the gun safe and out of the reach of persons not capable of exercising sufficient care in its handling. The failure to do so involved a significant risk of physical injury to a class of persons which included the plaintiff's son. The fact that the accidental shooting was precipitated by a third person (a minor) did not sever the causal chain between the defendant's negligence and the victim's injuries. A similar approach and result obtained in *Lynch v Nurdin*[9] where the defendant was held liable for his servant's negligence in leaving unattended a horse-drawn cart during which a seven-year-old who had climbed thereon was injured. In holding that the boy's intervening mischief did not amount to either contributory negligence or *novus actus interveniens*, Lord Denham C.J. effectively adopted a 'scope of the risk' approach as follows:

> For if I am guilty of negligence in leaving any thing dangerous in a place where I know it to be extremely probable that some other person will unjustifiably set it in motion to the injury of a third, and if that injury should be so brought about, I presume that the sufferer might have redress...If, for example, a gamekeeper...should rear his loaded gun against a wall in the play-ground of school boys whom he knew to be in the habit of pointing toys in the shape of guns at one another, and one of these should playfully fire it off at a schoolfellow and maim him, I think it will not be doubted that the gamekeeper must answer in damages to the wounded party.[10]

---

6 *Duce v Rourke* [1951] 1 WWR 305.
7 J. Fleming *The Law of Torts* (The Law Book Co. Ltd, 9th edn, 1998) 245.
8 (1816) 5 M & S 198. This case is examined in more detail in Chapter 2.
9 (1841) 1 QB 29. This case is examined in more detail in Chapter 2.
10 Ibid., 35.

Adopting a similar 'scope of the risk' approach, the Court of Common Pleas in *Collins v The Middle Level Commissioners*[11] refused to regard a plaintiff's attempt to mitigate his losses by breaching an act of parliament as a *novus actus* relieving the defendants of liability. In that case the defendants were required under an act of parliament to construct a cut with proper walls, gates and sluices to keep out the waters of a tidal river. They were also required to construct a culvert under the cut to carry off the drainage from the lands on the east to the west of the cut, and to keep it open at all times. Due to the negligent construction of the gates and sluices, the waters of the tidal river flowed into the cut and flooded the adjoining lands. The plaintiff and other land owners on the east side of the cut closed the lower end of the culvert, which prevented the waters overflowing their lands. However, the occupiers of the lands on the west side, believing that the stoppage of the culvert would be injurious to their lands, reopened it thereby allowing the waters through on to the plaintiff's land. The Court held that the defendant commissioners were liable for all of the damage caused to the plaintiff's land. That the plaintiff in closing the culvert may have acted in breach of a drainage statute in an attempt to prevent the flooding of his lands did not amount to a *novus actus* which would otherwise excuse the defendants 'from the natural consequences of their negligence'.[12] According to Brett J., 'the primary and substantial cause of the injury was the negligence of the defendants.'[13] Negligent construction of the gates and sluices raised the foreseeable risk that adjoining land owners would meddle with the culvert and cause the flooding of their lands.

The case of *Cobb v Great Western Railway*[14] raised for judicial consideration the issue of the extent to which a supplementary duty should be recognised to guard against risks which are unrelated to the main risk that the rule or norm was designed to address. There it was held that the defendant railway company which had negligently allowed a carriage to become overcrowded was not liable to the plaintiff for theft by pickpocketing by a third person who had deliberately exploited the vulnerable situation facilitated by the defendant's negligence. It could not be said that the norm or rule of conduct breached by the defendant was aimed at the prevention of theft.

Twentieth-century English cases began to link more specifically intervening causation issues with the duty-based 'scope of the risk' approach. For example, in *Northwestern Utilities Ltd v London Guarantee and Accident Co. Ltd*[15] Lord Wright considered that although the act of a third party may be relied on as a *novus actus*, the defendant may still be held liable in negligence if he failed in foreseeing and guarding against the consequences to his negligence of that third party's act. In *Philco Radio and Television Corporation v J. Spurling Ltd*[16] the Court of Appeal

---

11 (1869) LR 4 CP 279.
12 Ibid., 287 *per* Montague Smith J.
13 Ibid., 288.
14 [1894] AC 419. See also the Australian case of *Watts v Turpin* (1999) 21 WAR 402 where the failure of a neighbour to water the avocado trees of the accident victim was an independent and superseding cause of the loss for which the person who caused the accident was not liable.
15 [1936] AC 108.
16 [1949] 2 All ER 882 (CA).

rejected the defendants' *novus actus* plea through a careful examination of the content and scope of their duty of care. In that case packing cases containing dangerously inflammable celluloid film scrap were delivered by mistake by the defendants to the plaintiff's premises. Although no warning of their dangerous contents was given, the plaintiff's foreman recognised the material as inflammable and dangerous when some of it was taken out of one of the cases. He warned the workers in charge of the cases not to smoke near them and arranged with the defendants to deliver the cases to their proper destination. Before the cases were moved, however, a typist employed by the defendants approached the cases with a lighted cigarette and an explosion occurred causing significant damage. The Court of Appeal held that in the absence of evidence that the typist had deliberately set the scrap alight, the defendants had not discharged the onus of proving that the damage was caused by the intervening conduct of the typist. Tucker L.J. concluded, 'it was the duty of the defendants not to deliver this dangerous, inflammable material without warning, in such circumstances that damage might result from some mischievous or foolish act of some person on the plaintiff's premises.'[17]

The oft-cited decision of the English Court of Appeal in *Stansbie* v *Troman*[18] is a classic example of a situation where the defendant may be under an obligation as part of his or her original duty of care to take precautions to protect the plaintiff from not only the negligent, but even the intentional and criminal, acts of third parties.[19] This occurs where the negligence alleged against the defendant consists of the failure to take reasonable care to guard against the very eventuality which in fact materialised, and where the risk of intervening conduct is the reason for finding negligence against the defendant when sufficient preventive measures are not adopted. Thus, in *Stansbie* v *Troman*, Tucker L.J. stated:

> [T]he act of negligence itself consisted in the failure to take reasonable care to guard against the very thing that in fact happened. The reason why the decorator owed a duty to the householder to leave the premises in a reasonably secure state was because otherwise thieves or dishonest persons might gain access to them; and it seems to me that if the decorator was, as I think he was, negligent in leaving the house in this condition, it was as a direct result of his negligence that the thief entered by the front door, which was left unlocked, and stole these valuable goods.[20]

The Judicial Committee of the Privy Council has also effectively applied the duty-based 'scope of the risk' approach in a case involving a mischievous intervening act of a child plaintiff. In *Yachuk* v *Oliver Blais Co. Ltd*[21] a nine-year-old boy prevailed on an employee of the defendant company to sell him a small quantity of petrol by telling an untruthful statement. This was despite the fact that the employee entertained

---

17   Ibid., 885.
18   [1948] 2 KB 48 (CA). This case is examined in more detail in Chapter 5.
19   Some commentators argue that liability in such cases is essentially dependent on the defendant's original obligation and is far removed from the causation realm. See, for example, B. McMahon and W. Binchy *Irish Law of Torts* (Butterworths, 2nd edn, 1990) 51.
20   [1948] 2 KB 48, 52.
21   [1949] 2 All ER 150 (JCPC).

doubts as to the propriety of the sale. While re-enacting a scene he had recently witnessed at the cinema, the boy was seriously burned. The defendant contended that the plaintiff's deceitful representation and subsequent conduct severed the causal chain between the employee's negligence in selling the petrol to the boy and his sustaining the burning injuries. The Privy Council rejected the defendant's *novus actus* plea on the ground that the employee's negligence consisted in putting into the hands of a small, vulnerable and inexperienced boy a dangerous and explosive substance with which a reasonable and thoughtful person would have foreseen that a child was likely to injure himself. In delivering the judgment of the Board, Lord du Parcq observed, '[t]o put a highly inflammable substance into the hands of a small boy is to subject him to temptation and the risk of injury and this is no less true if the boy has resorted to deceit in order to overcome the suppliers' scruples.'[22] The Privy Council's approach to the determination of the *novus actus* plea reflected that of Denman C.J. in *Lynch* v *Nurdin*.[23]

That negligently caused injury may produce susceptibility in the plaintiff's condition and situation to further and aggravated injury was acknowledged by Eveleigh J. in *Wieland* v *Cyril Lord Carpets Ltd*.[24] The plaintiff suffered injury caused by the admitted negligence of the defendant. After hospital treatment the plaintiff was fitted with a neck collar which constricted the movement of her head. She was unable consequently to use her bi-focal spectacles properly and she suffered a fall while descending stairs, thereby sustaining further injuries. The defendant was also held liable for the effects of the later fall because they were considered to be attributable to the original negligence. According to Eveleigh J. the plaintiff's ability to negotiate stairs was impaired by the original motor vehicle accident and this impaired ability resulted in a fall suffered while undertaking normal daily activity.[25] Applying the duty-based approach to the intervening causation issue, His Lordship concluded, 'it is foreseeable that one injury may affect a person's ability to cope with the vicissitudes of life and thereby be a cause of another injury…'[26] The duty-based 'scope of the risk' approach has also been applied in the motor vehicle collision context by the Court of Appeal in *Rouse* v *Squires*.[27] It was held that the intervening and immediate cause of the death of a person assisting at the scene of an accident did not amount to a *novus actus* where the subsequent events fell within the range of foreseeable risks to be guarded against. As Cairns L.J. stated,

> [i]f a driver so negligently manages his vehicle as to cause it to obstruct the highway and constitute a danger to other road users, including those who are driving too fast or not keeping a proper lookout…then the first driver's negligence may be held to have contributed to the causation of an accident of which the immediate cause was the negligent

---

22 Ibid., 153.
23 (1841) 1 QB 29.
24 [1969] 3 All ER 1006 (QBD).
25 Ibid., 1008.
26 Ibid., 1010. Eveleigh J. also held that it was not unreasonable for her to descend the stairs on the occasion in question with the assistance of her adult son.
27 [1973] 1 QB 889 (CA).

driving of the vehicle which because of the presence of the obstruction collides with it or with some other vehicle or some other person.[28]

The 'scope of the risk' approach to intervening causation has also been endorsed by Oliver L.J. in *Lamb* v *Camden London Borough Council*[29] wherein His Lordship said that an intervening act of a third person over whom the defendant can exercise no control 'does not always break the chain [of causation] and, in particular, it will not do so where the very breach of duty relied on is the duty of the defendant to prevent the sort of intervention which has occurred…'[30] More recently Latham L.J. has applied the 'scope of the risk' approach in rejecting a defendant's *novus actus* plea. In *Forbes* v *Merseyside Fire and Civil Defence Authority*[31] a premature medical opinion leading to the plaintiff's early retirement and consequential financial loss was held not to have severed the causal chain, as 'what eventuated was exactly the type of event which fell within the risk area which the…defendant was under a duty to obviate.'[32]

The most recent and strongest endorsement of the 'scope of the risk' approach is to be found in the House of Lords decision in *Reeves* v *Commissioner of Police of the Metropolis*.[33] In that case a prisoner hanged himself in a police cell. The defendants were aware that he was a suicide risk, but the flap on the cell door had been left down allowing the prisoner to tie his shirt through the spy hole in the door and hang himself. The defendants conceded that a duty of care was owed to the prisoner but denied liability on the ground that his own act of suicide amounted to a *novus actus interveniens*. The House of Lords held that the suicide did not sever the causal chain as the death resulted directly from breach of a duty to prevent just such an act. It was not a superseding event but the very harm that the defendants were under a duty to prevent. As Lord Hope said:

> I do not see how what occurred in this case could be said to amount to a *novus actus interveniens*. There was no 'new' act here at all. The act by which the deceased killed himself was the very act which the commissioner was under a duty to prevent by not leaving the wicket gate open when the deceased was in his cell and thus providing him with the means of hanging himself. The chain of causation was not broken…Here the wrongful act was the cause of the harm because it created the opportunity for the deliberate act of self-harm. The suicide was a foreseeable consequence of the failure in duty which occurred when the deceased, who was a known suicide risk, was placed in a cell which provided him with the opportunity to carry out that act.[34]

Lord Hoffman noted the qualified nature of the general principle that 'the free, deliberate and informed act or omission of a human being, intended to exploit

---

28   Ibid., 898.
29   [1981] 1 QB 625 (CA).
30   Ibid., 640. In the *Lamb* case, the risk posed by the defendant negligently puncturing the water main was of damage to the foundations of the house caused by escaping water, not of squatters inhabiting and damaging it.
31   [2002] EWCA Civ 1067.
32   Ibid., para. 11.
33   [2000] 1 AC 360 (HL).
34   Ibid., 381. See also to the same effect the judgment of Lord Jauncey (at 374–5).

the situation created by a defendant, negatives causal connection.'[35] His Lordship observed:

> [T]here is an exception to this undoubted rule in the case in which the law imposes a duty to guard against loss caused by the free, deliberate and informed act of a human being. It would make nonsense of the existence of such a duty if the law were to hold that the occurrence of the very act which ought to have been prevented negatived causal connection between the breach of duty and the loss.[36]

Thus, an acceptance of the defendant's *novus actus* plea would render the duty of care ineffective. As we have seen in Chapter 5, the duty-based 'scope of the risk' approach has tended to be more consistently applied in intervening criminal misconduct causation cases.

Australia

As in England, Australian courts have had a long tradition of applying the 'scope of the risk' approach on a consistent and regular basis to resolve intervening causation issues. In one of its earliest cases,[37] the High Court of Australia relied on it to reject the defendant's *novus actus* plea that the overflow of a lavatory basin and consequential water damage to the plaintiff's goods had been caused by a deliberate mischievous act of an unknown third person. As O'Connor J. stated,

> [i]f the defendant had reason to suppose, having regard to the mode in which the building was occupied, and to the class of occupants and other persons to whom the lavatory would be accessible, that the plug-holes and waste pipes of the basins were likely to become choked from time to time by foreign substances left there accidentally or negligently, or placed there mischievously, it would be his duty to guard against the consequences of the plug-holes or waste pipes being choked in that way.[38]

Half a century later the High Court again applied the 'scope of the risk' approach in the context of a motor vehicle collision case. In the oft-cited case of *Chapman* v *Hearse*[39] the High Court rejected the defendant's *novus actus* plea that his negligent driving which caused a collision with another vehicle and triggered the intervention of a medically qualified 'rescuer' was superseded by the later negligence of another motorist in running down and killing that rescuer. In this type of situation, the first tortfeasor's negligence partially consisted of exposing a would-be rescuer to the risk of being injured by another tortfeasor's negligent driving. As the High Court said, 'there can be little doubt that it was reasonably foreseeable that subsequent injury by passing traffic to those rendering aid after a collision on the highway would be

---

35 Hart and Honore *Causation in the Law*, 136.
36 [2000] 1 AC 360, 367–8.
37 *Lothian* v *Rickards* (1911) 12 CLR 165. This case is examined in more detail in Chapter 3.
38 Ibid., 181. See also the judgment of Griffith C.J. (at 177).
39 (1961) 106 CLR 112. This case is examined in more detail in Chapter 3.

by no means unlikely.'[40] Soon after *Chapman* v *Hearse* was decided, the High Court had occasion to once again apply this duty-based approach to intervening causation issues in *Reg Glass* v *Rivers*.[41] There the plaintiff purchased and installed in his home a negligently manufactured burglar alarm system. The High Court rejected the defendant manufacturer's *novus actus* plea that the volitional conduct of the third party thief severed the causal chain on the ground that the theft of the plaintiff's goods was in these circumstances the very risk or eventuality that was to be guarded against. It was obvious that the scope of the manufacturer's duty of care extended to preventing this type of harm from occurring. And, in a number of decisions handed down by the High Court during the 1980s, it was held that there could arise out of the particular relationship between the parties a duty of care to guard against deliberate criminal conduct by third party strangers. So, in *Pitt Son & Badgery Ltd* v *Proulefco SA*,[42] the intruder's act of arson 'was the very kind which [the defendant] was obliged to take reasonable care to prevent'.[43]

State appellate and lower courts have followed the High Court's lead. In *Chomentowski* v *Red Garter Restaurant Pty Ltd*[44] the plaintiff employee-manager of a restaurant, who was attacked and robbed while depositing the restaurant's takings in the night-safe of a bank in the early hours of the morning, successfully sued the defendant employer for breach of its duty to take reasonable care for his safety. The New South Wales Court of Appeal rejected the defendant's *novus actus* plea to the effect that the attack and robbery were deliberate and voluntary acts of conscious volition which severed the causal chain. Mason J.A. aptly expressed the 'scope of the risk' approach in the following passage:

> The injury which the plaintiff sustained, although occasioned by deliberate human intervention, was the outcome of the very risk against which it was the duty of the defendants to safeguard the plaintiff as their employee. If, as was the case, it was the existence of that risk of injury which called for the exercise of care and the taking of precautions by the defendants, then the defendants' failure to take care may properly be regarded as the cause of the injury which occurred when the risk became an actuality.[45]

On the basis of such approach, it was held in *Mount Isa Mines Ltd* v *Bates*[46] that a reasonably foreseeable omission by the plaintiff worker to wear safety glasses did not amount to a *novus actus interveniens* but rather made it negligent for the defendant employer to fail to adopt a simple and inexpensive modification to machinery that would have avoided the risk of flying particles of metal. Thus the employer was held liable for an injury to the plaintiff's eye caused by the latter's failure to wear

---

40 Ibid., 121.
41 (1968) 120 CLR 516.
42 (1984) 153 CLR 644. This case is examined in more detail in Chapter 5.
43 Ibid., 648. See also the decision of the High Court of Australia in *Commonwealth Trading Bank of Australia* v *Sydney Wide Stores Pty Ltd* (1981) 148 CLR 304.
44 (1970) 92 WN (NSW) 1070 (NSWCA).
45 Ibid., 1086.
46 [1972–73] ALR 635.

safety glasses provided by the employer. And in *Parramatta City Council* v *Lutz*[47] where the defendant council had a duty of care to take steps to prevent an abandoned property from becoming a fire hazard but failed to do so, the New South Wales Court of Appeal rejected the council's plea that it should be excused from liability for the consequential destruction of a neighbouring cottage because an unknown third party had actually lit the fire.[48]

In *Curmi* v *McLennan*[49] the Supreme Court of Victoria (Appeal Division) held liable a houseboat owner who negligently gave teenagers using his houseboat access to an airgun which resulted in one of the teenagers shooting another in the eye. Gobbo J., who delivered the main judgment in the case, relied on the *Chomentowski* principle that in some situations a defendant may come under a duty of care not to expose the plaintiff to a risk of injury arising from deliberate or voluntary conduct and to guard against that risk. In the instant case the defendant's negligence in giving a group of high-spirited schoolboys access to an airgun in circumstances where they were entirely unsupervised at all times and without any guidance or instructions had generated the very risk of the type of injury which transpired. Similarly, in *Club Italia (Geelong) Inc.* v *Ritchie*[50] the Victorian Court of Appeal held that the organisers of a social function which got out of control owed a duty of care to an attending police officer. The plaintiff, a responding police officer who was severely beaten by some of the patrons, successfully sued the defendant club. Having held that the scope of the club's duty extended to protecting responding police officers from the criminal conduct of third parties, it would have been inconsistent to have upheld the club's argument that its liability should be extinguished by a successful *novus actus* plea when such third party intervention was the very thing it should have guarded against. The Supreme Court of Queensland (Trial Division) has recently examined and applied the 'scope of the risk' approach in a police pursuit case. In *Hirst* v *Nominal Defendant*[51] the plaintiff was an on-duty police officer driving a marked police car along a major highway at night. Upon witnessing a car speeding in the opposite direction, he performed a U-turn and began to pursue it while signalling with his lights for the driver to stop. During the course of the pursuit, the plaintiff lost control of the police car and collided with another vehicle. The plaintiff sued in negligence for damages for physical injuries and a post-traumatic stress disorder he allegedly sustained as a result of this collision. The nominal defendant (which was substituted for the unidentified speeding and negligent driver) pleaded *novus actus interveniens* on the basis that the collision was caused by the plaintiff's driving following his 'voluntary' decision to engage in the pursuit. Citing the speech of Lord Hoffman in *Environment Agency* v *Empress Car Co. (Abertillery) Ltd*[52] as well as drawing on the *Chomentowski* principle, McMurdo J. considered that the causal enquiry cannot be answered without reference to the particular content or scope of the duty of care

---

47 (1988) 12 NSWLR 293 (NSWCA).
48 Ibid., 311 *per* Kirby P.; 334 *per* McHugh J.A.
49 [1994] 1 VR 513.
50 (2001) 3 VR 447 (CA).
51 [2004] QSC 272.
52 [1999] 2 AC 22, 31–2.

owed by a defendant.[53] Here the content or scope of the duty of care owed by the unidentified driver was such that the latter knew, or at least should have known, that if he drove as fast as he did, there was a real prospect that the plaintiff would decide to pursue him and in doing so would drive so fast that he could lose control of the police car and cause injury to himself and others.[54] The type of loss sustained by the plaintiff was precisely the kind of damage which it was the driver's duty to avoid and the fact that his injuries stemmed from his own deliberate decision to engage in the pursuit did not amount to a *novus actus interveniens* on the basis of the holding of the House of Lords in *Reeves* v *Commissioner of Police of the Metropolis*.[55]

The two most recent and important decisions of the High Court of Australia to apply the duty-based 'scope of the risk' approach are *March* v *E. & M.H. Stramare Pty Ltd*[56] and *Bennett* v *Minister of Community Welfare*.[57] In the former case, the plaintiff driver was injured when his car ran into a truck which had been parked in a position where it straddled the centre line of a six-lane road. The collision occurred late at night and at a time when the truck's parking and hazard lights were illuminated. The plaintiff driver was under the influence of alcohol and driving at an excessive speed at the time of the accident. In an action in negligence for damages against the owner and driver of the truck, the court of first instance apportioned liability under apportionment legislation as to 70 per cent to the plaintiff and 30 per cent to the defendants. The intermediate appellate court dismissed the plaintiff's action on the ground that the plaintiff's own negligence was the sole effective cause of the accident. However, on further appeal to the High Court of Australia, the trial Judge's apportionment of liability was restored. The intervening causation issue concerned whether the plaintiff's intoxicated driving at an excessive speed broke the chain of causation between the truck driver's negligent parking and the plaintiff's accident-related injuries. Two High Court judges relied on the 'scope of the risk' approach to reject the defendants' *novus actus* plea. McHugh J. stated:

> That an intoxicated driver, driving at excessive speed and failing to keep a proper lookout, might collide with the parked truck was one of the risks which the defendants were obliged to reasonably foresee and guard against…Both the damage which the plaintiff suffered

---

53 [2004] QSC 272, para. 12.
54 Ibid., para. 14.
55 [2000] 1 AC 360. This decision was affirmed by the Queensland Court of Appeal in *Hirst* v *Nominal Defendant* [2005] 2 Qd R 133. In following *Medlin* v *State Government Insurance Commission* (1995) 182 CLR 1, the Court held that voluntary or deliberate conduct on the plaintiff's part did not necessarily sever the causal nexus so as to relieve a negligent defendant. It was necessary to have regard to the extent to which the plaintiff's voluntary conduct had been constrained by the defendant's misconduct and to consider whether it was reasonable for the plaintiff to make the choice which was the immediate cause of his loss. Accordingly, as the plaintiff's conduct was constrained by his legal duties as a police officer and the occurrence of the driver's unlawful conduct which it was the plaintiff's duty to prevent, the plaintiff's attempts to deal with the situation created by the unidentified driver did not break the causal chain but were adjudged both at first instance and on appeal to amount to contributory negligence (necessitating a one-third reduction in the plaintiff's damages).
56 (1990–91) 171 CLR 506.
57 (1992) 176 CLR 408.

and the manner of its occurrence were fairly within the risk created by the defendants' breach of duty.[58]

And according to Mason C.J.:

> In some situations a defendant may come under a duty of care not to expose the plaintiff to a risk of injury arising from deliberate or voluntary conduct or even to guard against that risk: see *Chomentowski* v *Red Garter Restaurant Ltd*. To deny recovery in these situations because the intervening action is deliberate or voluntary would be to deprive the duty of any content...As a matter of both logic and common sense, it makes no sense to regard the negligence of the plaintiff or a third party as a superseding cause or *novus actus interveniens* when the defendant's wrongful conduct has generated the very risk of injury resulting from the negligence of the plaintiff or a third party and that injury occurs in the ordinary course of things.[59]

Thus, both Mason C.J. and McHugh J. considered the scope of the truck driver's duty of care as extending to a duty to take reasonable care to prevent his parked truck from becoming a hazard to other inattentive road users, particularly negligent or intoxicated drivers like the plaintiff.[60]

In the *Bennett* case, the plaintiff was a ward of the State under the guardianship of the Director of Community Welfare. In 1973 the plaintiff lost several fingers when his hand came into contact with a circular saw while at a detention centre. The defendant conceded negligence as the plaintiff had not been properly instructed or supervised in the use of the saw and the saw had not been properly guarded. The Department of Community Welfare owed a duty of care to the plaintiff to enable him to obtain independent legal advice as to his legal position but this duty was never discharged. After leaving the Department upon attaining majority, the plaintiff obtained the advice of a barrister to the effect that he had no legal claim against the Department (advice which was erroneous because there was a real prospect of success). The plaintiff's claim therefore became statute-barred and he sued the Minister alleging a continuing failure to obtain for him independent legal advice and claiming damages for the loss of his common law right to sue for damages. On appeal to the High Court of Australia, the defendant's plea, that the independent and negligent legal advice which the plaintiff himself had received from the barrister in 1976 constituted a *novus actus interveniens*, was rejected. The High Court held that the defendant's negligence remained the legal cause of the plaintiff's loss since there would not have been a need for the plaintiff to seek legal advice from the barrister in 1976 if the Director had not breached his duty of care. Moreover the barrister's erroneous legal advice was based on incorrect and self-serving information provided by the Department.[61] Negligent legal advice was in these circumstances the very risk against which the Director had a legal duty to protect the plaintiff.[62] As Gaudron J.

---

58 (1990–91) 171 CLR 506, 537.
59 Ibid., 517–19 (footnote omitted).
60 See also the judgment of Deane J. (at 520–21).
61 (1992) 176 CLR 408, 414–15 (*per* Mason C.J., Deane and Toohey JJ.).
62 If, however, the barrister had provided correct legal advice which the plaintiff had chosen to ignore, a *novus actus* plea may well have succeeded if the court was satisfied that

observed, 'the question whether some supervening event broke a chain of causation which began with…an omission or a failure to perform a positive duty, is one that can only be answered by having regard to what would or would not have happened if the duty had been performed.'[63]

Canada

The Supreme Court of Canada has also applied the duty-based 'scope of the risk' approach to resolve intervening causation issues but its experience in doing so has been relatively limited compared with that of the High Court of Australia. In *Winnipeg Electric Railway Co. v Canadian Northern Railway Co. and Bartlett*[64] the deceased either jumped or fell off the back of a streetcar when it was negligently driven in front of an approaching train. According to Duff J., '[w]here there is a duty to take precautions to obviate a given risk the wrongdoer who fails in this duty cannot avoid responsibility for the very consequences it was his duty to provide against…'[65] However, not all risks may fall within the scope of the defendant's duty of care. In *Bradford v Kanellos*[66] a flash fire was negligently caused in a restaurant. A fire extinguisher was activated and gas was released which created a hissing sound. A patron shouted that gas was escaping and that there was a danger of an explosion. In the stampede that followed, the plaintiff was injured. The majority of the Supreme Court of Canada held against the plaintiff on the ground that her injury 'resulted from the hysterical conduct of a customer' and that such a reaction was not a consequence 'fairly to be regarded as within the risk created by the [defendant's] negligence in permitting an undue quantity of grease to accumulate on the grill'.[67] In a strong dissenting judgment, however, Spence J. (with whom Laskin J. concurred) said:

> I am not of the opinion that the persons who shouted the warning of what they were certain was an impending explosion were negligent. I am, on the other hand, of the opinion that they acted in a very human and usual way and that their actions…were utterly foreseeable and were part of the natural consequence of events leading inevitably to the plaintiff's injury.[68]

Lower Canadian courts have likewise applied the 'scope of the risk' approach to cases involving both intervening criminal and negligent conduct, albeit on a sporadic basis. In *Martin v McNamara Construction Co.*[69] employees of a construction company carelessly broke a fence enclosing a field in which, to their knowledge, cows were

---

the plaintiff's reasons for inaction were unreasonable.
    63 (1992) 176 CLR 408, 421. For a recent example of the application of the 'scope of the risk' approach by a member of the High Court of Australia, see the judgment of Gleeson C.J. in *Travel Compensation Fund v Tambree* (2005) 224 CLR 627, 640–41.
    64 (1920) 59 SCR 352.
    65 Ibid., 367.
    66 (1973) 40 DLR (3d) 578 (SCC).
    67 Ibid., 580. See also *Schlink v Blackburn* [1993] B.C.J. No. 2577, 18 CCLT (2d) 173 (C.A.).
    68 Ibid., 582.
    69 [1955] 3 DLR 51.

kept. One of them escaped through the gap in the fence onto the road and was struck by a negligent motorist. The Ontario Court of Appeal held that the defendant company could not escape responsibility by pointing to the subsequent negligent driving of the motorist since that event fell squarely within the range of foreseeable risks attributable to the situation generated by the employees' negligence. A similar case is *Holian v United Grain Growers*[70] where some mischievous boys took some fumigant tablets used to kill insects from the defendant's shed and placed them in the plaintiff's car as a 'stink bomb' causing illness to the plaintiff. The court imposed liability on the defendant since this theft and consequential injury were 'within the risk created by the negligence of the defendant in leaving the shed unlocked and unattended'.[71] Canadian courts have also held that the crimes of rape[72] and arson are to be foreseen and guarded against. In *Williams v New Brunswick*[73] a prisoner set fire to a lockup causing the death of 21 inmates. An action by the families of some of the deceased inmates succeeded against the defendant for negligently allowing the prisoner to obtain matches. Stratton C.J. concluded that the consequences of such negligence may 'fairly be regarded as within the ambit of the risk created by that negligence'.[74]

Like the English courts, Canadian courts have been reluctant to recognise a defendant's supplementary duty to guard against risks which are unrelated to the main risk or risks inherent in the particular duty of care. So, in *Duce v Rourke*[75] the court exonerated the negligent defendant motorist from liability for some tools stolen from the injured plaintiff's car after he had been taken to hospital. It could not be said that the norm of conduct violated by the defendant was aimed at the prevention of theft.[76]

New Zealand

The New Zealand Court of Appeal has had a long tradition in applying the duty-based 'scope of the risk' approach in resolving intervening causation issues. This tradition can be traced back to 1881 when the Court of Appeal decided *Reid v*

---

70   (1980) 11 CCLT 184 (Man. QB).

71   Ibid., 191.

72   *Q v Minto Management* (1985) 31 CCLT 158 (Ont. HC); *Jane Doe v Board of Police Commissioners for Metro Toronto* [1998] O.J. No. 2681, 39 O.R. (3d) 487 (Gen. Div.) (if police authorities use a woman as bait to catch a rapist, they may be held liable for that woman being raped by that rapist); *H.(M.) v Bederman* [1995] O.J. No. 3834, 27 CCLT (2d) 152 (Gen. Div.) (a doctor can be held liable for a sexual assault to a vulnerable patient by another patient).

73   (1985) 34 CCLT 299 (N.B.CA).

74   Ibid., 319. A defendant newspaper company was held partially liable for a theft from a vacant house because it failed to stop delivery of the newspaper during a vacation period, as instructed by the subscriber: *Crotin v National Post* [2003] O.J. No. 4583, 20 CCLT (3d) 316 (S.C.J.).

75   (1951) 1 WWR (NS) 305 (Alta).

76   The holding in *Duce v Rourke* is consistent with the English decision of *Cobb v Great Western Railway* [1894] AC 419 and the Australian decision of *Watts v Turpin* (1999) 21 WAR 402, but see *contra* the decision of the British Columbia Supreme Court in *Patten v Silberschein* [1936] 3 WWR 169.

Friendly Societies' Hall Company,[77] a case very similar on its facts to the Australian case of *Lothian* v *Rickards*.[78] In the *Reid* case, the plaintiff held a tenancy from the defendants of part of the ground floor of a building. On the upper floor there was a hand basin with a tap of water which was used by the defendants and certain other tenants. The tap and basin were so constructed that if the tap were turned full on, and the plug left in the basin, there was insufficient means of escape for the water. This having occurred, the water percolated to the ground floor and damaged the plaintiff's goods. There was no evidence to indicate whether the basin overflow had been caused by the wilful or merely negligent conduct of an unknown third person. The plaintiff did not use the tap and indeed was not aware of its existence until after the flooding of his goods. In an action for breach of contract for quiet enjoyment and in negligence, the defendants were held liable in damages. Prendergast C.J. formulated the relevant enquiry as follows:

> [T]he question to be considered is, whether there was negligence in not providing for the event of a wilful or negligent act of a third person. The damage was certainly not the result merely of an imperfection in the apparatus itself. There was manifestly the act of some person, and the question is, whether such an act and the consequences of it ought to have been anticipated and guarded against, and whether the not having guarded against the act the defendants are liable…[79]

The 'scope of the risk' approach was next relied on by the Court of Appeal in its 1945 decision in *John Mill and Co. Ltd* v *Public Trustee*[80] to reject the defendant company's *novus actus* plea in a case involving the death of a waterside worker in an industrial accident.[81] And in *McCarthy* v *Wellington City*[82] the Court of Appeal held that the deliberate acts of young boys in breaking open a safe and subsequently distributing detonators to other children did not amount to a *novus actus interveniens* on the grounds that such acts were reasonably foreseeable and ones which the defendant should have guarded against. Citing from the judgment of Tucker L.J. in *Stansbie* v *Troman*,[83] Turner J. considered the instant case as one 'where the act of negligence which is alleged against the defendant consisted in the failure to take reasonable care to guard against the very thing that in fact happened'.[84] McCarthy J. similarly held that the deliberate intervening acts of the boys in breaking open the safe and subsequently distributing the detonators did not sever the causal chain since such intervention was reasonably foreseeable and one which was required to be guarded against.[85] The 'scope of the risk' approach was also utilized by Woodhouse

---

77 (1881) 3 NZLR 238 (CA).
78 (1911) 12 CLR 165.
79 (1881) 3 NZLR 238, 247–8. See to the same effect the judgment of Williams J. (at 252).
80 [1945] NZLR 347 (CA).
81 See in particular the judgment of Sir Michael Myers C.J. (at 361–2).
82 [1966] NZLR 481 (CA).
83 [1948] 2 KB 48, 52 (CA).
84 [1966] NZLR 481, 517.
85 Ibid., 522.

J. (dissenting) in *Pallister* v *Waikato Hospital Board*[86] to find against the defendant hospital authority. That case concerned an action by a widow against the defendant for failing to prevent her suicidal husband from taking his life while the latter was under its care and control. The husband had been admitted to hospital because of suicidal tendencies and took his life while there. The majority of the Court of Appeal upheld the decision of the first instance court in which it had been held that the defendant had not been negligent. In an approach reminiscent of that used by the House of Lords in the later case of *Reeves* v *Commissioner of Police of the Metropolis*,[87] Woodhouse J. concluded that the defendant's breach of its duty of care was the legal cause of the husband's death since 'the impulse to suicide should be regarded as a causa sine qua non in the sense that it was a continuing situation and the one in respect of which the duty of care had arisen.'[88]

Other Jurisdictions

The 'scope of the risk' approach to intervening causation has been applied by the United States Supreme Court and is codified in the American Law Institute's *Restatement of the Law of Torts, Second*.[89] Section 442B. of the *Restatement* recites,

> [w]here the negligent conduct of the [defendant] creates or increases the risk of a particular harm and is a substantial factor in causing that harm, the fact that the harm is brought about through the intervention of another force does not relieve the [defendant] of liability, except where the harm is intentionally caused by a third person and is not within the scope of the risk created by the [defendant's] conduct.

The Supreme Court has rejected the defendant's *novus actus* plea in the context of the employer's duty to protect employees against the criminal acts of third parties. In *Lillie* v *Thompson*[90] the Supreme Court unanimously held in the plaintiff's favour on the following basis:

> [Defendant] was aware of conditions which created a likelihood that a young woman performing the duties required of [the plaintiff] would suffer just such an injury as was in fact inflicted upon her. That the foreseeable danger was from intentional or criminal misconduct is irrelevant; respondent nonetheless had a duty to make reasonable provision against it. Breach of that duty would be negligence, and we cannot say as a matter of law that [plaintiff's] injury did not result at least in part from such negligence.[91]

In terms of Section 442B. of the *Restatement*, although the plaintiff's serious and permanent physical injuries were caused by a violent and deliberate criminal attack,

---

86 [1975] 2 NZLR 725 (CA).
87 [2000] 1 AC 360 (HL).
88 [1975] 2 NZLR 725, 745.
89 (1965–79).
90 (1947) 332 US 459 (USSC). This case is examined in more detail in Chapter 5.
91 Ibid., 461–2.

such attack fell squarely within the scope of the risk generated by the defendant's failure to adopt and implement sufficient precautions to protect her.

The Irish Court of Appeal has also applied the 'scope of the risk' approach in a case involving accidental wounding by a firearm. In *Sullivan v Creed*[92] the defendant left a loaded gun at full cock standing inside a fence on his property adjacent to a public road. The defendant's 15-year-old son found the gun and, not realising that it was loaded, pointed it in play at the 16-year-old plaintiff who was on the road. The gun was discharged and the plaintiff lost an eye. The Court of Appeal upheld the decision of the King's Bench Division that the defendant was liable in negligence for damages. The defendant's conduct was characterised as gross negligence and the intervening negligence of his son was not considered sufficient to sever the causal chain. Walker L.J. considered that 'the law will attribute to [the defendant] a reasonable anticipation that all those who come that way, including the young, the careless, and the inexperienced, might see the gun, meddle with it, or use it carelessly in the highly dangerous condition in which he left it.'[93] His Lordship concluded that 'where, as in this case, the intervening act is almost a momentary one, arising immediately out of the negligence which gave occasion and opportunity for the intervening act, it is impossible to say that the original negligence has not been that to which the intervening act is to be attributed.'[94] FitzGibbon L.J. cited *Dixon v Bell*[95] as one of numerous cases which are authority for the proposition that leaving a dangerous chattel within the reach of others, without warning, creates a legal responsibility for the consequences of a negligent, reckless or even criminal act of a third person into whose hands the chattel has fallen.[96] His Lordship added, '[t]he anticipation of any misfortune which was not improbable as a consequence of his act was the defendant's duty, and every person who might not improbably be injured was within the scope of that duty.'[97]

Under German law, a critical factor in determining intervening causation issues is how the third-party intervention relates to the risk created by the defendant's negligence. If the intervention is no more than a realisation of such risk, then it can be imputed to be defendant. On the other hand, if the intervention is only coincidentally or randomly connected to the defendant's negligence, then the defendant cannot be made liable for the damage caused by the third party.[98] In one German case[99] the plaintiff's armoured vehicle was involved in a collision with another vehicle caused by the negligent driving of its operator. As a result of the accident, the armoured vehicle was overturned in a ditch alongside the road. The two occupants of the armoured vehicle escaped therefrom but were in shock. During a short period of time when the armoured vehicle was not under surveillance, two money containers

---

92 [1904] 2 IR 317 (CA).
93 Ibid., 349.
94 Ibid., 350.
95 (1816) 5 M & S 198.
96 [1904] 2 IR 317, 341.
97 Ibid.
98 Van Gerven, Lever and Larouche *Cases, Materials and Texts on National, Supranational and International Tort Law*, 429/30.
99 BGH, 10 December 1996, NJW 1997, 865.

were stolen from the vehicle and the plaintiff sought to recover the amount stolen from the civil liability insurer of the person who was responsible for the accident. The German court held that as the traffic accident had created a risk of theft which materialised through the action of a third party, the defendant insurer could be held liable for the loss of the money. The court reasoned as follows:

> The armoured vehicle was specifically designed to provide protection for the two money containers; that protection was lost when the vehicle was damaged as a consequence of the illegal overtaking maneuver [of the wrongdoer]...The theft of the two money containers from the scene of the accident became possible only when both means of safeguarding the contents of the armoured vehicle [armour and guards] were set aside. This means that...the damage arising from the subsequent intervention constituted the realization of a risk created by the wrongful conduct of the [person responsible for the accident]...[100]

Conclusion

The duty-based 'scope of the risk' approach to resolving intervening causation issues is one that appears to be increasingly preferred, particularly in the context of intervening criminal and deliberately inflicted harm by third persons. Indeed it may have a more natural fit in this realm but, despite the claimed benefits of this approach outlined at the beginning of this chapter, it may be a source of disquiet for those purists who maintain a strict separation or division of functions between the various elements of a negligence action, including duty of care and causation. By deferring to or substituting an assessment of the precise content and scope of the duty of care to resolve the intervening causation issues, attention is diverted from the calibration of intervening risks as 'foreseeable' or 'probable' which is arguably better adapted to evaluate the causal potency or impact of the defendant's breach of duty or lack thereof on the triggering or involvement of the intervening event. This could lead, and indeed has led, to conflicting decisions on the same facts[101] and an arbitrary inclusion or exclusion of intervening risks from the ambit of the defendant's duty of care on the basis of judicial policy preferences (or perhaps unreasoned assertion). However, the law has never pretentiously claimed to be a precise science and the application of the 'scope of the risk' approach without further refinement or development will continue to be somewhat of a forensic lottery.

---

100 Van Gerven, Lever and Larouche *Cases, Materials and Texts on National, Supranational and International Tort Law*, 429/30.

101 Compare, for example, the Canadian decisions *Duce* v *Rourke* (1951) 1 WWR (NS) 305 and *Patten* v *Silberschein* [1936] 3 WWR 169.

PART III
Operative Contexts

Chapter 8

Intervening Negligent Acts and Omissions

Introduction

As we have seen in Chapter 5, the common law's 'last human wrongdoer' doctrine once created an immunity for negligent defendants when the immediate cause of the plaintiff's injury was the intervening culpable act of a third party. As the force of the doctrine waned, this immunity was gradually lost. Defendants became increasingly liable for the criminal and deliberate acts of third parties[1] as well as for the negligent intervening conduct of plaintiffs and third parties. Nevertheless there is no absolute rule nowadays that all negligent intervening forces will or will not sever the causal chain. Such determination will turn on the facts and circumstances of each case. As contributory negligence, contribution and indemnity statutes have empowered the courts to allocate losses between tortfeasors and between the tortfeasor and the plaintiff, the last human wrongdoer doctrine has been displaced, thereby permitting judges to achieve a more equitable apportionment of damages. In the realm of intervening negligence, defendants now carry much more legal responsibility for its effects. This chapter will briefly examine a representative sampling of intervening negligence cases, as well as consider the effect of gross negligence or recklessness and negligent intervening omissions on the outcome of *novus actus* pleas. The majority of cases will involve intervening causation issues which arise out of motor vehicle accidents.

Ordinary Intervening Negligent Acts

The preponderance of intervening negligence cases do not result in a severance of the causal chain. This was the case even early on following the demise of the last wrongdoer doctrine. So, in *Byrne* v *Wilson*[2] the defendant, an omnibus operator, was held liable for the drowning of one of his passengers after the omnibus was negligently precipitated into a lock of a canal, notwithstanding the alleged intervening negligent act of an independent third person – the lock-keeper – in subsequently letting water into the lock. *Burrell Township* v *Uncapher*,[3] an 1887 decision of the Supreme Court of Pennsylvania, was the first case in which that court specifically considered the legal effect of an independent intervening negligent act committed by a third person. In that case the defendant township had negligently allowed the highway to remain in a dangerous condition by failing to guard a precipitous drop at the

---

1 See Chapter 5.
2 (1862) 15 Ir CLR 332. This case is examined in more detail in Chapter 2.
3 (1887) 117 Pa 353.

roadside. A third person negligently left a steam roller at the roadside and a second intervening force intervened when a horse which was pulling the plaintiff's carriage took fright at the steam roller and ran over the bank. The Supreme Court held that the fact that an injury to a highway user was caused by the combined effect of the unsafe condition of the road and the negligence of a third person is not sufficient to relieve the defendant township of liability for having failed in its duty to maintain the highway in proper repair.[4] An Irish court has similarly held a defendant company liable for negligently failing to construct a walkway around one of its construction hoardings, thereby forcing a pedestrian onto the roadway where the latter was struck by a car negligently driven by a motorist.[5] In a series of cases decided by the Supreme Court of Pennsylvania, it has been held that the negligent operation of an automobile in which the plaintiff was a passenger did not relieve from liability a defendant who had negligently left an unlighted truck parked on the highway. In *Kline v Moyer*[6] the Supreme Court held that an intervening negligent act will not become a superseding cause unless the intervening actor, having actual knowledge of the potential danger, subsequently acts in a manner which is considered unreasonably dangerous.

The Canadian courts have also been reluctant to relieve the defendant from liability in cases of intervening negligent acts. In *Fujiwara v Osawa*[7] the Supreme Court of Canada held that if a motorist steps on the accelerator instead of the brake to avoid an emergency created by another person, the original negligent actor remains liable. Likewise, when employees of the defendant company negligently allowed a cow to escape onto a highway where it was hit by a negligent motorist, the company cannot escape liability.[8] And in *Menow v Honsberger and Jordan House Ltd*[9] the Supreme Court of Canada held that if an intoxicated person is ejected from a hotel pub onto a busy highway and is struck by a car driven by a negligent motorist, the defendant hotel must share the blame.

The English and Australian courts have also required motorists to foresee and guard against the negligence of other motorists and to share in the apportionment of blame. So in *Chapman v Hearse*[10] the High Court of Australia upheld an apportionment of one-quarter of the blame against the original negligent actor for the death of a physician who was struck and killed by a negligent motorist after the physician had gone to assist a man lying on the roadway who had shortly before caused a motor vehicle collision through negligent driving. In 1973 the English Court of Appeal was called on to decide a similar case. In *Rouse v Squires*[11] on a frosty winter night an articulated lorry skidded into a jack-knife position, obstructing the nearside and centre lanes of the three-lane carriageway of a busy motorway. A motor vehicle being driven in the centre lane collided with the lorry and stopped

---

4   Ibid., 363.
5   *McKenna v Stephens and Hall* [1923] 2 IR 112.
6   (1937) 325 Pa 357.
7   [1938] SCR 170.
8   *Martin v McNamara Construction Co. Ltd* [1955] OR 523 (Ont. CA).
9   [1974] SCR 239.
10 (1961) 106 CLR 112. This case is examined in more detail in Chapter 3.
11 [1973] 1 QB 889 (CA).

with its rear lights on. Another lorry driver who had been following parked in the nearside lane just short of the jack-knifed lorry with headlights on to illuminate it. Shortly thereafter, the defendant, driving a lorry in the same direction with dipped headlights, came within view of the accident scene, braked upon seeing the parked lorry and moved into the centre lane. Upon realising that the centre lane was blocked, the defendant braked harder and skidded and collided with the parked lorry which was pushed forward, thereby knocking down and killing one Rouse who had been assisting at the accident scene. The plaintiff, the deceased's widow and legal representative of his estate, brought an action for damages under fatal accidents legislation against the defendant, alleging the latter had caused her husband's death. The defendant took third party proceedings against the driver and owners of the jack-knifed lorry, alleging that the negligent driving of that lorry had caused the accident and claiming contribution. At first instance the trial judge held that the accident and death were wholly attributable to the defendant's negligence on the ground that the defendant had driven extremely negligently, that he was not keeping a proper lookout, his speed was excessive in the prevailing conditions and that the accident scene was sufficiently lit to warn incoming drivers. Cairns L.J. dealt with the intervening causation issue as follows:

> If a driver so negligently manages his vehicle as to cause it to obstruct the highway and constitute a danger to other road users, *but not those who deliberately or recklessly drive into the obstruction*, then the first driver's negligence may be held to have contributed to the causation of an accident of which the immediate cause was the negligent driving of the vehicle which because of the presence of the obstruction collides with it or with some other vehicle or some other person.[12]

Accordingly, Cairns L.J. held that the third party driver's negligence contributed to Rouse's death to the extent of 25 per cent. Buckley L.J. also held that while the immediate cause of the accident was the defendant's negligent driving, there had been no break in the chain of causation between the third party driver's negligence and the accident. His Lordship considered that road users must anticipate that not all highway users will be maintaining a proper lookout and 'that the circumstances were not such as to be reasonably likely to bring to the notice of other users of the highway the existence and the extent of the hazard...in sufficient time to avoid an accident.'[13] Thus *Chapman* v *Hearse* and *Rouse* v *Squires* cumulatively support the proposition that a defendant whose negligence causes a highway collision may become liable for additional damage due to another motorist subsequently negligently piling into the wreckage or persons at the accident scene.

What about intervening negligence on the part of the plaintiff? With the demise of the last human wrongdoer doctrine and the emergence of apportionment legislation, courts have considered that a fairer way to deal with the plaintiff's intervening negligence is to reduce the award of damages on account of contributory negligence

---

12   Ibid., 898 (emphasis supplied).
13   Ibid., 901–2.

rather than treat the plaintiff's conduct as the sole cause of his or her loss.[14] The leading Australian authority for this proposition is the decision of the High Court of Australia in *March v E. & M.H. Stramare Pty Ltd*.[15] There the defendant's employee had negligently parked a truck in a dangerous position in the middle of a busy roadway and the plaintiff ran into the truck with his vehicle and was injured. It was found that the plaintiff was intoxicated and had been driving at an excessive speed at the time of the accident. The High Court held that road users owe a duty of care to all other road users, including the inattentive and those whose driving ability is impaired by alcohol. The trial Judge's apportionment of liability was upheld on appeal with the plaintiff's contributory negligence being assessed at 70 per cent. The defendant's plea that the plaintiff's intoxicated driving at an excessive speed constituted a *novus actus interveniens* was thus rejected.

Intervening negligent acts outside the motor vehicle collision context also generally have been held not to break the chain of causation. So, for example, the Ontario Court of Appeal has held in *Fetherston v Neilson and King Edward Hotel*[16] that when a guest negligently knocked over a light pillar at a New Year's eve dance, the defendant hotel was held liable because such a fixture was unsuitable for a crowded dance floor and because it had permitted overcrowding. Likewise, the Nova Scotia Court of Appeal refused to uphold the defendant's *novus actus* plea in a case involving intervening negligence. In *Smith v Inglis*[17] the plaintiff received a severe electric shock from a refrigerator manufactured by the defendant. The delivery man had negligently cut off the ground prong from the plug and the refrigerator components were improperly positioned so as to cause a short-circuit. The removal of the ground prong did not sever the causal chain as such prongs are commonly removed and, although this creates a risk by nullifying a safety device, the defendant should have foreseen that this might happen. Thus the manufacturer was not relieved of liability for having negligently manufactured the refrigerator.[18] Although the subsequent negligent interference with a safety device was the immediate cause of the plaintiff's shock, it merely activated a potential danger which already existed. The United States Sixth Circuit Court of Appeals has held that if a retailer and wholesaler were negligent in selling pork infected with trichinella, their negligence was the legally proximate cause of injuries sustained by the plaintiff who ate the pork, even though the negligence of a third person in not thoroughly cooking the meat may have contributed thereto.[19] And the English Court of Appeal has similarly refused to relieve the defendant of liability where the intervening negligence has activated rather than failed to eliminate a risk created by the defendant's negligence. In *Philco Radio and Television Corporation Ltd v J. Spurling Ltd*[20] the defendant carriers had negligently

---

14   *Jacques v Matthews* [1961] SASR 205; *Charlton v Public Trustee for the Northern Territory* (1967) 11 FLR 42.

15   (1991) 171 CLR 506. This case is examined in more detail in Chapter 7.

16   [1944] OR 470 reversed in part [1944] OR 621 (CA).

17   (1978) 83 DLR (3d) 215.

18   The Nova Scotia Court of Appeal was also of the view that the delivery man would be jointly liable for having removed the ground prong had he been sued.

19   *Troietto v G.H. Hammond Co.* (1940) 110 F 2d 135.

20   [1949] 2 All ER 882 (CA).

and mistakenly delivered a package containing highly inflammable celluloid film scrap to the plaintiff's premises. An employee of the plaintiff had approached the package with a lighted cigarette and caused a fire which caused extensive damage to the plaintiff's premises. The Court of Appeal held the defendants liable on the basis that the employee's conduct was negligent rather than deliberate.

There are, of course, cases in which the intervening negligence has been held sufficient to amount to *novus actus interveniens*. In *Doughty* v *Township of Dungannon*[21] the plaintiff's action against the defendant municipality was based on a claim for damages in negligence for damage to his truck when he attempted to cross a culvert on a slightly used and unimproved road. The day before the accident a driver, whose truck had become mired in mud near this bridge, had taken certain poles from the culvert to assist him in extricating his truck and failed to replace them in the culvert. On the assumption the defendant had been negligent, the Ontario court held that the conduct of the truck driver on the previous day broke the chain of causation in any event. The Supreme Court of Canada has similarly held, albeit by a 3:2 majority, in *Bradford* v *Kanellos*[22] that the intervening negligence of a restaurant patron in exclaiming that an explosion was about to occur (which, in fact, was not accurate) severed the causal link between the plaintiff's physical injuries and the defendant's negligence in permitting an excessive quantity of grease to accumulate on a cooking grill. The House of Lords has somewhat controversially held that the unreasonable act of the plaintiff in descending a steep staircase without assistance severed the chain of causation between his broken ankle and the defendant's employer's negligence which had caused an earlier injury and vulnerability to further damage.[23] And the English Court of Appeal has held in *Knightley* v *Johns*[24] that a police inspector's negligence in ordering the plaintiff to carry out the dangerous manoeuvre of riding through a tunnel against the traffic flow contrary to police standing orders for road accidents in tunnels amounted to a *novus actus interveniens*.

Intervening Gross Negligence/Recklessness

Courts are more inclined to uphold a *novus actus* plea where the intervening act was not merely negligent but reckless in quality. As Lord Hobhouse has observed in *Reeves* v *Commissioner of Police of the Metropolis*,[25] '[c]areless conduct may ordinarily be regarded as being within the range of normal human conduct when reckless conduct ordinarily would not.'[26] Section 447 (c) of the American Law

---

21 [1938] OR 684.
22 (1973) 40 DLR (3d) 578 (SCC). This case is examined in more detail in Chapter 7.
23 *McKew* v *Holland & Hannen & Cubitts (Scotland) Ltd* [1970] SC 20 (HL). The decision is controversial in the sense that it might have been fairer in the circumstances to apportion liability between the plaintiff and the defendant employer for the plaintiff's later injury in view of the statutory abolition of the complete common law defence of contributory negligence.
24 [1982] 1 All ER 851 (CA). This case is examined in more detail in Chapter 3.
25 [2000] 1 AC 360 (HL).
26 Ibid., 392.

Institute's *Restatement of the Law of Torts, Second*[27] provides in part that '[t]he fact that an intervening act of a third person...is done in a negligent manner does not make it a superseding cause of harm...if...the intervening act is a normal consequence of a situation created by the [defendant's] conduct and the manner in which it is done is not extraordinarily negligent.' Thus by implication the negligent quality of the intervening act may be so serious or the third person's conduct so reckless as to make it appear an extraordinary response to the situation created by the defendant and therefore a superseding cause or *novus actus interveniens*.[28] In the context of negligence law, as opposed to the criminal law, the concepts of recklessness and gross negligence are largely synonymous.[29] A person may be reckless if he or she commits an act involving an unjustifiable risk of injury to others, whether or not such risk is appreciated.[30] US courts have held that continued negligent action in the face of a known danger can amount to an extraordinarily negligent intervening and superseding cause, thereby relieving the defendant of liability.[31]

The English Court of Appeal has considered the effect of intervening recklessness in two relatively recent decisions. It will be recalled from earlier in this chapter that in *Rouse* v *Squires*[32] Cairns L.J. regarded 'those who deliberately or recklessly drive into the obstruction'[33] as tantamount to a *novus actus interveniens*. Buckley L.J. was similarly of the view that,

> ...when there is ample visibility and ample opportunity for the driver of an oncoming vehicle to see and appreciate the nature and extent of an obstruction and to take evasive action, then the obstruction does not constitute a danger, and in such a case there is a break in the chain of causation between the prior negligent act which caused the obstruction and the immediate consequences of the latter negligent act of a driver on the highway who causes an accident.[34]

These *obiter dicta* were considered by the Court of Appeal in its 1992 decision in *Wright* v *Lodge*.[35] There the respondent's car broke down on the eastbound carriageway of an unlit dual carriageway at night when visibility was very poor due to fog. The car came to a stop in the nearside lane of the carriageway and while the respondent was attempting to start it, an articulated container lorry driven by the appellant crashed into the back of it, causing a passenger in the rear seat of the car to be seriously injured. The lorry then veered out of control across the central reservation and came to rest on its side in the opposite westbound carriageway, where it was struck by three cars and a lorry. The driver of one of the cars was killed and

---

27 (1965–79).
28 Ibid., 480.
29 In *Shawinigan* v *Vokins* [1961] 1 WLR 1206, at 1214 Megaw J. defined 'recklessness' as 'gross negligence'.
30 B. McMahon and W. Binchy *Irish Law of Torts* (Butterworths, 2nd edn, 1990) 48.
31 L.H. Eldredge *Modern Tort Problems* (George T. Bisel, 1941) 221–2.
32 [1973] 1QB 889 (CA).
33 Ibid., 898. This comment was an *obiter dictum* since the Court of Appeal did not find recklessness or gross negligence on the facts.
34 Ibid., 901.
35 [1993] 4 All ER 299 (CA).

another driver was injured. At the time of the collision with the respondent's car, the appellant's lorry was found to have been travelling at an excessive speed. The injured driver and the personal representatives of the deceased driver sued the appellant and the respondent. The Court of Appeal upheld the finding of the court of first instance that the appellant had been driving recklessly in the prevailing circumstances and that such driving was the sole operative legal cause of the death and injuries. The contribution claims against the respondent were therefore dismissed. If the driver of a motor vehicle is involved in a collision with another vehicle partly as a result of his own negligence, he or she is not necessarily responsible for subsequent events which occur as the result of another driver's reckless driving which caused damage which would not have occurred if that driver had merely been driving negligently, since reckless driving stands in a different category from negligent driving. As Woolf L.J. observed, 'deliberate or reckless conduct is so obviously more blameworthy than [mere] carelessness.'[36] After having cited with approval the *obiter* remarks of Cairns L.J. in *Rouse* v *Squires*, Parker L.J. concluded that intervening recklessness may break the causal chain[37] and this was the case here on the facts. The appellant's act in driving at 60 miles per hour on a busy motorway in conditions of poor visibility was so reckless as to operate as a *novus actus interveniens*.

The Supreme Court of Canada has relieved defendants of liability where the plaintiff's own reckless conduct was held to be a *novus actus interveniens*. *Dallaire* v *Paul-Emile Martel Inc.*[38] concerned a civil liability action brought under Quebec law by the plaintiff to obtain damages for injuries he sustained when his foot got caught in a worm screw located in a conveyer used to remove manure from a poultry house. The plaintiff was 11 years old at the time of the accident and his leg injuries were so severe that his right leg had to be amputated. One of the defendants in the action was the equipment manufacturer. The sloping portion of the conveyer located outside the poultry house was covered by removable metal covers which were sometimes dislodged by strong winds. For three months prior to the accident the plaintiff's father failed to replace the metal covers which were lying on the ground beside the conveyer at the time of the accident. On the fateful day in question, the appellant was working outside the poultry house and had no work to do on the conveyer itself. His duties were to collect the manure and spread it on the fields. Despite this, the appellant straddled the conveyer trough when his right foot slipped and was caught by the worm screw. The Supreme Court held that the chain of causation had been broken by the plaintiff's own reckless conduct as well as by his father's failure to replace the metal covers. In delivering the judgment of the Court, Gonthier J. stated:

> The appellant was not unaware that the worm screw was dangerous when he straddled the trough. The trial judge noted in his reasons that the appellant is an intelligent person, that he could perceive the danger and had been warned of it by his father. I see no reason to

---

36 Ibid., 308–9.
37 Ibid., 305. See also the judgment of Evans-Lombe J. in *Barings plc (in liquidation)* v *Coopers & Lybrand (a firm)* [2003] EWHC 1319 (Ch); [2003] PNLR 639 for a discussion on the effect of reckless conduct on the causal chain.
38 [1989] 2 SCR 419.

disagree with the trial judge's opinion on this point: the appellant committed this rash act despite his father's warning. Failure to warn the appellant of the dangers involved in using the conveyer was therefore not the cause of the accident.[39]

Later in his judgment his Honour added:

> The appellant's accident did not occur because the conveyer was dangerous but rather because it was carelessly used. The users of equipment entailing dangers of which they are or should be aware have an obligation to use it carefully, in particular by using safety devices provided by the manufacturer. The conveyer was not dangerous when the metal covers were in place. The appellant and his father…caused the appellant's accident. The fact that the worm screw may have been dangerous was therefore not the cause of the appellant's accident, but merely occasioned it: the accident was rather due to the way in which the appellant and his father used the conveyer.[40]

Intervening recklessness has also been held to break the chain of causation in United States maritime law. In *Exxon v Sofec Inc.*[41] the owner of the oil tanker *Houston* that ran aground on a charted reef several hours after breaking away from a single point mooring (SPM) system sued the SPM's manufacturer seeking damages for loss of the tanker, cargo and oil spill cleanup. As a result of a severe storm, a chain linking the vessel to the SPM was severed. After conducting a bench trial in admiralty, the District Court at first instance found that the *Houston*'s captain's extraordinary negligence was the sole proximate and superseding cause of the tanker's grounding and this determination was affirmed on appeal to the United States Court of Appeals, Ninth Circuit. The District Court found that Captain Coyne acted unreasonably and in violation of maritime industry standards in a number of instances, including a failure to anchor properly, failure to request or accept assistance from the Coast Guard or other available ships, and his decision to linger unnecessarily in the vicinity of the shore. Although the breaking of the mooring chain imperilled the tanker ship, Captain Coyne had navigated it to a position of relative safety before these acts and omissions ultimately led to its stranding. The appellate court agreed with the District Court's finding that 'Captain Coyne had ample time, as well as opportunity and available manpower, to take precautions which would have eliminated the risk of grounding, and that his failure to do so amounted to extraordinary negligence, superseding any negligence of the defendants with regard to the breakout…'[42] And, in the medical negligence context, the High Court of Australia has held that only 'grossly negligent' medical treatment will sever the causal chain.[43]

---

39   Ibid., 426.
40   Ibid., 426–7.
41   (1995) 54 F 3d 570.
42   Ibid., 579.
43   *Mahony v J. Kruschich (Demolitions) Pty Ltd* (1985) 156 CLR 522, 530.

Intervening Negligent Omissions

What is the legal position in a situation where, after the defendant has been negligent and created a foreseeable and unreasonable risk of harm to another, a third person has the opportunity to avert the threatened harm by taking positive action? If such action were taken, it would prevent the defendant's negligence from causing the harm which has in fact occurred. In *Knightley* v *Johns*[44] Stephenson L.J. ventured the view that '[n]egligent conduct is more likely to break the chain of causation than conduct which is not; positive acts will more easily constitute new causes than inaction.'[45] A dictum of Goff L.J. in *Muirhead* v *Industrial Tank Specialities Ltd*[46] also suggests that where the intervening conduct consists of a negligent failure to prevent damage caused by the defendant's negligence, it may not constitute a *novus actus interveniens*.[47] This may be due to the fact, recently acknowledged by the Judicial Committee of the Privy Council,[48] that liability for omissions is less extensive than for positive negligent acts.

Section 452. (1) of the American Law Institute's *Restatement of the Law of Torts, Second*[49] essentially prescribes a rebuttable presumption against the judicial recognition of a *novus actus interveniens* in these circumstances in laying down the general rule that the failure of a third person to act to prevent harm is not a superseding cause of the harm, and so does not relieve the defendant of liability. Section 452. states:

1. Except as stated in Subsection (2), the failure of a third person to act to prevent harm to another threatened by the [defendant's] negligent conduct is not a superseding cause of such harm.
2. Where, because of lapse of time or otherwise, the duty to prevent harm to another threatened by the [defendant's] negligent conduct is found to have shifted from the [defendant] to a third person, the failure of the third person to prevent such harm is a superseding cause.

Subsection (2) of Section 452. acknowledges that in an exceptional case a negligent omission by a third person to prevent harm can amount to a *novus actus interveniens*. This can only occur where the entire responsibility for the situation has shifted to the third person whereby the defendant is relieved of liability. Shifted responsibility

---

44 [1982] 1 All ER 851 (CA).

45 Ibid., 865. See also F. Trindade and P. Cane *The Law of Torts in Australia* (Oxford University Press, 3rd edn, 1999) 495, citing *Australian Shipbuilding Industries (WA) Pty Ltd* v *Packer* (1993) 9 WAR 375; *O'Brien* v *Thorpe* (1987) Australian Torts Reports 69, 102 at 69, 112 *per* Derrington J.

46 [1986] QB 507, 533 (CA).

47 His Lordship did qualify this, however, by adding that a negligent omission has no causative effect unless it is 'a wholly independent cause of the damage, i.e. a *novus actus interveniens*'.

48 *Attorney General* v *Hartwell* (British Virgin Islands) [2004] UKPC 12, para. 25 (23 February 2004).

49 (1965–79).

may take the form of an express agreement between the defendant and the third person, by gratuitous promise or by fair implication from what was agreed upon.[50] Upon a clear understanding that the responsibility has been so shifted, the failure of the third person to act to prevent the threatened harm becomes a superseding cause or *novus actus*.

We shall deal first with those cases in which the courts have adhered to the general rule or rebuttable presumption against recognising *novus actus* in intervening negligent omission situations. Australian courts have fairly consistently refused to sustain *novus actus* pleas in these situations. In *Mount Isa Mines Ltd* v *Bates*[51] the court held that a foreseeable omission by the plaintiff to wear safety glasses made it negligent for the defendant employer to fail to adopt a simple, inexpensive modification of machinery that would have avoided the risk of flying metal particles. In such circumstances, the court held that the plaintiff's omission did not amount to a *novus actus*.[52] And in *Bennett* v *Minister of Community Welfare*[53] the High Court of Australia rejected the defendant's submission that the barrister's subsequent failure to provide the plaintiff with correct legal advice constituted a *novus actus interveniens* on the ground that such an intervening possibility was in these circumstances the very risk against which the Director of Community Welfare had a legal duty to protect the plaintiff.

The Canadian and English judicial approaches to resolving intervening causation issues in the context of negligent omissions have been more mixed. In the Canadian case of *Thompson* v *Toorenburgh*[54] the view was expressed that the failure to provide adequate medical treatment which would have saved an accident victim's life was not the same as committing an intervening act which caused her death. The British Columbia Court of Appeal held the defendant who caused the accident liable for the death, despite the inadequacy of the medical treatment provided by the hospital. As Robertson J.A. stated:

> Mrs Thompson would almost certainly have recovered if proper treatment had been applied speedily; the doctors failed to apply the treatment and so failed to save her life, but they did not cause her death. They failed to provide an *actus interveniens* that would have saved her life, but that is not the same as committing an *actus interveniens* that caused her death.[55]

On the other hand, another Canadian court in *Lamberty* v *Saskatchewan Power Corporation*[56] regarded the negligent failure of the defendant gas company to carry

---

50 *Restatement of the Law of Torts, Second* (ALI, 1965–79) 488.
51 [1972–73] ALR 635.
52 See also *Gardiner* v *Henderson & Lahey* [1988] 1 Qd R 125 (defendant does not cease to be liable for the immediate consequences of his or her actions if a third party has failed, negligently or otherwise, to take steps to avert loss or damage flowing from the defendant's negligence).
53 (1992) 176 CLR 408. This case is examined in more detail in Chapter 7.
54 (1975) 50 DLR (3d) 717 (BCCA).
55 Ibid., 721.
56 (1966) 59 DLR (2d) 246.

out any effective action to repair or isolate a gasline leak as so serious as to amount to a *novus actus interveniens*, thereby relieving the original defendants of liability for having interfered with the gasline.

English courts have considered the question whether a failure by a consumer to inspect a product or job for defects relieves a negligent manufacturer or contractor of liability. This issue was raised in *Herschtal* v *Stewart & Ardern Ltd*[57] where the plaintiff suffered injury caused by a defect in a car. The defendant motor engineers had reconditioned a car and supplied it to the plaintiff. The day after delivery a wheel came off as a result of the wheel nuts being improperly fastened. In determining when the possibility of an intermediate examination would have absolved the defendant from liability, Tucker J. held that a mere possibility of examination would not suffice; there must be a reasonable anticipation on the defendant's part that the plaintiff would examine the car such as would reveal the defect prior to its use.[58] The defendant motor engineers were held liable as it was held that they had no reasonable grounds for anticipating such an examination in the particular circumstances of the case. By contrast, an English court has held that a plaintiff's voluntary and unreasonable failure or omission to discharge a duty to mitigate his or her losses can give rise to a successful *novus actus* plea. In *McAuley* v *London Transport Executive*[59] the plaintiff sustained a cut left wrist in a workplace accident caused by the defendant employer's negligence. The plaintiff was taken to hospital but he unreasonably refused to have an operation on his wrist which would have assisted in restoring the plaintiff's left hand and wrist to full capacity. Without the operation, the condition of the plaintiff's left wrist deteriorated and he lost the use of his left hand. The court held that the plaintiff could not recover damages in relation to the loss of use of his left hand on the ground that this would not have occurred if he had not voluntarily and unreasonably refused to allow the doctors to operate on his left wrist.

The Irish courts have also considered the issue of when a negligent intervening omission should be considered to have severed the chain of causation. In *Crowley* v *A.I.B. and O'Flynn, Green, Buchan and Partners*[60] the plaintiff was seriously injured when he fell from the flat roof of premises owned by the A.I.B. The second-named defendants were the architects who had designed the roof without specifying the need for a railing around the roof. The High Court ordered the architects to pay 30 per cent of the damages for the roof's faulty design but this was reversed by the Supreme Court which held that the link between the architect's negligence and the plaintiff's injury had been broken by the fact that the defendant bank knew that boys regularly played on the unguarded roof but did not attempt to prohibit such conduct. The defendant bank's omission in this regard was held to constitute a *novus actus interveniens* which relieved the defendant architects of liability.

---

57   [1940] 1 KB 155.
58   Ibid., 170–71.
59   [1958] 2 Lloyds Rep 500.
60   [1988] I.L.R.M. 225.

Chapter 9

Extraordinary Natural Phenomena, Coincidences and Animals

Extraordinary Natural Phenomena

According to Holdsworth, it was settled in the reign of Edward III that if damage were caused to a barn by a sudden tempest, no writ of waste would lie against the tenant, even though the tenant had covenanted to restore the barn in good condition. A so-called 'act of God' provided a good defence to an action because the act causing the damage was not the act of the defendant.[1] Lord Westbury has defined an act of God as an event caused by the forces of nature 'which no human foresight can provide against, and of which human prudence is not bound to recognise the possibility.'[2] The concept of an act of God is largely synonymous with that of *novus actus interveniens*[3] and the phrase 'act of God' is still used by judges in today's legal vernacular.[4] An early text writer in the law of torts stated in 1903 that 'the defendant can never be liable when anything out of the natural and usual course of events unexpectedly arises and operates in such a way as to make the defendant's negligence, otherwise harmless, productive of injury.'[5] Acts of God include such natural phenomena as earthquakes, cyclones, lightning, tidal waves and landslides. At common law it has been held that extraordinary acts of nature will sever the causal chain provided they are overwhelming, unpredictable and in no manner linked to the defendant's negligence.[6] An intervening natural event will be treated as a cause of the plaintiff's loss where its occurrence was so unlikely in the circumstance that it must be considered a mere coincidence. By implication, the ordinary, as opposed to the extraordinary, operation of natural forces including weather conditions will not sever the causal chain since this must be anticipated and guarded against by the defendant. Legal responsibility is extinguished upon the occurrence of an event outside the range of ordinary experience, as human beings are only required to guard

---

1   W. Holdsworth *A History of English Law* Volume 3 (Methuen & Co. Ltd, 5th edn, 1942) 380.
2   *Tennent* v *Earl of Glasgow* (1864) 2 M (HL) 22, 26.
3   A.M. Dugdale and M.A. Jones (eds) *Clerk & Lindsell on Torts* (Sweet & Maxwell, 19th edn, 2006) [102], para. 2–80.
4   See the judgment of Lord Hoffman in *Environment Agency* v *Empress Car Co. (Abertillery) Ltd* [1999] 2 AC 22, 35 (His Lordship equated an 'act of God' with 'some extraordinary natural event').
5   M.M. Bigelow *The Law of Torts* (Cambridge University Press, 2nd edn, 1903) 376 (citing as an example a whirlwind arising on a quiet day which spreads a small fire).
6   J. Murphy *Street on Torts* (LexisNexis, 11th edn, 2003) 295.

against normal natural phenomena, not against unusual or extraordinary ones.[7] This distinction between the ordinary and the extraordinary has been recently affirmed by Lord Hoffman in *Environment Agency* v *Empress Car Co. (Abertillery) Ltd*.[8] French case-law has developed a similar principle whereby a defendant may be relieved of liability if the intervening event is external and constitutes *force majeure* in the sense that it is unforeseeable and unavoidable.[9] In common law jurisdictions a distinction is often drawn between intervening causes that are a reaction to the initial cause (by the plaintiff or third party) and intervening causes that are independent but operate in and on the situation created by the initial cause. The former type of intervening cause is usually a human action while the latter type tends to be some natural event.[10]

The operation of an intervening natural force will not absolve a defendant from liability if it can be considered a not abnormal incident of the risk created by him or her in the sense of being within 'the ordinary course of things'.[11] Thus loss caused by ice[12] can be attributed to the defendant who fails to take reasonable precautions to avoid its effect. However, a defendant is not held responsible for unprecedented frosts which cause water mains to burst despite the undertaking of reasonable and ordinary precautions. So, in *Blyth* v *The Birmingham Waterworks*[13] the defendant was not held liable for the flooding of the plaintiff's house allegedly due to the interference with the defendant's water pipes by '[o]ne of the severest frosts on record'.[14] The case turned on whether the defendant had been negligent. After formulating his classic definition of negligence, Alderson B. concluded:

> A reasonable man would act with reference to the average circumstances of the temperature in ordinary years. The defendants had provided against such frosts as experience would have led men, acting prudently, to provide against; and they are not guilty of negligence, because their precautions proved insufficient against the effects of the extreme severity of the frost of 1855…Such a state of circumstances constitutes a contingency against which no reasonable man can provide. The result was an accident, for which the defendants cannot be held liable.[15]

The tenor of the judgments in the case was such that even if the defendant had been guilty of negligence in some minor respects, the exceptional frost would still have been sufficient to sever the causal chain.

---

7   J. Fleming *The Law of Torts* (The Law Book Company Ltd, 9th edn, 1998) 249.

8   [1999] 2 AC 22, 35. Rule 442. (b) of the American Law Institute's *Restatement of the Law of Torts, Second* (1965–79) provides for the 'extraordinary-normal' distinction.

9   W. van Gerven, J. Lever and J. Larouche *Cases, Materials and Texts on National, Supranational and International Tort Law* (Hart Publishing, 2000) 464.

10 F. Trindade and P. Cane *The Law of Torts in Australia* (Oxford University Press, 3rd edn, 1999) 493.

11 J. Fleming, *The Law of Torts* (The Law Book Company Ltd, 9th edn, 1998) 247.

12 *Abbott* v *Kasza* [1975] 3 WWR 163; *Manchester Corporation* v *Markland* [1936] AC 360 (HL).

13 (1856) 11 Ex 781.

14 Ibid., 782.

15 Ibid., 784–5. See also *Sharp* v *Powell* (1872) LR 7 CP 253 (plaintiff's horse slipping on ice caused by extreme weather conditions considered too remote).

The extraordinary-ordinary or normal-abnormal distinction has also been applied by a US court to determine whether a sea squall amounted to a *novus actus interveniens*. In *Jacobson v Suderman and Young Inc. ('The Mariner')*[16] the Fifth Circuit Court of Appeals rejected the defendant's *novus actus* plea that a northerly sea squall severed the causal link between the defendant tug's negligent navigation and the plaintiff's loss. The Court considered that such a squall was not an extraordinary event in the particular locality at that time of year and the risk of such occurring ought to have been reasonably anticipated. According to Walker, Circuit Judge, who delivered the opinion of the Court, '[i]n the ordinary course of nature, such a squall or norther being likely to occur while the towage was in progress, the happening of such an ordinary operation of a force of nature...cannot be regarded as an independent cause.'[17] Thus a person is attributed with knowledge of the usual effect of ordinary natural conditions or forces upon his or her negligent conduct. The United States Supreme Court has likewise held that wind does not ordinarily amount to a *novus actus interveniens*. In *Louisiana Mutual Insurance Company v Tweed*[18] the Court rejected the plaintiff's submission that the accidental circumstance that the wind was blowing in a direction to favour the progress of the fire towards the plaintiff's warehouse constituted a new intervening cause so as to fasten the defendant with liability under an insurance contract. According to Miller J. who delivered the opinion of the Court:

> That may have been the usual course of the breeze in that neighborhood. Its force may have been trifling. Its influence in producing the fire in the [plaintiff's] warehouse was too slight to be substituted for the explosion as the cause of the fire.[19]

Having concluded that the true cause of the fire which burned down the plaintiff's warehouse was an explosion (liability for which the insurer was exempted under the terms of the contract of insurance), the defendant insurer was held not liable to make good such loss.

Lightning has been cited by text writers[20] and judges as another example of an act of God which can sever the causal connection. In *Environment Agency v Empress Car Co. (Abertillery) Ltd*[21] Lord Hoffman referred to a hypothetical example of a factory owner carelessly leaving a drum containing highly inflammable vapour in a place where it could be accidentally ignited. His Lordship expressed the *obiter* view that if the drum were struck by lightning, the owner's negligence could not be considered to be the legal cause of the explosion but only the provision of an occasion or situation upon which the coincidental extraordinary natural event could

---

16 (1927) 17 F (2d) 253.
17 Ibid., 254.
18 (1869) 7 Wall 44 (USSC).
19 Ibid., 52.
20 J. Murphy, *Street on Torts*, 294 (example cited of a child negligently injured while participating in a sports activity being struck by lightning while being wheeled across the playground to the waiting ambulance).
21 [1999] 2 AC 22 (HL).

operate.[22] There is no automatic rule, however, that lightning will always constitute a *novus actus interveniens*. In *Johnson v Kosmos Portland Cement Co.*[23] an oil barge belonging to the defendant company was tied to a dock while undergoing repairs when it was struck by lightning during a storm. An explosion occurred, killing all on board. The personal representatives of the deceased workers sued for damages under Kentucky fatal accidents legislation, alleging that the explosion was caused by the defendant's negligence in failing to provide the deceased workers with a safe working environment by not properly cleaning out the barge's hold so as to prevent the accumulation of gases. The Sixth Circuit Court of Appeals reversed the decision of the court of first instance that the lightning bolt which caused the explosion amounted to a *novus actus*. The majority of the Court of Appeals held that while the lightning strike was disconnected from the defendant's omission in the sense of not being dependent upon it or a force being put in motion by it, it was not 'self-operating' since the explosion would not have occurred had there been no accumulation of gases.[24] Simons, Circuit Judge, in delivering the majority judgment, said:

> Lightning is, at least at the time and place here involved, no extraordinary manifestation of natural force. Lightning strikes, and injury results. This is within our ordinary experience and observation. We take many precautions to avoid its injurious effect, insure and are insured against it.[25]

The defendant company was thus held liable for the deaths of the workers on the barge.

The issue whether heavy rainfall and flooding amount to a *novus actus interveniens* has been extensively litigated. In *Nichols v Marsland*[26] extraordinary rainfall, unprecedented in that area, which caused ornamental lakes to burst their embankments and flood adjoining land was held to be an act of God. Nevertheless, there are situations where the defendant has been held liable for failing to foresee and adequately guard against storm and flood damage.[27] In *Harrison v The Great Northern Railway Company*[28] Pollock C.B. did not consider an unusual rainfall to amount to a *novus actus interveniens*:

> [T]here was nothing in the weather of so extraordinary a character that the defendants were not bound to anticipate it. The storm, though unusual and extraordinary in a sense, yet as happening once in a year or few years was not unusual.[29]

---

22   Ibid., 30–31.
23   (1933) 64 F (2d) 193.
24   Ibid., 195.
25   Ibid., 196. Moorman, Circuit Judge, dissented on the ground that a lightning strike was unforeseeable in the circumstances and that it constituted a new outside intervening force which caused the explosion of inactive and dormant gas (at 197).
26   (1876) 2 Ex D 1.
27   *Re Armstrong and State Rivers and Water Supply Commission* [1952] VLR 187; *C.P.R. v Calgary* [1971] WWR 241 (Alta).
28   (1864) 3 H. & C 231; 159 ER 518.
29   Ibid., 238; 521.

The High Court of Australia has also considered the issue of when an excessive downpour of rain will amount to a *novus actus*. In *The Commissioner of Railways (Western Australia)* v *Stewart*[30] the defendant had constructed a railway embankment across a depression through which there ran streams carrying off surface water from a catchment on the higher side of the railway line. A heavy downpour of rain blocked culverts designed to carry off excess water and water subsequently banked back on to a private property, causing damage. The culverts originally provided were insufficient to carry off an exceptional fall of water. Although the fall in question was greater than had ever previously been experienced, it was found on the facts to be not so great that no reasonably prudent engineer would provide against it. Accordingly, the High Court of Australia held that the downpour did not amount to an act of God and the defendant was held liable for the negligent construction of the railway embankment. The intervention of the heavy rain was not considered of sufficient magnitude and intensity to break the causal chain.

In the context of whether natural phenomena sever the causal chain, the House of Lords has applied the distinction between normal and extraordinary events. In *Alphacell Ltd* v *Woodward*[31] the defendant company operated a paper manufacturing plant which involved maintaining tanks of polluted liquid near a river such that pollution would occur if they overflowed. There were pumps which were designed to draw off the liquid and prevent the tanks from overflowing. In late autumn, however, the pumps became choked with small pieces of vegetation and ceased to function, thereby causing an overflow. The House of Lords held that the pollution was caused by what the defendant failed to do. Although the pollution would not have occurred but for a natural event (the vegetation entering the pumps), that was not extraordinary. As Lord Pearson observed:

> There was not even any unusual weather or freak of nature. Autumn is the season of the year in which dead leaves, ferns, pieces of bracken and pieces of bramble may be expected to fall into water and sink below the surface and, if there is a pump, to be sucked up by it.[32]

Lord Salmon expressed the view that the holding would have been different if there had been an 'act of God' in the form of some extraordinary natural event.

The United States Supreme Court has considered the 'act of God' doctrine in the context of a common carrier's potential liability for damage to goods as a result of floods and storms. In *Memphis and Charleston Railroad Company* v *Reeves*[33] tobacco was transported pursuant to a contract through several railroad companies, including the defendant. While the defendant railroad company was engaged in transporting the tobacco, water flooded the track and entered a carriage, thereby damaging the tobacco. The evidence established 'one of the most sudden, violent and extraordinary floods ever known in that part of the country'.[34] The Supreme Court held that a

---

30 (1936) 56 CLR 520.
31 [1972] AC 824.
32 Ibid., 845.
33 (1870) 10 Wall 176 (USSC).
34 Ibid., 190.

common carrier assumes all risks except those caused by the public enemy or by an act of God (such as loss caused by extraordinary floods and storms). Provided the damage was immediately or proximately caused by an act of God, the defendant carrier will be relieved of liability unless the plaintiff proves that the defendant was negligent in not providing for the safety of the goods.[35] The Supreme Court further held that a carrier is also not liable for a loss attributable to an act of God where the carrier had contracted to carry the goods earlier than it did and, if it had done so, the goods would have escaped damage, on the ground that such a contractual non-compliance would have merely constituted a remote cause of such damage.[36]

Heavy weather at sea has also been held by the House of Lords to constitute a *novus actus interveniens*. In *Carslogie Steamship Co. Ltd* v *Royal Norwegian Government*[37] the motor vessel *Heimgar*, while lying at anchorage, was involved in a collision with the steamship *Carslogie*. It was conceded that the *Carslogie* was solely to blame for the accident. Owing to war restrictions, permanent repairs could not be carried out in the United Kingdom. After temporary repairs had been effected at Port Glasgow, the *Heimgar* proceeded to New York where permanent repairs were to be conducted. During the Atlantic crossing, the *Heimgar* experienced heavy weather and sustained considerable damage, thereby rendering the vessel unseaworthy. It was therefore necessary for the *Heimgar* to go into dry dock in New York to have the storm damage repaired, apart from the permanent repairs required by the collision damage. While in dry dock the collision repairs and storm damage repairs were carried out concurrently. It was agreed between the parties that ten days were required for the repair of the collision damage while 30 days were required to repair the storm damage. The question for decision was whether the owners of the *Carslogie* were liable for the loss of chartered hire for ten days while the vessel was in dry dock, in addition to the cost of repairs occasioned by the collision. The House of Lords held that the plaintiff could not succeed in its claim for the loss of use of the vessel for the ten days attributable to the collision damage because the *Heimgar* was in any event out of use at that time for the storm damage repairs. The defendants were not liable for the storm damage either because this damage, according to Viscount Jowitt, 'was not in any sense a consequence of the collision and must be treated as a supervening event occurring in the course of a normal voyage'.[38] The Atlantic storm had effectively operated as a *novus actus* which severed the link between the defendant's negligence and the plaintiff's loss of use of the *Heimgar* for ten days. Lord Morton concluded that 'the *Heimgar* ceased to be a potential money-making machine when she became unseaworthy owing to heavy weather...'[39] Yet this 'immobilisation' approach ignores the fact that the *Heimgar* would not have had to cross the Atlantic with the attendant perils but for the defendant's negligence and that its owners had adopted a reasonable course of

---

35 Ibid., 189.
36 This proposition has been codified by Rule 451 of the American Law Institute's *Restatement of the Law of Torts, Second* (1965–79).
37 [1952] AC 292 (HL).
38 Ibid., 299.
39 Ibid., 316. See to the same effect Viscount Jowitt (at 301).

action in so doing in the circumstances. More recently the English Court of Appeal has held that the unforeseeable collapse of the sea bed did not sever the causal link between the defendants' admitted negligence and the additional loss sustained by the plaintiffs.[40]

Does a fall in the market constitute such an unexpected and natural event as to sever the causal link between the defendant's negligence and the plaintiff's loss? This issue arose for determination in *Banque Bruxelles Lambert S.A.* v *Eagle Star Insurance Co. Ltd*.[41] The English Court of Appeal held that it was quite foreseeable by the defendants that if the borrower defaulted in repaying the loan, as indeed happened, the plaintiffs would have to sell the secured property and that its market value might have fallen in the meantime, such that the fall could not be considered as having 'broken the link between the valuer's negligence and the damage which the lender has suffered'.[42] The High Court of Australia has also considered a case in which a valuer negligently over-valued property for the purpose of the provision of a mortgage by the plaintiff on the security thereof, but where there had been a significant decline in property values before the fact of the over-valuation was discovered. In *Kenny & Good Pty Ltd* v *MGICA (1992) Ltd*[43] the High Court held that the valuer should be liable for the whole of the loss suffered by the plaintiff, including that attributable to the fall in market values, since the valuation had been a decisive factor in leading the plaintiff to act as it did.

Coincidences

In *Haber* v *Walker*[44] Smith J. referred to the following two examples of when an intervening event would be sufficient to sever the causal connection between the defendant's act or omission and the plaintiff's loss:

(a) human action that is properly to be regarded as voluntary, or
(b) a causally independent event the conjunction of which with the wrongful act or omission is by ordinary standards so extremely unlikely as to be termed a coincidence...[45]

---

40   *Humber Oil Terminal Trustee Ltd* v *Owners of the Ship 'Sivand'* [1998] 2 Lloyd's Rep 97 (CA). This case is examined in more detail in Chapter 3.
41   [1995] 2 WLR 607 (CA). The facts of this case appear in Chapter 3.
42   Ibid., 636 (*per* Sir Thomas Bingham M.R.). On appeal to the House of Lords, it was held that the valuer in such circumstances should be liable only for the difference between the valuation given and the true value of the property at the time of the valuation: [1997] AC 191.
43   (1999) 199 CLR 413.
44   [1963] VR 339 (Supreme Court of Victoria – Full Court).
45   Ibid., 358. Smith J. relied extensively on the analysis of causal principles put forward by H.L.A. Hart and A.M. Honore in the first edition of *Causation in the Law* (1959). See now Hart and Honore *Causation in the Law* (2nd edn, 1985) pp. 103–17; 123–34; 151–2; 157–9.

Section 442. (c) of the American Law Institute's *Restatement of the Law of Torts, Second*[46] refers to 'the fact that the intervening force is operating independently of any situation created by the [defendant's] negligence' as an important consideration 'in determining whether an intervening force is a superseding cause of harm to another'.

Thus, a defendant is not responsible for the consequences of a so-called 'coincidence' primarily on the basis of notions concerning personal responsibility. A favourite example used by text writers is that of a pedestrian injured by a negligent motorist who is later struck by a falling roof tile upon entering the hospital.[47] What marks this event a coincidence is not the fall of the tile but rather that the plaintiff should be within its range (as a consequence of the defendant's negligence) at the precise and random moment when it fell.[48] In *Environment Agency* v *Empress Car Co. (Abertillery) Ltd*[49] Lord Hoffman cited a hypothetical example of a factory owner carelessly leaving a drum containing highly inflammable vapour in a place where it could easily be accidentally ignited. If the drum was struck by lightning, the ensuing explosion would not have been caused by the owner's negligence as it merely provided an occasion for the harm. According to Lord Hoffman, the lightning happening to strike at that time and place would constitute a coincidence.[50] In the realm of case-law, the 'coincidence' principle was the basis of the decision in *Woods* v *Duncan*[51] involving the submarine *Thetis*. Although the painters had negligently obstructed the test-cock of the torpedo tube, the disaster was due to the coincidence that the torpedo officer had opened the inside door of the tube for an unusual purpose and at a moment when the bow-cap was open to the sea. That liability does not extend to an exceptional or abnormal conjunction of events is illustrated by a US case involving an unlawful highway obstruction. In *O'Neill* v *City of Port Jervis*[52] the deceased was directed to take a detour which passed close to a landing strip where he was struck by a falling aircraft. The defendant was held not liable because the chances of being hit by an airplane are negligible.

Also, according to Glanville Williams,[53] '[a] defendant is not liable merely because his negligence has brought his victim into a temporal and spatial position where he encounters an ordinary hazard of life, the negligence not imposing a handicap upon him in meeting the hazard.' So when an Australian rugby league football player whose jaw was broken went to play in England to regain match fitness but broke his leg while there, it was held that the fractured leg was not a consequence of

---

46 (1965–79).

47 See the judgment of Lord MacDermott in *Hogan* v *Bentinck West Hartley Collieries (Owners) Ltd* [1949] 1 All ER 588, 601 for other examples of coincidences. The authors of the *Review of the Law of Negligence: Final Report* (Commonwealth of Australia, 2002) (the 'Ipp Review') discuss the 'coincidence principle' at para. 7.45.

48 J. Fleming *The Law of Torts* (The Law Book Company of Australasia Pty Ltd, 2nd edn, 1961) 200.

49 [1999] 2 AC 22 (HL).

50 Ibid., 30–31.

51 [1946] AC 401.

52 (1930) 171 NE 694 (N.Y.).

53 G. Williams 'Causation in the Law' [1961] *Cambridge Law Journal* 62, 81.

the broken jaw which did not make him more vulnerable to a fractured leg, even though he would not have been in England and playing at that time but for the broken jaw.[54] Once again in the hypothetical context, if a doctor fails to warn a patient of a material risk of a surgical intervention and the patient would not have undergone the operation if warned and then a different risk, against which there was no need to warn, occurs, such as lightning striking the operating theatre, the doctor would not be liable for the patient's injury.[55] An application of Section 442. (a) of the *Restatement of the Law of Torts, Second* would support this conclusion. It provides in effect that the fact that an intervening force brings about harm different in kind from that which would otherwise have resulted from the defendant's negligence is an important consideration in determining whether that event is a superseding cause of the plaintiff's injury.

Animals

Can an animal owner who negligently fails to control it be liable for damage it thereby causes to others or can the owner successfully plead that the animal's conduct amounts to a *novus actus interveniens*? In Holdsworth's *A History of English Law*[56] it is stated that since the reign of Henry VII English common law has maintained the rule that damage done by a dog was not actionable unless the master knew beforehand of its savage tendency. This rule was extended in its application to other animals, including horses. In *Cox* v *Burbidge*[57] the defendant's horse was grazing on the footpath of a road on which the plaintiff, a five-year-old boy, was playing. Suddenly the horse struck out and kicked him in the face, injuring him severely. The plaintiff sued the defendant by his next friend in an action for negligence, alleging the defendant's failure to take proper precautions to guard against this type of incident occurring. The plaintiff's action failed on account of an insufficiency of evidence on the issue of breach of duty and whether the horse had been known to be vicious. However, several judges took the opportunity to make some useful observations by way of *obiter dicta* on the law in this area. Erle C.J. said:

> [T]he owner of an animal is answerable for any damage done by it, provided it be of such a nature as is likely to arise from such an animal, and the owner knows it. Thus in the case of a dog, if he bites a man or worries sheep, and the owner knows that he is accustomed to bite men or to worry sheep, the owner is responsible; but the party injured has no remedy unless the scienter can be proved…But, if the horse does something which is quite contrary to his ordinary nature, something which his owner has no reason to expect he will do, he has the same sort of protection that the owner of a dog has: and everybody knows that it is not at all the ordinary habit of a horse to kick a child on a highway.[58]

---

54   *Canterbury Bankstown Rugby League Football Club Ltd* v *Rogers* (1993) Australian Torts Reports 81-246.
55   This hypothetical is discussed in various parts of the judgment of Hayne J. in *Chappell* v *Hart* (1998) 195 CLR 232.
56   W. Holdsworth, *A History of English Law* Volume 3, 381.
57   (1863) 13 CB (NS) 430.
58   Ibid., 436–7.

Williams J. agreed with these propositions and added that the plaintiff's action could not succeed because he had failed to prove that the defendant knew beforehand of his horse's vicious propensity.[59]

The contemporary common law rule continues to be that an animal owner or keeper is liable for the normal behaviour of animals under his or her control, but not for their unpredictable actions.[60] In *Aldham v United Dairies (London) Ltd*[61] the English Court of Appeal held that a milkman who left his horse unattended for a long while in the street ought to foresee that it might become restless and be aggressive to a passer-by. On the other hand, the owner of a bullock, in the absence of knowledge of its vicious propensity, is not liable if it viciously attacks a cyclist after having escaped from the owner's control.[62] Interventions by animals will not ordinarily amount to a *novus actus interveniens* for sound public policy reasons.[63] The original *Restatement of the Law of Torts* produced by the American Law Institute addressed this issue. Rule 443 provided in effect that an intervening act of an animal which is considered a normal response to the stimulus of a situation created by the defendant's negligence is not a superseding cause of the plaintiff's injury. As we have just seen, however, the English common law will permit the plaintiff to recover damages notwithstanding the unpredictable, abnormal and vicious nature of the animal's behaviour in those cases where the plaintiff can discharge the scienter requirement.

Disease Contracted Because of Lowered Vitality Attributable to the Defendant's Negligence

What is the legal position where the plaintiff is injured by the defendant's negligence and his or her immune system is adversely affected, leading to the onset of life-threatening diseases and other conditions? Should the defendant also shoulder legal responsibility for the subsequent aggravation of the plaintiff's situation? Where the intervening event is the onset of a natural event such as a disease or other serious illness, it would appear that it will only amount to a *novus actus interveniens* where its occurrence was not precipitated by, or attributable to, the defendant's breach of duty.[64] Rule 458 of the *Restatement of the Law of Torts, Second* provides that '[i]f the [defendant] is liable for another's injury which so lowers the other's vitality as to render him peculiarly susceptible to a disease, the [defendant] is also liable for the disease which is contracted because of the lowered vitality.'

---

59   Ibid., 439. Proving that the keeper of an animal was actually aware of its dangerous disposition is known as 'the scienter'. The requisite knowledge must relate to the particular propensity which caused the damage. Thus, if a horse bites a person, it is not sufficient to prove that it was known to bite other horses: *Glanville* v *Sutton* [1928] 1 KB 571.

60   J. Fleming *The Law of Torts* (The Law Book Company Ltd, 9th edn, 1998) 250.

61   [1940] 1 KB 507 (CA). See also *Fleming* v *Atkinson* [1959] SCR 513; *Kirk* v *Trerise* (1979) 103 DLR (3d) 78; G.L. Williams *Liability for Animals* (Cambridge University Press, 1939).

62   *Lathall* v *Joyce & Son* [1939] 3 All ER 854.

63   *Arneil* v *Paterson* [1931] AC 560.

64   *Neall* v *Watson* (1960) 34 ALJR 364 (onset of pneumonia).

This particular issue has confronted the English courts on a number of occasions in the context of contested claims under accident insurance policies. In *Isitt* v *The Railway Passengers Assurance Company*[65] the assured fell down at a railway station and dislocated his shoulder. He was insured under a policy granted by the defendant company against 'death from the effects of injury caused by the accident'. He was immediately taken home and put to bed but died less than one month later, having been all the time confined to his bedroom. Although the defendant conceded that the assured's fall amounted to an 'accident' within the meaning of the policy, it argued that a natural event had intervened to sever the causal connection between the fall and the assured's death. In a case stated in a reference under the defendant's special Act, the umpire was asked to determine as a question of fact whether the pneumonia from which the assured died was directly caused by the accident. The umpire found as a fact that the pneumonia from which the deceased died was not caused directly by the accident, but was pneumonia resulting from cold. The umpire also found, however, that the assured would not have died as and when he did if it had not been for the accident. The assured had suffered significant pain and discomfort as a result of the accident. He was also very restless and unable to bear heavy or warm clothing and consequently was reduced to a state of debility in which he was more susceptible to cold than he would have been but for the accident. The umpire also found that the assured's catching cold and the onset of the fatal pneumonia were both due to his lowered vitality brought about by the effects of the accident. The Court of Queen's Bench held that the assured's death was due to 'the effects of injury caused by accident' within the meaning of the policy. Huddleston B. considered that the facts as stated by the umpire demonstrated that although the injury sustained in the fall was not the immediate or proximate cause of the assured's death, the death did ensue from the natural consequences of the injury. As the terms of the insurance contract did not require death to be immediately caused by the accident, the plaintiff was held entitled to recover the insurance proceeds.[66] Wills J. similarly held that the assured's death was due to the natural consequences of the injury rather than to any foreign or independent intervening cause.[67] This disposition appears consistent with the principle contained in Section 458 of the *Restatement of the Law of Torts, Second*.

In response to the *Isitt* decision, the English insurance industry tightened the wording of their accident insurance policies, and whether this initiative succeeded in law in circumventing the effect of *Isitt* was raised for determination before the English Court of Appeal in *In the Matter of an Arbitration Between Etherington and the Lancashire and Yorkshire Accident Insurance Company*.[68] Pursuant to the terms of an accident insurance policy, the defendant undertook to pay the legal personal representatives of the insured a capital sum if, during the currency of the policy, the insured should sustain any accidental bodily injury leading directly to the insured's death within three months of accident. The policy also contained a proviso, however,

---

65 (1889) 22 QBD 504.
66 Ibid., 510–11.
67 Ibid., 512–13.
68 [1909] 1 KB 591 (CA).

excepting all cases where the direct or proximate cause of death 'is disease or other intervening cause, even although the disease or other intervening cause may itself have been aggravated by such accident, or have been due to weakness or exhaustion consequent thereon, or the death accelerated thereby'. The insured sustained a heavy fall from his horse while hunting and was soaked through to the skin due to the damp and moist conditions. The effect of the shock and the wet clothing was to lower the vitality of his system which led to the onset of fatal pneumonia in his lungs within two days of the accident. The Court of Appeal held that the insured's death was directly caused by an accident within the meaning of the policy, and that as this case fell outside the proviso, the defendant was consequently liable under the policy. As Kennedy L.J. observed:

> [W]ithin a few hours of the accident a condition in the region of the lung was set up which no one can say was not a result of the accident, and which was really the birth of pneumonia. It is not a case of a new disease or other cause which intervenes. The fatal pneumonia was a 'sequela' of the accident against the consequences of which it was the object of the policy to insure.[69]

Vaughan Williams L.J. held that the phrase 'direct or proximate cause' covered in such a case 'not only the immediate result of the accident, but also all those things which may fairly be considered as results usually attendant upon the particular accident in question'.[70] Although both the *Isitt* and *Etherington* cases did not result from injury produced by any person's negligence, it is submitted that their underlying principles are equally applicable to such cases as well.

Infection of Injuries Caused by the Defendant's Negligence

The courts have also considered the issue of whether post-accident infection of an injury or wound caused by the defendant's negligence can amount to a *novus actus interveniens*. In *Dunham* v *Clare*[71] the applicant's husband sustained a foot injury during the course of his employment with the defendant. Twenty-five days later he died of blood-poisoning caused by a very rare form of disease called phlegmonous erysipelas. The English Court of Appeal held that in a claim under the *Workmen's Compensation Act 1897* an applicant must prove that the worker's death resulted in fact from an injury sustained in a workplace accident, no matter how improbable death may have been in the circumstances. The erysipelas was not held to constitute a new act intervening between the workplace accident and the death. In another worker's compensation claim case,[72] Bankes L.J. formulated the relevant test to be whether the worker's condition is in fact due to the original injury aggravated by infection or disease or, conversely, is the worker's condition due to infection or disease quite independent of the original injury?

---

69   Ibid., 603.
70   Ibid., 598.
71   (1902) 71 LJKB 683 (CA).
72   *Doolan* v *Henry Hope & Sons Ltd* (1918) 11 BWCC 93; 87 LJKB 671 (CA).

Subsequent cases have held that so long as the infection or disease was directly caused by the original injury, the former does not have to manifest instantaneously or within the scope of the employment. So, in the New Zealand case of *Burnett* v *Wairoa Co-operative Meat Company Ltd*[73] involving a traumatic injury complicated by subsequent infection, the court stated:

> [T]he sudden and rapid development of the disease of the eye, and the dirty and greasy state of the plaintiff's cap, point to the infection having been introduced at the time the abrasion was caused, but we do not think it is necessary to decide this point. The cases cited are authority for the proposition that so long as there is not *novus actus interveniens* the plaintiff's right to compensation is not affected whether the infection was introduced by the substance causing the abrasion or entered later. There is no suggestion in the present case of *novus actus interveniens*, and the chain of causation is not broken in any way. The injury complained of was directly due to the original abrasion, aggravated by infection introduced by natural causes then or later.[74]

Collinson v *Manvers Main Collieries Ltd*[75] and *Martin* v *Moore*[76] both involved an employee suffering a minor injury at work (respectively a hand blister and a knitting-needle finger prick). The site of the wound became infected in each case and in both cases the court held that it did not matter whether the micro-organisms which entered the wounds and caused sepsis entered the wounds in the course of the employment or independently of it. It was sufficient for an entitlement to compensation that the initial wound arose in the course of employment. As long as the infection was attributable to the original injury, the integrity of the causal connection would be preserved.

The Australian courts have also considered the effect on the causal chain of intervening infections. In *Adelaide Chemical and Fertilizer Company Ltd* v *Carlyle*[77] Dixon J. rejected the defendant company's argument that the deceased's death was not caused by the burns he received from negligently-stored acid but rather from septicaemia arising from a streptococcal infection entering through the tissue broken down by the burns. According to Dixon J.:

> Such an infection…cannot be considered a new and independent cause. It is a recognized danger to which traumatic injury exposes the sufferer and is regarded as part of the possible consequences of the infliction of a wound.[78]

A recent decision of the Supreme Court of Tasmania (Full Appellate Court) has followed the High Court's approach in the worker's compensation context. In *Woolfe* v *Tasmania (Department of Health and Human Services)*[79] the applicant for worker's compensation was employed by the defendant as a nurse. As part of her

---

73   [1921] NZLR 981.
74   Ibid., 985.
75   (1937) 30 BWCC 280.
76   [1946] IR 1; (1945) 39 BWCC Supp 12.
77   (1940) 64 CLR 514. This case is examined in more detail in Chapter 4.
78   Ibid., 534.
79   [2001] TASSC 66.

work duties, she was obliged to use a chemical hand-cleaning product called Hexol. She alleged that the use of Hexol would often cause an outbreak of dermatitis on her hands. On one occasion she noted an area of broken skin on one of her fingers which she considered to be another outbreak of dermatitis. Ten days later she noticed an area of white skin at the location of the cracked skin and, believing this to be indicative of infection, she attended a physician. Fearing the onset of septicaemia, she was hospitalised on the same day and underwent treatment including surgery for a serious infection later identified as streptococcus pyogenes. The applicant was left with a residual disability in her finger for which she claimed compensation under the *Workers' Rehabilitation and Compensation Act 1988* for a 'dermatitis 2d infection'. According to the medical evidence, the continued use of Hexol caused dermatitis which broke down the skin barrier causing secondary infection leading to total incapacity for a significant period. The applicant's compensation claim was dismissed by the Workers' Rehabilitation and Compensation Tribunal on the ground that although her dermatitis was contracted during the course of her employment, her incapacity was not caused by that condition but rather by the secondary infection, and there was no evidence to suggest that this infection occurred in the course of her employment. Cox C.J. held that the Tribunal had misdirected itself by treating the infection as totally distinct from the dermatitis and as a *novus actus interveniens*. Relying on the above-mentioned *Burnett*, *Collinson* and *Martin* cases, the learned Chief Justice held that the applicant's work-related dermatitis had caused her incapacity, notwithstanding that the immediate cause of her incapacity was the secondary infection which had most likely been contracted outside the course of her employment.[80] Crawford J. entertained no doubt that but for the dermatitis, the applicant would not have acquired the secondary infection which led, in turn, to her incapacity.[81]

The case-law drawn from various jurisdictions has consistently held to the proposition, then, that post-injury infection will not constitute a *novus actus interveniens*. Such infections are normal rather than extraordinary incidents of physical injury and so long as they can be medically certified to have been triggered by the original trauma, the defendants will not be relieved of liability therefor.

---

80   Ibid., para. 6.
81   Ibid., para. 23.

Chapter 10

Maritime Incidents

Novus actus interveniens has been pleaded from time to time in cases involving collisions between ships and it is argued that either the response taken to the emergency created or intervening heavy weather has severed the causal connection between the original negligence and the ultimate injury. As we shall see in the following brief survey of maritime case-law in this particular (and narrow) context, if one vessel, due to the negligent navigation of another vessel, is placed under the so-called 'heavy hand of the casualty', the reasonable conduct of those in charge of the victim vessel in seeking to mitigate loss will not be regarded as absolving the defendant from responsibility for loss sustained as a result of measures reasonably taken in the emergency situation generated by the defendant's negligence.[1]

An early and leading case establishing that proposition is the decision of the English Court of Appeal in *The City of Lincoln*.[2] The barque *Albatross* was run into by the steamer *City of Lincoln* in the North Sea. As a result of the collision the starboard quarter of the barque was severed, resulting in the loss of essential navigational equipment. Though the navigation of the barque was thereafter quite difficult, the master of the *Albatross* made for the Thames River, steering by a replacement compass which he had found in the hold. Owing to the loss of the navigational equipment, the *Albatross* ran aground and was consequently necessarily abandoned. The registrar held that as the barque's grounding had not been caused by any negligence of those on board, the defendants (the owners of the *City of Lincoln*) were liable for the damages sustained by the owners of the *Albatross*. Although the court of first instance reversed the registrar's decision on the ground that there had been negligence by the master of the *Albatross*, on further appeal, the Court of Appeal restored the registrar's decision on the basis that the grounding of the barque was a natural consequence of the defendant's negligence. All three judges of the Court of Appeal accepted the registrar's conclusion that there had been no negligence by those on the *Albatross*. According to Lord Esher M.R., the negligent navigation of the *City of Lincoln* did not merely damage the *Albatross* but it had the further devastating effect of depriving the captain of the *Albatross* of essential navigational equipment. The grounding of the barque was due to the loss of such equipment which was, in turn, 'the direct result of the wrongful act of the defendants'.[3] As the Master of the Rolls observed, '[i]f the defendants have done a wrongful act, whereby the plaintiffs or their servants have been deprived of the means of averting an accident

---

1 J. Fleming *The Law of Torts* (The Law Book Company Ltd, 9th edn, 1998) 248.
2 (1889) 15 PD 15 (CA).
3 Ibid., 17.

which subsequently happens, the defendants are responsible for it...'[4] Lindley L.J. considered that 'the reasonable conduct of those who have sustained the damage, and who are seeking to save further loss' must be regarded as a consequence as 'in the ordinary course of things' would flow from the defendant's negligence.[5] And Lopes L.J. could not identify any 'intervening independent moving cause' between the defendant's fault in placing the barque 'in a position of the utmost peril' and the barque's grounding.[6] Thus, the defendant's liability was extended to the entire loss of the barque.[7]

The decision of the House of Lords in *Owners of Steamship Singleton Abbey* v *Owners of Steamship Paludina*[8] provides a rare example of a *novus actus* plea succeeding (not on one but on two counts) albeit by a slender majority. In the early morning hours of a November day in Valetta Harbour, Malta, three vessels – the *Paludina*, the *Singleton Abbey* and the *Sara* – were moored to a quay and anchored. There was a strong wind blowing at the time and a swell in the harbour. At 8 a.m. the *Paludina* dragged her anchors and the fore part of the vessel fell down upon the *Singleton Abbey* and remained in contact with her. At 11 a.m. the *Paludina* attempted to extricate herself from the *Singleton Abbey* with the assistance of two tugs but in the process broke away from her moorings and tore the *Singleton Abbey* away from her short moorings. The *Singleton Abbey* in turn fell down upon the *Sara* and cast her adrift. The *Singleton Abbey* and the *Sara* then manoeuvred in the harbour under their own steam to keep away from the shore. Twenty minutes later the *Sara*, which had got up steam and was struggling to get out, got under the starboard quarter of the *Singleton Abbey*. The revolving propeller of the *Singleton Abbey* struck the *Sara*, as a result of which the *Sara* was sunk. The *Paludina* was clear of both ships at the time. In an action by the *Singleton Abbey* against the *Paludina*, a question arose as to whether the *Paludina* was also liable for the final collision between the *Singleton Abbey* and the *Sara*. The President of the Probate, Divorce and Admiralty Division found that the final collision was directly caused by the negligence of the *Paludina*. This decision was reversed in part by the Court of Appeal which held that the master of the *Singleton Abbey* was negligent in not stopping his engines in time to avert the collision with the *Sara*. On further appeal to the House of Lords, it was held by a 3:2 majority[9] that the final collision was not directly caused by the negligence of the *Paludina*, but that the action of the *Sara* constituted a *novus actus interveniens* severing the causal link between the *Paludina*'s original negligence and the *Sara*'s sinking. It was further held by two of the majority judges – Lord Sumner and Lord Blanesburgh – in concurring with the Court of Appeal that the miscalculation of the master of the *Singleton Abbey* in not stopping his engines sooner also broke the chain

---

    4   Ibid.
    5   Ibid., 18.
    6   Ibid., 19.
    7   See also *The Guildford* [1956] P 364 and compare *The Fritz Thyssen* [1968] P 255 (unreasonable refusal to accept aid).
    8   [1927] AC 16 (HL).
    9   Lord Sumner, Lord Carson and Lord Blanesburgh forming the majority (Viscount Dunedin and Lord Phillimore dissenting).

of causation. The *ratio decidendi* is perhaps best expressed in the judgment of Lord Blanesburgh who considered that the negligence of the *Sara* could not be rationally explained in light of the facts that it had the whole harbour in which to manoeuvre and the final collision occurred 20 minutes after the *Sara* and *Singleton Abbey* were cast adrift.[10] Although the *Paludina*'s original negligence may have created the occasion for the final collision, the subsequent careless navigation of the *Singleton Abbey* and the *Sara* was the more immediate and proximate cause thereof.[11] Lord Carson held that the chain of causation between the *Paludina*'s initial negligence and the *Sara*'s sinking had been severed by the latter vessel failing to make proper use of her steam power.[12] In concluding that the negligence of the master of the *Singleton Abbey* in not stopping its engines sooner amounted to a *novus actus interveniens*, Lord Sumner distinguished *The City of Lincoln* from the instant case on the ground that in the former case '[t]he hand of the original wrongdoer was still heavy on [the victim] ship' whereas in the latter case the master had full use of the navigational equipment of an undamaged ship in broad daylight with steam up.[13] As we have seen in the previous chapter, the House of Lords has also held in *Carslogie Steamship Co. Ltd v Royal Norwegian Government*[14] that an extraordinary natural phenomenon such as heavy weather at sea can also amount to a *novus actus interveniens*, apart from the subsequent negligent navigation of other vessels.

By contrast, there may be cases where the earlier negligence may create a situation of difficulty which is still operating at the time of the later negligence. As in *The City of Lincoln*, the hand of the original wrongdoer may still weigh heavy on the victim ship. Another example is *The Calliope*.[15] Having been involved in a collision with the *Carlsholm* (for which the latter ship was partly to blame), the *Calliope* found itself diverted from its original course. In order to regain that course, the *Calliope* had to perform an exceptionally difficult turning manoeuvre and, in so doing, was held to be negligent. Nevertheless, the *Carlsholm* was found to be partially responsible for the further damage to the *Calliope*. Even though by skilful navigation the *Calliope* could have avoided the damage, the hand of the *Carlsholm* was considered by the court to be still heavy on the ship.

The other leading maritime law decision of the House of Lords involving an intervening causation issue was handed down one year after its decision in *The Paludina*.[16] Like *The Paludina*, *The Metagama*[17] was also decided by a 3:2 majority, the latter case establishing that a not unreasonable error of judgement in difficult circumstances will not amount to a *novus actus interveniens* relieving the defendant

---

10 [1927] AC 16, 36.
11 Ibid.
12 Ibid., 35.
13 Ibid., 26–7. Lord Sumner rejected the proposition that the *Paludina* had put the *Singleton Abbey* in a situation of 'alternative danger' since such doctrine had never been extended in its application to a situation of danger to property (as opposed to human beings): ibid., 28–9. The doctrine of alternative danger will be examined in detail in Chapter 15.
14 [1952] AC 292 (HL).
15 [1970] P 172.
16 [1927] AC 16 (HL).
17 (1927) 138 LT 369 (HL).

of liability. The *Metagama* involved a collision between the *Baron Vernon*, owned by the Kelvin Shipping Company, and the *Metagama*, owned by the Canadian Pacific Railway Company. The collision occurred on 25 May 1923 in the River Clyde and liability for the collision was admitted by the owners of the *Metagama*. After the collision an unsuccessful attempt was made to beach the *Baron Vernon* on the south bank. Its engines were reversed and it was beached stern first on the north bank. The *Baron Vernon* remained there for 40 minutes until it slipped off with the falling tide and drifted across the River Clyde until its stern caught the south bank. The stern was swung down the River Clyde and the *Baron Vernon* assumed a parallel position with it. The *Baron Vernon* remained in that position until 27 May when the flood tide caught its port quarter and swung its stern into the south bank. The *Baron Vernon* sank rapidly into the mud such that it became impossible to conduct salvage operations at a reasonable cost and salvage attempts were consequently abandoned. In June 1923 The Clyde Navigation Trustees undertook the operation of removing the *Baron Vernon* pursuant to the exercise of their statutory powers and in July 1924 the vessel was finally raised and removed to a Glasgow dock. The Trustees sued the owners of the *Baron Vernon* for salvage expenses and the collateral question of the amount of damages the owners of the *Metagama* were liable to pay to the owners of the *Baron Vernon* arose for consideration. The owners of the *Metagama* contended that the negligence of those in charge of the *Baron Vernon* subsequent to the collision resulted in the latter vessel changing its position from one of comparative safety (from which salvage might have been more expeditiously and cheaply undertaken) into the final difficult position. It was further contended that reasonable seamanship demanded that the engines of the *Baron Vernon* should have been kept running and that these acts and omissions were new and independent intervening events which severed the causal chain. The owners of the *Baron Vernon* argued that it had not been proven that a reasonable master or pilot would have kept the engines running in the circumstances prevailing at the time.

The Lord Ordinary allowed the owners of the *Baron Vernon* to recover only such damage as was proved to have arisen from the collision, including the reasonable cost of salvage from the first position. The Second Division of the Scottish Court of Session held the *Metagama* responsible for the whole damage and the owners of the *Metagama* appealed to the House of Lords before which it was argued that a *novus actus interveniens* broke the chain of causation between the *Metagama*'s conceded original negligence and the final debacle. Viscount Haldane, in delivering the leading majority judgment, held that the defendants had not discharged the burden of proving that the chain of causation had been broken. In order to discharge such burden, the defendants must prove 'that the breach in the chain was due to unwarrantable action and not merely to action on an erroneous opinion by people who have *bona fide* made a mistake while trying to do their best...'[18] It was the duty of those on board the *Baron Vernon* to do all they could to mitigate their loss but, according to Viscount Haldane, 'they do not fail in this duty if they only commit an error of judgment in deciding on the best course in difficult circumstances.'[19] In

---

18   Ibid., 370.
19   Ibid.

reaching his conclusion, Viscount Haldane relied on several propositions which had been laid down and applied by Lindley L.J. in *The City of Lincoln*:[20]

> When a collision takes place by the fault of the defending ship in an action for damages, the damage is recoverable if it is the natural and reasonable result of the negligent act, and it will assume this character if it can be shown to be such a consequence as in the ordinary course of things would flow from the situation which the offending ship had created. Further, what those in charge of the injured ship do to save it may be mistaken, but if they do whatever they do reasonably, although unsuccessfully, their mistaken judgment may be a natural consequence for which the offending ship is responsible...Reasonable human conduct is part of the ordinary course of things, which extends to the reasonable conduct of those who have sustained the damage and who are seeking to save further loss.[21]

Thus, it would seem that reasonable defensive action to minimise loss in a difficult situation is within the scope of the risks generated by the original negligent navigation.

The legal propositions laid down by the Court of Appeal in *The City of Lincoln* and adopted by Viscount Haldane in *The Metagama* were reaffirmed and applied by the Court of Appeal in *Lord* v *Pacific Steam Navigation Co. Ltd (The Oropesa)*.[22] At about 3 a.m. on 4 December 1939 the *Manchester Regiment* and the *Oropesa* collided in the mid-Atlantic in gale conditions. According to the nautical assessors, the collision inflicted so much damage on the *Manchester Regiment* that the ship would not have had sufficient buoyancy to keep afloat due to a rapid flooding of the engine-room. Captain Raper, the master of the *Manchester Regiment*, considered that the best course of action was to send off 50 (out of a total crew of 74) in three lifeboats, leaving behind one lifeboat and 24 of the remaining crew. He then decided to travel to the *Oropesa* himself with as many men as could be spared from the *Manchester Regiment* in order to arrange with the captain of the *Oropesa* for distress messages to be sent out and for salvage assistance. Having left behind seven crew members on the *Manchester Regiment*, Captain Raper set off for the *Oropesa* in the remaining lifeboat with 16 men. Approximately half an hour later, the boat capsized in the gale and nine of the crew, including Lord, the son of the plaintiffs, drowned. A collision action was brought in the Admiralty Court in which blame was apportioned four-fifths to the *Manchester Regiment* and one-fifth to the *Oropesa*. The plaintiffs, the parents of the deceased man Lord, sued for damages, as administrators of their son's estate, for loss of expectation of life and as dependants on their deceased son's earnings under *Lord Campbell's Act 1843*. An appeal was brought from a decision in the plaintiffs' favour at first instance. The Court of Appeal dismissed the appeal on the ground that Captain Raper's action was taken to save the lives of those for whom he was responsible and was therefore reasonable in the circumstances and that, accordingly, his actions did not sever the causal chain between the *Oropesa*'s negligence and Lord's drowning. In delivering the main judgment of the Court of Appeal, Lord Wright required that '[i]t must always be shown that there is something which I

---

20   (1889) 15 PD 15 (CA).
21   (1927) 138 LT 369, 370.
22   [1943] 1 All ER 211 (CA).

will call ultroneous, something unwarrantable, a new cause coming in disturbing the sequence of events, something that can be described as either unreasonable or extraneous or extrinsic.'[23] Emphasising the perilous situation[24] Captain Raper had been placed in by the negligent navigation of the *Oropesa* and having cited *The City of Lincoln* and *The Metagama* decisions, Lord Wright considered that 'the heavy hand of the casualty' was still resting on Captain Raper when he set off on his ill-fated crossing to the *Oropesa*. Captain Raper had done nothing which could be considered outside the exigencies of the emergency situation and both he and Lord had acted reasonably in the dire circumstances they faced. Even if Captain Raper was acting under a mistaken impression and was not doing quite the right thing, his mistake or error of judgement might be regarded as the natural consequence of the emergency in which he had been placed by the negligence of the *Oropesa*.[25] For sound and obvious public policy reasons, rescue attempts in emergency situations created by a defendant's negligence are not as likely to be held to sever the causal chain, even if such rescue efforts entail a heightened risk of further damage.[26]

The US courts have also had occasion to apply the doctrine of superseding cause in the maritime context. One of the leading cases involved a plea that the gross negligence of a tanker captain severed the causal chain and thereby relieved the defendants of liability. *Exxon* v *Sofec Inc.*[27] concerned the stranding on a charted reef of the Exxon *Houston* nearly three hours after breaking away from a single point mooring system owned and operated by the defendants. The *Houston*, a steam propulsion oil tanker, was engaged in delivering oil into the defendants' submerged pipeline via floating hoses when a heavy storm caused a break in the chafe chain linking the tanker to the single point mooring system. Immediately after the breakout, the United States Coast Guard contacted the *Houston* to ascertain whether it needed assistance, but because he was advised assistance vessels would not arrive within two hours, the *Houston*'s Captain Coyne refused the offer, believing the problem would be resolved within that time. Over a period of some 100 minutes prior to the stranding, as the District Court at first instance found, Captain Coyne made a series of ill-advised acts and omissions which included the following:

- failure to regularly chart the tanker's position on the chart by means of navigational fixes;
- failure to call another officer to the bridge for assistance shortly before the stranding;
- failure to anchor properly;

---

23 Ibid., 215. The use of the term 'unwarrantable' can be traced to Viscount Haldane's judgment in *The Metagama* (1927) 138 LT 369, 370 (HL).

24 With his vessel in the mid-Atlantic, helpless, and without any means of propulsion in a heavy sea with a strong gale blowing, Captain Raper faced a more difficult proposition than that encountered by the master of the *Albatross* in *The City of Lincoln* (1889) 15 PD 15 (CA).

25 [1943] 1 All ER 211, 216 (*per* Lord Wright).

26 M. Lunney and K. Oliphant *Tort Law: Text and Materials* (Oxford University Press, 2000) 212.

27 (1995) 54 F 3d 570 (Ninth Circuit Court of Appeals).

- failure to request assistance from the Coast Guard or other available ships;
- initiating a disastrous final turn to the right towards the shore which resulted in the tanker's stranding at a time when the storm was threatening to push the tanker ashore.

The Exxon Company, as owner of the *Houston*, sued the defendants for damages for loss of the tanker, loss of its cargo and for oil spill cleanup costs. The District Court entered judgment for the defendants at first instance after conducting a bench trial in admiralty. It was found by the District Court that Captain Coyne's extraordinary negligence was the sole proximate and superseding cause of the *Houston*'s grounding. The enumerated acts and omissions amounted to violations of statutory and maritime industry standards and constituted unreasonable and reckless conduct in the circumstances. Although the breaking of the mooring chain imperilled the *Houston*, it successfully avoided that peril by heading out to sea to a position of relative safety. Captain Coyne's conduct after reaching that position was characterised by the District Court as extraordinary negligence and a superseding cause which extinguished the defendants' liability for negligence causing the breakout. The District Court also found that the fact that the *Houston* grounded almost three hours after the breakaway was 'highly extraordinary'. The United States Ninth Circuit Court of Appeals dismissed Exxon's appeal, holding that the District Court's finding of Captain Coyne's extraordinary negligence being the sole proximate and superseding cause of the *Houston*'s damage should not be disturbed.

The finding of *novus actus* by the courts in *Exxon* v *Sofec Inc.* parallels the decision of the House of Lords in *The Paludina*[28] where the *Sara* and the *Singleton Abbey* had reached a position of safety (having had the whole harbour to manoeuvre in) and the final collision did not occur until some 20 minutes after the original negligence by the *Paludina*.[29] However, the situation generated by the defendant's negligence in *Exxon* v *Sofec Inc.* is clearly distinguishable from cases like *The City of Lincoln*[30] and *The Oropesa*[31] since Captain Coyne in the former case had, as the District Court found, ample time, as well as opportunity and available resources, to take precautions which would have eliminated the risk of grounding on the charted reef. By contrast, the masters of the respective vessels in the latter two cases had been virtually deprived of their essential navigational equipment and were effectively left to fend for themselves. This largely explains the different legal conclusions on the *novus actus* issue.

To conclude this brief survey of the maritime case-law on *novus actus interveniens*, it would appear that courts will focus their attention on a number of factors in considering whether the causal link has been severed. These include, but are not limited to, the extent to which the victim ship is imperilled by the defendant's negligence (or, in the judicial vernacular, still operating under 'the heavy hand of

---

28 [1927] AC 16 (HL).

29 As in *Exxon* v *Sofec Inc.*, Lord Blanesburgh considered the possibility that the *Sara*'s chain-breaking conduct amounted to gross negligence: [1927] AC 16, 36.

30 (1889) 15 PD 15 (CA).

31 [1943] 1 All ER 211 (CA).

the casualty'), an *ex post facto* assessment of how reasonable or otherwise was the intervening conduct of the victim ship's captain in responding to the emergency situation created by the defendant's negligence, the extent to which the core navigational equipment of the victim ship has been disabled by the defendant's negligence, characterisation of the conduct of the victim ship's captain (ranging along a continuum from mere error of judgement to gross negligence), the length of time which elapsed between the original negligence and infliction of the ultimate damage, whether the victim ship could have, and did, reach a position of relative safety before the infliction of such damage, whether those on board the victim ship acted within or outside the exigencies of the emergency, and the human and property interests at stake. A balancing of these considerations in the context of the unique facts and circumstances of each case will assist in resolving the intervening causation issue.

Chapter 11

The Suicide Cases

Introduction

Tragically it happens from time to time that victims of negligently-caused road and workplace accidents take their own lives within one or two years after the accident. Courts have been confronted with both remoteness of damage and causation issues in deciding whether the defendant should be held liable not only for the initial accident injuries but for the suicide as well. In such circumstances, should the act of suicide be deemed a *novus actus interveniens*, relieving the defendant of liability for the death itself?

As we shall see in this chapter, early case-law considered that if a person in such a situation took their own life intentionally while in full possession of their mental faculties, the suicide was generally considered to have been caused, for legal purposes, by their own voluntary action rather than the original accident, regardless of the compelling nature of their despair.[1] The position was different, however, if the accident victim committed suicide involuntarily while insane and that insanity was directly caused by the accident injuries rather than by brooding over the accident and its *sequelae*. This distinction between a sane and insane state of mind has been recently and rightly discredited. After surveying the development of the case-law in this context from the leading common law jurisdictions, this chapter will conclude with some suggestions concerning future directions the law might take in terms of law reform.

England

This issue first arose in England under the *Workmen's Compensation Acts* where the case-law developed thereunder was concerned with the question whether the suicide of the worker, out of whose death the claim arises, should be treated as a *novus actus interveniens* so as to defeat the claim. Under the workers' compensation legislation which granted a statutory right to compensation where death 'results from' a work-related injury, it was settled early on that it is irrelevant to inquire whether the death was a reasonably foreseeable or a natural or probable result of the injury; the question is simply a causal one which ascertains whether or not the causal chain has been severed. This proposition was laid down in the influential judgment of Collins M.R. in *Dunham v Clare*.[2] Although not a suicide case, the following statement of

---

1 J. Fleming *The Law of Torts* (The Law Book Company of Australasia Pty Ltd, 2nd edn, 1961) 204.
2 [1902] 2 KB 292 (CA).

the Master of the Rolls has come to be taken as prescribing the rule to be applied in cases under the workers' compensation legislation:

> In the present case there was admittedly an accident causing injury and the only question is whether death in fact resulted from the injury. If death resulted from the injury it is not relevant to say that death was not the natural or probable consequence thereof. The question whether death resulted from the injury resolves itself into an inquiry as to the chain of causation. If the chain of causation is broken by a *novus actus interveniens*, so that the old cause goes and a new one is substituted for it, that is a new act which gives a fresh origin to the after-consequences...The only question to be considered is: Did the death or incapacity in fact result from the injury? The County Court judge by inquiring whether death was the natural or probable consequence of the injury has applied the wrong standard...If no new cause, no *novus actus interveniens* intervenes, death has in fact resulted from the injury.[3]

This passage was cited with approval in the judgment of the Scottish Court of Session in *Malone* v *Cayzer Irvine & Co.*[4] which involved the suicide of a worker following upon an injury sustained in the course of his employment. There the Court of Session was only concerned with the issue of whether the death was the direct result of the workplace injury, it being considered irrelevant whether the suicide was the natural or probable or foreseeable consequence of the accident. It was further held that the death of a worker might be proved to have resulted from the workplace injury by adducing evidence that the suicide was committed as a result of insanity and that the insanity was a direct result of the injury. The views of the respective courts in the *Dunham* and *Malone* cases were accepted in later cases, including the decision of the English Court of Appeal in *Withers* v *London, Brighton & South Coast Railway Company*.[5] There it was held that in order to qualify as a compensatory death claim, it must be proved not only that the suicide was the result of insanity, but also that the insanity was directly and strictly the result of the injury. As Warrington L.J. observed, it is not sufficient to prove that the insanity was the result of clinical depression caused by the fact of the accident and its *sequelae*, including resultant enforced idleness and brooding. The insanity must have been occasioned by the injury itself rather than by the consequences of the injury.[6] These decisions also established that it was not necessary for the claimant to show the insanity to have satisfied the strict *McNaghten*[7] test applied in the criminal law sphere, and that it was a question of

---

3   Ibid., 295–6.
4   (1908) 1 BWCC 27; [1908] SC 479.
5   [1916] 2 KB 772; 9 BWCC 616 (CA).
6   See also *Marriott* v *Maltby Main Colliery Co.* (1920) 90 LJKB 349; *Coulter* v *Coltness Iron Co.* [1938] SC 720; *Church* v *Dugdale & Adams Ltd* (1929) 22 BWCC 444, 449 (*per* Lord Hanworth M.R.).
7   The *McNaghten* Rule of criminal responsibility states essentially that if the accused was possessed of sufficient understanding when he committed the criminal act to know what he was doing and to know that it was wrong, he is responsible therefor, but if he did not know the nature and quality of the act or did know what he was doing but did not know that it was wrong, he is not criminally responsible: H. Black *Black's Law Dictionary* (West Publishing Co., Revised 4th edn, 1968) 1101.

degree whether the mental condition was sufficient to prevent the deceased's act in committing suicide from severing the causal chain. The rationale of these cases appears to be that a suicide is not a chain-breaking voluntary act, for the purposes of legal causation, if the accident victim was acting under the pressure of a mental disorder produced by the accident itself which prevented the worker from exercising a free and independent choice.

The vexed issue of whether suicide severs the causal chain has also arisen for the consideration of the English courts in the context of fatal accidents legislation. Pursuant to a statute of 1846 generally known as *Lord Campbell's Act*,[8] a limited measure of protection was accorded to dependants who had lost close relatives in fatal accidents. This statutory remedy for wrongful death makes it a wrong, at the suit of certain designated relatives, to cause the death of a human being 'by a wrongful act, neglect or default, which is such as would (if death had not ensued) have entitled the party injured to maintain an action and recover damages in respect thereof...' In the unreported case of *Cavanagh v London Transport Executive*[9] the deceased suffered injuries, including brain damage, as a result of a road accident. He committed suicide 16 months after the accident. His widow's action under the *Fatal Accidents Acts 1846–1908* succeeded before Devlin J. who held that the chain of causation was not broken by the fact that the husband took his own life while apparently legally sane. His Lordship held that the accident was a cause of the husband's suicide on the basis of a finding that an irrational state of mind arising from his head injuries falling short of certifiable insanity impelled the husband to his fateful self-destructive decision.[10] One year later, Pilcher J. adopted the same approach in *Pigney v Pointer's Transport Services Ltd*.[11] In that case a lorry driver sustained head injuries as the result of an accident in the course of his employment as a servant of the defendants. The injuries induced a condition of acute anxiety neurosis. Three months later he instituted proceedings against the defendants alleging that the accident had been caused through their negligence. Some 18 months after the accident and before his action had come on for trial, Mr Pigney hanged himself as a result of neurosis. His widow continued his action and also brought a second action under the *Fatal Accidents Acts 1846–1908*. After finding that the defendants had breached their duty of care, Pilcher J. applied the discredited *Polemis* rule[12] and held that the plaintiff's damage was 'directly traceable' to the defendants' negligence and not due to the operation of independent causes. According to the learned judge, if Mr Pigney had been insane at the time of his death as adjudged under the *McNaghten* Rules and his insanity had been attributable to the accident, the chain of causation would clearly have remained intact.[13] However, although he found that the deceased took

---

8   Now *Fatal Accidents Act 1976*.

9   *The Times* (23 October 1956).

10   Devlin J. tacitly adopted the view that whether or not the suicide was reasonably foreseeable in the circumstances was irrelevant under fatal accidents legislation. Only causation need be considered.

11   [1957] 1 WLR 1121.

12   *In re Polemis and Furness, Withy & Co.* [1921] 3 KB 560 (CA).

13   [1957] 1 WLR 1121, 1124.

his life in a fit of depression brought about by a condition of acute anxiety neurosis induced by the accident and accident injuries which the deceased had sustained 18 months earlier, Pilcher J. considered that when the deceased hanged himself he was not insane under the *McNaghten* Rules in that he must have known what he was doing when he took his own life and that he was doing wrong.[14] Notwithstanding the finding that Mr Pigney's suicide could not reasonably have been foreseen by the defendants,[15] Pilcher J. ruled that the causal chain still remained unbroken despite the finding that the deceased's acute anxiety neurosis fell short of the *McNaghten* requirements of insanity. At the time the decision was handed down, it was severely criticised by the late Professor John Fleming for imposing liability on the defendants 'even though the deceased was legally sane when he took his life and no less than 18 months had elapsed since the accident in question.'[16] However, as we shall see, case-law in a number of jurisdictions has since developed along similar lines such that the technical sane-insane distinction has been undermined as a touchstone for determining the outcome of a *novus actus* plea in this context.

Whether the suicide of a prisoner can amount to a *novus actus interveniens* has been considered by the Court of Appeal and the House of Lords. In *Kirkham* v *Chief Constable of the Greater Manchester Police*[17] the Court of Appeal held that when the defendant's negligence is such as to create a risk of suicide because of a prisoner's

---

14   Ibid., 1123. An intentional act of self-destruction not committed under the influence of insanity was felonious at that time (*felo de se* or felon or murder of himself).

15   Reasonable foreseeability not being required by the Court of Appeal in *Polemis*.

16   J. Fleming 'Liability for Suicide' (1957) 31 *Australian Law Journal* 587. But see now the decision of the English Court of Appeal in *Corr* v *IBC Vehicles Ltd* [2006] 3 WLR 395. In 1996 the claimant's husband was employed by the defendant as a maintenance engineer when he suffered severe head injuries in an accident caused by malfunctioning machinery. Following reconstructive surgery, he began to suffer post-traumatic stress disorder causing him to lapse deeper into depression. He committed suicide six years after his work accident. The claimant, as the deceased's widow, brought proceedings against the defendant employer under the *Fatal Accidents Act 1976*. Although the defendant admitted that the accident had been caused by its negligence, it denied liability for the suicide. The Court of Appeal (Ward L.J. dissenting, but not on the intervening causation issue) reversed the first instance decision which had rejected the claim on the ground that the suicide had not been reasonably foreseeable in the circumstances. It was held on appeal that the type of harm on which the claimant founded her claim was the deceased's depression, which the defendant conceded to have been a foreseeable consequence of its negligence; that suicide should no longer be regarded as necessarily breaking the causal chain; and that there was no break in such chain in the instant case as the evidence clearly established that there was no other cause than the depression that impelled the husband to suicide. According to Ward L.J. (at pp. 412–13), the deceased's conduct was not 'wholly unreasonable' and could not be characterised as the 'free and informed' act of a human being. Rather, the suicide was caused by a sense of hopelessness directly traceable to the workplace accident and its effects. See also Sedley L.J. (at p. 421) ('Once liability has been established for the depression, the question in each case is whether it has been shown that it was the depression which drove the deceased to take his own life.') And Wilson L.J. (at p. 426) (a suicide caused by pressures or feelings produced by the accident and its effects should not be regarded as a *novus actus*). An appeal to the House of Lords is pending.

17   [1990] 2 QB 283 (CA).

psychiatric illness, the suicide of that prisoner will not sever the causal chain. The police had failed to pass on to the prison authorities information that the prisoner in question was suffering from clinical depression and was suicidal. A *novus actus* plea could not prevail in circumstances where the defendant had a duty to prevent the prisoner from committing suicide.[18] The House of Lords has more recently examined this issue in *Reeves v Commissioner of Police of the Metropolis*.[19] In that case a prisoner hanged himself in a police cell. The defendants were aware that he was a suicide risk, but the flap on the cell door had been left down allowing the prisoner to tie his shirt through the spy hole in the door and hang himself. In an action brought under the *Fatal Accidents Act 1976*, the defendants conceded that a duty of care was owed to the prisoner but denied liability on the ground that his own act of suicide was a voluntary act done while of sound mind and, as such, severed the causal chain between the breach of their duty and the prisoner's death. The majority of the House of Lords rejected the *novus actus* plea as the death resulted directly from a breach of duty to prevent just such an act. It was not a superseding event but the very harm that the defendants were under a duty to prevent. It was further held that the duty to guard against the risk of prisoner suicide applied to all prisoners, whether they were of sound or unsound mind (the trial judge having found the deceased to have been of sound mind at the time of his death).[20] Nonetheless, the plaintiff's awarded damages were reduced by 50 per cent under the *Law Reform (Contributory Negligence) Act 1945* on the ground that the term 'fault' within the meaning of Section 4 thereof included intentional as well as negligent acts. Since the deceased had responsibility for his own life, and since his intentional act was committed while of sound mind and proved to be a substantial cause of his death, the defence of contributory negligence succeeded. Lord Hobhouse dissented:

> If [the deceased prisoner], knowing that the police officers had put him in a cell with a defective door and had failed to close the hatch, then voluntarily and deliberately, in full possession of his faculties, made the rational choice to commit suicide, principle and language say that it was his choice which was the cause of his subsequent death. He was not, on the judge's findings, acting under any disability or compulsion. He made a free choice: he is responsible for the consequence of that choice.[21]

---

18   See also *Knight v Home Office* [1990] 3 All ER 237.
19   [2000] 1 AC 360 (HL).
20   See the judgments of Lord Hoffman (ibid., 368) and Lord Hope (ibid., 385).
21   Ibid., 396. The majority decision of the House of Lords in *Reeves* contrasts sharply with that of the Supreme Court of Victoria in *Rigg v State of New South Wales* (1993) Australian Torts Reports 81-230. There, the plaintiff, aged almost 18, had a considerable criminal record and history of suicide attempts. He was suspected of burglary and arrested by New South Wales police who were advised by Victorian police of his criminal record, drug problem and previous psychiatric treatment, but not of his tendency to attempt suicide. The plaintiff was left alone in the exercise yard for about 10 minutes and unsuccessfully attempted to hang himself with a blanket, leaving him with permanent brain damage. The Court held that the police officers had not breached their duty of care to the plaintiff, but even if they had, the sole cause of the plaintiff's injuries was his own action in attempting to take his own life, an action which could not reasonably have been foreseen by the officers. One would have thought that

The decision of the House of Lords is significant in at least two respects. Firstly, it has discredited the historical distinction between a sane and insane state of mind in resolving the *novus actus* issue, at least in the custodial context. Secondly, it has endorsed the proposition that the deceased may have been contributorily negligent in bringing about his or her own demise, at least to the extent that he or she was not operating at the material time under a completely diminished mental capacity.

Australia

The leading Australian case on when an act of suicide will sever the causal chain is the decision of the Supreme Court of Victoria (Full Court) in *Haber* v *Walker*.[22] This case concerned an action brought under Section 16 of the *Wrongs Act 1958* by the plaintiff on her own behalf and that of her children on account of the death of her husband. The deceased was injured in a motor vehicle collision allegedly caused by the defendant's negligence. He received treatment for those injuries in hospital first in the surgical ward and then later in the psychiatric ward and finally as an out-patient. He suffered severe brain damage, one-sided facial paralysis, distorted vision, interference with the sense of smell, hearing impairment, defective memory and concentration, impaired co-ordination, and irritability and aggressiveness. The husband was greatly distressed by his appearance, his mental and physical impairment and his incapacity to earn money to support his family. He suffered from fits of deep depression and a sense of futility concerning the apparent hopelessness of his condition. After one unsuccessful suicide attempt in hospital, the deceased ended his life by hanging himself while considered insane under the *McNaghten* Rules as found by the jury. Although the jury found that the husband's suicide was not something which the defendant could reasonably be expected to have foreseen, it also found that his death was caused by the accident for which the defendant was responsible. On appeal, the Supreme Court of Victoria upheld the decision in the plaintiff's favour by a majority judgment. In an action under fatal accidents legislation, the test of liability is whether the death was caused by the wrongful act, neglect or default of the defendant. Accordingly, the plaintiff is not required to prove that the deceased's death by suicide was reasonably foreseeable by the defendant, but merely that his death was a consequence of the defendant's negligence. The majority held that the husband's act of suicide did not sever the causal chain, notwithstanding the lapse of 17 months from the accident. According to Lowe J., if the act of suicide was committed while insane under the *McNaghten* Rules, as was the case here, the causal chain remains intact.[23]

---

the plaintiff's age, vulnerability and psychiatric condition relative to the deceased prisoner in *Reeves* would have produced the opposite conclusion on the *novus actus* issue.

22 [1963] VR 339.

23 Ibid., 351–2. Whether any less degree of mental disturbance in the actor would suffice to preserve the integrity of the causal chain was not definitively resolved by Lowe J. although His Honour did express the *obiter* view that 'something less than legal insanity' might be sufficient. See also *Zavitsanos* v *Chippendale* [1970] 2 NSWR 495.

Smith J., the other majority judge, observed that a 'voluntary' act of a third person or the plaintiff may constitute a *novus actus interveniens* where such act is taken in the exercise of a free choice unencumbered by the pressure of any mental disorder attributable to the defendant's negligence.[24] In the instant case, however, the causal chain remained intact as the act of suicide was not truly voluntary in nature. The insanity produced by the accident and its injuries deprived the husband of a free choice concerning whether to live or die.[25] As has been observed by some commentators, the husband's decision to commit suicide was predominantly conditioned by the situation in which the defendant's negligence placed him, because the very manner in which he made decisions had been altered by that situation.[26] The *Haber* case was considered by a Queensland court in *Richters* v *Motor Tyre Service Proprietary Ltd*.[27] There the plaintiff was the estate of a woman who committed suicide 26 months after being injured in a car accident in which her husband had been killed. Apart from physical injuries, she suffered considerable pain and discomfort and was left with a permanent disability in two of her limbs. She subsequently developed a state of morbid depression, a recognisable psychiatric illness, as a result of her injuries and her husband's death and it was contended that when she took her own life it was the result of such depression which in turn had been caused by the accident. A claim was brought under the Queensland fatal accidents legislation for loss of dependency on her husband wherein damages were awarded for the period between the respective deaths.[28] However, on a separate cause of action in negligence for the deceased woman's personal injuries, a claim for damages for loss of expectation of life was rejected because her suicide was not considered a reasonably foreseeable consequence of her personal accident injuries and her husband's death. Her unforeseeable suicide thus amounted to a *novus actus interveniens*. Nevertheless, on similar facts, the Queensland Court of Appeal has recently applied the reasonable foreseeability criterion less strictly in *Lisle* v *Brice*[29] and held the suicide was both foreseeable and causally related to the defendant's negligence.

---

24 Ibid., 359.

25 Ibid., 361.

26 M. Davies and I. Malkin *Torts* (LexisNexis Butterworths, 4th edn, 2003) 92. See also *Telstra Corporation Ltd* v *Smith* (1998) Australian Torts Reports 81-487 (where the New South Wales Court of Appeal held that the plaintiff's attempted suicide was sufficiently causally connected to the defendant's negligence to give rise to liability).

27 [1972] Qd R 9.

28 The test for liability under successive versions of *Lord Campbell's Act 1846* being whether the death was caused by the defendant's wrongful act, there being no requirement to prove that the suicide was reasonably foreseeable.

29 [2002] 2 Qd R 168 (CA). See also *Telstra Corporation Ltd* v *Smith* [1998] Australian Torts Reports 81-487 (NSWCA); *NSW Insurance Ministerial Corporation* v *Myers* (1995) 21 MVR 295 (NSWCA). Compare *AMP General Insurance Ltd* v *RTA* (2001) 22 NSWCCR 247 (NSWCA) where it was held that the defendant was not legally responsible for the victim's suicide over five years after the accident but only a few days after a vigorous cross-examination in court had brought on severe depression, the latter amounting to a *novus actus interveniens*. Spigelman CJ stated (at 257) that '[a]ctions involving the deliberate infliction of self-harm should generally be regarded as "independent and unreasonable" and as a break in the sequence of events that

New Zealand

New Zealand courts have also considered the issue of the degree or extent of insanity necessary to prove that the suicide of the defendant's victim was not caused by the deceased's own wrongful act. In the early case of *McFarland* v *Stewart*[30] it was held that it was necessary to show that at the time the act of suicide was committed, the deceased was insane within the meaning of the *McNaghten* Rules; otherwise, the suicide would sever the causal chain if the deceased was sane at the material time.

The *McNaghten* Rules were also applied by the New Zealand Court of Appeal in *Murdoch* v *British Israel World Federation (New Zealand) Inc.*[31] The victim, a tram-driver, was crushed between his tram and a vehicle driven by the defendant's servant, whose negligence was not in issue. The victim remained in hospital for nine months following the accident. Apart from an amputated leg, he suffered other injuries, helplessness and dependence upon others. His wife gave evidence that from the date of the accident her husband increasingly suffered from anxiety and depression and personality change. The medical evidence established that the victim suffered from melancholia from the time of the accident, that melancholia is a condition accompanied by a propensity to commit suicide, and that a person suffering from melancholia would be unable to appreciate whether committing suicide was wrong. Sixteen months after the accident the victim committed suicide and, in an action by his dependants under the *Death by Accident Compensation Act 1908*, the issue for the Court of Appeal was whether the defendant's negligence or the deceased's own act had been the cause of his death. The majority of the Court considered themselves bound by the decision in *McFarland* v *Stewart* and held that although the deceased knew the nature and consequences of his action, there was sufficient medical evidence to support a finding that at the time he committed suicide, the deceased suffered from melancholia to such an extent that he was unable to appreciate that his act of suicide was wrong. The majority further held that, where a bright and cheerful man changed his outlook and personality within a few months after receiving shocking injuries, it was a reasonable inference that the mental change and insanity which led to his suicide were caused by the accident-related injuries he had received. Thus, the majority were satisfied that the causal chain remained intact and the defendant was therefore liable. Had the majority approach in *Murdoch* been applied in the English decision of *Pigney* v *Pointer's Transport Services Ltd*,[32] Mr Pigney's suicide when he was not insane at the material time would have constituted a *novus actus interveniens*.

---

may otherwise constitute a causal chain for the purpose of attributing legal responsibility.' And see *Sarkis* v *Summitt Broadway Pty Ltd Trading As Sydney City Mitsubishi* [2006] NSWCA 358 (no lack of new and extraneous causes intervening between the motor vehicle accident and the victim's suicide); *Holdlen Pty Ltd* v *Walsh* [2000] NSWCA 87 (in the context of workers' compensation legislation, 'Suicide, while deliberate, may often (but not always) be the product of a will so overborne or influenced by the worker's circumstances that it should not be regarded as an intentional act breaking the chain of causation': *per* Giles J.A. at para. 37).

30   (1900) 19 NZLR 22.
31   [1942] 61 NZLR 600 (CA).
32   [1957] 1 WLR 1121.

The sane-insane distinction is arguably inappropriate in those cases where institutions like hospitals, asylums and prisons owe a duty of care to guard patients and inmates from harming themselves because the risk of self-harm in such an environment is the very reason for finding negligence against the defendant for failure to adopt appropriate precautions.[33] In *Pallister* v *Waikato Hospital Board*[34] the widow of a man who had been admitted to hospital because of suicidal tendencies and who had taken his own life while in hospital sued the defendant hospital board for negligence in failing to take sufficient steps to guard against that very eventuality. The majority of the New Zealand Court of Appeal dismissed the widow's action under the *Deaths by Accidents Compensation Act 1952* on the ground that the plaintiff had not proven on a balance of probabilities that the defendant's servants had been negligent. Woodhouse J., who dissented on the question whether there was evidence that the defendant board had been negligent, rejected the argument that the voluntary act of the deceased in throwing himself from the window of a hospital was a new and independent cause of his death. His Honour stated:

> I am unable to accept that submission. It seems clear to me that the consequences of the negligence in this case were in no way interrupted or superseded by the act of the deceased. The risk that he would attempt to commit suicide and in particular, by jumping from a high window, was the very risk to be guarded against. It was the precise and only reason for the sort of precautions that unwisely were removed. Once it has been decided that the removal of those precautions amounted to negligence it would be a remarkable result to hold that the effect of the negligence had been exhausted at the very moment that the foreseeable result of it occurred. The concept of a *novus actus interveniens* does not embrace foreseeable acts in respect of which the duty of care has specifically arisen.[35]

Accordingly, the defendant's failure to discharge its duty of care in these circumstances was 'directly responsible' for Mr Pallister's death.[36] The approach of Woodhouse J. is consistent with that taken by the majority of the House of Lords in *Reeves* v *Commissioner of Police of the Metropolis*.[37] Richmond J., one of the majority judges, expressed the *obiter* view that had there been a failure by the defendant hospital board to use reasonable care to guard Mr Pallister against his known suicidal tendencies, that failure would have been an effective or substantial cause of his death.[38]

---

33 See the Canadian cases of *Stadel* v *Albertson* [1954] 2 DLR 328 (Sask. C.A.) and *Lepine* v *University Hospital* (1964) 50 DLR (2d) 255. This is also the prevailing US approach: see 11 *American Law Reports* 2d 775–800; contra *McFarland* v *Stewart* (1900) 19 NZLR 22.
34 [1975] 2 NZLR 725 (CA).
35 Ibid., 741–2.
36 Ibid., 745.
37 [2000] 1 AC 360 (HL).
38 [1975] 2 NZLR 725, 736. For a comment on the *Pallister* case, see Coote 'Suicide and the Claim of Dependants' [1976] NZLJ 54.

Canada

Canadian courts have also adopted a similar approach to suicide cases in the institutional context. Where suicidal tendencies are absent,[39] hospitals will not be held liable, but if these tendencies are actually known or they were reasonably foreseeable in the circumstances, liability will be imposed. So, in *Villemure* v *L'Hopital Notre-Dame*[40] a hospital and a psychiatrist were held liable for the suicide of a patient. And, in cases of prisoner suicide, it appears from the decision of the British Columbia Court of Appeal in *Funk* v *Clapp*[41] that the *novus actus interveniens* doctrine does not necessarily sever the causal chain between a breach of their duty of care to prisoners by prison authorities and the suicide of a prisoner in their charge. Seaton J.A. considered that *novus actus* could not aid the defendant where the deceased had committed suicide in his cell by hanging himself from the top of his cell door with his own belt two hours after he had been arrested, on the ground that the negligence complained of consisted in the failure to take reasonable care to guard against the very thing that happened.

In terms of actions brought by dependants under fatal accidents legislation, the Canadian courts have maintained the sane-insane distinction such that acts of suicide committed in lucid and sane moments will sever the causal chain and thereby relieve the defendant of liability. *Swami* v *Lo (No. 3)*[42] raised a claim by the widow of a man who committed suicide as a result of injuries suffered in a motor vehicle accident caused by the defendant's negligence. The deceased's injuries had caused severe pain which led to a state of depression, culminating in the suicide. Gould J. refused the widow's claim for compensation under the *Families Compensation Act*, R.S.C.C. 1960. His Honour found that the deceased was sane when he took his own life and held that under fatal accidents legislation the plaintiff must satisfy the reasonable foreseeability requirement.[43] Gould J. held that the suicide was not an injury of the type or extent which the defendant could reasonably have foreseen, and that the death was brought about by the act of the plaintiff himself – a *novus actus interveniens* – for which the defendant cannot be held responsible.[44] And in *Robson* v *Ashworth*[45] Galligan J. denied compensation to the family of a medical patient who committed suicide while sane on the grounds that it is a 'well-recognised rule of public policy that survivors of a person who commits suicide are not entitled to

---

39 *Stadel* v *Albertson* [1954] 2 DLR 328.
40 (1972) 31 DLR (3d) 454.
41 (1986) 68 DLR (4th) 229.
42 (1979) 11 CCLT 210 (B.C.); 105 DLR (3d) 451.
43 *Contra Pigney* v *Pointer's Transport Services Ltd* [1957] 1 WLR 1121 which was decided before the *Wagon Mound* cases decided by the Judicial Committee of the Privy Council: [1961] AC 388 (No. 1); [1967] 1 AC 617 (No. 2).
44 (1979) 11 CCLT 210, 216. Gould J. expressed the *obiter* view that if an injury to the husband's head had triggered a mental disturbance that culminated in suicide, the plaintiff's argument may have carried more weight. Compare *Hayes Estate and Hayes* v *Green and Green* (1983) 30 Sask R 166 (liability imposed for a foreseeable suicide).
45 (1985) 33 CCLT 229 (Ont.H.C.) affirmed (1987) 40 CCLT 164 (Ont. C.A.).

benefit from the suicide'.[46] His Honour indicated that it would be different if the person committed suicide while insane.

The leading Canadian decision on whether the suicide of a 'hypersensitive' person will sever the causal chain is the Ontario Court of Appeal decision in *Cotic v Gray*.[47] The plaintiff's husband suffered serious injuries when the motor vehicle he was driving collided with another motor vehicle, whose driver, whose negligence had caused the accident, was killed. Prior to the accident, the plaintiff's husband was subject to emotional upset and fits of severe depression. Following the accident his condition degenerated from a neurotic to a psychotic condition and he committed suicide 16 months later. The plaintiff, the deceased's widow, brought an action for damages for the benefit of herself and her two infant children for wrongful death against the other driver's estate under the *Fatal Accidents Act*, R.S.O. 1970.[48] At the trial before a jury of the plaintiff's action, the defendant admitted liability for the accident and the parties agreed that the only question to be reserved for the jury was whether the defendant's negligence caused or contributed to the death of the plaintiff's husband. The Ontario Court of Appeal dismissed the defendant's appeal from the trial Judge's judgment for the plaintiff following upon an affirmative answer to that question from the jury. The defendant had argued that the husband's suicide constituted damage of a different character which the reasonable person in the defendant's position would not have foreseen and, as such, amounted to a *novus actus interveniens*. In the course of his judgment, Lacourciere J.A., who delivered the leading judgment in the case, noted the interconnectedness in this case of remoteness of damage-foreseeability issues, the 'egg-shell' or 'thin skull' doctrine[49] (concerning the deceased husband's vulnerability to a post-accident psychotic episode by reason of his history of mental illness), and the *novus actus interveniens* plea. After a comprehensive and detailed review of English and Commonwealth case-law, His Honour held that it was unnecessary to decide whether the deceased's suicide was foreseeable as the defendant was required to take his victim as he finds him, and there was sufficient evidence before the jury to justify its answer that the accident, while not necessarily the sole cause, was a direct and substantial cause of the husband's suicide. Wilson J.A. added, '[u]ndoubtedly as a factual matter the deceased's psychiatric condition played a role in his subsequent suicide but the law would be taking away with one hand what it had given with the other if it were to

---

46   Ibid., 250. In *Pigney v Pointer's Transport Services Ltd* [1957] 1 WLR 1121, another case involving the suicide of an accident victim who was found to be sane at the time of death, Pilcher J. held that although it was against public policy to allow the personal representative of a suicide to succeed in a derivative claim (since that would permit a felon to benefit his or her own estate), it was not against public policy to allow a widow of a suicide to prosecute a statutory cause of action under fatal accidents legislation since no benefit accrued thereby to the estate of the deceased husband.

47   (1981) 124 DLR (3d) 641.

48   Prior to his suicide, the husband had commenced an action for property damage and personal injuries suffered by himself, his wife and their two infant children and this action had been settled prior to trial by the administrator *ad litem* of the deceased driver's estate.

49   *Dulieu v White & Sons* [1901] 2 KB 669, 679 (*per* Kennedy J.).

permit the victim's peculiar vulnerability to break the causal chain...'[50] Thus, it would appear under Canadian law that if the suicide of an accident victim may be said to be the result of a pre-disposing neurosis that flares up after, and as a consequence of, an accident attributable to the defendant's negligence, then that negligence may still be deemed a legally operative cause of the suicide.

The United States of America

Whether the act of suicide severs the causal chain between the defendant's negligence and the death of the accident victim has arisen for consideration by US courts on numerous occasions. The traditional or orthodox judicial view is that self-destruction is a new and independent agency rather than a normal or reasonably foreseeable incident of the risk for which a negligent defendant would be responsible, unless it is the result of an uncontrollable impulse or accomplished in a delirium or frenzy attributable to that negligence, so as to prevent the deceased from appreciating the nature of the act and its consequences.[51] Thus, even if a deceased person's act of suicide has been committed under the pressure of a mental disorder caused by the defendant's negligence, the death is not considered to be the consequence of that negligence, except in those circumstances where the deceased lacked knowledge and appreciation of the act and its consequences or was subjected to an irresistible impulse.

In the early case of *Scheffer* v *Washington City Railroad Co.*[52] the United States Supreme Court required the plaintiff in a fatal accidents legislation claim to prove not only an unbroken chain of causation but also that the death by suicide was the 'natural and probable consequence' of the defendant's negligence. The Supreme Court held that both Scheffer's insanity and his suicide amounted to superseding causes of his death as such condition and event were not 'naturally and reasonably to be expected' from his injury on the train resulting from the negligence of the defendant railway officials. Another early case of *Daniels* v *New York Railroad*[53] concerned an action under a wrongful death statute for the death by suicide of a person made insane as a result of a collision caused by the negligence of the defendant company's servants. In delivering the judgment of the Supreme Court of Massachusetts, Knowlton C.J. stated:

> We are of opinion that the liability of a defendant for a death by suicide exists only when the death is the result of an uncontrollable impulse or is accomplished in delirium or frenzy caused by the collision and without conscious volition to produce death, having knowledge of the physical nature and consequences of the act. An act of suicide resulting from a moderately intelligent power of choice, even though the choice is determined by a disordered mind, should be deemed a new and independent efficient cause of the death...

---

50 (1981) 124 DLR (3d) 641, 673. See also *Wright Estate* v *Davidson* (1992) 88 DLR (4th) 698, 705 (B.C.) (accident victim's suicide considered a *novus actus interveniens* since the decedent had full volition at the time of her self-destructive act).

51 J. Fleming 'Liability for Suicide' (1957) 31 *Australian Law Journal* 587, 589. The US case-law is reviewed in the leading decision of *Arsnow* v *Red Top Cab Co.* (1930) 159 Wash. 137.

52 (1882) 105 US 249 (USSC).

53 (1903) 183 Mass 393.

By the middle of the twentieth century, the US judicial position was expressed in the *American Reports*[54] as follows:

> Where an action is brought under a wrongful death statute the general rule is that suicide constitutes an intervening force which breaks the line of causation from the wrongful act to the death and therefore the wrongful act does not render defendant civilly liable. However where the wrongful act produces such a rage or frenzy that the person injured by the defendant's wrongful act, destroys himself during such rage or frenzy, or in response to an uncontrollable impulse, the act is, according to many dicta, considered as within a part of the line of causation from the defendant's wrongful act to the suicide and defendant's act is held to be the proximate cause of the death.

More recently, the US position appears to be that although the act of suicide is still viewed as an intentional or wilful intervening act which generally or presumptively relieves the defendant of liability, where a person with known suicidal tendencies is placed in the care of prison authorities or other custodians, the failure of the latter to take reasonable precautions to prevent suicide of inmates may constitute a direct and proximate cause of their death.[55]

Section 455 of the American Law Institute's *Restatement of the Law of Torts, Second*[56] addresses the issue of the defendant's liability for acts performed during insanity caused by the defendant's negligent conduct in the following terms:

> If the [defendant's] negligent conduct so brings about the delirium or insanity of another as to make the [defendant] liable for it, the [defendant] is also liable for harm done by the other to himself while delirious or insane, if his delirium or insanity
>
> (a) prevents him from realizing the nature of his act and the certainty or risk of harm involved therein, or
> (b) makes it impossible for him to resist an impulse caused by his insanity which deprives him of his capacity to govern his conduct in accordance with reason.

According to the Commentary on Clause (b), this clause applies where the other's insanity does not deprive him or her of capacity to realise the nature or consequences of their act but the act is done under an irresistible impulse because the insanity has prevented their reason from controlling their actions.[57] However, the fact that the defendant's negligence causes harm to another which results in recurrent attacks of extreme melancholia does not render the defendant liable for death or other harm which the other deliberately inflicts upon himself or herself during a lucid period in an effort to commit suicide because of a dread of the increasingly frequent recurrence of such attacks.[58]

---

54 *American Law Reports* (Annotated) (2nd series, 1950) vol. 11 751, 754, 756.
55 *Sudderth v White* (1981) 621 SW 2d 33 (Court of Appeals of Kentucky); *McLaughlin v Sullivan* (1983) 461 A 2d 123 (Supreme Court of New Hampshire); *Watters v T.S.R. Inc.* (1990) 904 F 2d 378 (US Court of Appeals, Sixth Circuit). See also *Molton v City of Cleveland* (1988) 839 F 2d 240 (the deceased's suicide being foreseeable and within the scope of the risk, it was not deemed to be an independent intervening cause).
56 (1965–79).
57 *Restatement of the Law of Torts, Second* (ALI, 1965–79) 494.
58 Ibid.

Conclusion

As we have seen in this chapter, the five common law jurisdictions surveyed have traditionally relied on the sane-insane distinction to help resolve the intervening causation issue arising in suicide cases. Put simply, liability will be imposed on defendants if their negligence generated such a degree of insanity as to impel their victim to suicide; wilful self-destruction by sane persons, on the other hand, will sever the causal chain and relieve defendants of liability. However, such distinction has fallen out of favour, at least in the institutional context, with the House of Lords as we have seen in their recent decision in *Reeves* v *Commissioner of Police of the Metropolis*.[59] And one wonders what sort of future this distinction has in a more general context in light of the vexed question at what point a person becomes sufficiently insane that the causal chain remains intact and secures the defendant's liability.

What are the alternatives, then? It has been suggested that all suicide cases should be handled in the same way. Accident victims are rendered susceptible to depression, one potential result of which is suicide in extreme cases. As Professor Linden points out, rarely does one take one's own life except when one's mental stability has been affected and, therefore, despite its rarity, suicide might be held not too remote, and negligent defendants might be required to compensate for it whether the victims are insane or not.[60] Nevertheless, as a double-edged sword, justice cuts both ways and the concern might be raised that defendants would be burdened under this approach with excessive liability disproportionate to their civil culpability.

Yet another alternative approach that might be considered is that of contributory negligence as was relied on recently by the House of Lords in *Reeves*. This approach involves a balancing of interests between the various parties. Although there is considerable sympathy for the suicide victims and their surviving dependants, there is also reason to be concerned at imposing on defendants civil responsibility for the deaths of their victims, even though it is by their own hands. Reliance on the notion of contributory fault as a compromise solution arguably affords judges a wider discretion in reaching just results in individual cases. Where victims are lucid and commit suicide without sufficient cause, the courts may allocate part, or perhaps all, of the loss to what they consider to be the contributory fault of the victims.[61] On the other hand, where the victims were so insane that they could not be held legally responsible for the suicide, their surviving dependants may recover in full.

---

59 [2000] 1 AC 360 (HL).
60 A. Linden and B. Feldthusen *Canadian Tort Law* (Butterworths, 8th edn, 2006) 420.
61 Ibid.

Chapter 12

Professional Malpractice

Introduction

This chapter will be devoted primarily to the operation of the *novus actus interveniens* doctrine in the context of medical malpractice where a plaintiff's injuries are exacerbated by subsequent medical treatment which he or she receives for those injuries. Other themes which will be examined include the operation of the doctrine in cases involving the unreasonable refusal to accept medical treatment, wrongful birth claims, and negligence by members of the legal profession.

We shall turn first to cases involving medical negligence. Hospitals and health carers are often involved in situations where the patient presents with injuries which are attributable to the defendant's negligent conduct. Such situations typically include motor vehicle and industrial accidents. However, as a result of the negligence of the hospital and/or health carer, some further damage is sustained by the plaintiff. In such a case, provided a plaintiff acts reasonably in seeking and accepting medical treatment and the original injury is exacerbated by negligence in the administration of the medical treatment, it is the generally accepted view of most common law jurisdictions surveyed in this book that the negligent medical treatment will not be regarded as a *novus actus interveniens* relieving the original defendant of liability for the aggravated injuries, because the original injury may be regarded as carrying some risk that medical treatment might be negligently administered. In those cases where negligent medical treatment is deemed to be a recognisable risk for which an accident victim might hold the original defendant responsible, the plaintiff will be permitted to recover from the original defendant (or his or her insurer) full damages both for the accident-related injuries as well as for the aggravated injuries attributable to the medical negligence, subject to the right of the original defendant to seek contribution and apportionment of damages from the negligent health carers in relation to the aggravated injuries.[1] On the other hand, where the injured plaintiff receives inexcusably bad or grossly negligent medical treatment or advice, such treatment will break the causal chain and the negligent health carer (or insurer) is solely responsible for any exacerbation of the plaintiff's injuries. While the original defendant would remain fully responsible for the accident-related injuries, he or she would not carry any legal responsibility for the aggravated, medically-related injuries.

---

1 *Scout Association of Queensland* v *Central Regional Health Authority* (1997) Australian Torts Reports 81-450.

The United States of America

The long-held and orthodox approach of the US case authorities is to generally hold a negligent defendant liable for injuries which have been exacerbated by subsequent medical treatment, even though such treatment was negligent in the actionable sense. The only qualifications to this general presumption appear to be intentional misconduct, recklessness or gross negligence on the part of the health carer. The law on this point has been put in the leading case of *Thompson v Fox*[2] as follows:

> Doctors, being human, are apt occasionally to lapse from prescribed standards, and the likelihood of carelessness, lack of judgment or of skill, on the part of one employed to effect a cure for a condition caused by another's act, is therefore considered in law as an incident of the original injury, and, if the injured party has used ordinary care in the selection of a physician or surgeon, any additional harm resulting from the latter's mistake or negligence is considered as one of the elements of the damages for which the original wrongdoer is liable.

Thus, generally speaking, actionable or ordinary (as opposed to gross) negligence will not sever the causal chain and the original wrongdoer will also be held responsible for the aggravated, medically-related injuries.

This distinction between ordinary and extraordinary negligence has been maintained in Section 457 of the American Law Institute's *Restatement of the Law of Torts, Second*[3] which states:

> If the negligent actor is liable for another's bodily injury, he is also subject to liability for any additional bodily harm resulting from normal efforts of third persons in rendering aid which the other's injury reasonably requires, irrespective of whether such acts are done in a proper or a negligent manner.

According to the *Restatement*'s accompanying commentary, the damages assessed against the defendant include not only the injury originally caused by the defendant's negligence but also the harm resulting from the manner in which the medical, surgical or hospital services are rendered, irrespective of whether those services are negligently rendered or not, so long as the negligence, if any, is a recognisable risk which is inherent in the human fallibility of those who render such services.[4] As for a rationale for imposing additional liability on the defendant, if the latter knows or should know that his or her negligence may result in harm sufficiently severe to require health care services, the defendant 'should also recognise [negligently-administered health care services] as a risk involved in the other's forced submission to such services, and having put the other in a position to require them, the [defendant] is responsible for any additional injury resulting from the other's exposure to this risk.'[5] By way of illustration, if A's negligence causes serious harm to B requiring B to be taken to a hospital, and a surgeon improperly diagnoses the case and performs

---

2   (1937) 192 A 107, 108 (Pa).
3   (1965–79).
4   *Restatement of the Law of Torts, Second* (ALI, 1965–79) 496–7.
5   Ibid.

an unnecessary operation or, after proper diagnosis, performs a necessary operation carelessly, there is no break in the causal chain and A's negligence is also a legal cause of the additional harm which B sustains.

The *Restatement* commentary also makes it clear that the original defendant is not answerable for harm caused by medical misconduct which is 'extraordinary' in the sense of falling outside the risks which are normally recognised as inherent or incidental in the necessity of submitting to medical treatment.[6] While mere medical misadventure or actionable negligence will not sever the causal chain, recklessly unreasonable medical treatment will. Nor will the original defendant be liable for harm resulting from negligent treatment of a disease or injury which is not due to the defendant's negligence, even though the plaintiff takes advantage of being in hospital to have it treated.[7]

Australia

Australian courts, including the High Court, have consistently held over a long period that only gross medical negligence will sever the causal chain, thereby relieving the original defendant of liability for the aggravated medically-related injury. Otherwise, ordinary actionable medical negligence, or something less like medical misadventure, will not sever the chain and the defendant, along with the negligent health carers, will be responsible therefor. This is the approach adhered to in a long line of workers' compensation cases which have held that the total condition of a worker whose compensable injury is exacerbated by medical treatment, reasonably undertaken to alleviate that injury, is to be causally attributed to the workplace accident.[8] The leading decision is that of the Supreme Court of South Australia in *South Australian Stevedoring Company Limited* v *Holbertson*.[9] That case involved an employer's appeal from an arbitrator's award under the *Workmen's Compensation Act 1932* (S.A.). The employer had unsuccessfully applied for termination of the weekly payment to the respondent worker on the ground that his incapacity at that time was not due to the workplace accident (in which a piece of timber had fallen on his arm, fracturing it) but to improper medical treatment. Following the accident, the worker had been taken to hospital where his arm was placed in a cast but, due to an undetected misalignment of the bones, his left hand and arm had been rendered useless for the purpose of any work. The employer contended that with proper medical treatment the worker would have made a full recovery within four months of the accident, and that since then the ongoing incapacity had been solely attributable to

---

6   Ibid., 498.
7   Ibid. So, for example, if A negligently fractures B's arm forcing B to go to hospital for treatment and, while there, an examination reveals that he is suffering from a hernia, and B decides to take advantage of being in hospital to have a hernia operation performed which is negligently carried out by the surgeon, A is not liable for harm done to B by the hernia operation.
8   See *Lindeman Ltd* v *Colvin* (1946) 74 CLR 313, at 321 (*per* Dixon J.) and *Migge* v *Wormald Bros Industries Ltd* [1972] 2 NSWLR 29, at 48 (NSWCA) (*per* Mason J.A.).
9   [1939] SASR 257.

the medical treatment. The arbitrator held at first instance that the existing incapacity was not referable to any impropriety in medical treatment. The Supreme Court held that the onus rested on the employer to prove *novus actus interveniens*[10] and that the critical issue was whether the employer had demonstrated that the present incapacity was due to the manner in which the worker's injury had been medically treated or whether it can fairly be regarded as resulting from the workplace accident. Napier J., in delivering the Court's judgment, stated:

> The respondent was taken to the hospital, where he was treated by fully qualified practitioners, who acted according to the best of their ability and judgment. In spite of that, by some mistake – either a blunder or an error of judgment – the treatment was ineffective and the arm is useless. It seems to us that it is unnecessary to inquire whether the respondent has a cause of action for negligence against the hospital or any of the doctors who attended him…But it is sufficient to say that there was, in our opinion, no evidence of any gross negligence – any grave departure from the standard of reasonable skill and care – in the treatment of the injury.[11]

And later His Honour added:

> As a matter of common sense we think that a mistake of this kind is a *sequelae* [*sic*] of the injury. When a man gets his arm broken all that he can do is to get it set by a competent practitioner, and he has to take the risk of the doctor making a mistake. If the treatment is so obviously unnecessary or improper that it is in the nature of a gratuitous aggravation of the injury, it may be possible to find the cause of the incapacity without relating it back to the original injury, but in the case of slight negligence…we think that it is impossible to say that the chain of causation is broken…We think that it would be monstrous if the Act, which insures the workman against the consequences of his own negligence, should leave him uninsured against *sequelae* of this kind, in a case where his own conduct has been beyond criticism. It seems to us that, as a matter of reason and justice, the risk of the treatment being less skilful than it might have been is one of the risks of any employment that involves the risk of an injury that requires treatment…[12]

This distinction between ordinary and gross medical negligence which has been applied in Australian workers' compensation cases has also been applied in cases involving the tort of negligence. In the ordinary case where efficient medical services are available to an injured plaintiff and provided he or she acts reasonably in seeking medical treatment, the original injury can be regarded as carrying some risk that such treatment might be negligently given.[13] Nevertheless, the original injury does not carry the risk of medical treatment or advice that is 'inexcusably bad'[14] or 'completely outside the bounds of what any reputable medical practitioner might prescribe'.[15]

---

   10   Citing *Bower* v *Meggitt and Jones* (1916) 86 LJ (KB) 463.
   11   [1939] SASR 257, 263.
   12   Ibid., 264.
   13   *Lawrie* v *Meggitt* (1974) 11 SASR 5, 8; *Beavis* v *Apthorpe* (1962) 80 WN (NSW) 852, 858; *Moore* v *A.G.C. (Insurances) Ltd* [1968] SASR 389, 394.
   14   *Martin* v *Isbard* (1946) 48 WALR 52, 56 (*per* Walker J.).
   15   *Lawrie* v *Meggitt* (1974) 11 SASR 5, 8 (*per* Zelling J.).

It has since been held that a mere error of judgement or medical misadventure will not sever the causal chain. In *Liston v Liston*[16] the plaintiff sustained back injuries in a car accident caused by the defendant's negligence. Her surgeon recommended a laminectomy which was correctly performed but ultimately unsuccessful and which added to her injuries. The plaintiff was left with a permanent back disability. Although expert evidence cast doubts upon the necessity or prudence of the operation, the Supreme Court of South Australia held the defendant liable for the consequential disability. According to Zelling J., even if the surgeon had made an error of judgement in recommending the operation, the defendant could have reasonably foreseen that the plaintiff would accept the surgeon's advice and that further injury might result from error in medical treatment. His Honour could not find any negligence on the surgeon's part and thus no *novus actus interveniens* was established.

The leading case authority in Australia is the High Court's decision in *Mahony v J. Kruschich (Demolitions) Pty Ltd*.[17] There a worker sued his employer for damages for personal injuries sustained by him in the course of his employment. The employer sought contribution from the worker's doctor under Section 5(1)(c) of the *Law Reform (Miscellaneous Provisions) Act 1946* (N.S.W.), alleging that his negligent medical treatment had caused or contributed to the worker's continuing incapacities. In the course of its unanimous judgment, the High Court stated:

> A negligent tortfeasor does not always avoid liability for the consequences of a plaintiff's subsequent injury, even if the subsequent injury is tortiously inflicted. It depends on whether or not the subsequent tort and its consequences are themselves properly to be regarded as foreseeable consequences of the first tortfeasor's negligence.[18]

And the High Court later added:

> When an injury is exacerbated by medical treatment…the exacerbation may easily be regarded as a foreseeable consequence for which the first tortfeasor is liable. Provided the plaintiff acts reasonably in seeking or accepting the treatment, negligence in the administration of the treatment need not be regarded as a *novus actus interveniens* which relieves the first tortfeasor of liability for the plaintiff's subsequent condition. The original injury can be regarded as carrying some risk that medical treatment might be negligently given…[19]

The High Court also observed that the original injury does not carry the risk of 'grossly negligent medical treatment or advice'[20] but, as in the case of so many other courts, did not offer any assistance as to how such negligence might be differentiated from ordinary actionable medical negligence. In the High Court's view, the former type of negligence, being unforeseeable, would sever the causal chain whereas the latter, being foreseeable, would not.

---

16 (1981) 31 SASR 245.
17 (1985) 156 CLR 522.
18 Ibid., 528.
19 Ibid., 529.
20 Ibid., 530.

The *Mahony* case has been subsequently applied by Australian state courts. In *Scout Association of Queensland* v *Central Regional Health Authority*[21] the plaintiff suffered a hip injury as a result of the Scout Association's negligence. As a result of the Health Authority's failure, through its doctors, to diagnose the plaintiff's injury as a hip injury, the plaintiff developed necrosis of the hip. The court held that the Scout Association was not relieved of liability for the hip necrosis as it was considered that the negligent medical treatment was not sufficiently gross to operate as a *novus actus interveniens*. In the result, the Health Authority was found to be 70 per cent responsible for the necrosis while the Scout Association was found to be 30 per cent responsible. The New South Wales Supreme Court has also applied the *Mahony* distinction between ordinary and gross medical negligence in its unreported decision in *Aquilina* v *N.S.W. Insurance Ministerial Corporation*.[22] The plaintiff sued the defendant for compensation for injuries and continuing back pain sustained in two motor vehicle accidents. He also sued two doctors for injuries sustained during a surgical operation necessitated by the two car accidents. During exploratory surgery, the surgeon perforated the plaintiff's right internal iliac artery. Because of the failure by the surgeon and anaesthetist to resuscitate the plaintiff earlier, the plaintiff suffered a cardiac arrest and brain damage. The issue presented to the Court was to determine whether the defendant was liable to compensate the plaintiff not only for the car accident injuries but for the additional incapacities flowing from the negligently performed surgery. Applying the *Mahony* decision, the Court held that the defendant was liable for both (subject to its right to seek contribution against the doctors) on the ground that the doctors' negligence did not amount to gross negligence in the circumstances and that the original car accident injuries carried some risk that negligent medical treatment might be given.[23]

Canada

The Canadian case-law appears somewhat bifurcated on the issue of what degree of medical negligence will sever the causal chain. One strand of authority regards ordinary actionable medical negligence as sufficient to amount to a *novus actus*

---

21 (1997) Australian Torts Reports 81-450.

22 New South Wales Supreme Court No. 12379/92; 11572/92, 5 December 1994.

23 The approach taken by the Australian courts in *Vieira* v *Water Board* [1988] Australian Torts Reports 80-166 demonstrates that it may be possible to decide the *novus actus* issue without the need to categorise the quality of the medical negligence. In that case the plaintiff's hand was injured in a workplace accident and an orthopaedic surgeon, who mistakenly suspected that the plaintiff was suffering from an elbow condition, performed an ulnar nerve transfer to relieve that condition. While the plaintiff had not suffered elbow pain before the operation, he experienced pain in his elbow after the operation, although the pain in his hand had stopped. The New South Wales Court of Appeal affirmed the trial Judge's decision not to hold the defendant liable for the elbow condition on the ground that the workplace injury had not caused it. The elbow pain suffered post-operatively was caused by the intervening medical treatment in the surgeon mistakenly believing that the elbow condition had been caused by the accident. This was not a case of unsuccessful medical treatment being performed to relieve accident-caused symptoms but of treatment performed to relieve symptoms unrelated to the accident.

interveniens while another line of cases is authority for the proposition that the original injury carries some risk of ordinary medical negligence for the defendant. The leading case for the former line of authority is the 1941 decision of the Ontario Court of Appeal in *Mercer* v *Gray*.[24] There the child plaintiff was struck by the defendant's automobile and received fractures of both legs. One of the plaintiff's fractured legs became worse when her doctors mistakenly failed to cut her cast soon enough after a cyanosed condition became evident. At trial the defendant successfully contended that the aggravation of the leg injury due to the lack of skill in the medical treatment could not be attributable to the defendant. The Court of Appeal remitted the case for a new trial on the ground that 'if reasonable care is used to employ a competent physician or surgeon to treat personal injuries wrongfully inflicted, the results of the treatment, even though by an error of treatment the treatment is unsuccessful, will be a proper head of damages.'[25] However, McTague J.A., in delivering the Court's judgment, added:

> There may be cases where the medical or surgical treatment is so negligent as to be actionable. This would be in effect *novus actus interveniens* and the plaintiff would have his remedy against the physician or surgeon.[26]

This approach distinguishes between innocent errors of judgement and actionable mistakes and indeed there may often be a fine line between the two. The problem can be perceived as to whether the damage was the result of the normal incident of the risk created by the defendant's conduct. As medical attention has usually been treated as such a normal risk, it is difficult to understand why bad surgery should be in any other category.[27] As one American commentator has remarked, 'it would be an undue compliment to the medical profession to say that bad surgery is no part of the risk of a broken leg.'[28]

Subsequent cases have applied the *Mercer* v *Gray* distinction and held that the original injury carries only the risk of *bona fide* medical error and that ordinary actionable medical negligence is sufficient to sever the causal chain.[29] So, for example, in *Watson* v *Grant*[30] liability was imposed on the original wrongdoer for the consequences of improper (presumably non-negligent) medical treatment when two unnecessary operations were performed on the injured plaintiff. As Aikens J. explained:

> [I]f A injures B, it is reasonably foreseeable that B will seek advice and treatment for his injuries...it is foreseeable that B will seek advice and treatment from...a qualified doctor. The reasonable man, in my opinion, would be aware that a doctor may err in diagnosis or in treatment, or both, without the patient...having any reason to suppose he is being badly

---

24   [1941] 3 DLR 564.
25   Ibid., 567.
26   Ibid., 568.
27   'Negligence-Causation-*Novus Actus Interveniens*' (1941) 19 *Canadian Bar Review* 610 [author unstated].
28   *Prosser on Torts* (2nd edn) 273.
29   *Block* v *Martin* (1951) 4 DLR 121 (Alta S.C.).
30   (1970) 72 WWR 665 (B.C.).

advised or treated...there is inherent risk that B may suffer further loss or injury because of *bona fide* error on the part of the doctor...the great majority of people who are injured or are ill are well aware that the doctor chosen may make some mistake in diagnosis or treatment, but are driven by necessity to accept the risk. It seems to me plain that it is reasonably foreseeable that a person injured to the extent that medical help is required, is driven to accept risk of medical error.[31]

Implicit in His Honour's judgment is the categorisation of the improper medical treatment as medical misadventure falling short of actionable medical negligence. In a later case, Lacourciere J.A. of the Ontario Court of Appeal similarly observed, '[e]very tortfeasor causing injury to a person placing him in the position of seeking medical or hospital help, must assume the inherent risks of complications, *bona fide* medical error or misadventure...'[32] Two more recent cases have held that a radiologist's failure to diagnose the plaintiff's shoulder injury as a shoulder dislocation and to prescribe appropriate medical treatment amounted to chain-breaking intervening actionable medical negligence, thereby relieving the original wrongdoer (or the statutory compensation fund) of responsibility for the aggravation of the injury thereby caused.[33]

A second line of case-authority has emerged since *Mercer* v *Gray* was decided in 1941. Some Canadian courts have moved closer to the approach adopted by their US and Australian counterparts in their willingness to also impose liability on the original wrongdoer for actionable medical negligence (falling short of gross negligence). So, for example, in *Kolesar* v *Jeffries*[34] Haines J. indicated that an original defendant may be held liable for the subsequent negligence of a doctor or hospital which aggravates a plaintiff's injuries 'unless it is completely outside the range of normal experience'. This test implies that certain instances of actionable medical negligence might well be compensable as falling within the realm of reasonable foreseeability but that more serious and egregious instances would fall beyond the range of foreseeability and thus amount to a *novus actus interveniens*.[35] Other Canadian cases adopting this approach include *Katzman* v *Yaeck*[36] and *Price* v *Milawski*.[37] In the latter case Arnup J.A. of the Ontario Court of Appeal held that one negligent doctor could be held liable for the additional loss caused by another doctor's negligence where the first doctor negligently records incorrect details in a patient's medical record such that it is foreseeable that later another doctor may negligently rely on the accuracy of such record.

---

31 Ibid., 672.

32 *Papp* v *Leclerc* (1977) 77 DLR (3d) 536, 539. His Honour added that the onus rests on the defendant to prove that intervening actionable medical negligence has broken the chain of causation (ibid.).

33 *Rehak* v *McLennan* [1992] O.J. No. 1202 (Q.L.) (Gen. Div.); *Mitchell* v *Rahman*, [2002] MBCA 19 (Man. C.A.).

34 (1976) 9 OR (2d) 41, 43 (Ont. H.C.J.).

35 As we have seen, this approach was adopted by the High Court of Australia in *Mahony* v *J. Kruschich (Demolitions) Pty Ltd* (1985) 156 CLR 522.

36 (1982) 136 DLR (3d) 536.

37 (1977) 82 DLR (3d) 130, 141–2 (Ont. C.A.).

A third category of Canadian case dealing with intervening improper medical treatment has not found it necessary to adopt a strict classification of the medical error as between mere misadventure, ordinary negligence or gross negligence. This has occurred particularly in cases involving omissions. In *Thompson* v *Toorenburgh*[38] a woman with a minor heart condition received injuries in an accident caused by the defendant's negligence. She was treated for lacerations at the hospital and released. She returned to hospital later the same evening and died of a pulmonary oedema precipitated by the accident. It was clear from the evidence that proper medical treatment at the time of the readmission could have saved her life. The original defendant was still held liable for her death. Although there was no specific finding on whether the medical error was negligent or non-negligent,[39] Kirke Smith J. did not consider that the causal chain had been severed. This conclusion was affirmed by the British Columbia Court of Appeal on the ground that the failure to provide an *actus interveniens* which would have saved an accident victim's life was not the same thing as committing an *actus interveniens* that caused her death.[40] And in *Davidson* v *Connaught Laboratories*[41] Linden J. held that a pharmaceutical company's warnings concerning a rabies vaccine were 'inadequate and unreasonable in the circumstances'[42] but that the failure by doctors to disclose material risks associated with the vaccine resulted in the failure of the plaintiff to prove causation. It was not the doctors' practice to discuss neurological side-effects with their patients for fear that the latter might refuse what the former considered as necessary treatment. The *novus actus interveniens* consisted of an independent judgement of the doctors which was interposed between the manufacturer's negligent warnings and the plaintiff's injury.

England

In the recent Court of Appeal decision in *Rahman* v *Arearose Ltd*[43] Laws L.J. observed, '[t]he English authorities are, with deference, somewhat equivocal upon the question'[44] of what degree of intervening medical negligence is required to sever the causal chain between the negligence of the original wrongdoer and the plaintiff's injury.

Early English authorities adhered to the view that gross negligence would amount to a *novus actus interveniens*. In the workers' compensation case of *Rocca* v *Stanley Jones & Co.*[45] a worker's arm had been fractured and had been treated in hospital, but there had been gross negligence on the part of the casualty officer. The arm was not placed in splints but only bound up and the worker had been allowed to return to work. On these facts the arbitrator held that the employers were not liable for

---

38   (1972) 29 DLR (3d) 608 (B.C.).
39   On the facts it is difficult to conclude that the error was mere medical misadventure.
40   *Thompson* v *Toorenburgh* (1975) 50 DLR (3d) 717, 721 *per* Robertson J.A.
41   (1980) 14 CCLT 251 (Ont. H.C.J.).
42   Ibid., 276.
43   [2001] QB 351 (CA).
44   Ibid., 366.
45   (1914) 7 BWCC 101.

incapacity resulting from the medical treatment administered by the casualty officer and the Court of Appeal held, in turn, that the arbitrator's decision had proceeded from a correct interpretation and application of the law. Since then, however, and up until recently, the English case-law has been characterised by a persistent refusal by the courts to concede that negligent medical treatment can be a recognisable risk for which an accident victim might hold the original wrongdoer responsible.[46] In the 1944 decision of the Court of Appeal in *Rothwell* v *Caverswall Stone Co. Ltd*,[47] another workers' compensation case, Du Parcq L.J. reviewed the relevant cases and summarised their legal effect as follows:

> [N]egligent or inefficient treatment by a doctor or other person may amount to a new cause and the circumstances may justify a finding of fact that the existing incapacity results from the new cause, and does not result from the original injury.[48]

Thus, ordinary actionable medical negligence falling short of gross medical negligence would suffice to sever the causal chain. Only medical misadventure or *bona fide* medical error would keep the chain intact.

The leading authority on this issue is the 1949 decision of the House of Lords in *Hogan* v *Bentinck West Hartley Collieries (Owners) Ltd*,[49] another workers' compensation case. The worker, a miner, suffered from a congenital defect – two top joints to his right thumb, the additional joint forming a false thumb in addition to his normal thumb. His false thumb was fractured in a workplace accident and, despite the worker returning to work, the thumb continued to be painful. The worker was sent to hospital by his own doctor where it was discovered that the fracture had not united, and an operation was advised and performed for the removal of the false thumb and the top joint of the normal thumb. On an application by the worker for compensation under the *Worker's Compensation Act 1925* on the ground of pain in the stump, the county court judge, sitting as an arbitrator thereunder, accepted the view of the medical witnesses that the operation was a proper one to cure the congenital deformity but not to cure the pain caused by the workplace accident, and compensation was refused on the ground that the incapacity then existing was due, not to the accident, but to an 'ill-advised' operation. The question before the House of Lords was whether the worker's incapacity resulted from the original workplace injury or the operation. By a majority of three to two,[50] the Law Lords held that the inappropriate medical treatment operated as a *novus actus interveniens*. On a true construction of Section 9 (1) of the *Act* which required that the incapacity for work results from the workplace injury, it was for the arbitrator to determine as a fact whether or not the incapacity existing at the date of the arbitration resulted from the original accident or from the operation. As there was sufficient evidence on which the arbitrator could properly find that the incapacity resulted from the

---

46   J. Fleming 'Liability for Suicide' (1957) 31 *Australian Law Journal* 587, 588.
47   [1944] 2 All ER 350 (CA).
48   Ibid., 365.
49   [1949] 1 All ER 588 (HL).
50   Lords Simonds, Normand and Morton forming the majority with Lords Reid and MacDermott in dissent.

operation, there was no misdirection and no ground for interfering with his award. The majority adopted as a correct statement of the existing law on the issue the above-cited passage from the judgment of Du Parcq L.J. in the *Rothwell* case. Lord Normand stated the principle as follows:

> I start from the proposition, which seems to me to be axiomatic, that if a surgeon, by lack of skill or failure in reasonable care, causes additional injury or aggravates an existing injury and so renders himself liable in damages, the reasonable conclusion must be that his intervention is a new cause and that the additional injury should be attributed to it and not to the original accident. On the other hand, an operation prudently advised and skilfully and carefully carried out should not be treated as a new cause, whatever its consequences may be.[51]

In a forceful dissent, Lord Reid reluctantly accepted previous authority that intervening medical treatment could constitute a *novus actus* but insisted that only 'grave lack of skill and care'[52] could sever the causal chain. Any negligence falling short of that would be attributable to the original wrongdoer and the health carers. As a workers' compensation case, it should be noted that *Hogan* is merely persuasive in the context of the tort of negligence.[53]

The law on this point as stated in the *Rothwell* and *Hogan* cases appears to have been endorsed by the Judicial Committee of the Privy Council in *Algol Maritime Limited* v *Acori*.[54] There the plaintiff was employed by the defendants under a seaman's employment contract and suffered a back injury from a fall during the course of his employment. One of the questions raised on appeal was whether a laminectomy operation performed on the plaintiff after the date of the accident severed the causal chain between the accident and the plaintiff's disability. The trial Judge had made the following findings:

> In my view the operation was an integral and ongoing part of [the plaintiff's] treatment as perceived by the doctors in Spain who were treating the plaintiff and does not constitute a *novus actus interveniens*. The operation with hindsight and in the opinion of the expert medical witness Mr Wade...ought not to have been attempted where there was no evidence of sciatic pain and not so soon after the injury was sustained. However that is not to say

---

51 [1949] 1 All ER 588, 596.

52 Ibid., 607. See *Conley* v *Strain* [1988] IR 628. The proposition that only medical treatment so grossly negligent as to be a completely inappropriate response to the injury inflicted by the defendant should operate to break the causal chain was approved by the Court of Appeal in *Webb* v *Barclays Bank plc and Portsmouth Hospitals NHS Trust* [2001] EWCA Civ 1141; [2002] PIQR P8; [2001] Lloyd's Rep. Med. 500 at [55] (the subsequent negligence of a surgeon in advising the plaintiff to undergo an above-the-knee amputation of her leg did not 'eclipse' the defendant employer's original wrongdoing). Thus, if the plaintiff acts reasonably in seeking or accepting treatment, negligence in performing the treatment will not necessarily sever the causal chain relieving the first tortfeasor from liability for the plaintiff's aggravated condition as the original injury can be regarded as carrying some risk that medical treatment might be negligently given.

53 Professor Fleming has argued that the same conclusion would follow *a fortiori* in cases of common law negligence. See J. Fleming 'Liability for Suicide', 588.

54 [1997] UKPC 38 (21 July 1997) (Gibralter).

that the doctors treating the plaintiff were negligent in any way...Their intervention did not break the proximate chain of causation.[55]

Their Lordships refused to interfere with the finding that the laminectomy did not break the chain of causation, and held that the lower courts had not erred in directing themselves in accordance with the law as laid down in the *Rothwell* and *Hogan* cases. Here, the medical treatment amounted to mere medical misadventure, but their Lordships indicated that if the medical treatment had been negligently performed, it might amount to 'a new and separate cause of the injury in which case the chain of causation...might be broken'.[56]

The English Court of Appeal has had occasion to deal with intervening medical negligence in a number of cases. In *Robinson* v *The Post Office*[57] the plaintiff technician slipped and injured his leg through the defendant employer's negligence. To guard against infection a test dose of anti-tetanus serum was administered. Instead of waiting the usual time of half an hour for a reaction, a doctor administered the full shot after only one minute. The plaintiff subsequently developed a severe reaction to the anti-tetanus shot owing to a rare allergy and this resulted in encephalitis and brain damage. The Court of Appeal held that the doctor was not liable in negligence as it was most unlikely that a proper test dose would have disclosed the plaintiff's allergy. Thus the failure to wait the prescribed time before administering the anti-tetanus shot did not cause the plaintiff's injury and could not, therefore, constitute a *novus actus interveniens*. In its 2002 decision in *Forbes* v *Merseyside Fire and Civil Defence Authority*[58] the Court of Appeal held that a *bona fide* medical error of judgement was not sufficient to sever the causal chain, without making any reference to the *Rothwell* and *Hogan* cases. The plaintiff was a divisional commander of the Merseyside Fire and Civil Defence Authority who sustained a groin strain and a hernia while undergoing a lifting strength test under the supervision of the second defendant. Due to his injuries, the plaintiff was ultimately retired by the first defendant and he claimed damages both for the negligently-caused injury itself and for the consequential financial loss as a result of his early retirement. The second defendant argued that she should be liable only for damages attributable to the injuries themselves and that she should not be liable for the consequential financial loss on the ground that the Authority had acted on negligent advice tendered to it by its occupational health doctor. It was alleged that when the early retirement decision had been taken, insufficient time had elapsed since the accident to make it possible to reach an appropriate conclusion concerning the prospects of the plaintiff being able to continue to work. It was also argued that subsequent reports of medical experts had concluded that there was no sufficient disability to have justified the Authority's decision to retire the plaintiff. Latham L.J. accepted the trial Judge's conclusion, however, that the advice of the doctors was neither negligent nor unreasonable but was rather furnished in good faith. At most the advice amounted to an error of judgement which could not be considered sufficient

---

55   Ibid., para. 8.
56   Ibid., para. 9.
57   (1974) 2 All ER 737 (CA).
58   [2002] EWCA Civ.1067.

to sever the causal chain. Accordingly, the second defendant was also responsible for the plaintiff's financial loss. The conclusion of the Court of Appeal on the *novus actus* issue could well have been accommodated by an application of the rule laid down in the *Rothwell* and *Hogan* cases. It would appear that that rule remains good law in England today.[59] Perhaps as a matter of procedural fairness, the approach of the US and Australian courts, in holding that intervening negligent medical treatment can be a recognisable risk for which an accident victim might hold the original wrongdoer responsible, is preferable. As Professor Linden has observed, it is confusing and somewhat arbitrary to make liability for the intervening medical error turn on whether or not there is actionable negligence.[60] It may be harsh to require an injured plaintiff to undertake two actions to recover full damages when the original defendant triggered the chain of events. It might be preferable to hold the original defendant liable for medical negligence (falling short of gross negligence) who could then sue the negligent health carers for contribution. The original defendant would thus, and for good reason, bear more of the procedural burden, and the plaintiff's recovery would be facilitated more expeditiously.

Refusal to Accept Medical Treatment as *Novus Actus Interveniens*

A line of English workers' compensation cases has considered the employer's contention that the worker's incapacity is the result of unwillingness to undergo medical treatment rather than of the workplace accident itself. This culminated in the case of *Steele* v *Robert George & Co.*[61] in which the House of Lords held that where the worker's refusal has been unreasonable, he or she is not entitled to compensation. As Viscount Simon L.C. stated:

> [T]he Workmen's Compensation Acts do not contain any express provision that the weekly payment during incapacity shall come to an end, or be reduced, if the workman unreasonably refuses to undergo a surgical operation or other medical treatment for the purpose of ending, or diminishing, the incapacity. This ground of relief to the employer is based on the view that, if the proximate cause of the continuing incapacity is the unreasonable refusal of a workman to avail himself of surgical or medical skill, it can no longer be said that the incapacity 'results from the injury' within the meaning of the Workman's Compensation Act, 1925, s. 9, after the time when the rejected remedy might be confidently expected to bring about a cure.[62]

---

59   But see the Court of Appeal decision in *Webb* v *Barclays Bank* [2001] EWCA Civ 1141 mentioned at n. 52 *supra*. The decision of the High Court of Australia in *Mahony* v *J. Kruschich (Demolitions) Pty Ltd* (1985) 156 CLR 522 was referred to but neither endorsed nor rejected by Laws L.J. in his judgment in *Rahman* v *Arearose Ltd* [2001] QB 351, 366 (CA). As for intervening pharmaceutical negligence, the Court of Appeal has held in *Prendergast* v *Sam & Dee Ltd* [1989] 1 Med LR 36 that a pharmacist's foreseeable negligence in misreading a doctor's prescription and supplying the patient with the wrong drug did not sever the causal chain from the doctor's initial negligence in writing an illegible prescription.
60   A. Linden and B. Feldthusen *Canadian Tort Law* (Butterworths, 8th edn, 2006) 416.
61   [1942] 1 All ER 447 (HL).
62   Ibid., 448.

The test of reasonableness was also relied on by Starke J. in his judgment in *Adelaide Chemical and Fertilizer Company Limited* v *Carlyle*.[63] There the deceased, an acid burn victim, did not follow advice given to him in hospital to seek the assistance of a doctor on the following day but, in His Honour's view, the evidence did not establish any fault on the part of the deceased or his wife that might otherwise have severed the causal chain. According to Starke J., '[a]fter treatment at the Adelaide Hospital, the deceased did not report to the nearest doctor next day, as advised, but his wife treated him to the best of her ability with tannemol, which a chemist advised her was a proper treatment for burns, as in fact it was, and she called in a doctor so soon as unexpected complications developed.'[64] The defendant was thus not relieved of responsibility for the deceased's death. Later Australian cases involving a refusal to accept medical treatment have also considered as determinative whether the plaintiff's refusal is reasonable in the prevailing circumstances. In *Walker-Flynn* v *Princeton Motors Pty Ltd*[65] it was held to be relevant evidence for the jury to consider that the plaintiff's refusal to use contraceptives to mitigate the damage further pregnancies would cause to her crushed pelvis arose because the plaintiff was a Catholic and rejected birth control. The jury concluded she acted reasonably and the causal chain thus remained intact. In *Boyd* v *SGIC*,[66] however, a decision by the son of a Jehovah's Witness to refuse a blood transfusion in order to placate his father was held to be an unreasonable failure to mitigate damage.[67]

The Ontario Court of Appeal has adopted a somewhat different approach in two cases decided in the 1980s. In *Ippolito* v *Janiak*[68] and *Brain* v *Mador*[69] it was held that when accident victims unreasonably refuse medical treatment their damages will be reduced because of failure to mitigate their loss, but they will not be denied compensation (as they otherwise would in the wake of a successful *novus actus* plea). The burden would appear to be on the defendant to prove that the plaintiff's refusal to mitigate was unreasonable.[70] A contrary authority is the decision of the Judicial Committee of the Privy Council in *Selvanayagam* v *University of West Indies*.[71]

---

63   (1940) 64 CLR 514. This case is examined in more detail in Chapter 4.
64   Ibid., 528.
65   (1960) SR (NSW) 488.
66   [1978] Qd R 195.
67   The cases are not readily distinguishable apart from the plaintiff's less serious condition in *Walker-Flynn*. For a Canadian decision involving refusal of a blood transfusion see *Hobbs* v *Robertson* (2004) 243 DLR (4th) 700 where the Supreme Court of British Columbia refused to hold a surgeon liable for the death of a patient due to blood loss when the patient had signed a document releasing the surgeon and hospital from 'any responsibility whatsoever' for complications arising from the patient's refusal to accept blood. The effective cause of death was the patient's refusal to accept blood rather than the surgeon's negligence in creating the circumstances in which a life-saving blood transfusion became necessary.
68   (1981) 18 CCLT 39.
69   (1985) 32 CCLT 157. See also *Gray* v *Gill* [1993] B.C.J. No. 2289, 18 CCLT (2d) 120, 133 (S.C.); but *cf.* where a refusal to mitigate is deemed reasonable: *Engel* v *Kam-Ppelle Holdings Ltd* [1993] S.C.J. No. 4, 15 CCLT (2d) 245.
70   *Janiak* v *Ippolito* [1985] 1 SCR 146; *Munce* v *Vinidex* [1974] 2 NSWLR 235 (CA).
71   (1983) 1 All ER 824 (JCPC).

There the plaintiff university lecturer was injured when he fell into an unguarded ditch. Although he was rendered virtually unemployable, he refused to undergo a recommended operation which was said to have 'quite good' chances of enabling him to return to work within six months. The plaintiff's refusal was prompted by his awareness that his diabetes increased the risk of infection. The Privy Council held that the onus of proving the reasonableness of his refusal, and failure to comply with the duty to mitigate his damage, lay upon the plaintiff. The plaintiff discharged this onus as the medical advice was merely one factor among many to be weighed in determining whether the refusal was reasonable.

Wrongful Birth Claims and Plaintiff's Failure to Mitigate Damage Through Termination of Pregnancy

Wrongful birth actions originate where it is claimed that there has been a negligent failure of contraception, sterilisation or abortion. A plaintiff can institute proceedings against the medical practitioner who failed to prevent her conception and pregnancy. The critical issues to be resolved by the courts include whether damages should be awarded to the mother for the birth of the child as a result of the failure of the contraception device or negligently-tendered contraception advice and, if so, what heads of damage are recoverable. In terms of causation, the issue arises as to whether the mother's refusal to terminate the pregnancy, or persistence in having intercourse in the knowledge of such medical negligence, amounts to a *novus actus interveniens* relieving the medical practitioner of liability.

Some courts have adopted a strict and cautious approach to the intervening causation issue, as illustrated in the decision of the New South Wales Court of Appeal in *CES v Superclinics (Aust.) Pty Ltd*.[72] In that case doctors negligently failed to detect a young woman's pregnancy. When her pregnancy was finally diagnosed, she was too far along in her pregnancy to have an abortion. She claimed damages against the doctors for the cost of raising her healthy child. The Court of Appeal dismissed her 'wrongful birth' claim for various reasons, one of which was the characterisation of the plaintiff's own conduct in not giving up her newborn child for adoption as a *novus actus interveniens*. According to Priestley J.A.:

> The point in the present case is that the plaintiff chose to keep her child. The anguish of having to make the choice is part of the damage caused by the negligent breach of duty, but the fact remains, however compelling the psychological pressure on the plaintiff may have been to keep the child, the opportunity of choice was in my opinion real and the choice made was voluntary. It was this choice which was the cause, in my opinion, of the subsequent cost of rearing the child.[73]

---

72 (1995) 38 NSWLR 47.
73 Ibid., 84–5. In the US case of *Albala v City of New York* (1981) 445 NYS 2d 108 (CA), the infant plaintiff was conceived after her mother's uterus had been perforated and after she had had an abortion and also after a malpractice claim for the perforated uterus had been commenced by her mother. Wachtler J. held that no cause of action for the pre-conception tort was cognisable as the mother was in the best position to avoid the damage to her child.

A more plaintiff-sensitive and empathetic approach has been taken by the English courts. In *Emeh v Kensington, Chelsea and Westminster Area Health Authority*,[74] the plaintiff underwent sterilisation. Despite this she conceived again but did not discover the pregnancy until well into the second trimester. She refused to undergo a lawful abortion to avoid a further operation. The trial Judge held that she was not entitled to recover the cost of bringing up her congenitally abnormal child because her refusal to terminate the pregnancy was unreasonable and, as such, amounted to a *novus actus*. The Court of Appeal reversed this judgment, recognising that abortion at such a late period in the pregnancy was attended by trauma and risk. Slade L.J. held that, except for the most exceptional circumstances, a choice to refuse termination of pregnancy could not be regarded as unreasonable.[75] Where the defendant has negligently created the plaintiff's dilemma, he or she should not be permitted to successfully claim that the plaintiff acted unreasonably in deciding on how to respond to that dilemma.[76]

In *McFarlane v Tayside Health Board*[77] the House of Lords confirmed that the failure to undergo a termination of pregnancy or the failure to give up the child for adoption following birth did not break the chain of causation between a negligently performed sterilisation operation or negligent advice as to its success and the birth.[78] This case involved the first plaintiff regaining his fertility after a vasectomy. The operation was carried out skilfully and with due care and the plaintiffs were advised to adopt contraceptive measures until sperm samples had been analysed. Five months after the operation, the surgeon advised the first plaintiff that his sperm counts were negative and that contraceptive measures were no longer necessary. The plaintiffs acted on this advice but the second plaintiff again became pregnant and gave birth to a healthy daughter. The plaintiffs sued the defendant claiming negligence in the compilation of the seminal analysis record and in advising the plaintiff that he could dispense with contraceptive measures when the defendant had not received two samples which tested negative for motile sperm. Although the defendant was not relieved of responsibility on the basis of a successful *novus actus* plea, their Lordships did limit the recoverable heads of damages. A similar conclusion was reached on the intervening causation issue in the Australian case of *Melchior v Cattanach*.[79] There the female plaintiff had undergone a sterilisation procedure which proved to be ineffective. It was alleged that the defendant medical practitioner negligently failed to warn her of the possibility that the operation may not be effective and that such negligence was a material cause of her pregnancy.

---

74 [1984] 3 All ER 1044 (CA).
75 Ibid., 1053.
76 Ibid.
77 [1999] 3 WLR 1301 (HL).
78 Ibid., 1311, 1317, 1339 and 1347. Likewise where a child develops a rare condition which is considered to be a natural and foreseeable consequence of childbirth: *Groom v Selby* [2001] EWCA Civ 1522; [2002] Lloyd's Rep. Med. 1. But it may be otherwise in the case of disabilities due to an infection arising after the perinatal period since the risk of disablement to an otherwise healthy child is one of life's vicissitudes: A.M. Dugdale and M.A. Jones (eds) *Clerk & Lindsell on Torts* (Sweet & Maxwell, 19th edn, 2006) [114], para. 2–103.
79 [2000] QSC 285 (23 August 2000).

Holmes J. rejected the arguments that the failure of the plaintiffs to give up their child for adoption or to terminate the pregnancy was either a *novus actus interveniens* or a failure to mitigate damage. Rather than an interruption in the causal chain, such failures were more of a failure to interrupt such chain. According to His Honour, one could not assume that resorting to abortion or adoption would be less catastrophic than the decision to keep the child. In effect, then, the decision of the plaintiffs could not be said to be unreasonable in the circumstances.

By contrast, where a plaintiff knows that she is not sterile following a failed sterilisation operation and decides nevertheless to engage in sexual intercourse without taking contraceptive measures, the causal chain between the negligent performance of the surgery and the subsequent birth of the child will be held to be severed. The plaintiff's unreasonable conduct will be deemed to constitute a *novus actus interveniens*.[80]

Intervening Negligence by Members of the Legal and Accounting Professions

Most professional malpractice cases involving intervening causation issues are drawn from the medical field but a few such cases arise from time to time in the legal field. We have already examined two such cases in earlier chapters. In *Roberge v Bolduc*[81] the Supreme Court of Canada held that the intervening negligent legal advice of a notary in the context of a title search did not amount to a *novus actus interveniens* as the initial negligent legal advice tendered by the defendant notary had necessitated the plaintiff's seeking a second legal opinion and such course of action was not unreasonable in the circumstances. And in *Bennett v Minister of Community Welfare*[82] the High Court of Australia rejected the defendant's plea

---

80   *Sabri-Tabrizi* v *Lothian Health Board* 1998 SLT 607, 610–11, citing *The Oropesa* [1943] P 32, 39 (*per* Lord Wright); *McKew* v *Holland and Hannen and Cubitts (Scotland) Ltd* [1969] 3 All ER 162. But see *Pidgeon* v *Doncaster Health Authority* [2002] Lloyd's Rep. Med. 130 (County Court) where the judge distinguished *Sabri-Tabrizi* and *McKew*. There the plaintiff was negligently advised in 1988 that a smear test for cervical cancer was normal when it actually showed pre-cancerous abnormalities. A further test in 1997 resulted in a diagnosis of cervical cancer. During the intervening period the plaintiff had received four letters from the defendants' cervical cancer screening programme about the need to have a smear test. Although she had been aware that she could develop cervical cancer, the plaintiff had not undergone further testing because she found it painful and embarrassing. The plaintiff's failure to undergo further smear testing was held not to sever the causal chain. *Sabri-Tabrizi* and *McKew* were distinguished on the basis that in those cases the plaintiffs were aware of their particular condition whereas Ms Pidgeon did not know of her condition and had been reassured by the 1988 test result. As the Court observed, there was 'an important difference between a claimant indulging in behaviour against a background of known vulnerability, whether it be weakness of the leg or ability to conceive, and a claimant failing to take steps which may reveal a condition, if in fact present, having previously been reassured that it was not present' (at [23]). Although her failure was not 'so utterly unreasonable' as to sever the causal chain, Ms Pidgeon was adjudged to be two-thirds contributorily negligent.

81   [1991] 1 SCR 374. This case is examined in more detail in Chapter 4.

82   (1992) 176 CLR 408. This case is examined in more detail in Chapter 7.

that the intervening negligent legal advice tendered to the plaintiff by a barrister amounted to a *novus actus*. The defendant's negligence remained the legal cause of the plaintiff's loss since there would have been no need for the plaintiff to request the barrister's legal opinion if the defendant had properly discharged his duty of care. Negligent legal advice was the very risk against which the defendant had a legal duty to protect the plaintiff.

Another case involving the negligence of both accountants and solicitors has emanated from Queensland. In *O'Brien* v *Thorpe Nominees Pty Ltd*[83] the plaintiff company approached accountants (the second defendants) seeking to find a secure investment. The accountants introduced the plaintiff to a property developer who wished to borrow money and approached their solicitors (the first defendants) to arrange the loan. The accountants were aware that the developer had serious liquidity problems and had had difficulty borrowing from other sources, but failed to inform the plaintiff and the solicitors of this. The developer's property was already mortgaged and, as a second mortgage was not satisfactory to the plaintiff, the accountants recommended mortgage insurance as an added security in order to further the transaction. A provisional agreement for the loan was made but the solicitors were instructed not to proceed without first obtaining mortgage insurance. The loan was then finalised by the solicitors and the money was advanced to the developer. However, no mortgage insurance had been obtained. Because of the urgency of the matter, the solicitors merely obtained an undertaking that the premium for the mortgage insurance would be paid. Neither the plaintiff nor the accountants were told that no insurance had been obtained. On the developer's default in the loan's repayment, the plaintiff lost the entire amount advanced to the developer. The plaintiff sued the accountants and solicitors in negligence. The trial Judge held that both the accountants and the solicitors had been negligent, and rejected the accountants' contention that the solicitors' negligence amounted to a *novus actus interveniens*. The trial Judge considered that the solicitors' negligence was of a general kind which had been reasonably foreseeable. An appeal and cross-appeal by the solicitors and accountants to the Supreme Court of Queensland (Full Court) was dismissed. It was held on the analogy of *Mahony* v *J. Kruschich (Demolitions) Pty Ltd*[84] that the solicitors' negligence was not so 'inexcusably bad' as to exonerate the accountants from liability. Responsibility was attributed one-third to the accountants and two-thirds to the solicitors. Underlying factors supporting the rejection of the *novus actus* plea included the fact that the solicitors' intervention had not only been foreseeable but had been intended by the accountants, the degree of urgency concerning the transaction, and the lack of critical information supplied to the solicitors. The accountants' duty extended to the giving of full and proper advice to the solicitors and the accountants' negligence continued to operate after the solicitors' negligence had occurred.

In 2005 the High Court of Australia considered whether the continued illegal trading activities of a travel agent severed the causal chain between the negligent

---

83 (1987) Australian Torts Reports 80-143, *sub. nom. Thorpe Nominees Pty Ltd* v *Henderson & Lahey* [1988] 2 Qd R 216 (FC).

84 (1985) 156 CLR 522.

misstatements of an accountant and an auditor and the financial loss suffered by the plaintiff. In *Travel Compensation Fund* v *Tambree*[85] an accountant and auditor respectively prepared and audited the financial statements of a travel agent for two successive financial years, knowing that those statements would be submitted to the plaintiff Travel Compensation Fund for the purpose of maintaining the agent's participation in the Fund. The statements were false and misleading and failed to reveal a significant trading loss. On 23 February 1999 the agent's participation in the Fund was terminated. Her licence was thereby also terminated, but she continued trading unlawfully from the same premises until the Department of Fair Trading closed them on 20 April 1999. The Fund paid to persons who had dealt with the travel agent compensation amounting to some $143,000, all but $13,000 of which related to moneys paid to the agent during the time she was engaged in illegal trading. The plaintiff Fund sought to recover from the defendants, the accountant and auditor, the larger sum as common law damages arising from their negligence and misleading and deceptive conduct. The High Court held that the agent's continued trading, after her participation in the Fund had been terminated, did not sever the causal connection between the defendants' negligent conduct and the plaintiff's loss, on the ground that had the defendants acted properly, the plaintiff would not have suffered any loss following 23 February 1999 because the regulatory steps that were taken on 20 April 1999 to stop the agent from trading would have been taken much sooner. Moreover, the plaintiff's reliance on the accuracy of the financial statements was considered reasonable in the circumstances.[86] Gleeson C.J. preferred to adopt a 'scope of the risk' approach in resolving the intervening causation issue.[87] According to the Chief Justice, the travel agent's continued illegal trading did not transcend 'the scope of the risk against which the [plaintiff] attempted to obtain protection' since the risk that an insolvent agent would keep trading until forced to close down 'was part of the risk against which the [plaintiff] was seeking to protect itself when it considered the financial statements...'[88]

---

85 (2005) 224 CLR 627.
86 Ibid., 644 (*per* Gummow and Hayne JJ).
87 Ibid., 641. See Chapter 7 for a full examination of the 'scope of the risk' approach.
88 Ibid., 640.

Chapter 13

Rescue of Persons and Property

Introduction

In the 1880 decision of the Court of Common Pleas in *Scaramanga & Co.* v *Stamp*[1] Cockburn C.J. observed:

> The impulsive desire to save human life when in peril is one of the most beneficial instincts of humanity…it is of the utmost importance that the promptings of humanity in this respect should not be checked or interfered with by prudential considerations as to injurious consequences.[2]

Since that time, courts in various common law jurisdictions have transposed these observations of Cockburn C.J. from a maritime perils context into a general context. Eventually the courts developed the common law such that a negligent defendant is now under a duty of care to would-be rescuers who come to the aid of a third person imperilled by the defendant's negligence.[3] The rationale for the imposition of such a duty of care to the rescuer was because the tortfeasor ought reasonably to have had the rescuer in contemplation as being exposed to the risk of injury in seeking to extricate the third person from the perilous situation created by the defendant's negligence.[4] In extending legal protection to would-be rescuers, public policy is served in the sense of encouraging (or, at least, not discouraging) acts of rescue.

In earlier times rescuers fared badly in the courts. Both voluntary assumption of risk[5] and causation[6] were invoked to regularly deny them compensation. In terms of the intervening causation issue, it was held that the rescuer's 'voluntary' act in attempting the rescue severed the causal chain.[7] Later cases came to recognise that spontaneous action taken under pressure and out of a sense of duty ought not to be characterised as 'voluntary' in the true sense.[8] Today the critical question is whether

---

1 (1880) 5 CPD 295. This case laid down that deviation in the course of a voyage in order to save life is an excuse for apparent breach of the terms of a charter party.
2 Ibid., 304.
3 *Haynes* v *Harwood* [1935] 1 KB 146 (CA); *Baker* v *T.E. Hopkins & Son Ltd* [1959] 3 All ER 225 (CA).
4 A.L. Goodhart 'Rescue and Voluntary Assumption of Risk' (1934) 5 *Cambridge Law Journal* 192, 197–8.
5 *Kimball* v *Butler Bros* (1910) 15 OWR 221 (Ont. CA); *Cutler* v *United Dairies (London), Ltd* [1933] 2 KB 297 (CA).
6 *Anderson* v *Northern Railway Company* (1875) 25 UCCP 301 (CA); *Evenden* v *Manning Shire Council* (1929) 30 SR (NSW) 52 (FC).
7 *Evenden* v *Manning Shire Council* (1929) 30 SR (NSW) 52 (FC).
8 *Haynes* v *Harwood* [1935] 1 KB 146 (CA).

the rescuer's intervention is a foreseeable and normal response to the peril created by the defendant's negligence and it is held to be such as a general principle.[9] Absent gross negligence or recklessness on the rescuer's part,[10] a reasonably attempted act of rescue will not amount to a *novus actus interveniens* and the defendant will thus not be allowed to be absolved from responsibility to the rescuer for the injurious consequences flowing from a danger which he or she had created. In rescue cases where the plaintiff's conduct has been considered particularly meritorious by the courts, the law has sympathetically stretched foreseeability to what Professor Fleming terms a 'transparent fiction'.[11]

Development of the Case-Law

The earliest instances of damages being awarded to rescuers occurred in North America in the early part of the twentieth century. In the 1910 Canadian case of *Seymour* v *Winnipeg Electric Railway*[12] the Manitoba Court of Appeal refused to follow earlier authority and held, on a demurrer, that a rescuer could recover damages from a negligent wrongdoer. Richards J. observed, 'the trend of modern legal thought is toward holding that those who risk their safety in attempting to rescue others who are put in peril by the negligence of third persons are entitled to claim such compensation from such third persons for injuries they receive in such attempts.'[13] This is *a fortiori* in the case of the infirm and the helpless. The breakthrough in the United States of America occurred eleven years later in *Wagner* v *International Railroad Company*[14] where Cardozo J. articulated observations which have since been adopted throughout the common-law world:

> Danger invites rescue. The cry of distress is the summons to relief. The law does not ignore these reactions of the mind in tracing conduct to its consequences. It recognises them as normal. It places their effects within the range of the natural and probable. The wrong that imperils life is a wrong to the imperilled victim; it is a wrong also to his rescuer. The risk of rescue, if only it be not wanton, is born of the occasion. The emergency begets the man.

Since then, the US courts have taken the view that the defendant's act is not only a wrong to the person imperilled, but also to the rescuer because the wrongdoer ought to have foreseen that his or her act would cause the rescuer to embark on a risky rescue. Indeed, some courts have regarded such altruism as not only foreseeable but natural and probable.[15] Section 294 of the American Law Institute's *Restatement of the*

---

    9   *Chapman* v *Hearse* (1961) 106 CLR 112.
    10   As for which see later in this chapter.
    11   J. Fleming *The Law of Torts* (The Law Book Company Limited, 9th edn, 1998) 248, citing *Urbanski* v *Patel* (1978) 84 DLR (3d) 650. See also *Chapman* v *Hearse* (1961) 106 CLR 112. Both cases will be discussed later in this chapter.
    12   (1910) 13 WLR 566 (Man. CA).
    13   Ibid., 588.
    14   (1921) 232 NY 176, 180.
    15   *Liming* v *Illinois Central Railway* (1890) 81 Iowa 246.

Law of Torts, Second[16] states in substance that an act or omission which negligently puts a third person in peril subjects the defendant to liability to others who are led by their perception of the third person's peril to bring themselves within reach of the dangerous effects of the defendant's conduct. The rescuer's act in attempting to rescue the third person is not generally regarded as a superseding cause relieving the defendant of liability.

Despite these North American developments, the Full Court of the Supreme Court of New South Wales still denied recovery in a 1929 case to the personal representative of a school teacher who had drowned in his attempt to rescue a 12-year-old girl who was one of his students. In *Evenden* v *Manning Shire Council*[17] the Court held that the conduct of the deceased constituted a *novus actus interveniens*, rejecting the plaintiff's contention that the deceased 'of necessity' plunged into the water in endeavouring to save a child imperilled by the defendant's negligence. Halse Rogers J., in delivering the Court's judgment, said:

> The [plaintiff] has, in my view, confounded a moral with a legal obligation…From a legal point of view, no damage resulted to the deceased from the negligence of the defendant. Undoubtedly such negligence created the emergency in which he had to act, and likewise, but for such negligence he would not have met his death. But between the negligence of the defendant and the death of the deceased, there is a *novus actus interveniens*, the voluntary determination of the deceased to attempt to save life. The negligence of the defendant did not affect him at all except by way of moral compulsion, and his death cannot be said legally to result from such negligence.[18]

This somewhat legalistic and technical approach began to be displaced in England, following closely on the heels of the North American developments. In *Brandon* v *Osborne Garrett and Company Ltd*[19] the plaintiffs, husband and wife, were in a shop when a portion of the glass skylight dislodged and fell towards the husband. On seeing it falling, the wife immediately and instinctively clutched her husband's arm and tried to pull him out of harm's way but was herself injured. In holding in favour of the plaintiffs, Swift J. said, 'if [the wife] did something which a reasonable person in the circumstances ought not to have done she would not be entitled to damages, but if what she did was done instinctively and was in the circumstances a natural and proper thing to do, I think she is entitled to recover.'[20] And in *Cutler* v *United Dairies (London), Ltd*[21] Slesser L.J. observed by way of an *obiter dictum*,[22] '[t]here may be cases, where, for example, a man sees his child in great peril in the street and, moved

---

16 (1965–79).
17 (1929) 30 SR (NSW) 52 (FC).
18 Ibid., 58.
19 [1924] 1 KB 548 (CA). This case is examined in more detail in Chapter 6.
20 Ibid., 552.
21 [1933] 2 KB 297 (CA). This case is examined in more detail in Chapter 5.
22 As Professor Goodhart has pointed out in his article 'Rescue and Voluntary Assumption of Risk' (1934) 5 *Cambridge Law Journal* 192, 200–201, the plaintiff in *Cutler* is more accurately characterised as a volunteer rather than as a rescuer.

by paternal affection, dashes out and holds a runaway horse's head in order to save his child, and is injured; there is no *novus actus interveniens*.'[23]

In 1935 the English courts finally set their imprimatur on the North American developments in upholding the claim of a rescuer. In *Haynes v Harwood*[24] a police constable was injured when he attempted to stop runaway horses which posed an imminent threat to a woman and several children. Distinguishing the *Cutler* case on the ground that no person or property was there imperilled by the defendant's negligence, the trial Judge held in the plaintiff's favour as a police officer is 'expected to' aid those in danger 'in pursuance of a duty'.[25] The Court of Appeal affirmed the decision, with Greer L.J. declaring, 'it would be a little surprising if a rational system of law in those circumstances denied any remedy to a brave man who had received his injuries through the original default of the defendant's servant.'[26] The Court of Appeal also held a rescuer's act not to amount to a *novus actus* in *Ward v T.E. Hopkins & Son Ltd*[27] where a fatal accidents legislation claim was allowed. There, a doctor perished while attempting the rescue of two workers who had been trapped in a well as a result of the defendant's negligence. Morris L.J. stated, '[t]hose who put others in peril can hardly be heard to say that they never thought that rescue might be attempted or be heard to say that the rescue attempt was not caused by the creation of the peril.'[28] Willmer L.J. added:

> In my judgment, it was a natural and probable result of the wrongdoing of Mr Hopkins that, in the likely event of someone being overcome by the carbon monoxide poisoning a doctor would be called in, and that such doctor, having regard to the traditions of his profession, would, even at the risk of his own safety, descend the well for the purpose of attempting a rescue. Unless it can be shown, therefore, that Dr Baker displayed such an unreasonable disregard for his own safety as to amount to negligence on his part...I do not think it can be said that his act constituted a *novus actus interveniens*.[29]

By 1961, Australian law had fallen into line with these developments in England and North America. In *Chapman v Hearse*,[30] although argument was addressed to the High Court of Australia that the negligent driving of Hearse constituted a *novus actus interveniens*, it was not even contended that Dr Cherry's own act in going to Chapman's assistance could also amount to a *novus actus*.

---

23 [1933] 2 KB 297, 306. The plaintiff's voluntary act in acceding to a request to help pacify the runaway horse was regarded as a *novus actus interveniens* or alternatively as a voluntary assumption of risk.
24 [1934] 2 KB 240; affirmed [1935] 1 KB 146 (CA). This case is examined in more detail in Chapter 5.
25 [1934] 2 KB 240, 250.
26 [1935] 1 KB 146, 152.
27 [1959] 1 WLR 966 (CA).
28 Ibid., 975–6.
29 Ibid., 982.
30 (1961) 106 CLR 112. This case is examined in more detail in Chapter 3.

Negligent Rescue Attempts

If a reasonably undertaken rescue attempt will not sever the causal chain, will a negligent rescue attempt do so? And, if so, will ordinary negligence suffice or must gross negligence or recklessness on the part of the rescuer be proven on the evidence?

Authority for the proposition that wanton disregard for the rescuer's own safety will sever the causal chain is to be found in the judgment of Cardozo J. in *Wagner v International Railroad Company*[31] where His Honour stated, '[t]he risk of rescue, if only it be not wanton, is born of the occasion.' This appears to be the position taken in the American Law Institute's *Restatement of the Law of Torts, Second*.[32] In the commentary accompanying Section 443,[33] it is stated, 'if the third person officiously intervenes when his incompetence is so great that any ordinary person would realize the grave danger of meddling with the situation, his interference may be regarded as so extraordinary as to relieve the [defendant] from liability.'[34] English case-law appears to be more equivocal on the point. There is some limited authority by analogy to be found in the judgment of Scrutton L.J. in the *Cutler*[35] case for the proposition that the causal chain will be severed where the rescuer's reaction to the danger is grossly foolish and disproportionate. There His Lordship, after referring to the plaintiff's acknowledgment of the danger involved in assisting to pacify the horse, stated:

> In those circumstances the ordinary and natural consequence that any man must foresee, if he tries to hold a runaway and restless horse, is that he may be injured by it. If he sustains injury in those circumstances it results from his own intervention.

Two members of the Court of Appeal considered this issue in *Ward v T.E. Hopkins & Son Ltd*.[36] In a rather guarded expression of opinion, Morris L.J. considered that '[i]f a rescuer acts with a wanton disregard for his own safety it might be that in some circumstances it might be held that any injury to him was not the result of the negligence that caused the situation of danger.'[37] Willmer L.J. also appeared to require gross negligence on the rescuer's part to sever the causal chain when His Lordship quoted with apparent approval the above-mentioned passage from the judgment of Cardozo J. in the *Wagner* case.[38] However, later in his judgment, Willmer L.J. appeared to imply that something falling below gross negligence would suffice to break the causal chain when he stated, '[u]nless it can be shown, therefore,

---

31   (1921) 232 NY 176, 180.
32   (1965–79).
33   Section 443 states in substance that the intervention of a force which is a normal consequence of a situation created by the defendant's negligent conduct is not a superseding cause of the plaintiff's injury.
34   *Restatement of the Law of Torts, Second* (ALI, 1965–79) 473.
35   [1933] 2 KB 297, 304.
36   [1959] 1 WLR 966 (CA).
37   Ibid., 977.
38   Ibid., 981.

Dr Baker displayed such an unreasonable disregard for his own safety as to amount to negligence on his own part...I do not think it can be said that his act constituted a *novus actus interveniens*.'[39] In another case coming before the Court of Appeal four years later, Lord Denning M.R. appears to have adopted the US approach in requiring gross negligence before the causal chain will be severed. *Videan* v *British Transport Commission*[40] involved the death of a stationmaster who was killed by a carelessly driven trolley while attempting to rescue a child trespassing on a railway line. According to the Master of the Rolls:

> Whoever comes to the rescue, the law should see he does not suffer for it. It seems to me that, if a person by his fault creates a situation of peril, he must answer for it to any person who attempts to rescue the person who is in danger...The rescuer may act instinctively out of humanity or deliberately out of courage. But whichever it is, so long as it is not wanton interference, if the rescuer is killed or injured in the attempt, he can recover damages from the one whose fault has been the cause of it.[41]

The decision of the Court of Appeal in *Knightley* v *Johns*[42] provides one of the few recent instances where the actions of rescuers were held to have severed the causal chain. In that case, the defendant successfully argued that the actions of the police in dealing with an emergency triggered by a motor vehicle accident in a highway tunnel, particularly the instructions of the police inspector, had severed the causal chain between the defendant's negligent driving and the plaintiff's injuries. After citing the above-mentioned authorities, Stephenson L.J., who delivered the main judgment in the case, did not make any specific finding on whether the police inspector's conduct amounted to gross negligence, although such a finding might be inferred in the following passage from His Lordship's judgment:

> In my judgment, too much happened here, too much went wrong, the chapter of accidents and mistakes was too long and varied, to impose on Mr Johns liability...The ordinary course of things took an extraordinary course...But would [the defendant] anticipate such a result as this from so many errors as these, so many departures from the common sense procedure prescribed by the standing orders for just such an emergency as this?[43]

The defendant motorist was therefore relieved of liability for the damages claimed by the rescuer police constable who had acted on the police inspector's negligent instructions.

It would appear that, on the balance of authority, the defendant will only escape liability for the damage suffered by the rescuer if the rescue attempt was doomed to failure from the beginning or if the risk assumed by the rescuer was grossly disproportionate to the purpose of the rescue.[44] There is an obvious and sound public

---

39 Ibid., 982.
40 [1963] 2 All ER 860 (CA).
41 Ibid., 868.
42 [1982] 1 All ER 851 (CA). This case is examined in more detail in Chapter 3.
43 Ibid., 866.
44 As would be the case in an attempt to retrieve a suitcase from a burning vehicle liable to explode at any moment: W. van Gerven, J. Lever and J. Larouche *Cases, Materials and*

policy argument for requiring proof of gross negligence before holding that the causal chain has been severed (the effect of such holding being a denial of recovery by the rescuer or his or her personal representatives). Rescuers should not be unduly discouraged from attempting to save life and property in peril, as they would be if ordinary negligence sufficed to interrupt the causal connection. It must be borne in mind that rescuers often act in difficult circumstances, and the pressures and lack of time to reflect on the situation created by the negligently-caused emergency situation can produce understandable and forgivable errors of judgement on the rescuer's part. For these reasons, legislatures have often protected rescuers whose negligence has fallen short of gross negligence.

Rescue of Property

As long ago as the 1890s US and Canadian courts extended the rescue cases to cover instances where the plaintiff had exposed himself or herself to risk in attempting to save either his or her own or a third person's property which had been endangered by the defendant's negligence. *Liming* v *Illinois Central Railway*[45] is a leading authority on this point. There the defendant railway company negligently set fire to some grass. When the plaintiff went to a barn to save some horses belonging to a neighbour, he was caught by the rapidly-expanding fire and was badly burned. The Court said:

> [The plaintiff] was under no legal obligation to protect the property of his neighbor; yet his attempt to do so was entirely lawful, and was most praiseworthy. If he had failed to make a reasonable effort to save it, he would have merited the censure and contempt of his neighbors...Under the circumstances of the case, it was the natural and probable result of the wrong of the defendant.

A number of other US cases have held that it is reasonable and proper for persons to defend their property from negligently-lit fires by 'backburning' operations and that such attempts to rescue their property from disaster do not amount to a superseding cause of any subsequent loss. For example, *Lowden* v *Shoffner Mercantile Co.*[46] involved an action against the trustees of a railway company for damages for the destruction of the plaintiff's warehouse by fire. In the course of carrying out their duties, the defendant's employees negligently commenced a fire near the plaintiff's warehouse. In order to prevent the spread of the fire to the warehouse, several of the plaintiff's employees commenced backburning operations. The Eighth Circuit Court of Appeals rejected the defendant's contention that the lighting of the backfires amounted to a superseding cause of the plaintiff's loss on the ground that such action in mitigation of damage 'was reasonable and proper under the circumstances'.[47]

Texts on National, Supranational and International Tort Law (Hart Publishing, 2000) 429/40 – 429/41.

    45   (1890) 81 Iowa 246; 47 NW 66, 68 (Supreme Court of Iowa).
    46   109 F 2d 956 (8 Cir 1940).
    47   Ibid., 958–9. See also *McKenna* v *Baessler* (1892) 86 Iowa 197; 53 NW 103 (Supreme Court of Iowa).

The Supreme Court of Canada has also held that reasonable steps taken by a plaintiff in defence of his or her own property will not amount to a *novus actus interveniens*. In *Town of Prescott* v *Connell*[48] the majority of the Supreme Court of Canada rejected the defendant's *novus actus* plea that the plaintiff's voluntary act of attempting to restrain the horses after they had been frightened by the negligence of the defendant's servants had been the sole legal cause of his injuries. Rather, the plaintiff's conduct was characterised as an instinctive and reasonable response to an emergency situation created by negligence for which the defendant was responsible. Sedgewick J. considered the plaintiff's unsuccessful attempt to regain control of his horses as 'the natural or probable result' of that negligence.[49] The holding in each of these cases is consistent with the principle laid down in Section 445 of the *Restatement of the Law of Torts, Second*[50] which states, '[i]f the [defendant's] negligent conduct threatens harm to another's person, land, or chattels, the normal efforts of the other or a third person to avert the threatened harm are not a superseding cause of harm resulting from such efforts.'

The principle that reasonable efforts to rescue property from imminent harm or to prevent further damage thereto has also been judicially supported in England. In the maritime context, Viscount Haldane has stated in *The Metagama*:[51]

> ...what those in charge of the injured ship do to save it may be mistaken, but if they do whatever they do reasonably, although unsuccessfully, their mistaken judgment may be a natural consequence for which the offending ship is responsible...Reasonable human conduct is part of the ordinary course of things, which extends to the reasonable conduct of those who have sustained the damage and who are seeking to save further loss.[52]

It has been held in *D'Urso* v *Sanson*[53] that a guard who was injured while trying, in the course of his employment, to extinguish a fire in his employer's premises may recover damages.

Medical Rescue

An interesting and difficult issue arises in cases where measures are taken (usually by close relatives) some time after an accident or event to help the victim after consultation with medical specialists. Are such measures, taken voluntarily and after due reflection, sufficient to sever the causal chain or can the damage sustained by the Good Samaritan, as it were, be attributed to the defendant's negligence?

---

48   (1893) 22 SCR 147. This case is examined more closely in Chapter 2.
49   Ibid., 161–3.
50   (ALI, 1965–79) 475.
51   (1927) 29 Lloyd's List Law Reports 253 (HL). This case is examined in more detail in Chapter 10.
52   Ibid., 254.
53   [1939] 4 All ER 26. See also *Hyett* v *Great Western Railway Company* [1947] 2 All ER 264 which is examined in Chapter 4.

This issue arose for consideration in the Canadian case of *Urbanski* v *Patel*.[54] During a sterilisation procedure (tubal ligation) performed on a young woman, the doctor negligently removed her only kidney, believing he was removing an ovarian cyst. Her father then donated a kidney to his daughter but the transplanted kidney was rejected and the daughter remained on dialysis. The father successfully sued the doctor for the damage he had suffered which was associated with the donation of his kidney. The Manitoba Queen's Bench held that the father's act of attempted rescue did not amount to a *novus actus interveniens* as it was not truly volitional, and moreover should have been reasonably foreseen by the defendant doctor. The father's moral and paternal compulsion overrode the orthodox arguments that he had voluntarily incurred the loss and, unlike the usual rescue situation, had acted after due deliberation.[55]

It is interesting to note that the German courts have addressed the same issues on very similar facts in another kidney donation case.[56] The plaintiff, 13 years old at the time, was injured while playing sport and was taken to hospital. Because of a suspected intra-abdominal injury, the surgeon performed a laparotomy. Having found that the left kidney was damaged, he decided to remove it. The plaintiff had been born without a right kidney, and as a result of the removal of her left kidney, she had to be put on dialysis. A few weeks after the accident, after having consulted physicians, the plaintiff's mother decided that she would donate a kidney to her daughter. Unlike the *Urbanski* case, the kidney transplant was successful. The mother assigned her legal rights against the defendant surgeon to her daughter, who sued for the material damage sustained by her mother. The critical issue in the litigation was whether the mother's decision to donate a kidney to her daughter had severed the causal chain between the surgeon's negligence in removing the daughter's only kidney and the damage suffered by her mother. It was argued on behalf of the defendant surgeon that the mother had freely decided after due reflection to donate the kidney some time after his negligence and outside an emergency situation, and that accordingly the mother's conduct did not constitute a true rescue. The BGH upheld the judgment of the intermediate appellate court which had in turn upheld the decision of the court of first instance to allow the plaintiff's claim. After having recalled the principles developed in its case-law on rescue cases, the BGH stated:

> In the case at hand, those legal principles justify that the defendant be made answerable for the kidney donation and the injury to body and health suffered by the plaintiff's mother, since they are connected to conduct for which the defendant is responsible. The kidney donation arose specifically because [the defendant] injured the plaintiff and brought the plaintiff's mother into a situation in which she must have felt invited to make such a sacrifice for her child. Undoubtedly, the mother's behaviour must be praised highly from a moral perspective, and the law cannot help but approve of it and acknowledge it. From a medical perspective, it was justified to donate a healthy kidney in order to attempt to improve the physical condition and health of the plaintiff...

---

54 (1978) 84 DLR (3d) 650 (Man QB).
55 J. Fleming, *The Law of Torts* (The Law Book Company Limited, 9th edn, 1998) 248.
56 BGH, 30 June 1987, BGHZ 101, 215.

Contrary to the opinion of the [defendant], imputability cannot be denied on the ground that the plaintiff's mother did not decide to donate a kidney under the immediate pressure of an acute emergency, but rather had time to discuss it and to weigh the pros and cons carefully...It is after all not exceptional that a rescuer has enough time for reflection... Whether the injury suffered by the one who wanted to reduce...the damage still qualifies as rescue...must be assessed in the light of its relationship to the invitation and certainly also of the temporal and spatial dimensions. On the basis of the foregoing, a kidney donation to an injured child from a close relative – here the mother – will easily be seen as a response to an invitation *Herausforderung* to rescue the endangered life or health of the child. The mother's sacrifice is in substance linked with the menacing situation created by the physician when he removed the child's sole kidney.[57]

The BGH thus held the defendant surgeon to be responsible also for the injuries sustained by the plaintiff's mother, despite the mother's full knowledge of the material risks involved in the kidney donation and her informed consent thereto. The arguments are indeed finely balanced on this issue and the court's conclusion might not always be consistent with that reached in these two cases, depending on the facts and circumstances of each case and such factors as the urgency of the remedial medical intervention and temporal proximity to the accident or event which necessitated the original treatment. It remains to be seen whether courts will be sufficiently adventurous to stretch the rescue doctrine beyond these limits.

Self-Rescue

As in cases involving attempted rescue of other persons or their property, it would appear that the causal chain will not be severed where a person attempts to extricate himself or herself from a situation of danger or substantial inconvenience caused by the defendant's negligence, provided the 'self-rescue' attempt is reasonable in the circumstances and does not involve disproportionate risks. Authority for this proposition may be found in the decision of the English Court of Appeal in *Sayers v Harlow Urban District Council*.[58] The plaintiff visited a public lavatory owned by the defendant and faced the unenviable dilemma of being unable to get out when the lock of the toilet door jammed. She was injured while trying to climb out. Although the Court of Appeal held that the plaintiff had been contributorily negligent, her self-rescue attempt was not adjudged to be a *novus actus interveniens*. All three members of the Court of Appeal[59] were satisfied that Mrs Sayers had acted reasonably in the circumstances.

---

57 Translation by A. Hoffman and Y.P. Salmon as extracted in Van Gerven, Lever and Larouche *Cases, Materials and Texts on National, Supranational and International Tort Law*, 429/39 – 429/40.

58 [1958] 1 WLR 623 (CA). This case is examined in more detail in Chapter 4.

59 Lord Evershed M.R., Morris and Ormerod LL.J.

Chapter 14

Children

Introduction

Generally speaking, the case-law has evolved over the past two centuries to the point that a negligent defendant may no longer hide behind the conduct of children.[1] Intervening conduct by a third party not responsible, or at least not fully responsible, for his or her own actions will be much less likely to constitute a *novus actus interveniens*.[2] Thus, an act of a child is much less likely than an act of an adult to sever the causal chain, even though the child may have been acting deliberately at the time.[3] In considering an attempt to draw a distinction between loss caused to the plaintiff by failure to control an adult of full capacity and loss caused by failure to control a child, Lord Reid has observed, '[a]s regards causation, no doubt it is easier to infer *novus actus interveniens* in the case of an adult...'[4]

A young child's inherent inability to recognise and appreciate risks is central to a consideration of whether his or her conduct should relieve the defendant of liability. A child's innocence and lack of experience may result in his or her perceiving as attractive or alluring a situation which an older person would rightly regard as a situation of danger. The case authorities are replete with judicial observations to this effect. For example, Lord Sumner has observed:

> Children acting in the wantonness of infancy...may be and often are only links in the chain of causation extending from such initial negligence to the subsequent injury. No doubt each intervener is a *causa sine qua non* but unless the intervention is a fresh, independent cause, the person guilty of the original negligence will still be the effective cause, if he ought reasonably to have anticipated such interventions and to have foreseen that if they occurred, the result would be that his negligence would lead to mischief.[5]

More recently, Lord Hobhouse has pointed out that child plaintiffs act under a disability through a lack of age and experience and that '[b]oth as a matter of causation and the attribution of responsibility, their conduct does not (without more) remove the responsibility of the defendant or transfer the responsibility to the child plaintiff...'[6]

---

1 P. Kaye *An Explanatory Guide to the English Law of Torts* (Barry Rose Law Publishers Ltd, 1996) 283.
2 *Weld-Blundell v Stephens* [1920] AC 956, 985.
3 A. M. Dugdale and M.A. Jones (eds) *Clerk & Lindsell on Torts* (Sweet & Maxwell, 19th edn, 2006) [107], 2–91.
4 *Home Office v Dorset Yacht Co. Ltd* [1970] AC 1004, 1030 (HL).
5 *Latham v Johnson & Nephew Ltd* [1913] 1 KB 398, 413 (CA).
6 *Reeves v Commissioner of Police of the Metropolis* [2000] 1 AC 360, 394–5.

A long line of cases involving children stretching back some two centuries has gradually established the principle that 'a person who holds out a temptation to a child cannot reproach it with yielding to that temptation, if it merely indulges its natural instinct of meddling with attractive objects.'[7] Those defendants who are aware of, or ought to anticipate, the presence of children within the range of their own operations are not relieved from liability for injury caused by the children in the pursuit of their natural instincts of curiosity, misjudgement and mischief.[8] We shall now turn to examine the evolution of the case-law concerning when, if at all, the intervening conduct of children can amount to a *novus actus interveniens*, thereby relieving the defendant from liability.

The Development of the Case-Law

The 1816 case of *Dixon* v *Bell*[9] is an early authority dealing with the liability of a firearms owner for an accidental shooting allegedly caused by the owner's want of care. In that case, the defendant had left a loaded gun with another man and sent his young servant girl to collect it, with a message to this man to remove the priming. This he did but not effectively. The servant returned home with the gun and, believing that the priming had been removed so that the gun could not be discharged, pointed it at the plaintiff's son, a child, and pulled the trigger. The gun discharged and put out the child's right eye. The defendant was held liable in an action upon the case. Lord Ellenborough C.J. considered that the defendant had not done enough to render the gun safe and harmless.[10] Thus, the intentional act of the child servant in firing the gun did not sever the causal chain and relieve the defendant from liability since the outcome fell squarely within the scope of what the defendant should have anticipated and guarded against.

The next significant case of *Lynch* v *Nurdin*[11] is one of the first of many cases to consider children's propensity for mischief and their lack of experience and judgement and the extent to which these qualities impact on *novus actus* and contributory negligence pleas. In that case the defendant's cart was parked in a London street. The driver left the horse and cart without any supervision for about half an hour. The plaintiff, a six-year-old boy, and several other children began playing about the cart. During the driver's absence, the plaintiff climbed upon the cart and another boy proceeded to lead the horse on which caused the plaintiff to fall off. He was then run over by the cart and suffered a fractured leg. The owner of the cart was sued and it was argued on the defendant's behalf that the driver's alleged negligence in leaving the horse and cart unattended could not be considered the legal cause of the plaintiff's injury; rather, the effective and immediate cause of his injury was his

---

7   J.G. Fleming *The Law of Torts* (The Law Book Company of Australasia Pty Ltd, 2nd edn, 1961) 198.

8   *Glasgow Corporation* v *Taylor* [1922] 1 AC 44, 67 (*per* Lord Sumner); *Thompson* v *Bankstown Corporation* (1953) 87 CLR 619, 631.

9   (1816) 5 M & S 198.

10   Ibid., 199.

11   (1841) 1 QB 29.

trespass on the defendant's chattel. This argument was rejected. Although the causal potency of the boy's conduct in relation to his injury was significant, the degree of self-care to be expected of a normal six-year-old boy was 'very small indeed'.[12] As Lord Denman C.J. observed:

> [The plaintiff] merely indulged the natural instinct of a child in amusing himself with the empty cart and deserted horse...The most blameable carelessness of [the defendant's] servant having tempted the child, he ought not to reproach the child with yielding to that temptation. He has been the real and only cause of the mischief. He has been deficient in ordinary care: the child, acting without prudence or thought, has, however, shewn these qualities in as great a degree as he could be expected to possess them. His misconduct bears no proportion to that of the defendant which produced it.[13]

The defendant's *novus actus* and contributory negligence pleas were therefore rejected. The cart driver had, in effect, a duty to guard against the very risk of injury which eventuated. The vulnerability of the class of potential victims of such neglect –young children – no doubt factored significantly in Lord Denman's reasoning.[14]

Several English decisions soon followed the *Lynch* case which denied recovery to child plaintiffs whose intervening conduct was held to constitute either contributory negligence on their part or a *novus actus interveniens*. *Hughes v Macfie*[15] is an example of a case making virtually no allowance for the fact that the plaintiff was a child of tender years. The defendants carried on the business of sugar refiners and, for that purpose, occupied a warehouse on one side of a street into which their cellar opened. The cellar opening was covered by a large wooden flap or lid when not required for the delivery of sugar casks. On the day of the accident the defendant's servants had removed the flap for the purpose of lowering some casks into the cellar and had leant it against the wall in a nearly upright position. The plaintiff, a five-year-old child, climbed upon the flap and in jumping down caught the flap with his jacket and pulled it over upon himself, thereby sustaining injuries. In denying recovery to the child plaintiff, Pollock C.B. stated:

> Had [the plaintiff] been an adult, it is clear that he could have maintained no action. He would voluntarily have meddled for no lawful purpose with that which, if left alone, would not have hurt him. He would therefore...have contributed by his own negligence to his damage. We think the fact of the plaintiff being of tender years makes no difference. His touching the flap was for no lawful purpose...[16]

---

12   Ibid., 36.
13   Ibid., 38.
14   Contrast *Donovan v Union Cartage Co.* [1933] 2 KB 71 (recovery denied to child falling from an unhorsed van left unattended in the street). But see *Haynes v G. Harwood & Son* [1935] 1 KB 146 (CA) where the mischievous act of a boy in throwing a stone at the horses was not held to constitute a *novus actus interveniens* severing the causal connection between the negligence of the servant driver in leaving them unattended and the plaintiff rescuer's injury.
15   (1863) 2 H & C 744.
16   Ibid., 749.

It is respectfully submitted that this case would be decided differently today. Given the location of the accident adjacent to a busy public street, it was not beyond the reasonable anticipation of the defendant's servants that such an incident involving children could occur and it would today be considered well within the scope of the risk to be guarded against.[17]

Another questionable decision is that of the Court of Exchequer in *Mangan* v *Atherton*.[18] The defendant, a whitesmith, customarily displayed goods for sale in a public street on market days. On the day of the accident, he displayed a machine for crushing oil-cake, unfenced and without superintendence. The machine was operated by an unsecured handle and the cogs which worked the crushing rollers were exposed. The plaintiff, a four-year-old boy, together with his seven-year-old brother and other young boys, walked past the machine on their way home from school. While one of the boys was turning the handle, the plaintiff, at his brother's direction, placed his fingers in the cogs which crushed them so badly that they had to be amputated. The defendant successfully appealed against the jury's verdict for the plaintiff, having contended on the basis of *Hughes* v *Macfie* that the plaintiff's own act was the accident's *causa causans*. The Court of Exchequer[19] held against the plaintiff on the ground that no negligence had been proven. Martin B. went on to observe by way of an *obiter dictum* that even if the defendant had been negligent, the accident was directly caused by the act of the plaintiff himself.[20] The findings of the Court of Exchequer on both the negligence and *novus actus* issues have been subsequently judicially criticised, and rightly so. In *Clark* v *Chambers*[21] Cockburn C.J. characterised the defendant's conduct in *Mangan* v *Atherton* as 'negligence of a very reprehensible character' and considered the determination of the *novus actus* plea in the defendant's favour to be in conflict with previous case authorities.[22]

A more realistic approach to the foibles of childhood was taken by the English Court of Appeal in *Williams* v *Eady*[23] where the defendant, a schoolmaster, was held liable to one of his pupils for an injury resulting from the careless act of another boy in handling phosphorous. Although the phosphorous bottle had been locked up, the key had been found surreptitiously and left lying around. It was found by one of the boys and the bottle was retrieved. One of the boys put a lighted match into the bottle and replaced the stopper. When he later opened it to look at it, the bottle burst and the plaintiff was injured. The Court of Appeal upheld the jury's verdict for the plaintiff, not regarding the actions of the boys as severing the causal link between the schoolmaster's negligence in not taking sufficient precautions to secure the phosphorous and the boy's injury. Lord Esher M.R. considered that the schoolmaster was bound to take notice of the ordinary nature of young boys and their tendency to do mischievous acts. Considering the well-established duty of care owed by teachers

---

17 See Chapter 7 generally.
18 (1866) LR 1 Ex 239.
19 Comprised of Martin B. and Bramwell B.
20 (1866) LR 1 Ex 239, 240.
21 (1878) 3 QBD 327.
22 Ibid., 339.
23 (1893) 10 Times LR 41.

to their students, it could be said once again that what happened here fell squarely within the range of risks reasonably to be guarded against, and so the duty of care could not be undermined by upholding the *novus actus* plea. By contrast, in the 1903 decision of the Court of Appeal in *McDowall* v *Great Western Railway Company*[24] Vaughan Williams L.J. was prepared to find by way of an *obiter dictum* that the negligent conduct of some boys in trespassing on a railway siding and releasing the brake of a brake-van which led to a level crossing accident did constitute a *novus actus interveniens* despite the defendant railway company's knowledge of previous episodes of boys breaking into vans or trucks on the same part of the railway line.[25]

A series of cases has considered the involvement of children in accidental shootings and whether their intervening conduct supersedes the defendant's negligence in not adequately securing the gun in question. The Irish Court of Appeal has applied the 'scope of the risk' approach in such a case. In *Sullivan* v *Creed*[26] the defendant left a loaded gun at full cock standing inside a fence on his property adjacent to a public road. The defendant's 15-year-old son found the gun and, not realising that it was loaded, pointed it in play at the 16-year-old plaintiff who was on the road. The gun was discharged and the plaintiff lost an eye. The Court of Appeal upheld the decision of the King's Bench Division that the defendant was liable. The defendant's conduct was characterised as gross negligence and the intervening negligence of his son was not considered sufficient to sever the causal chain. Walker L.J. considered that 'the law will attribute to [the defendant] a reasonable anticipation that all those who come that way, including the young, the careless, and the inexperienced, might see the gun, meddle with it, or use it carelessly in the highly dangerous condition in which he left it.'[27] FitzGibbon L.J. was content to decide the case on the basis of the principle laid down in the venerable English decision of *Dixon* v *Bell*.[28] That adults may be held liable for injury caused by the intervening negligence of children in mishandling firearms has been established in other jurisdictions as well. In the English case of *Newton* v *Edgerley*[29] the defendant farmer allowed his 12-year-old son to have a gun. The defendant advised his son not to take the gun off the farm and not to handle it in the presence of others, but failed to instruct him on the proper handling of the gun while in the company of others. The son disobeyed his father and went shooting with neighbouring boys aged 14. The boys walked in single file and the son carried his loaded and cocked gun with its barrel pointed to the ground. The boy walking behind the defendant's son, in an endeavour to take it from him, pulled the trigger, resulting

---

24 [1903] 2 KB 331 (CA).
25 Ibid., 338. Contrast, however, the Canadian decision of *Geall* v *Dominion Creosoting Co.* (1917) 555 CR 587 where the employees of the defendant company had negligently left four cars of the British Columbia Electric Railway in such a position that they should have anticipated that the boys from a nearby school might do just what they did, release these cars and thereby cause damage. Unlike the *McDowall* case, the company was held liable in these circumstances. The result in *Geall* is more in line with the contemporary trend in the case authorities.
26 [1904] 2 IR 317 (CA).
27 Ibid., 349.
28 (1816) 5 M & S 198.
29 [1959] 3 All ER 337.

in a heel injury to the plaintiff boy who was walking in front. In the plaintiff's action for damages, the defendant was held liable in negligence for having allowed his son to have a gun without instructing him on how to handle it while others were present. Lord Parker C.J. held that the act of the other boy in mishandling the gun did not constitute a *novus actus interveniens* because this was just the sort of thing that was likely to happen and which the defendant had in mind when instructing his son not to handle the gun in the presence of others.

In its 1994 decision in *Curmi v McLennan*[30] the Supreme Court of Victoria (Appeal Division) held responsible a houseboat owner who negligently gave teenage boys using his houseboat access to an airgun which resulted in one of them shooting another in the eye. The Court held that in some circumstances a defendant may come under a duty of care not to expose the plaintiff, or someone belonging to his or her class, to a risk of injury arising from deliberate or voluntary conduct, and to guard against such risk. The defendant's negligence in giving a group of high-spirited schoolboys access to an airgun in circumstances where they were entirely unsupervised at all times and without any guidance or instructions had generated the very risk of the type of injury which transpired. The boy's act of shooting the plaintiff was thus not held to amount to a *novus actus*. The mischievous acts of children firing loaded guns have also been attributed by Canadian courts to those who negligently create the opportunities for their dangerous conduct.[31]

Courts have also dealt with many situations, apart from firearms, where the plaintiff or a third party is injured by the intervening negligent use of, or interference with, dangerous objects by children. An important point of principle in this regard was laid down by the House of Lords (Ireland) in its 1909 decision in *Cooke v Midland Great Western Railway of Ireland*.[32] There the defendant railway company kept a turntable unlocked (and therefore dangerous for children) on their land close to a public road. The defendant's servants knew that children were in the habit of trespassing and playing with the turntable, to which they obtained easy access through a gap in a fence which the defendant was bound by statute to maintain. A four-year-old child was seriously injured while playing with other children on the turntable. In an action brought by the injured boy's father and next friend, the House of Lords affirmed that there was sufficient evidence for a jury to make a finding of actionable negligence against the defendant,[33] and that such negligence was the immediate cause or *causa causans* of the boy's injury. Lord Collins relied on the virtually identical decision of the United States Supreme Court in *Railroad Co. v Stout*[34] to find in the plaintiff's favour. After observing that those of tender age are less capable of caution and therefore of contributory negligence, His Lordship stated,

---

30 [1994] 1 VR 513.

31 *Edwards v Smith* [1941] 1 DLR 736; *Bishop v Sharrow* (1975) 8 OR (2d) 649; *Ingram v Lowe* (1975) 55 DLR (3d) 292 (Alta C.A.). See also in a different but related context *Whelan v Parsons & Sons* [2005] N.J. No. 264, 33 CCLT (3d) 24 (C.A.) (beer bottles thrown at bus by youths gathered at a take-out restaurant).

32 [1909] AC 229.

33 The particulars of negligence consisting of failure to maintain adequate fencing and omission to secure the turntable in a fixed position.

34 (1873) 17 Wall. (US) 657.

'[t]empting or even allowing children to make a plaything of a dangerous machine without taking adequate, or indeed any, precautions against the probable danger of mischief through their imprudence is a form of benevolence which ought not to be encouraged.'[35] Lord Atkinson also noted the propensity of children of tender years to trespass on land and meddle with chattels, attributable to their 'very inquisitive and frequently mischievous disposition'.[36] Later in his judgment His Lordship formulated the general principle that 'if the owner of any premises on which dangerous and alluring machines or vehicles...are placed gives leave to boys of a mischievous and intermeddling age, or to children of such tender years as to be quite unable to take care of themselves, to enter upon the premises, he will be...responsible for any injury...'[37] Pursuant to this principle, a *novus actus* plea will not succeed where a mischievous boy starts up a car and subsequently causes injury.[38] Nor will the plea succeed where a snowmobile is mishandled by children.[39] Similarly contractors engaged on demolition work must guard against the danger of children trespassing on a private site over the week-end despite repeated warnings-off, and anticipate the likelihood that, by interfering with the remaining structure which is known to be unsafe, the child trespassers will bring a wall down upon themselves.[40] And in *Harris* v *Toronto Transit Commission*[41] the Supreme Court of Canada did not find a *novus actus interveniens* when a child's arm, protruding from a bus window, was fractured when the bus collided with a pole. In imposing partial liability, the Court stated that the bus driver 'should have foreseen the likelihood of child passengers extending their arms through the window, notwithstanding the warning'.[42]

The same general principle applies to situations where children meddle with dangerous substances such as inflammable liquids, explosives and poisons. The Judicial Committee of the Privy Council has applied a duty-based 'scope of the risk' approach in a case involving a mischievous intervening act of a child plaintiff. In *Yachuk* v *Oliver Blais Co. Ltd*[43] a nine-year-old boy prevailed on the servant of the defendant company to sell him a small quantity of petrol by telling an untruthful statement. This was despite the fact that the employee entertained doubts as to the propriety of the sale. While re-enacting a scene he had recently witnessed at the cinema, the boy was seriously burned. The defendant contended that the plaintiff's deceitful representation and subsequent conduct severed the causal chain between the employee's negligence in selling the petrol to the boy and the burning injuries. The Privy Council rejected the defendant's *novus actus* plea on the ground that the employee's negligence consisted in putting into the hands of a small, vulnerable and inexperienced boy a dangerous and explosive substance with which a reasonable

---

35   [1909] AC 229, 241–2.
36   Ibid., 237.
37   Ibid., 238.
38   *Martin* v *Stanborough* (1924) 41 TLR 1.
39   *Ryan* v *Hickson* (1975) 7 OR (2d) 352; *Hoffer* v *School Division of Assiniboine South* [1973] 6 WWR 765.
40   *Davis* v *St Mary's Demolition Co.* [1954] 1 All ER 578.
41   [1967] SCR 460.
42   Ibid., 465 (*per* Ritchie J.).
43   [1949] 2 All ER 150 (JCPC).

and thoughtful person would have foreseen that a child was likely to injure himself. In delivering the judgment of the Board, Lord du Parcq observed, '[t]o put a highly inflammable substance into the hands of a small boy is to subject him to temptation and the risk of injury and this is no less true if the boy has resorted to deceit in order to overcome the supplier's scruples.'[44] This approach to determining the *novus actus* plea reflected that taken by Lord Denman C.J. in *Lynch* v *Nurdin*.[45] The limited knowledge of the child plaintiff of the inflammable properties of petrol was held to preclude a finding both of contributory negligence and *novus actus interveniens*.

New Zealand and Canadian courts have followed this lead. In *McCarthy* v *Wellington City*[46] the defendant operated a quarry on which it kept detonators. The New Zealand Court of Appeal held that it had negligently failed to adequately secure them as boys had managed to break open the safe in which they were kept. The boys took the detonators home and one of the boys gave them to a younger brother who later gave some to the nine-year-old plaintiff who was injured while playing with them. The Court held that it was a foreseeable consequence of the defendant's negligence that the detonators could pass through the hands of children who had not entered the quarry and therefore the *novus actus* plea could not succeed. And in the Canadian case of *Holian* v *United Grain Growers*[47] where some mischievous boys took some fumigant tablets used to kill insects from the defendant's shed and placed them in the plaintiff's car as a 'stink bomb' causing illness to the plaintiff, the court imposed liability since the theft and subsequent injury were 'within the risk created by the negligence of the defendant in leaving the shed unlocked and unattended'.[48]

The US courts have also adhered to the principle that where a dangerous article is negligently left by a defendant where it is likely to be found by children, the conduct of children who find the article and are injured by it is not an intervening or superseding cause of the injury so as to relieve the defendant of liability. One who deals with children must anticipate their normal behaviour and the defendant is held liable in such circumstances under the general rule that a negligent defendant is responsible for all of the consequences of the negligence which ought reasonably to have been foreseen. *New York Eskimo Pie Corporation* v *Rataj*[49] involved an action for damages by a 15-year-old female plaintiff for serious and permanent injuries she received from the explosion of a bottle in which dry ice had been placed by children. The ice had been thrown into the street by an employee of the defendant ice cream manufacturer. The Third Circuit Court of Appeals held that the defendant was charged with knowledge of the expansive properties of dry ice in its transition from a solid to a gaseous state within a confined space, as well as the propensity of children to be attracted by these properties without appreciating the attendant dangers. Accordingly, the defendant's argument that the children's meddling with the dry ice constituted the proximate cause of the plaintiff's injuries was rejected,

---

44 Ibid., 153.
45 (1841) 1 QB 29.
46 [1966] NZLR 481 (CA).
47 (1980) 11 CCLT 184 (Man. Q.B.).
48 Ibid., 191.
49 (1934) 73 F 2d 184 (3 Cir.).

and liability was imposed on the defendant on the ground that a person of ordinary intelligence in the defendant's position would have foreseen the explosion of the bottle containing the dry ice as the 'natural and probable outcome' of any negligence in not disposing of the dry ice more carefully.

Another significant and illustrative US case in this context is the decision of the Third Circuit Court of Appeals in *American Mutual Liability Insurance Company v Buckley & Co., Inc.*[50] There the Buckley Company, a contractor, was excavating for the foundation of a school and its employees negligently left dynamite caps used to detonate dynamite lying on a pile of lumber. A 13-year-old boy picked up a cap notwithstanding that one of his companions warned him to leave it alone. The boy threw the cap into a bonfire which went out and the cap did not explode. On approaching the remains of the fire to investigate further, the cap exploded and the boy sustained serious injuries. The defendant company's insurers argued that although the dynamite caps had been left in a dangerous position due to the negligence of its insured's employees, the injured boy's deliberate actions in trying to explode the cap amounted to a *novus actus interveniens*. In rejecting this argument, the Court relied on the decision of the Supreme Court of Pennsylvania in *Fehrs v McKeesport*[51] which applied the doctrine of 'attractive nuisance' whereby a child of tender years brought into contact with an attractive nuisance may be expected to behave dangerously or irresponsibly with it. In delivering the Court's opinion in the *Fehrs* case, Simpson J. stated, '[w]ith reference to dangerous articles negligently left where they are likely to be found by children, in the majority of the cases, the courts do not treat their acts as intervening causes, but hold that the result must have been, or at least ought to have been, foreseen, and consequently the defendant is held liable...'[52] Thus, in the instant case, the Court did not consider the causal chain to have been severed by the boy's deliberate act intending to explode the dynamite cap since it was deemed to be a normal response to the stimulus of a situation created by the negligence of the defendant's employees.

Conclusion

This brief and illustrative overview of the development of the case-law over the past two centuries concerning the involvement of children in intervening causation issues establishes as a general rule that the deliberate acts of children are less likely than those of adults to sever the causal chain. This is so even where the child plaintiff is considered to have been contributorily negligent.[53] Those case authorities which hold to the contrary tend to have been decided in the nineteenth and early part of the twentieth centuries.[54] Even today, however, the acts of children can in some circumstances amount to a *novus actus interveniens*. In *Dallaire v Paul-Emile Martel*

---

50   (1941) 117 F 2d 845 (3 Cir.).
51   (1935) 318 Pa 279.
52   Ibid., 280.
53   *Harris v Toronto Transit Commission* [1967] SCR 460.
54   *Hughes v Macfie* (1863) 2 H & C 744; *Mangan v Atherton* (1866) LR 1 Ex 239; *McDowall v Great Western Railway Company* [1903] 2 KB 331 (CA).

Inc.[55] the Supreme Court of Canada held that the reckless conduct of an 11-year-old plaintiff severed the causal chain on the basis that the boy was aware through a warning from his father that it was dangerous to use the machinery in question in the particular manner in which he did.

Apart from cases of gross negligence, however, courts will take a lenient view of the intervening behaviour of children in terms of its causal potency *vis-à-vis* the ultimate injury. This is due to the lack of experience, judgement, skill and circumspection to be attributed to children of tender years. Nevertheless, the concept of childhood encompasses a significant range of ages, and what might present as an alluring trap to a three-year-old could well be considered an obvious danger to a 12-year-old. In this regard, the following passage from the American Law Institute's *Restatement of the Law of Torts* is apt:

> A child of tender years is not required to conform to the standard of behaviour which it is reasonable to expect of an adult, but his conduct is to be judged by the standard of behaviour to be expected from a child of like age, intelligence and experience. A child may be so young as to be manifestly incapable of exercising any of those qualities of attention, intelligence and judgment which are necessary to enable him to perceive a risk and to realise its unreasonable character. On the other hand it is obvious that a child who has not yet attained his majority may be as capable as an adult of exercising the qualities necessary to the perception of a risk and the realisation of its unreasonable character. Between these two extremes there are children whose capacities are infinitely various.[56]

This concept of rising levels of 'functional capacity' until the age of majority or 'years of discretion' are attained has been recognised by domestic courts[57] and is an integral part of the United Nations-sponsored *Convention on the Rights of the Child 1989*. Thus, generally speaking, the older the child is at the time when the intervening conduct occurs, the more likely it is that it will constitute a *novus actus interveniens*, particularly if the conduct is rash or reckless in nature. That said, it will normally be the case that the intervening conduct of children will not sever the causal chain as the 'scope of the risk' doctrine[58] gains increasing judicial recognition in this area.

---

55   [1989] 2 SCR 419. This case is examined in more detail in Chapter 8.

56   *American Restatement of the Law of Torts* para. 283. See to the same effect a passage from the treatise *The Common Law* (1881) by Oliver Wendell Holmes (pp. 108–9).

57   See, for example, the judgment of Kitto J. in *McHale* v *Watson* (1966) 115 CLR 199.

58   See Chapter 7 and cases mentioned earlier in this chapter.

Chapter 15

Escaping from Danger and Inconvenience

Introduction

Perhaps it is useful to begin this chapter with an illustrative example in order to set the context for the examination of the case-law to follow. The operator of a tram fails to observe an oncoming train before crossing a set of railway tracks. One of the tram's passengers, who is standing on its rear platform, sees the oncoming train and, fearing an imminent collision, jumps off the platform and sustains serious physical injuries. In the meantime, however, the tram operator has seen the train, accelerates and succeeds in getting the tram safely across the railway line just as the train rushes by. No other tram passengers are injured. Should the injured passenger's act in jumping from the tram be considered a *novus actus interveniens* in these circumstances?[1]

Courts have addressed this intervening causation issue by developing the so-called doctrine of 'alternative danger'. It has been concisely expressed by a judge of the Supreme Court of Canada as follows:

> Persons who in a sudden emergency are distracted by terror, and thus between two causes choose the wrong one, are not disentitled to recover. The very state of incapacity to judge calmly is produced by the defendant's negligent act.[2]

An English judge has said, 'if the negligence of [the defendant] puts [the plaintiff] in a situation of alternative danger, that is to say, if he will be in danger by remaining still, and in danger if he attempts to escape, any injury that he may sustain in so doing is a consequence of the [defendant's] negligence...'[3] Section 444 of the American Law Institute's *Restatement of the Law of Torts, Second*[4] likewise effectively states that an act done by another in normal response to fear or emotional disturbance created by the defendant's negligence does not constitute a superseding cause of the harm or a *novus actus interveniens*.

Generally speaking, the conduct of the plaintiff or a third party will not amount to a *novus actus interveniens* where it is a panic or instinctive reaction to a situation

---

1   *Winnipeg Electric Railway Co.* v *Canadian Northern Railway Co. and Bartlett* (1920) 59 SCR 352.
2   *Town of Prescott* v *Connell* (1893) 22 SCR 147, 163 *per* Sedgewick J.
3   *Adams* v *The Lancashire and Yorkshire Railway Company* (1869) LR 4 CP 739, 742 *per* Montague Smith J.
4   (1965–79).

of immediate or imminent danger created by the defendant's negligence.[5] Where the defendant's negligence has placed the plaintiff or a third party in a situation of 'alternative danger', if such person acts reasonably in the agony of the moment, that act will not sever the causal chain between the defendant's negligence and that person's injuries.[6] And we shall see later in this chapter that out of the doctrine of alternative danger has emerged what may be called a doctrine of 'alternative convenience' whereby 'if the inconvenience is very great and the danger run in avoiding it very slight, it may not be unreasonable to incur that danger.'[7] As we shall observe in the next two sections, normal human reactions, such as fear of imminent injury to oneself or the desire to extricate oneself from a significant inconvenience, are sufficiently within the realm of foreseeability to make the defendant liable for injury sustained as the result of another responding to them in a normal and reasonable manner.[8]

The Development of the Case-Law on Escaping from Danger

Our examination begins with the time-honoured 'Squib Case' of *Scott* v *Shepherd*[9] which is the first of a long line of cases to hold the defendant liable where, in a situation of imminent peril caused by the wilful or negligent act of the defendant, the plaintiff has taken not unreasonable action, instantaneously and without sufficient time for reflection, to avoid the consequences of the defendant's negligence. As will be recalled from Chapter 2, the intervention of bystanders who tossed away the lighted squib thrown by the defendant did not exculpate him from liability to the plaintiff who was ultimately injured by that squib. It was held to be no defence to the person who first threw the squib that the plaintiff would have suffered no loss had not a third party picked it up and thrown it again after the defendant had thrown it, because the third party, in throwing it, was acting instinctively, involuntarily and in self-preservation. It was the act of the defendant that placed the intervening third parties in such an excited and terror-stricken state of mind that they quite naturally blindly threw away the object which threatened so much damage. *Scott* v *Shepherd* paved the way for the development of the 'alternative danger' doctrine by indirectly endorsing the principle that the acts of persons who are distracted by terror in a sudden emergency and fail to choose the best option should not result in the defendant being relieved of liability.

---

5   A.M. Dugdale and M.A. Jones (eds) *Clerk & Lindsell on Torts* (Sweet & Maxwell, 19th edn, 2006) [111], para. 2–98.

6   R. Balkin and J. Davis *Law of Torts* (LexisNexis Butterworths, 3rd edn, 2004) 335.

7   *Adams* v *The Lancashire and Yorkshire Railway Company* (1869) LR 4 CP 739, 742 *per* Montague Smith J. If the risk taken by the plaintiff is disproportionate to the necessities of the particular situation, it may be a matter of degree whether such unreasonable conduct should disentitle the plaintiff to recovery or, at least, full recovery on the basis of his or her contributory negligence. See *Sayers* v *Harlow Urban District Council* (1958) 1 WLR 623 (CA).

8   J. Fleming *The Law of Torts* (The Law Book Company of Australasia Pty Ltd, 2nd edn, 1961) 197.

9   (1773) 2 W Bl 892. This case is examined in more detail in Chapter 2.

In terms of its origins, the alternative danger doctrine may be more directly traced to the 1816 case of *Jones* v *Boyce*.[10] This was an action on the case against the defendant, a coach proprietor, for allegedly failing to provide a safe and proper means of conveyance such that the plaintiff, an outside passenger, felt obliged, in order to avoid imminent danger, to jump off the coach, thereby sustaining a broken leg. The coach did not overturn, however. The jury found a verdict for the plaintiff. In his address to the jury, Lord Ellenborough set out the principle that if A negligently places B in such a dangerous situation that B is forced of necessity to adopt a 'perilous alternative' and B's adoption of that alternative is not unreasonable in the circumstances, A remains responsible for the consequences of B's choice. However, Lord Ellenborough added the significant qualification that 'if the plaintiff's act resulted from a rash apprehension of danger, which did not exist, and the injury which he sustained is to be attributed to rashness and imprudence, he is not entitled to recover.'[11] Thus, a prudent precaution adopted for the purpose of self-preservation would not sever the causal chain; a rash and imprudent act not justified by the circumstances would amount to a *novus actus interveniens* absolving the defendant of liability.

Jones v *Boyce* has since become the leading authority for the proposition that the original tortfeasor is not relieved of liability where the person imperilled by his or her negligence makes a reasonable attempt to escape the danger. This principle has become firmly established in a series of cases where a passenger jumps from a moving vehicle which the driver has negligently allowed to get out of control. Liability has been established notwithstanding that the passenger would have remained unscathed had he or she remained in the vehicle.[12] In this type of case, the victim is presented with a sudden choice of 'jump or not to jump' without having the luxury of due reflection on the risks involved in pursuing each alternative.[13] The US courts have held that a decision to jump to avoid imminent peril, which proved to be fatal, did not constitute a *novus actus interveniens* even though such decision was unsafe. So in *Sandri* v *Byram*[14] the plaintiff's decedent jumped from a motor car being operated on the railroad right of way, when a collision with another car at a street crossing seemed imminent. The Circuit Court of Appeals formulated the appropriate legal test to be applied as follows:

> Did he jump to escape what would have seemed, to an ordinary prudent person, situated as he was, an impending peril, caused by the negligence of [the defendant]? If he did, the chain of causation leading from [the defendant's] act to [the decedent's] death is not broken by decedent's choice of an unsafe course in an emergency.[15]

---

10   (1816) 1 Stark 493.
11   Ibid., 495.
12   *Malleys Ltd* v *Rogers* (1955) 55 SR (NSW) 390; *De Alba* v *Freehold Investment Co.* (1895) 21 VLR 204.
13   *The Paludina* [1927] AC 16, 29 *per* Lord Sumner.
14   (1929) 30 F 2d 784 (Circuit Court of Appeals, Sixth Circuit).
15   Ibid., 786.

The Irish courts have also dealt with 'alternative danger' cases and have focused on whether a reasonable person in the plaintiff's position would have adopted a similar course of action.[16] In adopting this objective test, the Irish courts have ignored the plaintiff's personal idiosyncrasies at the time of the accident. The objective test was applied in *Kingston* v *Kingston*[17] where the defendant was taking his family on a seaside outing and, while driving down a steep incline, exclaimed that he had lost his brakes. The plaintiff, the defendant's wife, who was sitting in the passenger seat, jumped from the car and sustained injuries. However, the defendant succeeded in safely bringing the car to a halt and none of the children travelling in the car at the time suffered any injury. The Supreme Court refused to disturb the jury's finding that the plaintiff had been guilty of contributory negligence.[18] In finding that a reasonable person would not have acted as she did in such circumstances, Walsh J., delivering the Court's judgment, stated, '[t]he test does not...permit to be taken into account the pre-accident nervous or anxious condition of the plaintiff which was peculiar to her only.'[19] The doctrine of alternative danger has also been applied by an Australian court in a case where a plaintiff bystander, confronted by danger created by a negligently-caused collision, ran for safety and thereby suffered injury which would not have occurred if she had remained where she was.[20]

The English decision of *Brandon* v *Osborne Garrett and Company Ltd*[21] can be regarded as an extension of the application of the alternative danger doctrine to a rescuing spouse. There, the plaintiffs, husband and wife, were in a shop when a portion of the glass skylight dislodged and fell towards the husband. On seeing it falling, the wife immediately and instinctively clutched her husband's arm and tried to pull him out of harm's way but was herself injured. In holding in the plaintiff's favour, Swift J. stated, 'if [the wife] did something which a reasonable person in the circumstances ought not to have done she would not be entitled to damages, but if what she did was done instinctively and was in the circumstances a natural and proper thing to do, I think she is entitled to recover.'[22] Although it appears from the case report that the plaintiff wife was not herself in a position of peril before her rescue attempt, Swift J. considered the instant case to be 'covered in principle by the statement of the law in *Jones* v *Boyce*'.[23] His Lordship regarded as immaterial the distinction between self-rescue attempts and acts undertaken for the preservation of spouses, children and 'even of a friend or stranger'.[24]

The mere fact that a plaintiff is aware of a risk of danger and deliberately elects to take it will not necessarily break the causal chain. A defendant who negligently creates a dangerous situation will remain liable where a plaintiff, fully aware of the danger, risks incurring it, if a reasonable person in the circumstances would have

---

16   *Hogg* v *Keane* [1956] IR 155, 158.
17   102 ILTR 65 (Sup. Ct, 1965).
18   At the time a complete defence.
19   102 ILTR 65, 68.
20   *Parry* v *Yates & Griffin* (1963) WAR 42.
21   [1924] 1 KB 548.
22   Ibid., 552.
23   Ibid.
24   Ibid.

risked incurring it. The 1848 case of *Clayards* v *Dethick*[25] raised this very issue of what effect the plaintiff's knowledge of a dangerous situation and the incurring of risks inherent therein should have on the defendant's liability in negligence. It was held that the defendant's negligence in failing to fence off a trench was not excused merely because the plaintiff knew that some danger existed through the defendant's neglect and assumed the risk posed by such danger in order to pursue his livelihood. Thus, the defendant was not relieved from liability on the basis of contributory negligence, voluntary assumption of risk or *novus actus interveniens*. According to Patteson J. the critical question was whether the danger was so obvious and great that no sensible prudent person could have assumed the inherent risks.[26] Coleridge J. stated that the plaintiff was not obliged to abstain from pursuing his livelihood because there was some danger, and formulated the appropriate jury question to be whether the plaintiff acted as a person 'of ordinary prudence would have done, or rashly and in defiance of warning'.[27] Underlying their judgments is the notion that whether or not the causal link between the defendant's negligence and the plaintiff's injury is severed depends on the extent to which the conduct of the author of the intervening event – in this case the plaintiff – is judicially deemed to be reasonable or normal in the circumstances.[28] A similar approach was taken by the House of Lords in *A.C. Billings & Sons Ltd* v *Riden*.[29] There the defendant contractors had obstructed the approach to a house, so that it became impassable. Alternative access was through an adjoining property and this route involved some danger. The plaintiff, appreciating this, availed herself of this route and was injured. The House of Lords held the contractors liable on the basis that a defendant who negligently creates a dangerous situation will be liable even though a plaintiff, fully aware of the danger, risks incurring it, if a reasonable person in the same position would have risked incurring it. The *Clayards* and *Riden* decisions are thus authority for the proposition that a not unreasonable assumption of even a significant risk of danger will not amount to a *novus actus interveniens*.

The Development of the Case-Law on Escaping Situations of Significant Inconvenience

In delivering the judgment of the court in *Robson* v *North Eastern Railway Co*.[30] Field J. observed,

> it has been long established that, if a person by a negligent breach of duty exposes the person towards whom the duty is contracted to obvious peril, the act of the latter in endeavouring to escape from the peril, although it may be the immediate cause of the injury, is not the less to be regarded as the wrongful act of the wrongdoer: *Jones* v *Boyce*; and this doctrine has, we think, been rightly extended in more recent times to a 'grave inconvenience'…

---

25   (1848) 12 QB 439. The facts of this case are examined in Chapter 2.
26   Ibid., 446.
27   Ibid., 447.
28   This notion has been fully explored in Chapter 4.
29   (1958) AC 240.
30   (1874–75) LR 10 QB 271, 274.

This extension of the 'alternative danger' doctrine to situations of grave or significant inconvenience has taken place mainly in the context of injuries to railway passengers. *Adams v The Lancashire and Yorkshire Railway Company*[31] concerned an action to recover damages for personal injuries sustained by the plaintiff through the alleged negligence of the defendant railway company. The plaintiff was a passenger on one of the defendant's trains. He sat next to the carriage door but could have sat further away from the door had he chosen to do so as there were only two or three passengers in the carriage at the time. Shortly after the journey began, the carriage door flew open due to a defective door lock attributable to the defendant's negligence. The plaintiff shut and fastened the door but shortly afterwards it again flew open and he shut and fastened it again. This occurred three times and on the fourth occasion the plaintiff fell out of the train while holding the door shut and trying to fasten it. The Court of Common Pleas overturned a verdict in the plaintiff's favour and held that the defendant was not liable. The plaintiff's injury was not considered to be the necessary or natural result of the company's negligence since the inconvenience the plaintiff would have suffered if he had not attempted to shut the door was slight compared with the considerable peril incurred in his attempt to shut it. The inconvenience was not so great as to make it reasonable for the plaintiff to place himself in such a perilous situation since the train would have arrived at the next station in three minutes and the plaintiff could have changed his seat to a safer one. Ryles J. held that although the accident would not have happened but for the defendant's negligence, '[such] negligence, however, was neither the immediate nor the effective cause of the accident; that cause was the act of the plaintiff, in trying to shut the door…'[32] Brett J. attempted to formulate a general principle that 'if the inconvenience is so great that it is reasonable to get rid of it by an act not obviously dangerous, and executed without carelessness, the person causing the inconvenience by his negligence would be liable for any injury that might result from an attempt to avoid such inconvenience.'[33] Such principle was not satisfied on the instant facts, however, and Brett J. denied the plaintiff a remedy on the ground of his contributory negligence. Montague Smith J. distinguished *Jones v Boyce*[34] on the basis that the doctrine of alternative danger had no application to the facts of the instant case. By 'voluntarily' undertaking to shut the door, the plaintiff exposed himself to significant danger when he was not suffering any tangible inconvenience. Thus the plaintiff's repeated attempts to shut the door were unreasonable in the circumstances and constituted a superseding cause of his own injury.[35]

What of the train passenger who is forced by the negligence of the defendant railway company to descend from the train carriage in less-than-ideal conditions? In *Rose v North Eastern Railway*[36] a passenger descended from his carriage

---

31   (1869) LR 4 CP 739.
32   Ibid., 741.
33   Ibid., 744.
34   (1816) 1 Stark 493.
35   (1869) LR 4 CP 739, 742–3. As we saw in Chapter 4, unreasonable intervening conduct has since been held on many occasions to sever the causal chain.
36   (1876) 2 Ex D 248, 251 (CA).

which had stopped beyond the platform. Cockburn C.J. identified the relevant considerations as follows:

> If the passenger is satisfied that the train is going on, and there is apparently no alternative but to get out, he must do as best he can. Of course, if he is careless in getting out and is thereby injured, it is his own fault, but if he does his best and yet sustains injury, the company will not have done what was incumbent on them to do, and will be liable.

In its 1973 decision in *Caterson v Commissioner of Railways*,[37] the High Court of Australia considered the extension of the application of the 'alternative danger' doctrine in this context. The plaintiff, accompanied by his 14-year-old son, had driven a friend some 40 miles to a railway station, in order that the friend might catch a long-distance express train. The plaintiff carried the friend's luggage into the carriage, and as he was leaving the carriage he noticed that the train had started to move. No one in the carriage heard any warning that the train was about to depart. The next scheduled stop was some 80 miles away. The train was not travelling very fast when the plaintiff, thinking of his son on the platform 40 miles from home, jumped on to the platform and was injured. The plaintiff's action for damages for personal injuries against the Commissioner for Railways succeeded at first instance, the court having rejected the Commissioner's argument that the plaintiff's voluntary act in jumping from the train severed the causal chain. This disposition was affirmed on appeal to the High Court of Australia. Gibbs J. held that the plaintiff's conduct of jumping from the carriage was 'in the ordinary course of things' and 'the very kind of thing' likely to happen as a result of the defendant's negligence.[38] Moreover, the plaintiff's conduct was not unreasonable:

> No one could doubt that it would be negligent to jump from a train travelling at full speed simply to avoid the inconvenience of being carried on to another station. On the other hand, a person who wishes to avoid being carried on to a distant station might not unreasonably jump out from a train which was travelling very slowly.[39]

As for the doctrine of alternative danger, Gibbs J. had this to say:

> It was said that…the doctrine of alternative danger, and of which *Jones v Boyce* is an early example, has no application unless the plaintiff has been placed by the defendant's negligence in a position in which he has to choose between two dangers; it will never be reasonable, so it was said, to take a risk of injury merely to avoid an inconvenience, however great. I cannot agree with that submission which seems to me inconsistent with the decisions in *Robson v North Eastern Railway Co.*…and *Sayers v Harlow Urban District Council*. Where a plaintiff has by reason of the negligence of the defendant been so placed that he can only escape from inconvenience by taking a risk, the question whether his action in taking the risk is unreasonable is to be answered by weighing the degree of inconvenience to which he will be subjected against the risk that he takes in order to try to escape from it…[40]

---

37 (1973) 128 CLR 99.
38 Ibid., 110.
39 Ibid., 112 *per* Gibbs J.
40 Ibid., 111.

It is submitted with respect that this passage accurately reflects the current law on the doctrine of 'alternative inconvenience'.

The English Court of Appeal has taken a similar approach in a case involving a plaintiff's self-rescue attempt. In *Sayers* v *Harlow Urban District Council*[41] the plaintiff visited a public lavatory owned by the defendant and became incarcerated when the lock on the toilet door jammed. For the next 10 minutes or so she tried unsuccessfully to attract attention. She then decided to try to climb out by standing on the revolving toilet roll holder which rotated, causing her to slip and fall and sustain injury. Although the Court of Appeal held the plaintiff to have been contributorily negligent, her self-rescue attempt was not adjudged to be a *novus actus interveniens*. All the judges[42] of the Court of Appeal considered the plaintiff to have been acting reasonably in these particular circumstances. The inconvenience caused to the plaintiff was appreciable and she had not taken any risk which was disproportionate to the necessities of her situation. Lord Evershed M.R. distinguished *Adams* v *The Lancashire and Yorkshire Railway Co.*[43] on the ground that the degree of inconvenience suffered by Mrs Sayers far exceeded that experienced by the unsuccessful Mr Adams.[44] Moreover, the risk of falling out of a moving train was described by the Master of the Rolls as 'hazardous in the extreme'.[45]

Conclusion

As we have seen in this chapter, the 'alternative danger' doctrine was introduced by the common law towards the end of the eighteenth century[46] and extended in its application to situations of grave or significant inconvenience around the middle of the nineteenth century.[47] Generally speaking, normal and not unreasonable reactions to the defendant's negligent conduct, such as fear of imminent injury to oneself or the desire to extricate oneself from significant inconvenience, will not sever the causal chain. In relation to the former human reaction, this will be particularly so where the reactive behaviour has occurred instinctively in the agony of the moment. As regards the latter human reaction, whether or not there is sufficient time for due deliberation in terms of a 'cost-benefit' analysis,[48] the position appears to be that the touchstone

---

41 [1958] 1 WLR 623 (CA).
42 Lord Evershed M.R. and Morris and Ormerod LL.J.
43 (1869) LR 4 CP 739.
44 As the accident occurred in July, it was not suggested that Mr Adams was cold or exposed to any draughts. The train was due to arrive at the next station in three minutes and he could have taken a seat further away from the faulty carriage door.
45 [1958] 1 WLR 623, 628. A Canadian court has examined the causal impact of the desire to avert harm or escape an inconvenience in *Abbott* v *Kasza* (1976) 71 DLR (3d) 581 (backing truck angled across highway).
46 (1773) 2 W Bl 892.
47 *Robson* v *North Eastern Railway Co.* (1876) LR 10 QB 271.
48 *Caterson* v *Commissioner for Railways* (1973) 128 CLR 99 (instinctive reaction); *Sayers* v *Harlow Urban District Council* [1958] 1 WLR 623 (CA) (sufficient time for reflection).

of 'reasonableness' will involve a weighing of the degree of inconvenience caused to the plaintiff against the risks inherent in escaping the inconvenience. So long as the risks undertaken are not disproportionate to the degree of inconvenience sought to be avoided, the causal chain will remain intact.

Chapter 16

Negligence Causing Susceptibility to Later Harm

Introduction

What is the situation when a person sustains physical injury through another's negligence and subsequently sustains further physical injury in an accident allegedly due to his or her weakened condition caused by that negligence? In some situations the original tortfeasor may be liable for certain ulterior consequences such as where the plaintiff falls and sustains injury during convalescence. Section 460 of the American Law Institute's *Restatement of the Law of Torts, Second*[1] presents the following legal disposition:

> If the [defendant] is liable for an injury which impairs the physical condition of another's body, the [defendant] is also liable for harm sustained in a subsequent accident which would not have occurred had the other's condition not been impaired, and which is a normal consequence of such impairment.

According to the commentary accompanying Section 460, it applies only where the later accident is a normal consequence of the original injury. Thus, where the injured person attempts to make normal use of the injured part of his body by walking on a leg which has been broken after it has mended sufficiently to permit the attempt, and he or she is further injured by a second fall resulting from its weakened condition, the second injury is a normal consequence of the original impairment, and the defendant's negligence will be deemed to have been the legal cause of the later injury as well. Where, however, the injured person unnecessarily or unreasonably attempts to walk a short time after the leg is fractured, the second injury becomes an abnormal consequence for which the defendant will not be held responsible. In such cases the contributory negligence of the injured person will reduce the award of damages,[2] although it may be that the conduct of the plaintiff is so wholly unreasonable and reckless as to amount to a *novus actus interveniens*, thereby barring recovery of damages altogether for the later injury.[3]

---

1   (1965–79).

2   *Restatement of the Law of Torts, Second* (ALI, 1965–79) 501; M.A. Millner '*Novus Actus Interveniens*: The Present Effect of Wagon Mound' (1971) 22 Northern Ireland Legal Quarterly 168, 176–9; *Sayers* v *Harlow Urban District Council* [1958] 1 WLR 623 (CA).

3   A.M. Dugdale and M.A. Jones (eds) *Clerk & Lindsell on Torts* (Sweet & Maxwell, 19th edn, 2006) [109] – [110] paras 2–96 and 2–97.

In the cases which follow, a significant period of time often elapses between the tortfeasor's original negligence and the accident producing the later injury. This tends to encourage defendants to contend that a *novus actus* has occurred but such an argument has been rightly rejected, particularly where the effects of that negligence are ongoing.[4]

The Development of the Case-Law

The courts tend to agree that the issue of whether the original tortfeasors should remain liable for the later injury turns on the degree to which the post-negligence conduct of the plaintiff is perceived to be reasonable or normal in the circumstances. However, this judicial determination is difficult to predict in individual cases, as we shall see in this section.

Canadian courts have permitted plaintiffs to recover damages from the defendant for the later injury as well. In *Block* v *Martin*[5] a negligently-injured plaintiff fell while fishing and fractured his leg. The court held that the fracture would not have occurred unless the earlier injury was unhealed and such earlier injury remained a 'definite, contributing, predisposing cause'.[6] Australian and English courts have similarly so held. In *Pyne* v *Wilkenfeld*[7] the plaintiff was injured in a motor vehicle accident caused by the defendant's negligence. She later suffered further injuries when she stumbled on uneven ground, because she was wearing a surgical collar to support her neck as a result of her accident injuries and the collar restricted her vision by preventing her from seeing immediately in front of her. The Supreme Court of South Australia held that her further injuries were also caused by the defendant's negligence since she would not have stumbled if she had not been wearing the surgical collar, which she would not have been wearing but for the first accident. The intervening fall was attributable to the ongoing effects of the defendant's negligence.

The English case of *Wieland* v *Cyril Lord Carpets Ltd*[8] raised virtually identical facts and issues. The plaintiff, a bus passenger, received a jarring neck injury as a result of an accident admittedly caused by the defendant's negligence. An attending specialist prescribed a collar for her neck which was then fitted. She wore bi-focal glasses and the position of her neck in the collar deprived her of her usual ability to adjust herself automatically to the bi-focals. This produced some unsteadiness. While descending a flight of stairs with the assistance of her adult son, she fell and injured her ankles. Eveleigh J. held that there was no break in the causal chain on the ground that it had not been unreasonable for her in these circumstances to descend

---

4 *McCarthy* v *Wellington City* [1966] NZLR 481, 497 (*per* Tompkins J.); *Smith* v *Auckland Hospital Board* [1965] NZLR 191, 222 (*per* T.A. Gresson J.).

5 [1951] 4 DLR 121 (Alta).

6 Ibid., 126. See also *Boss* v *Robert Simpson (Eastern) Ltd* (1968) 2 DLR (3d) 114, 126 (*per* Coffin J.) (defendant is liable for later falls which are not the result of the plaintiff being 'careless or negligent').

7 (1981) 26 SASR 441.

8 [1969] 3 All ER 1006 (QBD).

the stairs with the assistance of her son.[9] The defendant was thus held liable for the additional injuries caused by the fall as they were still within the risk created by the defendant, rather than attributable to danger to which the plaintiff had unreasonably or deliberately exposed herself. Eveleigh J. stated, 'it is foreseeable that one injury may affect a person's ability to cope with the vicissitudes of life and thereby be a cause of another injury…' and held that 'the injury and damage suffered because of the second fall are attributable to the original negligence of the defendant…'[10]

The New South Wales Court of Appeal has recently upheld a plaintiff's claim for damages for later injuries in two cases. In *Kessey* v *Golledge*[11] the plaintiff was involved in a motor vehicle accident in 1992 as a result of the defendant's admitted negligence. This aggravated an existing condition of spondylolisthesis. Four years later the plaintiff fell in the course of her employment and further aggravated her back injury. The defendant argued that the 1996 workplace fall amounted to a *novus actus interveniens* on two grounds. First, it was contended that whatever problems had been caused to the plaintiff by the 1992 accident, they had resolved prior to the 1996 workplace accident and that the plaintiff's problems as from the date of the second accident were solely attributable to the effect of the workplace accident operating on the pre-existing condition of spondylolisthesis. Second, it was argued that the plaintiff's conduct in tripping over some books which had been left on the floor constituted careless or unreasonable conduct which severed the causal chain. The Court of Appeal rejected both submissions. The defendant had failed to discharge the onus of proving an absence of evidence linking the motor vehicle accident and the workplace accident. The Court of Appeal agreed with the trial Judge's finding that as a result of the injuries sustained in the motor vehicle accident, the plaintiff's back was vulnerable to pain and disability and that the 1996 workplace accident could not be causally disentangled from the 1992 accident. As for the defendant's second submission, the Court of Appeal distinguished the House of Lords decision in *McKew* v *Holland & Hannen & Cubitts (Scotland) Ltd*[12] on the ground that there was no evidence that the plaintiff was acting carelessly or unreasonably at the time of the later accident. The defendant was thus also held liable for the injuries sustained in the later workplace accident. A similar result was reached one year later when the New South Wales Court of Appeal decided the case of *Expokin Pty Ltd* v *Graham*.[13] The plaintiff, a nurse, slipped and fell in the defendant's supermarket, sustaining a right-knee injury. Although the plaintiff returned to work one week later, she continued to experience recurring painful symptoms with little sign of improvement. Some nine months later, she twisted her knee in an incident at work and, following another workplace mishap, was forced to cease her employment. At trial the defendant argued that the later workplace twisting injury was in no way connected to the original injury sustained in the supermarket fall and, as such, constituted a *novus actus interveniens*. The trial Judge rejected this submission and concluded instead that the later injury

---

9   Ibid., 1008.
10 Ibid., 1010.
11 [1999] NSWCA 424.
12 [1970] SC 20 (HL). This case is examined in detail in Chapters 3 and 4.
13 [2000] NSWCA 267.

was caused by instability in her right knee attributable to the original accident. His Honour relied on *State Government Insurance Commission* v *Oakley*[14] where it was held that the defendant is liable if the further injury results from a subsequent accident which would not have occurred had the plaintiff not been in the physical condition caused by the defendant's negligence. The defendant had failed to discharge the onus of proving that there was another self-sufficient cause entirely unrelated to his or her negligence. Accordingly, the defendant was held liable not only for the supermarket injuries (for which liability was admitted) but for the later workplace injury as well.

There is also a line of cases denying recovery to the plaintiff for damages relating to injuries sustained in later accidents. Perhaps the leading authority is the House of Lords decision in *McKew* v *Holland & Hannen & Cubitts (Scotland) Ltd.*[15] There the plaintiff workman sustained an injury in a workplace accident admittedly due to his employer's fault. His left leg was thereby weakened and on several occasions it became numb and he lost control of it for a short period. Some three weeks after the accident he went to inspect a house of which he had been offered the tenancy, accompanied by his wife and a relative. On leaving the premises and in the course of descending a steep staircase which lacked a handrail, his left leg went numb. Fearing that he might fall, the plaintiff jumped to the bottom of the staircase, sustaining further injury. In an action brought by the plaintiff against the employer for damages in relation to both accidents, the House of Lords held that the defendant employer was not liable for the injury sustained in the second accident, on the ground that the plaintiff had acted unreasonably in descending the staircase as he did, thus amounting to a *novus actus interveniens*. As Lord Reid stated:

> In my view the law is clear. If a man is injured in such a way that his leg may give way at any moment, he must act reasonably and carefully. It is quite possible that in spite of all reasonable care his leg may give way in circumstances such that as a result he sustains further injury. Then that second injury was caused by his disability, which in turn was caused by the defender's fault. But if the injured man acts unreasonably, he cannot hold the defender liable for injury caused by his own unreasonable conduct. His unreasonable conduct is *novus actus interveniens*. The chain of causation has been broken and what follows must be regarded as caused by his own conduct and not by the defender's fault or the disability caused by it.[16]

The effect of a successful *novus actus* plea in such circumstances is, of course, to deny any recovery of damages for the later injury. The House of Lords refused to view the case as one of contributory negligence on the plaintiff's part necessitating an apportionment of damages between the plaintiff and the defendant for the later injury. This is a curious approach inasmuch as the plaintiff's second accident was

---

14 (1990) Australian Torts Reports 81-003. See also *Skea* v *NRMA Insurance Ltd* [2005] ACTA 9 (Supreme Court of the Australian Capital Territory – Court of Appeal) where Crispin P. stated (at para. 5), 'It is open to a defendant to attempt to show that some or all of the plaintiff's continuing disabilities are not attributable to the initial illness but to subsequent non-compensable stresses. However, in that event, the defendant bears the onus of "disentangling" the non-compensable from the compensable components of his or her condition…'

15 [1970] SC 20 (HL).

16 Ibid., 25.

attributable to two concurrent causes – the original workplace accident (which left the plaintiff's left leg in a weakened and more vulnerable state as a result of the defendant's negligence) and the plaintiff's carelessness. As Professor Linden has pointed out,[17] if injured plaintiffs act negligently and fall, they cannot be expected to be treated in the same way as if they had been careful. But neither should they automatically be denied compensation for the additional later injury. The fairer solution is to apportion liability and to reduce plaintiffs' damages awards to the extent that their negligence contributed to their later injury.[18] The lack of any reference to the *Law Reform (Contributory Negligence) Act 1945* in the judgments of their Lordships in the *McKew* case is thus somewhat perplexing. Nevertheless, the tenor of those judgments would suggest that a defendant will normally be liable for a later injury which has been caused by a weakness or predisposition to injury attributable to the defendant's negligence where the plaintiff has been exercising ordinary prudence in his or her daily activities at the time of the later injury.

Canadian and Australian courts have denied recovery of damages for later injuries where the plaintiff has shown a disregard for his or her own safety and welfare. In the Canadian case of *Priestley* v *Gilbert*[19] the plaintiff's leg was seriously injured in an accident caused by the defendant driver's gross negligence. Upon becoming intoxicated at a Christmas party, the plaintiff began dancing and, owing to weakness in his leg from the accident injury, he fell and fractured his leg again. In refusing his claim for damages arising from the second fracture, Osler J. stated:

> ...[T]here is an onus upon a person who knows or should know of a physical weakness to act reasonably and carefully and to protect himself from harm...[T]o get up and dance on this occasion was not a reasonable action in his condition...and the principle of *novus actus interveniens* protects the defendant from responsibility for that injury.[20]

Such an approach mirrors that taken by Lord Reid in the *McKew* case and suffers from the same shortcoming concerning the failure to consider the possibility of holding the plaintiff contributorily negligent. Similarly, in the Australian case of *Nicolson* v *Tucker*[21] the plaintiff sued the defendant for damages for injuries arising out of a motor vehicle accident. As a consequence of his injuries, the plaintiff underwent an operation to insert a dowel into his cervical spine. Two weeks later, as a result of lifting a motorised lawnmower to a height of five feet, the dowel split and the plaintiff was required to undergo another operation. The Supreme Court of South Australia held that the plaintiff's action in lifting the mower, thereby splitting the dowel, amounted to a *novus actus interveniens*, and the defendant was thus not responsible for the later injury and second operation. The plaintiff had acted in

---

17   A. Linden and B. Feldthusen *Canadian Tort Law* (Butterworths, 8th edn, 2006) 407.
18   Various other commentators have also criticised the House of Lords on this point. See, for example, A. Palmer 'Causation in the High Court' (1993) 1 *Torts Law Journal* 9, 14; F. Trindade and P. Cane *The Law of Torts in Australia* (Oxford University Press, 3rd edn, 1999) 494, n. 81; M.A. Millner '*Novus Actus Interveniens*', 178–9.
19   [1972] 3 OR 501 (Ont.).
20   Ibid., 508.
21   (1984) Australian Torts Reports 80-512.

complete disregard for his own welfare and his act could not have been reasonably foreseen by the defendant. In contrast to the *Priestley* case, the negligence of the plaintiff in *Nicolson* was more reckless and, for that reason, the successful *novus actus* plea (as opposed to a finding of contributory negligence) in the latter case could perhaps be more easily defended. The *McKew* 'reasonableness' test will not apply, however, where the plaintiff is compelled to assume the risk of further injury as part of his or her employment. In *State Government Insurance Commission* v *Oakley*[22] the plaintiff nurse had received an injury to her right arm and shoulder in a motor vehicle accident caused by the defendant's negligence. This left her with a residual disability causing her to rely only on her left arm in lifting patients. In lifting a patient she suffered further injury for which she claimed damages. The defendant motorist who was responsible for the first injury was also held liable for 50 per cent of the later injury since the ongoing effects of the first injury were held to have contributed to it.

Conclusion

It is difficult to formulate precise conclusions in this particular area of intervening causation. This is due in part to each case turning on its own set of facts and circumstances and the fact that it is often a matter of degree. Temporal considerations are also important; often a significant period of time elapses between the negligently-caused accident and the subsequent accident or event. The causation enquiry therefore can become quite murky and complex as other plausible contributing factors are identified and raised by the defendant. However, the following three propositions do enjoy general support amongst the case authorities where the defendant's negligence causes an injury and the plaintiff subsequently suffers a further injury.

First, where the later injury results from a subsequent accident which would not have occurred had the plaintiff not been in a physically vulnerable or weakened condition caused by the defendant's negligence, the added damage will be considered to have been caused by that negligence.[23] This is so provided the plaintiff was not acting unreasonably in terms of regard for his or her well-being at the time of the second accident or event. As King J. stated in *Australian Eagle Insurance Company Ltd* v *Federation Insurance Ltd*:[24]

> If, at the time of the second accident...the [plaintiff's] condition is still unhealed or unstable and the incapacity would not have occurred but from that unhealed or unstable condition, the incapacity must be regarded as resulting from the first accident as well as from the second accident. Moreover, when the second accident is a mere aggravation or recurrence of the injury sustained in the first accident and is brought about by ordinary and reasonable conduct on the part of the [plaintiff], the consequent incapacity must, in my opinion, be regarded as the result of the first accident as well as from the second accident.

---

22   [1990] Australian Torts Reports 81-003.
23   *State Government Insurance Commission* v *Oakley* (1990) Australian Torts Reports 81-003, p. 67, 577 (*per* Malcolm C.J.).
24   (1976) 15 SASR 282, 292.

Second, where the further injury results from a subsequent accident which still would have occurred had the plaintiff been in normal health, but the damage sustained is greater because of aggravation of the earlier injury, the additional damage resulting from the aggravated injury should be treated as having been caused by the defendant's negligence.[25] Third, where the further injury results from a subsequent accident which would have occurred had the plaintiff been in normal health and the damage sustained in the later accident does not include any aggravation of the earlier injury, the later accident and further injury should be regarded as causally independent of the defendant's negligence.[26] As King J. said in *Australian Eagle Insurance Company Ltd v Federation Insurance Ltd*,[27] '[i]f, at the time of the second accident, the physical consequences of the first accident have stabilized to the degree that they can fairly be regarded as spent and as leaving only a vulnerability to injury from future trauma, the incapacity flowing from the second accident cannot be regarded as the result of the first accident but must be regarded as the second accident only.' And as Lord Reid has observed in *Hogan v Bentinck West Hartley Collieries (Owners) Ltd*,[28] '[i]f liability to pay compensation is to cease, not only must a new cause of incapacity come in, but the old must go out: there must no longer be any causal connection between the injury by accident and the present incapacity.'

---

25   *State Government Insurance Commission v Oakley* (1990) Australian Torts Reports 81-003, p. 67, 577 (*per* Malcolm C.J.); *GIO v Aboushadi* (1999) Australian Torts Reports 81-531; *Fishlock v Plummer* [1950] SASR 176.
26   *State Government Insurance Commission v Oakley* (1990) Australian Torts Reports 81-003, p. 67, 577 (*per* Malcolm C.J.).
27   (1976) 15 SASR 282, 292.
28   [1949] 1 All ER 588, 605 (HL).

Chapter 17

Miscellaneous Operative Contexts

Introduction

The *novus actus interveniens* doctrine has operated from time to time in sundry other contexts. Each such other context does not of itself warrant its own chapter but collectively they may be dealt with conveniently within one chapter, although their subject-matter may be somewhat unrelated. The nine operative contexts to be examined in this chapter include: conduct necessary to exercise legal rights or privileges tortiously impeded, dangerous chattels, negligent inspection, institutional liability, defamation/republication, drug addiction, spousal desertion, plaintiff's fraud and passing off.

Conduct Necessary to Exercise Legal Rights or Privileges Tortiously Impeded

A defendant who wrongfully impedes the exercise of another's legal rights or privileges cannot assert as a superseding cause the plaintiff's normal and reasonable efforts to remove the impediment or to exercise the right or privilege notwithstanding its existence.[1] This legal principle was firmly established in the nineteenth century[2] and has been codified in Section 446 of the American Law Institute's *Restatement of the Law of Torts, Second*[3] which states:

> If the [defendant] intentionally or negligently impedes the exercise of another's rights or privileges, the other's normal efforts to remove the impediment or to exercise the right or privilege notwithstanding its existence are not a superseding cause of harm resulting from such efforts.

Thus, if a defendant falsely imprisons another, such act will be regarded as the legal cause of any injury the plaintiff sustains in any reasonable effort to escape therefrom.[4]

In the 1848 case of *Clayards* v *Dethick*[5] the defendant partially obstructed a right-of-way which the plaintiff cab proprietor relied on in pursuing his livelihood.

---

1 J. Fleming *The Law of Torts* (The Book Company Limited, 9th edn, 1998) 249.
2 *Clark* v *Chambers* (1878) 3 QBD 327; *Clayards* v *Dethick* (1848) 12 QB 439.
3 (1965–79).
4 The adoption of an unreasonably dangerous means of escaping from such an imprisonment may entail a finding of contributory negligence against the plaintiff: see *Sayers* v *Harlow Urban District Council* [1958] 1 WLR 623 (CA) (not a false imprisonment case but the principle would still apply).
5 (1848) 12 QB 439. This case is examined in more detail in Chapter 2.

In leading his horse along this right-of-way, the horse fell into an unfenced trench and died. It was held that the defendant's negligence in failing to fence off the trench was not excused merely because the plaintiff knew that some danger existed and assumed the risk posed by such danger in order to pursue his calling. Coleridge J. stated that the plaintiff was not obliged to abstain from pursuing his livelihood because there was some danger involved and the court appeared satisfied that the plaintiff had not acted unreasonably in the circumstances.[6] The 1878 case of *Clark* v *Chambers*[7] involved the plaintiff losing an eye when it came in contact with a spiked barrier placed across a footpath as he was lawfully passing along it. The barrier had originally been placed by the defendant across a roadway but it had been relocated without authority by a third person across the footpath. The Court of Queen's Bench held that the defendant, having unlawfully placed a dangerous object across a roadway, was liable for the injury occasioned by it to the plaintiff, notwithstanding that the immediate cause of the accident was the intervening act of a third party in repositioning that object across the footpath. *Clark* v *Chambers* has been applied by the Supreme Court of Ireland in *Cunningham* v *MacGrath Brothers*.[8] There the plaintiff was injured when a ladder fell on her. The ladder had originally been left by the defendant outside a shop, causing a partial obstruction of the footpath. Some unknown person had then moved the ladder round a corner into a small side street where the accident occurred. In the plaintiff's public nuisance action for damages for her personal injuries, the defendant argued that the intervention of the unknown person in moving the ladder from a position of relative safety to a position of danger constituted a *novus actus interveniens*. The Supreme Court rejected the defendant's plea. In delivering the Court's judgment, Kingsmill Moore J. stated:

> I am of opinion that the test to be applied is whether the person responsible for creating the nuisance should anticipate as a reasonable and probable consequence that some person in pursuance of his rights would attempt to abate the nuisance and in so doing would create a danger. Applying this test it seems to me that [the defendant] should have anticipated as reasonable and probable that someone…would remove the ladder and put it somewhere near in a position where it would be less of an obstruction but might constitute more of a danger.[9]

In *Weld-Blundell* v *Stephens*[10] Lord Sumner endorsed the decision in *Clark* v *Chambers* and accepted the principle that the conduct of persons acting reasonably in the exercise or the defence of their rights between the defendant's negligence and the plaintiff's injury will not ordinarily amount to a *novus actus interveniens*.[11]

---

6   See also the decision of the House of Lords in *A.C. Billings & Sons Ltd* v *Riden* (1958) AC 240.
7   (1878) LR 3 QBD 327. This case is examined in more detail in Chapter 2.
8   [1964] IR 209.
9   Ibid., 215.
10 [1920] AC 956, 984 (HL).
11 Also citing *The Sisters* (1876) 1 PD 117; *Halestrap* v *Gregory* (1895) 64 LJ (QB) 415.

Spousal Desertion after a Disfiguring or Debilitating Accident

What is the situation where a spouse is injured through another's negligence and the other spouse deserts him or her due to disfigurement, disability or personality change? Does the other spouse's decision to end the relationship constitute a *novus actus interveniens* relieving the defendant of liability for other heads of damage such as pain and suffering and certain expenditure? The resolution of this question may ultimately turn on a judicial value judgement.[12]

Older case authority has denied pain and suffering damages for marital breakdown where a defendant motorist was held not liable in an action for personal injury damages when the plaintiff's wife, believing him to be no longer capable of sexual intercourse, deserted him and took with her the children of the marriage.[13] More recent case-law would suggest that the possibility of desertion by a partner following a disfiguring, disabling or personality-altering accident is sufficiently commonplace today in light of changing social mores for it to be perceived as not abnormal and foreseeable.[14] Thus, the *novus actus* plea will rarely succeed now in this context.

Drug and Alcohol Addiction

Difficult problems arise for courts concerning the causal effects of conduct on the plaintiff's part where that conduct may be perceived as an inappropriate social response to difficulties faced by the plaintiff which have been caused by an earlier injury attributable to the defendant's negligence. New South Wales courts have faced more than their fair share of cases in this regard. The position would appear to be that a plaintiff who takes to alcohol or drugs to alleviate accident-associated pain, thereby aggravating the harm he or she suffers as a result of the defendant's negligence, may recover damages for that aggravated harm on the basis that such a reaction was reasonably foreseeable or involved an involuntary response on the plaintiff's part.

In *Havenaar* v *Havenaar*[15] the New South Wales Court of Appeal distinguished between, on the one hand, voluntary consumption of alcohol after an accident which would sever the causal chain (even if foreseeable) and, on the other hand, involuntary consumption where there was no other available way of relieving the pain.[16] Drug addiction, however, poses more serious problems for the courts. In *State Rail Authority of New South Wales* v *Wiegold*[17] the plaintiff was a maintenance linesman employed by the defendant. He was injured during the course of his work when he

---

12   R. Balkin and J. Davis *Law of Torts* (LexisNexis Butterworths, 3rd edn, 2004) 337.
13   *Cameron* v *Nottingham Insurance Co. Ltd* [1958] SASR 174.
14   *Encev* v *Encev* (SC (Vic), BC 9706275, unreported) at 3133; *Jones* v *Jones* [1985] QB 704 (CA); *Hird* v *Gibson* [1974] Qd R 14 (FC). See also H. Luntz *Assessment of Damages* (4th edn, 2002) [2.7.6].
15   [1982] 1 NSWLR 626 (CA).
16   *Commonwealth* v *McLean* (1997) 41 NSWLR 389 (CA); *New South Wales Insurance Ministerial Corporation* v *Myers* (1995) 21 MVR 295 (NSWCA) (injuries led to depression, excessive alcohol consumption and attempted suicide).
17   (1991) 25 NSWLR 500 (NSWCA).

fell down a railway embankment at night due to a defective torch with which he had been supplied by the defendant employer. After the accident the plaintiff was unable to work and he received worker's compensation payments. However, he began to worry about how he would be able to support his family once his entitlement to these payments expired. He began to grow Indian hemp, intending to produce and sell marijuana, but was arrested, convicted and imprisoned. Applying the so-called 'but-for' test, the trial Judge held that the plaintiff's imprisonment had been caused by the defendant's negligence. On appeal, a majority of the New South Wales Court of Appeal held that, as a matter of policy, it was inappropriate to hold that the plaintiff's imprisonment was caused by the defendant's negligence. Rather, the plaintiff's voluntary and rational decision to resort to drug-related crime constituted a *novus actus interveniens*. Samuels J.A. reasoned:

> If the plaintiff has been convicted and sentenced for a crime, it means that the criminal law has taken him to be responsible for his actions, and has imposed an appropriate penalty. He or she should therefore bear the consequences of the punishment...If the law of negligence were to say, in effect, that the offender was not responsible for his actions and should be compensated by the tortfeasor, it would set the determination of the criminal court at naught...Hence, the application of the simple 'but for' test to determine causation would be singularly inappropriate in this case. In all of the circumstances, it would be quite unreal to find that the [defendant] caused the [plaintiff] to engage in criminal conduct.[18]

Another contemporaneous case to come before the New South Wales Court of Appeal involved the plaintiff's drug addiction. In *Yates* v *Jones*[19] the 17-year-old plaintiff was injured in a motor vehicle accident caused by the defendant's negligence. Her injuries included chest pains. She was hospitalised and, according to her evidence, given insufficient pain relief medication to relieve her discomfort. A 'casual acquaintance' visited her in hospital and suggested she try some heroin as pain relief. At first she resisted but agreed on his third visit and he then injected her with the drug. She subsequently developed a heroin addiction which she supported by criminal activity, including theft and prostitution. Although her claim succeeded at trial, a majority of the New South Wales Court of Appeal denied that part of her claim for damages concerning her subsequent drug addiction. Samuels J.A. held that the course of events leading to the plaintiff agreeing to take heroin was not reasonably foreseeable while Meagher J.A. concluded that the drug dealer's conduct and the plaintiff's own conduct was deliberate and voluntary in nature and amounted to *novus actus interveniens*. While the majority were preoccupied with public policy considerations and the normative effect of the criminal law on civil liability, Kirby P. dissented on the basis that the plaintiff's own conduct was not truly volitional but rather the product of significant pain and consequent vulnerability. In the result, the defendant was not held responsible for the damages relating to the plaintiff's heroin addiction.[20]

---

18   Ibid., 514. Kirby P., in dissent, agreed with the trial Judge that the plaintiff should not be punished twice which a finding against civil liability would otherwise entail (at 505).

19   (1990) Australian Torts Reports 81-009 (NSWCA).

20   In so holding, the New South Wales Court of Appeal distinguished its earlier decision in *Grey* v *Simpson* (unreported, NSWCA, 3 April 1978) (in which the Court had held that it

Yates v *Jones* was distinguished in a later case before the New South Wales Court of Appeal. In *Goodsell* v *Murphy*[21] the plaintiff was injured in a motor vehicle accident, sustaining neck, head and knee injuries. Her hospital treatment included morphine. When she left the hospital she was still in considerable pain. Prior to the accident, the plaintiff had a history of heroin addiction. Within days of her hospital discharge, the plaintiff arranged for a friend to purchase heroin for her and she then resumed taking heroin. At trial the plaintiff successfully argued that the accident was a contributing factor in her relapse to addiction and she was awarded damages therefor. On appeal, a majority of the Court of Appeal[22] agreed with the trial Judge's finding on causation. The majority considered that while she did have a history of drug use, evidence was accepted at first instance that it was the pain stemming from the accident that led her to ask a friend to acquire the heroin three days after discharge from hospital. Their Honours factually distinguished *Yates* v *Jones* upon which the defendant relied. In *Yates* the Court of Appeal was not satisfied with the plaintiff's argument that she used heroin for pain relief after her accident, given she had not used it before and did not have experience of its palliative effect. In the instant case, however, the plaintiff had used heroin before the accident and was aware of its apparent palliative attraction.

Passing Off Actions

Generally speaking, in an action for 'passing off' taken pursuant to statute, the plaintiff must be able to show that the act complained of constitutes a misrepresentation. The defendant's conduct must have occurred in the course of trade and have been made to prospective customers or to the consuming public in such a way as to deceive them into believing that there is some type of connection between the goods and services of the defendant and those of the plaintiff. The error or misconception in question must also have been caused by the defendant's conduct and not by other intervening events or circumstances for which the defendant is not responsible.[23] However, there is no doctrine of 'erroneous assumption' to the effect that the error or misconception on the prospective customer's or consumer's part

---

was open to the trial Judge to find that the plaintiff's heroin addiction was a direct result of psychological problems and severe pain stemming from his injuries). Compare *Rosenberger* v *Meanderham Pty Ltd* (unreported, Qld SC, Cullinane J., 7 October 1995, BC9502123) (plaintiff's drug abuse not only unforeseeable, but her decision to abuse drugs in the way she did unreasonable). There is also English case-authority for the proposition that a defendant is not liable for a plaintiff's voluntary, deliberate and informed decision to use heroin. In *Wilson* v *Coulson* [2002] PIQR P300 (QBD) the plaintiff alleged that brain damage sustained in a road traffic accident caused by the defendant's negligence had produced a personality change, which led to him becoming addicted to heroin. Harrison J. held that the defendant was not liable for further brain damage caused by a heroin overdose because the plaintiff's capacity to refuse to take heroin had not been affected by the defendant's negligence and, as such, his decision to use heroin had been voluntary, deliberate and informed.

21 (2002) Australian Torts Reports 81-671 (NSWCA).
22 Mason P. and Beazley J.A.
23 *Parkdale Custom Built Furniture Pty Ltd* v *Puxu Pty Ltd* (1982) 149 CLR 191.

automatically operates to sever the causal chain and thereby relieve the defendant of liability for the consequences of its conduct.[24]

Plaintiff's Fraud

The commission of fraud by the plaintiff will generally amount to a *novus actus interveniens*. However, rare exceptions do arise from time to time based on the particular facts and circumstances of the case. For instance, in *Krakowski* v *Trenorth*[25] the directors of the plaintiff company had knowingly furnished false replies in connection with a sale of the company's property to a third party, causing the sale to be set aside for fraudulent misrepresentation. These replies had been given on the advice of a solicitor employed by the defendants concerning the directors' duty of disclosure under the transaction. The fraud was found to be of a technical nature, there being no intention to deceive on the directors' part. In these circumstances it was held that the company's fraud did not interrupt the chain of causation.[26]

Negligent Inspection

Will intervening negligent inspection or omission to inspect relieve defendants such as manufacturers and contractors of their responsibility? At one time the unexplored possibility of intermediate inspection excused negligent defendants.[27] Increasingly, however, courts are refusing to grant salvation on the 'gospel of redemption' by inspection.[28] Contemporary law no longer allows a negligent manufacturer or contractor to escape responsibility on the ground that an intermediary failed to subsequently inspect the article or job, at least in cases where there was no reasonable likelihood of an effective examination which would have disclosed the defect.[29]

It would appear that a manufacturer cannot escape liability by claiming that it was considered probable that there would be an intermediate examination by another which would reveal a defect in the product. In *Herschtal* v *Stewart & Ardern Ltd*[30] the defendant motor engineers reconditioned a car and supplied it to the plaintiff. The day after delivery the wheel came off as a result of the wheel nuts being improperly fastened. The plaintiff was injured. In determining when the possibility of an

---

24 *Taco Co. of Australia Inc.* v *Taco Bell Pty Ltd* (1982) 42 ALR 177, 200 (FCA, Full Court).
25 (1996) Australian Torts Reports 81-401.
26 See also *The Duke Group* v *Pilmer* (1999) Australian Torts Reports 81-507 where it was held that where the directors of the plaintiff company had used a negligently-compiled valuation report on the asset value of another company in order to fraudulently obtain shareholder consent to a take-over of that other company, the directors' fraud did not insulate the valuer from liability in negligence.
27 *Donoghue* v *Stevenson* [1932] AC 562 (HL).
28 *Ives* v *Clare Brothers Ltd* [1971] 1 OR 417, 421–2 (*per* Wright J.).
29 J. Fleming *The Law of Torts* (The Law Book Company of Australasia Pty Ltd, 2nd edn, 1961) 201.
30 (1940) 1 KB 155.

intermediate examination would have absolved the defendant from liability, Tucker J. held that the test was not whether there was an opportunity or possibility for such examination prior to use. Rather, the question was whether the defendant had good reason to contemplate that an examination, which would have revealed the defect, would be carried out prior to use. Tucker J. held that the defendant had no reason to anticipate such an examination and found the defendant liable in negligence in failing to properly secure the wheel.[31] Thus it would appear that a manufacturer or contractor cannot successfully plead *novus actus interveniens* unless an intermediate examination was reasonably contemplated in the ordinary course of events.

This principle has also been applied against repairers leading to a joint tortfeasor situation. In *Grant* v *Sun Shipping Co. Ltd*[32] the repairers of a ship had removed hatch covers over the hold of the ship and had left without replacing them. The shipowners' employees failed to notice this and the hold remained uncovered at the time the plaintiff stevedore, believing the hatches to be closed, fell into it and was injured. Although the shipowners' employees might have discovered the danger by conducting a proper inspection, the House of Lords held that the repairers were not relieved from liability to the plaintiff by reason of the subsequent intervening negligence of the employees in failing to inspect. Both defendants were held to have causally contributed to the plaintiff's injuries. The *Grant* case was followed by the Alberta Court of Appeal in *Ostash* v *Sonnenberg*[33] where it refused to relieve one negligent defendant from liability on the ground that another defendant could have discovered the defect. Smith C.J. stated that '…there were separate acts of negligence on the part of two persons which directly contributed to cause injury and damage to the plaintiffs and that therefore they are entitled to recover from both of them.'[34] However, if someone actually discovers the defect and does nothing to minimise the inherent danger involved when he or she had the means to do so, that person may be made exclusively responsible on the basis of a successful *novus actus* plea by the original tortfeasor.[35]

Institutional Liability

The residents of hospitals, mental institutions, prisons and schools may render those who manage them liable for injuries to themselves and to third persons. A *novus actus* plea will seldom succeed in this type of situation since the intervening events will often be found to have come within 'the scope of the risk' against which the defendant 'keepers' are under a duty to guard against.[36]

In *Williams* v *New Brunswick*[37] a prisoner set fire to a lockup causing the death of 21 inmates. An action by the families of some of the deceased prisoners succeeded

---

31 Ibid., 170–71.
32 [1948] AC 549 (HL).
33 (1968) 67 DLR (2d) 311 (Alta C.A.).
34 Ibid., 328.
35 *Stultz* v *Benson Lumber* (1936) 6 Cal. App. 2d 688.
36 See Chapter 7.
37 (1985) 34 CCLT 299 (N.B.C.A.).

against the provincial government for negligence in allowing the prisoner to obtain matches. The New Brunswick Court of Appeal held that the consequences of the negligence may 'fairly be regarded as within the ambit of the risk created by that negligence'.[38] The act of the prisoner in lighting the fire did not amount to a *novus actus* in such circumstances. On the same basis the House of Lords has held that the Home Office owed a duty of care to the owner of a yacht which had been set in motion and damaged during an escape attempt by some Borstal boys who were working on an island in the custody of police officers.[39] And in *Carmarthenshire County Council v Lewis*[40] a school was held liable when a child ran out of a school yard and caused the death of a motorist who swerved to avoid him.

In the context of a hospital or mental institution charged with the care of patients where the risk of self-destruction is part of the risk which the defendant institution is under a duty to take reasonable care to prevent, Professor Fleming has observed that such an institution 'should, on principle, be responsible for a suicidal death, regardless of whether the inmate was legally insane or not, because the risk of such an occurrence is the very reason for calling the defendant negligent if he fails to adopt precautions against it.'[41] This is *a fortiori* as the defendant's knowledge of the inmate's suicidal tendencies increases. Hospitals and mental institutions have also been held liable for attacks by their patients and escapees on third persons.[42] In his dissenting judgment in *Pallister v Waikato Hospital Board*[43] Woodhouse J. of the New Zealand Court of Appeal discussed at length the basis of a hospital's duty of care in relation to a patient with known suicidal tendencies, and why the suicide of the plaintiff's husband could not in the circumstances be considered a new and independent cause of his death. The reasoning of Woodhouse J. has been adopted by the House of Lords in its 1999 decision in *Reeves v Commissioner of Police of the Metropolis*.[44] There a prisoner hanged himself in a police cell even though the defendants had been aware that he was a suicide risk. The defendants denied liability on the ground that the prisoner's suicidal act was a voluntary act done while of sound mind and, as such, severed the causal chain. The majority of the House of Lords rejected the *novus actus* plea as the death resulted directly from breach of a duty to prevent just such an act. It was not a superseding event but the very harm that the defendants were under a duty to prevent.

---

38   Ibid., 319. See also *Michaluk v Rolling River School* [2001] M.J. No. 122, 153 Man. R. (2d) 300 (C.A.) (foreseeable that Grade 8 student playing with wire could puncture his eye).

39   *Home Office v Dorset Yacht Co. Ltd* [1970] AC 1004 (HL). This case is examined in more detail in Chapter 7.

40   [1955] AC 549.

41   J. Fleming *The Law of Torts* (The Law Book Company of Australasia Pty Ltd, 2nd edn, 1961) 204.

42   *Lawson v Wellesley Hospital* [1978] 1 SCR 893; *Holgate v Lancashire Mental Hospitals Board* [1937] 4 All ER 19.

43   [1975] 2 NZLR 725 (CA). This case is examined in more detail in Chapter 11.

44   [2000] 1 AC 360 (HL). This case is examined in more detail in Chapter 11.

Defamation/Republication

Defamation is committed when the defendant communicates to a third person, usually by words, any matter which adversely affects the reputation of the plaintiff. This tort protects a person's interest in his or her own reputation.[45] Since the tort of defamation protects the opinion that others hold of a person, as opposed to one's estimation of oneself, an action will lie only when the defamatory matter is made known to someone other than the plaintiff. This element of the tort of defamation is known as 'publication'.[46] The question with which we are concerned is whether, once a defamatory remark has been uttered or published, an unauthorised republication of it constitutes a *novus actus interveniens*, thereby relieving the original defendant of liability for damages sustained by the unauthorised republication.

In *Ward* v *Weeks*,[47] an early slander case, the plaintiff alleged that the defendant had said to one Edward Bryce that the plaintiff 'is a rogue and a swindler' and that Bryce subsequently (without the defendant's authority) repeated the defamatory words (as the statement of the defendant) to one John Bryer. It was further alleged that prior to hearing the defamatory words, Bryer was about to sell goods on credit to the plaintiff who was about to commence business as a shopkeeper but, upon hearing the words, lost trust in the plaintiff and consequently refused to extend credit to him. Tindal C.J. held that the plaintiff had failed to establish causation, stating:

> Every man must be taken to be answerable for the necessary consequences of his own wrongful acts: but such a spontaneous and unauthorised communication cannot be considered as the necessary consequence of the original uttering of the words. For no effect whatever followed from the first speaking of the words to Bryce; if he had kept them to himself Bryer would still have trusted the plaintiff. It was the repetition of them by Bryce to Bryer, which was the voluntary act of a free agent, over whom the defendant had no control, and for whose acts he is not answerable, that was the immediate cause of the plaintiff's damage.[48]

Thus, the unauthorised republication was the effective and immediate cause of the plaintiff's injury, effectively severing the causal link between the defendant's slander and the plaintiff's injury. The causal chain was held to have been broken by the spontaneous and unauthorised conduct of a free and independent agent or third party.

Ward v *Weeks* has received the express approval of the majority of the House of Lords in *Weld-Blundell* v *Stephens*.[49] In that case the plaintiff employed the defendant, a chartered accountant, to investigate the affairs of a company. In a letter to the defendant accountant, the plaintiff made defamatory statements concerning two officers of that company. The defendant's partner negligently left the letter in the company's offices where it was found by a manager who made a certified copy

---

45 Balkin and Davis, *Law of Torts*, 545.
46 Ibid., 566.
47 (1830) 7 Bing 211.
48 Ibid., 215.
49 [1920] AC 956 (HL).

of it and communicated its contents to the officers who had been defamed. These officers obtained damages for libel from the plaintiff who sought to recover them from the defendant on the basis of his breach of contract or negligence. The issue became whether or not on these facts the actions of the manager amounted to a *novus actus interveniens* which relieved the defendant accountant of liability for the republication of the libel to the company officers. A majority of their Lordships relied on *Ward* v *Weeks* and held that the plaintiff's liability for damages for libel did not result from the defendant accountant's breach of duty but from the actions of the manager.[50]

The relationship between intervening causation issues and liability for republication of defamatory material arose for the consideration of the English Court of Appeal in *Slipper* v *British Broadcasting Corporation*.[51] The plaintiff, a former detective chief superintendent, was prominently featured in a film made and broadcast by the defendants which dealt with the plaintiff's unsuccessful attempt to bring back to England from Brazil Ronald Biggs for his part in the 1963 mail train robbery. The plaintiff brought actions in respect of both a press review of the film and its subsequent broadcast, claiming that he was portrayed in a defamatory manner. In his statement of claim, the plaintiff relied on the defendant's knowledge that the film was likely to be reviewed in the national press and claimed that passages from several such reviews which repeated the alleged defamatory sting of the film should be taken into account in the assessment of general damages. The defendant applied to strike out that portion of the plaintiff's statement of claim. The Court of Appeal held that there were no specific or special rules regarding republication peculiar to defamation and such issues fell to be decided in accordance with the ordinary principles governing intervening causation issues. The question whether the defendants anticipated that the press reviews would repeat the sting of the libel raised issues of foreseeability and 'natural and probable consequence' and constituted a question of remoteness of damage. Stocker L.J. observed:

> Further, in my view, the law relating to republication in defamation cases is but an example of the rules of *novus actus* in all cases of tort…In a defamation case where there has been republication the question whether or not there has been a breach in the chain of causation inevitably arises but such cases are not in a special category related to defamation actions but are examples of the problem and will fall to be decided on general principles and in the light of their own facts as established. All these cases cited, including *Ward* v *Weeks*, are examples, on their own facts, of cases concerned with *novus actus* – breaches of the chain of causation.[52]

Slade L.J. concluded, '[p]rima facie, the court will treat the unauthorised repetition of a libel as a *novus actus interveniens* breaking the chain of causation between

---

50 Lord Wrenbury considered *Ward* v *Weeks* to be 'good law' but accepted that a defendant could be liable not only if he had authorised repetition of a slander by a third party but also 'if from the surrounding circumstances it is to be inferred that he anticipated and wished that he should repeat it' (ibid., 999).
51 [1991] 1 QB 283 (CA).
52 Ibid., 296.

the original publication and the damage suffered by the injured party through the repetition or republication.'[53] Nevertheless His Lordship cautioned that every case must be decided on its own facts and that a number of case authorities 'seem to show that *on particular appropriate facts* the repetition of the sting of a libel by an unauthorised third party may be treated as the "natural" or the "natural and probable" consequence of the original publication, so as to expose the original publisher to a claim for damages in respect of the repetition...'[54] Thus, it would appear that where the republication is the voluntary and unauthorised act of a free agent, the defendant will not be liable for its effects where such republication is not the natural or probable consequence of the original publication.[55]

Dangerous Chattels and Substances

In those cases where a plaintiff has been injured by a dangerous article such as a firearm, poison or a highly inflammable substance, it will generally be more difficult (but not impossible) for the defendant to successfully plead *novus actus interveniens*. In *Dominion Natural Gas Co.* v *Collins & Perkins*[56] Lord Dunedin stated the classical position:

> It has...again and again been held that in the case of articles dangerous in themselves, such as loaded firearms, poisons, explosives and other things *ejusdem generis*, there is a peculiar duty to take precaution imposed upon those who send forth or instal such articles when it is necessarily the case that other parties will come within their proximity. The duty being to take precaution, it is no excuse to say that the accident would not have happened unless some other agency than that of the defendant had intermeddled with the matter.[57]

That greater care is required of the defendant concerning inherently dangerous chattels is illustrated by the long line of firearms cases which have consistently imposed liability on the defendant for having failed to take adequate precautions to secure the gun from being handled by others, including children. Where the plaintiff has been shot by a third party, the defendant has still been held liable, notwithstanding a *novus actus* plea, on the ground that such an intervening event fell squarely within the scope of the risk which someone in the defendant's position should have anticipated. Such judicial approach dates back to the 1816 case of *Dixon* v *Bell*[58] and has been followed subsequently by the Irish Court of Appeal in *Sullivan* v *Creed*.[59] The mischievous acts of children in accidentally discharging loaded firearms have also

---

53 Ibid., 301–2 citing *Ward* v *Weeks* (1830) 7 Bing 211 and *Weld-Blundell* v *Stephens* [1920] AC 956.
54 Ibid., 302 (emphasis in original).
55 *Ward* v *Weeks* (1830) 7 Bing 211, 215 *per* Tindal C.J.; *Weld-Blundell* v *Stephens* [1920] AC 956, 976 (*per* Lord Dunedin), 987 (*per* Lord Sumner), 999 (*per* Lord Wrenbury); *Slipper* v *British Broadcasting Corporation* [1991] 1 QB 283, 301–2 (*per* Slade L.J.).
56 [1909] AC 640 (JCPC).
57 Ibid., 646.
58 (1816) 5 M & S 198. This case is examined in more detail in Chapter 2.
59 [1904] 2 IR 317 (CA). This case is examined in more detail in Chapter 14.

been attributed by English and Australian courts to those who negligently create the opportunities for their dangerous conduct respectively in *Newton v Edgerley*[60] and *Curmi v McLennan*.[61] In the Australian case of *Hogan v Gill*[62] the plaintiff, a four-year-old boy, was playing at the defendant's house with the defendant's six-year-old son. The children were playing the game 'Cowboys and Indians'. The defendant's son went into his parents' bedroom, picked up a loaded .22 calibre rifle which the defendant had left there and shot the plaintiff in the head, the latter sustaining severe injuries. The Queensland Supreme Court held the defendant liable in negligence for the plaintiff's injuries on the ground that as he knew beforehand that the children liked to play such games, such an eventuality was reasonably foreseeable. Another recent Australian case concerning the negligent storage of a loaded rifle is *Muller v Lalic*.[63] There the defendant's adult son shot the plaintiff with a high-calibre, military-style rifle he had taken from a locked wardrobe in the defendant's home. The son had removed the gun from the locked wardrobe contrary to his father's express directions. In an action in negligence, the trial Judge held that the father had not been negligent in storing the rifle and that the son's act in disobeying his father and subsequent conduct constituted a *novus actus interveniens*. However, the New South Wales Court of Appeal held that the trial Judge erred in finding that the son's conduct amounted to a *novus actus* and in finding that the defendant had not been negligent, since he had left the firearm loaded when he had informed others that it was never loaded. His son had pulled the trigger, reasonably believing from what his father had told him that the gun was not loaded. Relying on the above-quoted passage from the judgment of Lord Dunedin in *Dominion Natural Gas*, Stein J.A., in delivering the Court's judgment, described a loaded firearm as 'an inherently dangerous chattel' in respect of which a higher degree of care is required.[64] An act of a third party which constitutes a more immediate cause of the plaintiff's injury than the defendant's negligence did not necessarily sever the causal chain in such circumstances.

The same strict standards will also be applied against those who deal in highly inflammable substances and explosives. In *Yachuk v Oliver Blais Co. Ltd*,[65] for instance, the Judicial Committee of the Privy Council held the defendant vicariously liable for the act of its servant for having sold to a nine-year-old boy a small quantity of petrol, even though the boy had resorted to deceit to procure the sale. In *Philco Radio and Television Corporation of Great Britain Ltd v J. Spurling Ltd*,[66] the defendants negligently delivered parcels of highly inflammable celluloid film scrap to the plaintiff's premises where a typist mischievously touched one of the parcels with a lighted cigarette, having no idea of its volatile properties. The English Court

---

60 [1959] 3 All ER 337. This case is examined in more detail in Chapter 14.
61 [1994] 1 VR 513 (Supreme Court of Victoria – Appeal Division). This case is examined in more detail in Chapter 14.
62 (1992) Australian Torts Reports 81-182 (Qld S.C.).
63 [2000] NSWCA 50.
64 Ibid., para. 32.
65 [1949] 2 All ER 150 (JCPC). This case is examined in more detail in Chapter 14.
66 [1949] 2 All ER 882 (CA).

of Appeal refused to regard her conduct as amounting to a *novus actus interveniens* and held the defendants liable for the ensuing conflagration which seriously damaged the plaintiff's premises. The New Zealand Court of Appeal has held a defendant quarry operator liable for injuries to a nine-year-old boy sustained by an exploding detonator, in circumstances where the defendant's negligence in failing to adequately secure the detonators provided an opportunity for other boys to steal them.[67]

The chain of causation may, however, be broken in exceptional cases. One such example is *Taylor* v *Rover Co. Ltd*.[68] A worker was blinded in one eye when a splinter flew off the top of a chisel he was hammering. The defendant employer had the chisel specially manufactured and the manufacturers relied on a third party (the second defendants) for heat treatment and hardening. Although the evidence established that the weakness of the chisel was caused by the third party's negligence, the court held that the third party was not liable for the plaintiff's injury on the basis that some weeks earlier, another worker had been injured in the same way by the same chisel. The defendant employer thus had actual knowledge that the chisel was dangerous and therefore should have withdrawn it from circulation. The defendant's omission in this regard severed the causal chain, thereby relieving the third party of liability.

Inadequate Warnings

A manufacturer may still incur liability for an inadequate warning where its product has come under the supervision and control of a third party, but that is not always the case. In *Anderson* v *Corporation of the City of Enfield; Turco (Aust.) Pty Ltd (Third Party)*[69] the plaintiff employee brought an action against the defendant employer claiming damages for personal injury resulting from coming into contact with a particular cleaning substance. The employer was found liable in negligence for leaving the substances in a drum unprotected and without a warning label. The employer sought to recover contribution from the manufacturer of the product, arguing that the inadequacy of the manufacturer's warning label had contributed to the plaintiff's injury. The manufacturer claimed, in turn, that the employer's negligence amounted to a *novus actus interveniens*. In delivering the judgment of the Supreme Court of South Australia, King C.J. stated that the manufacturer of an inherently dangerous product owes a duty to give an adequate warning to those into whose hands the product may come of its dangerous qualities.[70] His Honour held that the product labelling did not contain a sufficiently striking warning and that it was reasonably foreseeable that the defendant employer might not appreciate the significance of the warning and might therefore fail to take adequate precautions to protect its employees.[71] Both the employer and manufacturer were found to have contributed to the plaintiff's injury. Accordingly, the *novus actus* plea did not succeed.

---

67   *McCarthy* v *Wellington City* (1966) NZLR 481 (CA).
68   (1966) 2 All ER 181.
69   (1983) 34 SASR 472.
70   Ibid., 476.
71   Ibid., 480.

Another instance of a *novus actus* plea not succeeding in such circumstances is the New Zealand case of *Grant v Cooper, McDougall and Robertson Ltd*.[72] In that case the plaintiff sheep farmer had dipped his sheep with a sheep dip manufactured by the defendant. His sheep were poisoned. The jury found that the label on the dip was inadequate and that the dip was potentially dangerous without adequate instructions. Northcroft J. rejected the defendant manufacturer's argument that the plaintiff must have known that the dip was dangerous, its purpose being to kill insects, but that he had nevertheless elected to take the risk. His Honour held that the inadequacy of the label constituted a negligent failure to warn the plaintiff of the risks involved in using the dip and nothing in the plaintiff's conduct could be said to have severed the causal chain between the negligent omission and the poisoning of the sheep. The opposite conclusion was reached in the Australian decision of *Forbes v Olympic General Products (Qld) Pty Ltd*[73] where the intervening reckless and unreasonable conduct of the plaintiff's employer was held to have severed the causal chain linking a distributor's failure to warn and the plaintiff's injuries. The plaintiff was employed to assist in the insulation of a freezer compartment in the hold of his employer's fishing trawler. The employer approached a distributor of insulation material and purchased a recommended material. This material was highly flammable and had been supplied by the manufacturer, along with sheets of technical information, to the distributor in containers carrying prominent red and black labels warning of its flammability. No warning was provided, however, on the need for adequate ventilation when using the product in confined spaces, but the distributor was aware of this fact. The distributor repackaged the material and provided its own labels and information sheets. The distributor's repackaged material had no warning other than an 'inflammable' label. The employer asked the distributor to transfer the material into small tins, which were unlabelled, and declined the distributor's offer to label the tins. The plaintiff and the employer then applied the material to the hold of the trawler. The only ventilation in the hold was an open area on the deck above the hold but this was partly covered by a tray. On the second day of installing the insulation, the employer completely covered the opening to keep the sun off. Fumes in the hold ignited and an explosion occurred, resulting in life-threatening burns to 80 per cent of the plaintiff's body.

The plaintiff's action in negligence against the manufacturer and distributor was dismissed, the employer being held solely responsible for his injuries. The manufacturer was not liable because it had been the distributor's responsibility to package the material and provide warnings. Although the distributor was clearly in breach of its duty to the plaintiff in failing to warn of the need for adequate ventilation, it had not been established on the balance of probabilities that if the employer had been appropriately warned by the distributor, the plaintiff would not have been injured, since the employer had not demonstrated a concern for safety. Once he began using the product, he became aware of the need for ventilation but had not provided any but had instead actually inhibited it. The defendant employer's intervening negligence thus constituted a *novus actus interveniens*.

---

72 (1940) NZLR 947.
73 (1989) Australian Torts Reports 80-301.

What is the situation where the plaintiff uses a contaminated product despite having heard circulated rumours concerning its possible danger? In *Rolfe* v *Katanga Lucerne Mill Pty Ltd*[74] the New South Wales Court of Appeal rejected a *novus actus* plea in such circumstances. There the plaintiff's race horses contracted botulism after having consumed contaminated feed which had been supplied by the defendant. In delivering the Court's judgment, Santow J.A. held that mere rumour and carelessness on the plaintiff's part are not enough to sever the causal connection. The kind of knowledge that would suffice to break the chain of causation would include both actual knowledge on the plaintiff's part of the contamination or 'a deliberate hiding of the eyes' from that knowledge when the plaintiff had reasonable grounds to suspect the contamination.[75]

---

74 [2005] NSWCA 252.
75 Ibid., paragraphs 53 and 119.

PART IV
Conclusion

Chapter 18

The Influence of Contributory Negligence and Apportionment Legislation on Intervening Causation Issues

Introduction

As we have already seen, the author of an intervening act may be either a third person or the plaintiff. In the latter case, the question arises whether the negligent conduct of the plaintiff should be treated merely as contributory negligence, in which case the plaintiff will be awarded reduced damages under contributory negligence legislation, or as a *novus actus interveniens*, in which case the plaintiff will be denied damages altogether. As we shall see, this question may be a matter of degree.

In former times, and up until the mid-twentieth century in many jurisdictions, the contributory negligence of the plaintiff provided the defendant with a complete defence. It is not altogether clear why the common law took the rather drastic position that contributory negligence was a complete defence. On the facts of some cases, there might have been a causal notion that the plaintiff's own conduct constituted a *novus actus* which severed the causal connection between the defendant's negligence and the plaintiff's injury.[1] Some early cases appear to have considered that the plaintiff's contributory negligence negatived the causal connection between the defendant's negligence and the plaintiff's damage. *Butterfield* v *Forrester*[2] is one such example. There, the defendant, in the course of repairing his house, put a pole across part of the road, thereby obstructing it and committing a public nuisance. At dusk one evening, at a time when there was sufficient light to observe this obstruction from some 100 yards, the plaintiff left a public house and rode his horse very fast along the road. The plaintiff was injured when he and his horse fell after colliding with the pole. Bayley J. considered that if the plaintiff had used ordinary care for his own safety, he would have seen the obstruction in time and that the accident appeared to happen entirely from his own fault. Other early examples include *Hughes* v *Macfie*[3] where a five-year-old boy was denied recovery on the basis of his own negligence[4] and *Adams* v *The Lancashire and Yorkshire Railway Company*[5] where Brett J. considered that by

---

1 H. Luntz and D. Hambly *Torts: Cases and Commentary* (Butterworths, 4th edn, 1995) 354.
2 (1809) 11 East 60; 103 ER 926.
3 (1863) 2 H & C 744. This case is examined in more detail in Chapter 14.
4 Ibid., 749.
5 (1869) LR 4 CP 739. This case is examined in more detail in Chapter 2.

putting himself in peril by attempting to close the door of a moving railway coach, the plaintiff was contributorily negligent.[6]

Eventually, a judicial reaction transpired to the injustice of denying recovery to a negligent plaintiff, even in cases where the defendant's negligence far outweighed the plaintiff's contributory negligence.[7] This occurred in the form of the 'last opportunity' rule[8] whose rationale was to be found in the reaction of the courts to the harshness of the complete or all-or-nothing nature of the common law defence of contributory negligence. Prior to the enactment of legislation concerning contributory negligence and apportionment in the mid-twentieth century, the plaintiff's contributory negligence was regarded as defeating his or her claim entirely, unless it could be shown that, notwithstanding such negligence, the defendant had the last opportunity of avoiding the accident. The plaintiff was entitled to recover, despite his or her negligence, if the defendant had the last opportunity of avoiding the accident but negligently failed to do so.[9] So, in the 1842 case of *Davies* v *Mann*[10] the Court of Exchequer held that the plaintiff, who had left his donkey tethered in the road, was not barred by contributory negligence when the donkey was run down and killed by the defendant's wagon. As one commentator has observed:

> The 'last opportunity' doctrine was essentially a causal argument: in such cases the court held that the only 'real' or 'effective' cause of the damage was the conduct of the defendant; the contributory negligence of the plaintiff was regarded as no longer legally operative...Causal refinements of this kind led to a vast and complicated body of case law, most of which was rendered mercifully obsolete by the introduction of the Law Reform (Contributory Negligence) Act 1945...[11]

The last opportunity rule or doctrine was severely criticised by the High Court of Australia in *Alford* v *Magee*[12] and effectively died with the enactment of contributory negligence legislation.[13]

It was not only the judges who rebelled against the common law defence of contributory negligence. Parliamentarians shared their distaste for the harshness of the operation of the defence on the plaintiff, leading to legislative intervention in the form of the *Law Reform (Contributory Negligence) Act 1945* (England).[14] This legislation provides that:

---

6   Ibid., 744.

7   *Joslyn* v *Berryman* (2003) 198 ALR 137, 142 (HCA) (*per* McHugh J.).

8   Or 'last clear chance' rule as it is known in the United States of America.

9   *March* v *E. & M.H. Stramare Pty Ltd* (1990–91) 171 CLR 506, 511 (*per* Mason C.J.).

10 (1842) 10 M & W 547; 152 ER 588.

11 M.A. Millner '*Novus Actus Interveniens*: The Present Effect of Wagon Mound' (1971) 22 Northern Ireland Legal Quarterly 168, 171 (footnote omitted).

12 (1952) 85 CLR 437, 450–64.

13 Millner, '*Novus Actus Interveniens*', 171; *March* v *E. & M. H. Stramare Pty Ltd* (1990–91) 171 CLR 506, 513 *(per* Mason C.J.).

14 The English model, passed in 1945, has since been adopted throughout Australia and New Zealand.

Where any person suffers damage as the result partly of his own fault and partly of the fault of any other person or persons, a claim in respect of that damage shall not be defeated by reason of the fault of the person suffering the damage, but the damages recoverable in respect thereof shall be reduced to such extent as the court thinks just and equitable having regard to the claimant's share in the responsibility of the damage.

Henceforward, courts were no longer obsessed with identifying a single cause for accidents and injuries.[15] Since the enactment of apportionment legislation, there has been a diminishing tendency to exculpate defendants by a denial of causality, and the notions of multiple causation and responsibility have become increasingly entrenched.[16] As Mason C.J. of the High Court of Australia has observed:

[T]he courts are no longer as constrained as they were to find a single cause for a consequence and to adopt the 'effective cause' formula. These days courts readily recognize that there are concurrent and successive causes of damage on the footing that liability will be apportioned as between the wrongdoers.[17]

Contemporary Operation of *Novus Actus Interveniens* in the Concurrent Wrongdoers Context

Like the *Law Reform (Contributory Negligence) Act 1945*, the introduction of legislation allowing apportionment of damages between tortfeasors (by a process called contribution) in the form of the *Civil Liabilities (Contribution) Act 1978* (England) has affected judicial decision-making on whether an intervening negligent act will sever the causal chain. Where the act of a third party combines with the defendant's negligence to cause the plaintiff's harm, the third party and defendant are concurrent wrongdoers. Where several tortfeasors are in some way responsible for the same damage suffered by the plaintiff, it is rare for the court to hold that only one of them is the sole legal cause of that loss.[18] The decision of the High Court of Australia in *Chapman v Hearse*[19] and that of the English Court of Appeal in *Rouse v Squires*[20] are weighty authority for this proposition. Although the plaintiff may sue every party responsible for his or her injury, the principle of joint and several liability means that each tortfeasor is liable in full to the plaintiff. Accordingly, the plaintiff need only sue one tortfeasor, and it is then up to that tortfeasor to seek contribution from others whose fault may have contributed to the plaintiff's damage. They may be joined as a co-defendant in the plaintiff's action. Recklessness or gross negligence

---

15   B. McMahon and W. Binchy *Irish Law of Torts* (Butterworths, 2nd edn, 1990) 54.

16   J. Fleming *The Law of Torts* (The Law Book Company of Australasia Pty Ltd, 2nd edn, 1961) 202.

17   *March v E. & M. H. Stramare Pty Ltd* (1990–91) 171 CLR 506, 512.

18   M. Lunney and K. Oliphant *Tort Law: Text and Materials* (Oxford University Press, 2000) 210.

19   (1961) 106 CLR 112. This case is examined in more detail in Chapter 3.

20   [1973] 1 QB 889 (CA). This case is examined in more detail in Chapter 8. See also *Barber v British Road Services*, *The Times*, 18 November 1964 (CA) and *Harvey v Road Haulage Executive* [1952] 1 KB 120 (CA).

on the third party's part may, however, provide an exception to the general rule that the intervening negligence of a third party (against whom contribution is sought by the defendant) will not break the causal chain between the defendant's negligence and the plaintiff's damage.[21] Likewise, a third party may allege that the supervening act of the defendant is of such an extreme nature as to relieve him or her totally from responsibility for the plaintiff's damage. This argument has been accepted by the English Court of Appeal in its decision in *Wright* v *Lodge*[22] where the defendant's post-accident reckless driving was held to constitute a *novus actus interveniens*, thereby relieving the third party co-defendant of any responsibility.

Contemporary Operation of *Novus Actus Interveniens* in the Contributory Negligence Context

Where the plaintiff's act follows upon the defendant's negligence and the acts of both the plaintiff and the defendant contribute to the plaintiff's harm, the case is *prima facie* one of contributory negligence on the plaintiff's part, leading to an apportionment of damages between the two of them if the plaintiff is adjudged not to have been exercising reasonable care for his or her own protection.[23] It still remains open to the defendant to allege that the plaintiff's supervening act is of such nature as to relieve the defendant entirely from responsibility. Nevertheless, it is only in exceptional cases like recklessness or gross negligence that courts will deny any recovery to the plaintiff;[24] in most cases the courts will nowadays apportion liability between the plaintiff and the defendant on the basis of their respective degrees of fault.[25]

There remain some operative contexts in which the courts are reluctant to adjudge the plaintiff either to have been contributorily negligent or to have committed a *novus actus interveniens*. This is the case with young children who are deemed not to have sufficient knowledge or life-experience to be adjudged civilly culpable. So, for instance, the Judicial Committee of the Privy Council refused to support a finding of contributory negligence against a nine-year-old boy on the basis that 'it was the very property of gasoline which he neither knew, nor could be expected to know, which brought about his misadventure.'[26] Similarly, in *Lynch* v *Nurdin*,[27] the conduct of the six-year-old boy in trespassing on an unattended horse-drawn cart was held not to constitute either contributory negligence on his part or a *novus actus*. Although the causal potency of the boy's conduct in relation to his injury was significant, the degree of self-care to be expected of a normal six-year-old boy was 'very small indeed'.[28]

---

21 McMahon and Binchy, *Irish Law of Torts*, 54.
22 [1993] 4 All ER 299 (CA). This case is examined in more detail in Chapter 8.
23 McMahon & Binchy, *Irish Law of Torts*, 45.
24 See, for example, the decision of the Supreme Court of Canada in *Dallaire* v *Paul-Emile Martel Inc.* [1989] 2 SCR 419.
25 McMahon & Binchy, *Irish Law of Torts*, 54.
26 *Yachuk* v *Oliver Blais Co. Ltd* [1949] 2 All ER 150, 154 (JCPC).
27 (1841) 1 QB 29. This case is examined in more detail in Chapter 2.
28 Ibid., 36 (*per* Lord Denman C.J.).

Recently, the defence of contributory negligence has been invoked in suicide cases.[29] Arguments have been advanced[30] that tortfeasors should not be unduly burdened with civil responsibility for the self-inflicted deaths of their victims and that a reduced recovery to the families of suicide victims is appropriate on the basis that their fault contributed to the damages suffered. As Professor Linden has suggested:

> Where the victims were so insane that they could not be held responsible for the suicide, the families may recover in full. Where the victims are lucid, and commit suicide without sufficient cause, the courts may attribute part, or even all, of the loss to what they might hold to be the contributory fault of the victims.[31]

The House of Lords has recently employed this approach in *Reeves* v *Commissioner of Police of the Metropolis*[32] where the defendant's *novus actus* plea that the deceased's prison suicide was a deliberate act was rejected. Rather, it was held, the deceased had responsibility for his own life and since his intentional act while of sound mind was a substantial cause of his death, the defence of contributory negligence should succeed. Responsibility for the prisoner's suicide was apportioned equally between the deceased and the defendant and the damages reduced accordingly under the *Law Reform (Contributory Negligence) Act 1945*. Historically, the defence of contributory negligence was seldom invoked or allowed to succeed in such cases.

In the workplace accident context, the contributory negligence approach is preferred to a finding of *novus actus interveniens* against the plaintiff worker. In the Australian decision of *Mount Isa Mines Ltd* v *Bates*,[33] for example, the plaintiff miner suffered injury when he struck a metal drill with a hammer in order to release it. A piece of metal flew into his eye and blinded him. Safety goggles had been provided to the plaintiff as a precaution against this type of injury but the plaintiff had failed to wear them. Such failure was held to have been reasonably foreseeable, and the defendant employer did not escape liability since the plaintiff's intervening foreseeable act, albeit negligent, did not sever the causal chain. Liability was therefore apportioned equally between the plaintiff and the defendant. The US courts have also adopted this approach in the case of an injured worker. In the case of *Anderson* v *Baltimore & Ohio Railroad Company*,[34] the Second Circuit Court of Appeals refused to find in the defendant railroad company's favour when the plaintiff's testator had been struck and killed by a locomotive engine while performing his employment duties as a fireman on a pusher engine. The Court stated:

> Granting that he was negligent in not observing the approaching engine, his contributory negligence does not preclude recovery in an action based on violation of the statutory

---

29 See generally Chapter 11.
30 A. Linden and B. Feldthusen *Canadian Tort Law* (Butterworths, 8th edn, 2006) 420.
31 Ibid.
32 [2000] 1 AC 360 (HL).
33 (1972) 46 ALJR 408; [1972–73] ALR 635. See also the decision of the Queensland Court of Appeal in *Hirst* v *Nominal Defendant* [2005] QCA 65; 2 Qd R 133 (trial Judge's one-third reduction in damages made for the contributory negligence of an on-duty police officer engaged in a high-speed pursuit upheld).
34 (1937) 89 F 2d 629.

duty, unless his act can be deemed a new and superseding cause of the accident. It is not considered as such when it is a normal reaction to the situation created by the defendant's wrong.[35]

Courts have also tended to prefer a contributory negligence approach in road accident cases (in which case the plaintiff victim is allowed recovery of reduced damages) over a *novus actus* approach (which would deprive the plaintiff of any recovery). In *Harris v Toronto Transit Commission*,[36] the plaintiff child's arm, which was protruding from a bus window, was fractured when the bus collided with a pole. In imposing partial liability, the Supreme Court of Canada considered that the bus driver 'should have foreseen the likelihood of child passengers extending their arms through the window, notwithstanding the warning'.[37] In motor vehicle accidents, a plaintiff's failure to take reasonable care for his or her own safety will generally be judicially perceived as contributory negligence rather than as amounting to a *novus actus interveniens*. The decision of the High Court of Australia in *March v E. & H. Stramare Pty Ltd*[38] supports this proposition. The defendant's servant had negligently parked a truck in the centre of a busy roadway. The plaintiff motorist, who was intoxicated and exceeding the speed-limit at the material time, was injured when he collided with the stationary but properly illuminated truck. The Supreme Court of South Australia held by a majority that the 'real cause' of the collision had been the plaintiff's negligence and recovery was denied. On further appeal to the High Court of Australia, the trial Judge's apportionment of responsibility under the *Wrongs Act 1936* (S.A.) as to 70 per cent to the plaintiff and 30 per cent to the defendants was restored. The plaintiff's negligence did not constitute a *novus actus* in the circumstances since the negligent act of someone such as the plaintiff driving into the truck was the very thing the defendant's employee should have anticipated. The High Court held that the truck driver owed a duty of care to all road users, including those whose faculties had been impaired by alcohol. The plaintiff's 'intoxication and associated carelessness took him within the class of inattentive drivers to whom the truck represented the greatest hazard'.[39] Once it was accepted that the defendant's servant owed such a duty of care, he could not rely on the plaintiff's conduct as having severed the causal chain.

A contributory negligence view of the plaintiff's behaviour has also been preferred in other contexts. In Canada, for example, when a person unreasonably refuses medical treatment, damages will be reduced, rather than denied altogether, on account of a failure to mitigate his or her loss.[40] And the English Court of Appeal has applied the ordinary principles of contributory negligence, rather than the *novus actus* doctrine,

---

35   Ibid., 631.
36   [1967] SCR 460.
37   Ibid., 465 (*per* Ritchie J.). See also *Bohlen v Perdue and City of Edmonton* [1976] 1 WWR 364 (Alta); *Wickberg v Patterson* (1997) 145 DLR (4th) 263 (Alta CA).
38   (1990–91) 171 CLR 506.
39   Ibid., 521 (*per* Deane J.).
40   *Ippolito v Janiak* (1981) 18 CCLT 39 (Ont. C.A.); *Brain v Mador* (1985) 32 CCLT 157 (Ont. C.A.).

in *Sayers* v *Harlow Urban District Council*.[41] There, a woman was trapped in a public lavatory through the defendant's negligence and was injured while trying to rescue herself from this predicament by climbing out. Although her conduct was not considered as 'unwise or imprudent, or rash or stupid' in the circumstances, the Court of Appeal held that the plaintiff 'cannot be absolved from some measure of fault'[42] and accordingly found her to be 25 per cent contributorily negligent.[43] Implicit in the reasoning of the judgments of the members of the Court of Appeal is the notion that a finding of gross negligence or recklessness against the plaintiff would have resulted in a *novus actus* determination. A number of Australian decisions also support the approach that the fair way to deal with the plaintiff's intervening negligence is to reduce the plaintiff's damages on the basis of contributory negligence and not treat such negligence as the exclusive cause of the loss.[44]

Conclusion

Contributory negligence has been defined by Lord Denning M.R. as a person's carelessness in looking after his or her own safety where it ought to have been reasonably foreseen in the circumstances that if he or she did not act as a reasonable prudent person, he or she might sustain injury.[45] The defence of contributory negligence is no longer a complete defence and it is now possible under apportionment legislation to produce a fairer result by apportioning responsibility between the defendant and the plaintiff.[46] Once the court has determined that the defendant has breached a duty to take reasonable care for the plaintiff's safety, the plaintiff's intervening negligent or unreasonable conduct should not ordinarily lead to a finding of *novus actus interveniens*. Nevertheless, can a point be reached where the plaintiff has contributed to such an extent to his or her injuries that it necessitates a finding that the plaintiff's conduct constitutes a *novus actus*, thereby disentitling the plaintiff to any damages? Some commentators and judges are of the view that such a point is reached where the plaintiff's conduct can be fairly described as reckless or grossly negligent in nature.[47] If that is the case, the emergence of apportionment legislation has effectively restricted the scope of application of the *novus actus* doctrine in those cases where the plaintiff's conduct has not been adjudged to be reckless or grossly negligent in nature.

---

41   [1958] 1 WLR 623 (CA). This case is examined in more detail in Chapter 4.
42   Ibid., 632 (*per* Morris L.J.).
43   See also *Jebson* v *Ministry of Defence* [2000] 1 WLR 2055 (CA).
44   See *Jacques* v *Matthews* [1961] SASR 205; *Charlton* v *Public Trustee for the Northern Territory* (1967) 11 FLR 42.
45   *Froom* v *Butcher* [1976] QB 286, 291 (CA).
46   See the judgment of Lord Pearce in *Imperial Chemical Industries Ltd* v *Shatwell* [1965] AC 656 (HL).
47   A.M. Dugdale and M.A. Jones (eds) *Clerk & Lindsell on Torts* (Sweet & Maxwell, 19th edn, 2006) [109] – [110] paras 2–96 and 2–97; McMahon and Binchy *Irish Law of Torts*, 54; C.D. Baker *Introduction to Tort* (Law Book Co. Information Services, 2nd edn, 1996) 228; *Wright* v *Lodge* [1993] 4 All ER 299 (CA) (third party co-defendant).

Chapter 19

The Inter-relationship Between Remoteness of Damage and *Novus Actus Interveniens*

Introduction

In a negligence action, the plaintiff must prove on a balance of probabilities that he or she was owed a duty of care by the defendant and that the defendant's breach of that duty caused a type or kind of injury to the plaintiff which was not too remote in the circumstances. In 1961 the Judicial Committee of the Privy Council reaffirmed in *Overseas Tankship (UK) Ltd* v *Morts Dock & Engineering Co. Ltd (The Wagon Mound (No. 1))*[1] that the legal test for remoteness of damage is reasonable foreseeability. In delivering the Board's judgment, Viscount Simonds stated:

> Their Lordships...have been concerned primarily to displace the proposition that unforeseeability is irrelevant if damage is 'direct'. In doing so, they have inevitably insisted that the essential factor in determining liability is whether the damage is of such a kind as the reasonable man should have foreseen.[2]

As we have already seen in Chapter 7, intervening causation issues have been linked to issues concerning the content and scope of the particular duty of care owed. Similarly, as we shall see in this brief chapter, both judges and legal scholars[3] have acknowledged a significant link between *novus actus interveniens* and remoteness of damage questions. In the Canadian case of *Cotic* v *Gray*[4] Lacourciere J.A. observed that remoteness of damage arguments are 'interwoven with' the *novus actus interveniens* doctrine and that these two matters 'cannot conveniently be segregated'.[5] Eminent judges have referred in their judgments to these two matters almost as if they were interchangeable or synonymous concepts. For example, Lord Wright has stated:

> There are invoked certain well-known formulae, such as that the chain of causation was broken, that there was a *novus actus interveniens*. These somewhat august phrases, sanctified as they are by standing authority, only mean that there was not such a direct

---

1 [1961] AC 388 (JCPC).
2 Ibid., 426.
3 B. McMahon and W. Binchy *Irish Law of Torts* (Butterworths, 2nd edn, 1990) 45.
4 (1981) 124 DLR (3d) 641 (Ont. C.A.).
5 Ibid., 652.

relationship between the act of negligence and the injury that the one could be treated as flowing directly from the other. Cases have been cited which have shown a very great difference of opinion on what is the true answer in different cases to that question whether the damage was direct or, on the other hand, to use another phrase, was too remote.[6]

Yet, the two concepts of *novus actus* and remoteness should theoretically be perceived, and historically have been perceived, as distinct in terms of both their role as judicially-created limitation of liability devices and their application. As one commentator has pointed out, some of the *novus actus* cases may be perceived to be more a matter of remoteness of damage than of causation, in that the question was not truly whether the defendant had caused loss to the plaintiff notwithstanding that an intervening event had directly brought it about and but for which there would have been *no* damage, but instead whether the defendant *should be* liable for having 'caused' the *additional* type of loss to the plaintiff which arose as a result of the intervening event, and where the original damage would have occurred even without such event.[7]

Early English Case-Law

Hoey v *Felton*,[8] a false imprisonment case, is one of the earlier cases where a *novus actus* was held to have broken the chain of causation, although the court's reasoning also included a remoteness of damage analysis. The plaintiff, a cigar-maker, went to the defendant's shop for refreshment, in payment for which he tendered money which was found to be bad. Thereupon the defendant uttered a slander against the plaintiff and detained him in custody for half an hour. The special damage allegedly sustained by the plaintiff was that he lost an employment opportunity with a cigar manufacturer. He claimed that he felt so unwell in consequence of the slander and detention that he was obliged to go home, thereby missing a job interview. In delivering the court's judgment, Erle C.J. held that the type of damage sustained by the plaintiff was too remote in the circumstances:

> In the present case, we think it was too remote. The damage does not immediately and according to the common course of events follow from the defendant's wrong...The wrong would not have been followed by the damage, if some facts had not intervened for which the defendant was not responsible. Thus, there was the act of the plaintiff, who returned home instead of going to the factory and explaining...[9]

Thus, the plaintiff's decision to return home rather than attend the scheduled interview was deemed sufficient to constitute a superseding cause of his own loss.

---

6 Lord v *Pacific Steam Navigation Co. Ltd (The Oropesa)* [1943] 1 All ER 211, 213 (CA).

7 P. Kaye *An Explanatory Guide to the English Law of Torts* (Barry Rose Law Publishers Ltd, 1996) 287.

8 (1861) 11 CB (NS) 142.

9 Ibid., 146.

In the 1889 case *The City of Lincoln*[10] the English Court of Appeal similarly employed a combined *novus actus*/remoteness of damage approach. In that case the barque *Albatross* was run into the by the steamer *City of Lincoln* in the North Sea. The steamer was solely to blame for the accident. As a result of the collision the barque was damaged and essential components of its navigational equipment were lost. The captain of the barque immediately made for a port of safety, navigating the vessel as best he could in the difficult circumstances. Nevertheless, the barque was grounded and subsequently necessarily abandoned. The Court of Appeal held that the owners of the steamer were liable for the loss of the barque.[11] Two of the three judges who sat on the case also adopted a remoteness analysis. Lord Esher M.R. considered that '[i]f the defendants have done a wrongful act, whereby the plaintiffs…have been deprived of the means of averting an accident which subsequently happens, the defendants are responsible for it and such accident…is not too remote.'[12] And Lindley L.J. framed as one of the questions to be decided 'whether the loss of the ship was not too remote a consequence of the collision to render the owners of the *City of Lincoln* responsible for the loss of the *Albatross*.'[13]

Contemporary English and Canadian Case-Law

English and Canadian courts in particular have continued on occasion to utilize 'remoteness' terminology in the context of determining intervening causation issues. In *Pigney* v *Pointer's Transport Services Ltd*[14] Pilcher J. had to decide

> …whether the suicide of the deceased constituted a *novus actus interveniens* which serves to break the chain of causation between his injury and his death, or whether upon the ordinary principles which govern remoteness of damage in cases of tort, the death of the deceased man was caused by the injury he received due to the defendants' lack of care for his safety.[15]

Likewise, in *Sayers* v *Harlow Urban District Council*[16] Lord Evershed M.R. considered whether the damage suffered by the plaintiff in attempting to escape from a locked public lavatory was 'too remote' in the course of determining intervening causation and contributory negligence issues.[17] And in *Home Office* v *Dorset Yacht Co. Ltd*[18] Lord Reid appears to have characterised as a remoteness of damage question the legal implications of the intervening acts of the escaped Borstal trainees.[19]

---

10   (1889) 15 PD 15 (CA).
11   See Chapter 2 where the court's reasoning on the *novus actus* issue is explained in more detail.
12   (1889) 15 PD 15, 17.
13   Ibid.
14   [1957] 1 WLR 1121. This case is examined in more detail in Chapter 11.
15   Ibid., 1123.
16   [1958] 1 WLR 623 (CA).
17   Ibid., 625.
18   [1970] AC 1004 (HL).
19   Ibid., 1027.

Perhaps the most notorious recent example of a court preferring a remoteness of damage approach over a causal approach is the 1981 decision of the English Court of Appeal in *Lamb* v *Camden London Borough Council*.[20] There the defendants admitted liability in nuisance when a broken water main caused damage to the plaintiff's house. However, the critical issue in this case was whether additional damage to the house caused subsequently by squatters was too remote or unforeseeable to form part of the damages payable by the defendants. Although the reasoning of the members of the Court of Appeal was not directly concerned with intervening causation issues, the intentional and criminal acts of the squatters were interposed between the defendants' negligence and the plaintiff's injury. While remoteness concerns appeared to underpin the judgments of Lord Denning M.R. and Oliver L.J., Watkins L.J. was more explicit. Although His Lordship regarded the damage perpetrated by the squatters 'as reasonably foreseeable in these times', Watkins L.J. had 'the instinctive feeling that [such] damage is too remote'.[21] The squatters' behaviour was considered 'unreasonable conduct of an outrageous kind' and 'this kind of anti-social and criminal behaviour provides a glaring example of an act which inevitably...is too remote to cause a defendant to pay damages for the consequences of it.'[22] Despite a remoteness and public policy[23] analysis, the same conclusion could have been reached through a duty of care approach (that is to say, whose legal responsibility was it to keep the squatters out) and a consideration of whether the intervening events which occurred were fairly to be regarded as coming within the scope of risks to be guarded against by the defendants.[24] Indeed, all three judges of the Court of Appeal referred extensively in their judgments to Lord Reid's *obiter* views expressed in *Home Office* v *Dorset Yacht Co. Ltd* on intervening causation.

Since the *Lamb* case, English courts have continued to intermingle intervening causation and remoteness issues. So, for example, in *Knightley* v *Johns*,[25] Stephenson L.J., in delivering the main judgment of the Court of Appeal, regarded the police inspector's negligence as 'the real cause of the plaintiff's injury and made that injury too remote from the [defendant's] wrongdoing to be a consequence of it'.[26] The Court of Appeal held that the inspector's negligence amounted to a *novus actus interveniens* in the particular circumstances of the case. In *Meah* v *McCreamer*[27] the plaintiff had been injured in a motor vehicle accident caused by the defendant's intoxicated driving. As a result of sustaining serious head injuries and brain damage, the plaintiff experienced a marked personality change. Almost four years after the accident, the plaintiff sexually assaulted and maliciously wounded several women, and was sentenced to life imprisonment. It was held that since but for the injuries received in the accident and the resulting personality change, the plaintiff would not

---

20 [1981] 1 QB 625 (CA). This case is examined in more detail in Chapter 3.
21 Ibid., 647.
22 Ibid.
23 See the judgment of Lord Denning M.R.
24 See Chapter 7.
25 [1982] 1 All ER 851 (CA). This case is examined in more detail in Chapter 3.
26 Ibid., 866.
27 [1985] 1 All ER 367 (QBD).

have committed the criminal acts, he was entitled to damages to compensate him for being imprisoned. Thus, the plaintiff's crimes were not considered to constitute a *novus actus interveniens*. Nevertheless, it was further held that the defendant was not liable to reimburse the plaintiff for damages he was required to pay to the rape victim in respect of her injuries on the ground of excessive remoteness of that further damage rather than on causal principles.[28] And in *Slipper* v *British Broadcasting Corporation*[29] Stocker L.J. considered as a remoteness of damage question whether the defendant should be liable for an unauthorised libel republication.[30]

Some Canadian courts have preferred a remoteness over a causal approach when dealing with cases where articles are stolen from someone left unconscious on the road or otherwise incapacitated as a result of negligent driving. In such cases the court has considered the *extent* of the defendant's liability to be the critical issue, in circumstances where the defendant's liability for the original injury is uncontroversial. In *Patten* v *Silberschein*[31] the defendant negligently ran down the plaintiff, a pedestrian. While he lay unconscious, the plaintiff lost $80 from his pocket. Although the British Columbia Supreme Court considered that the claim for the lost money was 'too remote' in the sense of not being 'the natural and probable consequence of the defendant's act of negligence', nevertheless it felt obliged to follow the decision of the English Court of Appeal in *Re Polemis*[32] and awarded damages to the plaintiff for the lost money as well as for his other accident-related losses. In *Duce* v *Rourke*,[33] however, an Alberta court refused to follow the *Patten* case and relieved the negligent defendant of liability for the loss of some tools which had been stolen from the injured plaintiff's car after he was taken to hospital. The court considered that *Polemis* did not apply to the theft which was a 'consequence of some conscious intervening independent act, for which the defendant was in no wise responsible'. The court refused to hold that the intervening criminal act constituted a *novus actus interveniens* on the ground that the theft should have been foreseen and guarded against by the original wrongdoer.[34] On basically the same facts, the Alberta court, unlike its British Columbia counterpart in *Patten*, preferred to determine the issues by applying intervening causation principles.[35]

---

28 *Meah* v *McCreamer (No. 2)* [1986] 1 All ER 943.
29 [1991] 1 QB 283 (CA). This case is examined in more detail in Chapter 17.
30 Ibid., 296. The overlap of remoteness of damage and intervening causation issues is also well illustrated in the recent Court of Appeal decision in *Corr* v *IBC Vehicles Ltd* [2006] 3 WLR 395.
31 [1936] 3 WWR 169 (B.C.).
32 [1921] 3 KB 560 (CA). This case merely required a causal link regardless of the degree of foreseeability.
33 (1951) 1 WWR (NS) 305 (Alta).
34 Ibid., 305–6.
35 See also *Jones* v *Shafer* [1948] SCR 166, 177 (*per* Locke J.) (damages occasioned by the criminal act of a third person in the circumstances of that case considered too remote for recovery).

Conclusion

At common law causation and remoteness of damage issues have always been considered discrete elements of a negligence action in respect of which the plaintiff carries the onus of proving. A court is best placed to determine how the particular issue is to be categorised in terms of presenting primarily an intervening causation or a remoteness question. What is undesirable and, indeed, unconventional, however, is for a court to regard such issue as a mixed or hybrid issue and to apply both causal and remoteness issues to its resolution. Were the intervening causation and remoteness tests identical, few problems would arise, but, as we have seen in earlier chapters, the reasonable foreseeability test has long since been abandoned as the predominant *novus actus* test, having been replaced by notions of voluntariness, unreasonableness, probability/likelihood, and an examination of the content and scope of the duty of care.[36] A conscious separation of these matters will avoid confusion in legal analysis and provide greater consistency in judicial decision-making.

---

36 See Chapters 3–7.

Chapter 20

Conclusion

Intervening causation issues have proven difficult and challenging for judges and scholars alike. In terms of their resolution, these issues appear to defy the application of any single or universal test, prompting one eminent English Law Lord to confess, 'I find it very difficult to formulate any precise and all-embracing rule.'[1] Having said that, Lord Wright proceeded to hypothesise what he considered necessary to sever the causal chain as follows:

> It must always be shown that there is something which I will call ultraneous, something unwarrantable, a new cause coming in disturbing the sequence of events, something that can be described as either unreasonable or extraneous or extrinsic. I doubt very much whether the law can be stated more precisely than that.[2]

It is thus not easy to prognosticate from the cases what test should be applied in deciding whether an intervening event has broken the chain of causation, and to reconcile cases that have been previously decided. That there is no such all-embracing formula to cover all cases involving intervening causation issues is due in part to the varying nature of intervening events and their surrounding circumstances. Resolving *novus actus* issues involves a determination of mixed questions of fact and law.[3] Cases involving such issues are fact- and circumstance-sensitive. The High Court of Australia has said that whether the chain of causation has been broken is 'a matter of circumstance and degree'[4] and 'a matter of fact and degree'[5] to be decided on the facts of each particular case. The judgment of Lord Wright in *The Oropesa*[6] is replete with references to the determinative influence of fact and circumstance in resolving intervening causation issues.[7]

Apart from the fact-sensitive nature of intervening causation cases and the absence of an all-embracing legal test to resolve them, the influence of policy-driven and intuitive judicial approaches must be acknowledged. In determining tortious liability in a context where the plaintiff's injury has been occasioned by multiple

---

1 *Lord* v *Pacific Steam Navigation Co. Ltd ('The Oropesa')* [1943] 1 All ER 211, 213 (CA) (*per* Lord Wright).
2 Ibid., 215.
3 *Roberts* v *Bettany* [2001] EWCA Civ. 109, para.12 (*per* Buxton L.J.).
4 *Chapman* v *Hearse* (1961) 106 CLR 112, 122.
5 *Mahony* v *J. Kruschich (Demolitions) Pty Ltd* (1985) 156 CLR 522, 528.
6 [1943] 1 All ER 211 (CA).
7 M. Lunney and K. Oliphant *Tort Law: Text and Materials* (Oxford University Press, 2000) 207 (whether an intervening event will be held to break the chain of causation is said to 'depend very greatly on the precise factual context in question').

contributing causes, judicial policy choices are necessitated in determining whether, and to what extent, the defendant should be held civilly responsible.[8] An American commentator has observed that what a court is really concerned with in determining whether intervening events constitute a superseding cause is some rule of law which restricts liability short of requiring the defendant to pay for all the harm caused by the breach of duty, and that such a restrictive rule is inevitably based on policy considerations.[9] McHugh J. of the High Court of Australia has explicitly and candidly referred to intervening causation issues as requiring 'policy choices whose objects are to limit legal responsibility'.[10] In alluding to a rule that enables a court to make a value judgement that in the circumstances legal responsibility does not attach to the defendant even though his or her negligence was a necessary condition of the plaintiff's loss, McHugh J. observed:

> Whatever label is given to such a rule – 'common sense principles', 'foreseeability', '*novus actus interveniens*', 'effective cause', 'real and efficient cause', 'direct cause', 'proximate cause' and so on – the reality is that such a limiting rule is the product of a policy choice that legal liability is not to attach to an act or omission which is outside the scope of that rule even though the act or omission was a necessary precondition of the occurrence of damage to the plaintiff. That is to say, such a rule is concerned only with the question whether a person should be held responsible for an act or omission which ex hypothesi was necessarily one of the sum of conditions or relations which produced the damage…That a policy choice is involved in the use of some rules which limit liability for wrongful acts or omissions is obvious…The rule that a defendant is not liable for damage which has been brought about by an overwhelming supervening event ('a *novus actus interveniens*') is also a rule of policy…[11]

Policy choices arise at the 'legal causation' stage.[12] While 'factual causation' is concerned with assessing whether the defendant's negligence is a *conditio sine qua non* of the plaintiff's injury, that is, whether the harm would have occurred 'but for' that negligence, legal causation moves beyond the scientific and historical reconstruction of events to policy issues of whether the defendant should be civilly responsible. Although a court may be satisfied that the defendant's negligence satisfies the 'but

---

8   D. Rosenberg *The Hidden Holmes: His Theory of Torts in History* (Harvard University Press, 1995) 69. In *The Queen in right of British Columbia* v *Zastowny* (2006) 269 DLR (4th) 510 (BCCA), a case involving the effect on the causal chain of the plaintiff's intervening criminal conduct, Saunders J.A. said (at 538), '[t]he issue is primarily one of causation and the tempering effect of public policy…', while Smith J.A. referred (at 549) to 'the judicial policy underlying the application of the *novus actus* doctrine'.
9   L.H. Eldredge *Modern Tort Problems* (George T. Bisel Company, 1941) 209.
10   *March* v *E. & M.H. Stramare Pty Ltd* (1990–91) 171 CLR 506, 532.
11   Ibid., 530–31. And see the judgment of McHugh J. in *Allianz Australia Insurance Ltd* v *GSF Australia Pty Ltd* (2004–2005) 221 CLR 568, 586–7 where His Honour stated: 'Where several factors operate to bring about the injury to a plaintiff, selection of the relevant antecedent (contributing) factor as legally causative requires the making of a value judgement and, often enough, consideration of policy considerations. This is because the determination of a causal question always involves a normative decision' (footnote omitted).
12   See Chapter 1 for a discussion of 'factual causation' and 'legal causation'.

for' test of factual causation, a *novus actus* plea may succeed on policy grounds if the court finds in light of subsequent events that the defendant should not be held accountable for consequences beyond his or her control.[13] Of course, public policy being a double-edged sword, it may well transpire that a court identifies a sufficient policy reason for not sustaining a *novus actus* plea. As Professor Fleming has said, whether the defendant's conduct was not only a factual but also a legal cause of the plaintiff's harm 'depends…on the policy to be pursued in delimiting legal responsibility for negligent conduct'.[14] As the answer to the legal causation enquiry involves intuitive and evaluative judgements[15] based on the judicial application of various public policy considerations, attaining predictability and uniformity in intervening causation cases may be more of an art than an exact science.

Numerous decisions discussed in previous chapters raised important and, indeed, in some cases, controversial public policy issues. As we have seen, courts have been reluctant to find that the intervention of a rescuer amounts to a *novus actus interveniens* in order to encourage altruism or, at least, not to discourage would-be Good Samaritans.[16] Courts have also proceeded cautiously in cases where the accident victim aggravates his or her injuries through deliberate misconduct, by taking to alcohol or drugs or attempting suicide[17] as a means of dealing with pain and suffering. So in *Yates* v *Jones*[18] the majority of the New South Wales Court of Appeal characterised the plaintiff's act of agreeing to have heroin injected into her

---

13   A.M. Dugdale and M.A. Jones (eds) *Clerk & Lindsell on Torts* (Sweet & Maxwell, 19th edn, 2006) [101], 2–78; *Wright* v *Lodge* [1993] 4 All ER 299 (CA); *Rouse* v *Squires* [1973] 1 QB 889, 898, (reckless driving may sever causal chain).

14   J. Fleming *The Law of Torts* (The Law Book Co. of Australasia Pty Ltd, 2nd edn, 1961) 193.

15   Eldredge, *Modern Tort Problems*, 208; M. Jones 'Multiple Causation and Intervening Acts' (1994) 2 *Tort Law Review* 133.

16   See Chapter 13 and cases like *Chapman* v *Hearse* (1961) 106 CLR 112; *Haynes* v *G. Harwood & Son* [1935] 1 KB 146 (CA); *Ward* v *T.E. Hopkins & Son Ltd* [1959] 3 All ER 225 (CA); *Brandon* v *Osborne Garrett and Company Limited* [1924] 1 KB 548.

17   See Chapter 11.

18   (1990) Australian Torts Reports 81-009 (NSWCA). This case is examined in more detail in Chapter 17. See also *State Rail Authority of New South Wales* v *Wiegold* (1991) 25 NSWLR 500 (NSWCA) where Samuels J.A. observed (at 514) (in the context of whether the plaintiff's intervening criminal conduct severed the causal chain), '[i]f the law of negligence were to say, in effect, that the offender was not responsible for his actions and should be compensated by the tortfeasor, it would…generate the sort of clash between civil and criminal law that is apt to bring the law into disrepute.' The *Wiegold* case is examined in more detail in Chapter 17. And in the same context, the majority of the British Columbia Court of Appeal has recently endorsed this public policy principle in *The Queen in right of British Columbia* v *Zastowny* (2006) 269 DLR (4th) 510, 538 (*per* Saunders J.A.), 550 (*per* Smith J.A.) where the trial Judge's award of damages for loss of employment income while he was incarcerated was deemed to be contrary to the policy principle that the criminal and civil law should avoid clashing with each other. See also to the same effect the judgment of Fish J. (for the majority) in *H. L.* v *Canada (Attorney General)* (2005) 251 DLR (4th) 604; [2005] 1 SCR 401, para. 137 ('to compensate an individual for loss of earnings arising from criminal conduct undermines the very purpose of our criminal justice system').

(allegedly as pain relief) by a 'casual acquaintance' as a *novus actus interveniens*, having been influenced by its assessment of public policy considerations and the normative effect of the criminal law on civil liability. The courts have also faced difficult questions in cases involving wrongful birth and unwanted pregnancy claims. In *CES* v *Superclinics (Australia) Pty Ltd*[19] the New South Wales Court of Appeal rejected the plaintiff's claim for the cost of raising her child after doctors had negligently failed to detect her pregnancy on the ground that the plaintiff's decision to not give up her newborn child for adoption constituted a *novus actus interveniens*. By contrast, the English Court of Appeal held in *Emeh* v *Kensington and Chelsea and Westminster Area Heath Authority*[20] that the plaintiff's refusal to have an abortion in connection with an unwanted pregnancy was not so unreasonable in the circumstances to warrant a finding of *novus actus interveniens* or a failure to mitigate damage. Determining *novus actus* pleas by resorting to an assessment of the reasonableness or otherwise of the plaintiff's conduct involves judges in classifying human behaviour in value-laden ways.[21]

A leading example of the significant influence of policy considerations in determining intervening causation issues is the approach taken by Lord Denning M.R. in *Lamb* v *Camden London Borough Council*.[22] The main issue in that case was whether the defendant council should be liable not only for damage to the plaintiff's house caused by a negligently-ruptured water main but also for damage subsequently caused to the house by squatters inhabiting it in the plaintiff's absence. Lord Denning referred to the utility of the concepts of duty of care, remoteness of damage and causation as limitation of liability devices but added, 'ultimately it is a question of policy for the judges to decide.'[23] The Master of the Rolls then proceeded to hold against the plaintiff property owner on the ground that there was no good policy reason to charge the depredations of the squatters to council revenue rather than to the insurance company with whom the plaintiff no doubt had a policy covering the damage.[24] The defendant council had no right to enter and secure the building and it was therefore incumbent on the plaintiff to adequately insure or otherwise protect himself against the risk of squatters.[25] Thus, the responsibility for guarding against such risk lay with the householder rather than the council and the former had essentially failed without sufficient excuse to better mitigate her damage.[26] Deciding in such circumstances who should bear the burden of the loss clearly involves underlying judicial value judgements and 'almost intuitive judgments about degrees of culpability, often concealed in appeals to colourful epithets and common sense'.[27]

---

19 (1995) 38 NSWLR 47 (NSWCA).

20 [1984] 3 All ER 1044 (CA). This case is examined in more detail in Chapter 4.

21 F. Trindade and P. Cane *The Law of Torts in Australia* (Oxford University Press, 3rd edn, 1999) 497.

22 [1981] 1 QB 625 (CA).

23 Ibid., 636.

24 Trindade and Cane, *The Law of Torts in Australia*, 497.

25 *Lamb* v *Camden London Borough Council* [1981] 1 QB 625, 637.

26 C.D. Baker *Introduction to Tort* (Law Book Company Information Services, 2nd edn, 1996) 229.

27 Jones, 'Multiple Causation and Intervening Acts', 136.

Conclusion

Despite the fact-sensitive nature of intervening causation cases and the intrusion of policy considerations and value judgements, certain general principles or propositions may be extracted from the case-law with a reasonable degree of confidence. They are:

1. If the act of the third party is unforeseeable (which is not that common a finding in these times[28]), the defendant will not be liable.[29]
2. The causal connection between the defendant's negligence and the plaintiff's injury may be negatived by grossly negligent or reckless conduct.[30]
3. The causal connection may similarly be negatived by what the court perceives to be a particularly unreasonable or abnormal response of either the plaintiff or a third party to the defendant's negligence.[31]
4. If the intervening conduct was the very risk of injury against which it was the defendant's duty to guard against so as to prevent injury to the plaintiff or someone in his or her class, then the causal connection will not be severed (the so-called 'scope of the risk' approach).[32]
5. Even if the intervening conduct was not the very risk of injury against which it was the defendant's duty to guard against, the causal chain will still not be severed if the intervening conduct was in the ordinary course of things and the very kind of thing which was likely or probable to happen as a result of the defendant's negligence.[33]
6. If the third party's act is intended by the defendant or is an inevitable response to the defendant's negligence, then that negligence will still be considered to be the legally operative cause of the plaintiff's injury.[34]
7. Subject to (4) above, if the third party's act is criminal, intentional or deliberate, it is more likely to be considered a *novus actus interveniens* than negligent intervening conduct. Nevertheless, even an intentional act of suicide committed while of sound mind may not sever the causal connection if this was the very risk to be guarded against by the defendant.[35] Similarly, the common law of various jurisdictions is now prepared to impose civil liability on a defendant for negligently providing an opportunity for third parties to cause deliberate harm where the scope of the defendant's duty of care extends to taking precautions to guard against that very eventuality.[36]

---

28 See the last section of Chapter 3 for the effect the decision of the Judicial Committee of the Privy Council in *Overseas Tankship (UK) Ltd* v *The Miller Steamship Co. Pty Ltd (The Wagon Mound (No. 2))* appears to have had on the application of the test of reasonable foreseeability.
29 See Chapter 3.
30 See Chapters 8 and 12.
31 See Chapters 4 and 10.
32 See Chapter 7.
33 See Chapter 6.
34 B. McMahon and W. Binchy *Irish Law of Torts* (Butterworths, 2nd edn, 1990) 53.
35 See Chapter 11.
36 See Chapter 5.

8. In cases involving especially young children, a *novus actus* plea will seldom succeed.[37]
9. Subject to a finding of recklessness, intervention by a rescuer will not ordinarily amount to a *novus actus interveniens*.[38]
10. The ordinary, as opposed to the extraordinary or unusual, operation of natural forces including weather conditions will not sever the causal chain since this must be anticipated and guarded against by the defendant.[39]
11. A causally independent event, the conjunction of which with the defendant's negligence is by ordinary standards so extremely unlikely as to be termed a coincidence, will amount to a *novus actus interveniens*.[40]
12. A *novus actus* plea will not normally succeed where a person imperilled by the defendant's negligence and facing imminent harm takes reasonable but unsuccessful measures to avoid that harm and is thereby injured.[41] The same principle would appear to apply to situations of significant inconvenience attributable to the defendant's negligence.[42]
13. A *novus actus* plea will not normally succeed where the defendant's negligence has created a weakened or physically vulnerable state in the plaintiff and the plaintiff subsequently sustains additional injury attributable to that negligence. Where, however, the second injury has been contributed to in part by the plaintiff's conduct, damages may be reduced under contributory negligence legislation.[43]

To quote from Lord Wright once again, 'I doubt very much whether the law can be stated more precisely than that.'[44] To formulate an over-arching general principle or underlying rationale or common thread from a comprehensive examination of the intervening causation case-law is a daunting task. Perhaps Lord Simonds was on the right track when he observed in *Hogan* v *Bentinck West Hartley Collieries (Owners) Ltd*[45] that 'the [intervening causation] question can only be answered on a consideration of all the circumstances and, in particular, of the quality of that later act or event.' In terms of the quality of the intervening event, the question involves an assessment of how independent or divorced from the defendant's negligence is that event or, conversely, how closely has that negligence impacted on that event. This notion of 'significant influence' is a possible underlying rationale which might explain most, if not all, of the outcomes in intervening causation cases. Some have suggested that it may be preferable if courts were to examine the situation actually created by the defendant's negligence and consider the extent to which the intervening

---

37 See Chapter 14.
38 See Chapter 13.
39 See Chapter 9.
40 *Haber* v *Walker* [1963] VR 339, 358 (*per* Smith J.).
41 See Chapter 15.
42 Ibid.
43 See Chapter 16.
44 *Lord* v *Pacific Steam Navigation Co. Ltd ('The Oropesa')* [1943] 1 All ER 211, 215 (CA) (*per* Lord Wright).
45 [1949] 1 All ER 588, 593 (HL).

event is shaped by that situation.[46] Although the defendant's negligence is a *conditio sine qua non* of the intervening event because that event would not have occurred at all but for that negligence, the intervening event should still be regarded as a *novus actus interveniens* 'if there is anything significant about it that is not conditioned or shaped by the situation created by [the defendant's negligence]'.[47] Conversely, if the situation created by the defendant's negligence is more than a mere necessary condition of the intervening event in that it shapes or impacts on that event to a significant degree, then the intervening event should not be held to constitute a *novus actus interveniens*.

Thus, an intervening event will be considered 'extraneous' or 'extrinsic'[48] if it is not predominantly shaped or conditioned by the situation created by the defendant's negligence. The application of this notion of 'significant influence' may be demonstrated by considering two cases which were examined in previous chapters.[49] In *Haber* v *Walker*[50] the plaintiff's husband's decision to commit suicide was predominantly conditioned or shaped by the situation created by the defendant's negligence because the husband's thought processes and behaviour had been altered to a significant degree by that negligence. As we have seen in Chapter 11, however, that is not always the case as suicide, especially when committed by a person of sound mind a considerable period of time after the defendant's negligence, can be considered sufficiently volitional and a product of the exercise of free will to amount to a *novus actus interveniens*. And in *The Oropesa*[51] the decision of Captain Raper of the *Manchester Regiment* to cross to the *Oropesa* in a lifeboat was predominantly conditioned by the crisis situation created by the negligent operation of both ships. If, however, hypothetically speaking, Captain Raper had responded to that crisis situation by ordering the plaintiffs' son to attempt to swim to the *Oropesa* during a storm to convey a message, such a response could be considered a *novus actus interveniens* as such an order would not be conditioned predominantly by the defendant's negligence but rather by Captain Raper's unrealistic assessment of the dangers involved in such a crossing and a swimmer's chance of surviving it. Thus, where the intervening event and the defendant's negligence are so closely connected, as where the intervening event is significantly related to the state of things generated by the defendant's negligence, the defendant will remain liable. Otherwise, he or she will be relieved of liability through a *novus actus* finding. Further elaboration and expansion of this underlying rationale and the above-mentioned general principles are tasks which will no doubt continue to occupy (and challenge) future judges and scholars.

---

46 M. Davies and I. Malkin *Torts* (LexisNexis Butterworths, 4th edn, 2003) 91.
47 Ibid.
48 '*The Oropesa*' [1943] 1 All ER 211, 215 (*per* Lord Wright).
49 These examples are taken from Davies and Malkin, *Torts*, 91–2.
50 [1963] VR 339. This case is examined in more detail in Chapter 11.
51 [1943] 1 All ER 211 (CA). This case is examined in more detail in Chapter 10.

Index

abnormality. *see* normality; reasonableness test
absence of tests 6–7, 259
accident insurance policies 143–4
accidental shootings
    dangerous chattels and substances 237–8
    intervening conduct of children 203–4
    liability of firearms owners for 15–16
accounting professions, intervening negligence by 186–7
acts of god 133
    flooding 136–7
    lightning 135–6
addiction, drug and alcohol 229–31, 230n20
Alberta Court of Appeal 233
Alberta Supreme Court 41, 79
alcohol addiction 229
alternative danger doctrine 14, 15–16, 66, 209–17
American Law Reports 167
animals, interventions by 141–2
apportionment legislation 247–8
arson cases 79–80
    foresight test in Canada 41
attractive nuisance doctrine 207
    see also children, intervening conduct of
attributive causation 5
Australia
    contributory negligence 250
    contributory negligence of the plaintiff 246
    dangerous chattels and substances 238
    deliberate interventions 83–8
    drug and alcohol addiction 229–31, 230n20
    escape from danger 212
    escape from inconvenience 215
    extraordinary natural phenomena 139
    foresight test 43–6
    fraud by plaintiffs 232
    High Court of 43–4, 46, 62–4, 84–5, 87–8, 107–8, 110–11, 122, 124, 137, 139, 173, 185–7, 215, 250, 259
    inadequate warnings 239, 240–1
    infection of injuries 145
    intervening conduct of children 204
    intervening negligent legal advice 185–6
    intervening negligent omissions 130
    lower courts 45–6, 64
    medical negligence 171–4, 174n23
    negligence causing susceptibility to later harm 220, 221–2, 223–5
    New South Wales Court of Appeal 45, 64, 85–7, 108–9
    ordinary intervening negligent acts 122, 124
    prisoner suicides 159n21
    probability test 97–8
    reasonable foreseeability 32
    reasonableness test 62–4
    refusal to accept medical treatment 182
    rescue cases 191, 192
    scope of risk approach 107–12
    state courts 44–5
    suicide cases 160–1
    Supreme Court of New South Wales 191
    Supreme Court of Queensland 109, 238
    Supreme Court of South 45, 64, 220, 223–4, 239, 250
    Supreme Court of Victoria 84n102, 109, 159n21, 160, 204
    Victorian Court of Appeal 109
    wrongful birth claims 184–5

British Columbia Court of Appeal 80, 130, 164, 177
British Columbia Supreme Court 78
but for test 3, 5, 44

Canada
    Alberta Supreme Court 41, 79

British Columbia Court of Appeal 80
contributory negligence 250
deliberate intervention 77–81
fatal accidents legislation 164–5
foresight test 39–42
intervening conduct of children 206
intervening gross negligence 127–8
intervening negligence as *novus actus interveniens* 125
medical negligence 174–7
medical rescue 197
negligence causing susceptibility to later harm 220, 223
negligent inspection 232–3
nineteenth century case 23
Nova Scotia Court of Appeal 124
novus actus interveniens and remoteness of damage 253, 257
Ontario Court of Appeal 39, 40, 124, 165, 175
ordinary intervening negligent acts 122
prisoner suicide cases 164
rape and arson cases 79–80
reasonableness test 65–6
refusal to accept medical treatment 182
rescue cases 190
rescue of property 196
scope of risk approach 112–13
suicide cases 164–6
Supreme Court of 39, 40, 65–6, 77, 78, 96–7, 112, 122, 127–8, 185, 196, 208
car accidents. *see* motor vehicle accidents
causation, factual and legal 5–6, 260–1
Causation in the Law (Hart & Honore) 88, 101
chain of causation
  breaking by intervening gross negligence 127–8
  first English case to refer to 24–5
  impact of deliberate interventions 69–71
  impact of intentional criminal conduct 74–5
  intervening negligence as breaking 125
chattels and substances, dangerous 237–9
children, intervening conduct of 88–9, 199–200, 238
  and contributory negligence 17, 248
  and deliberate intervention 73
  development of case law 200–7
Civil Liabilities (Contribution) Act 1978 (England) 247

coincidences 139–41
concurrent wrongdoers 247–8
conduct necessary to exercise legal rights or privileges 227–8
contributory negligence
  and action of children 17
  defence of 10
  of the plaintiff 245–7, 248–51
Court of Common Pleas 103, 189
criminal intervention 45, 48–9, 70, 74–5, 81–3

dangerous chattels and substances 237–9
Davies, M. 49
defamation and publication 235–7
deliberate interventions
  Australia 83–8
  Canada 77–81
  French Cour de cassation 89
  impact on chain of causation 69–71
  intentional criminal conduct 74–5
  Ireland 89
  New Zealand 88–9
  Papua New Guinea 89
  rescue cases 73
  United Kingdom 71–7
dependent intervening force 9
direct consequence test (England) 13
disease contracted due to lowered vitality 142–4
drug addiction 229–31, 230n20
duty-based approach. *see* scope of risk approach

England
  cases during nineteenth century 14–25, 14–27
  cases prior to nineteenth century 13–14
  first case to refer to 'chain of causation' 24–5
  first decision based on probability 22
  medical negligence 177–81
  see also United Kingdom
English Court of Appeal 55, 73, 103–4, 105, 122–3, 124–5, 126–7, 139, 142, 147–9, 156, 158, 158n16, 177–8, 180–1, 192, 198, 202–3, 216, 236, 247–8, 250–1, 255
  foresight test 38
  probability test 92–4
escape from danger and inconvenience 209–10

development of case law (danger) 210–13
development of case law (inconvenience) 213–16
explosive substances 238–9
extraordinary natural phenomena 133–9

factual causation 5, 260–1
fatal accidents legislation 157–8, 164–6
firearms cases 237–8
    intervening conduct of children 203–4
    owner's liability for accidental shootings 15–16
Fleming, John 6, 7, 49, 234, 261
flooding 136–8
foresight test
    Australia 43–6
    Canada 39–42
    endorsement of 33
    Europe 48–9
    judicial initiative to dilute 50
    New Zealand 47–9
    plaintiff as author of intervening event 33–4
    and probability of event 32–9
    rejection of 33–5
    suitability of 35–8, 49–50
    United Kingdom 32–9
    United States of America (USA) 42–3
    use of 31–2
fraud by plaintiffs 232
French Cour de cassation
    deliberate interventions 89
    foresight test 48–9

Germany
    medical rescue 197–8
    Schutzzweck der Norm 101
    scope of risk approach 116–17
Goodhart, A.L. 8, 191n22

Hart, H.L.A. 88, 101
High Court of Australia 6–7, 43–4, 46, 48, 84–5, 87–8, 110–11, 122, 124, 137, 173, 185–7, 215, 247, 250, 259
History of English Law, A (Holdsworth) 133, 141
Holdsworth, W. 133, 141
Holmes, O.W. 31
Honore, T. 88, 101
hospitals
    institutional liability 234
    negligence of in suicide cases 163, 164
House of Lords 77, 94–5, 106–7, 125, 137, 138, 148–9, 149–50, 158, 178–9, 184, 213, 222, 233, 234, 235, 249

inadequate warnings 239–41
independent intervening force 9
infection of injuries 144–6
inflammable substances 238–9
injure, intent of defendant to 16
inspection, negligent/omission of 232–3
institutional liability 233–4
insurance policies 143–4
intervening causation 3–4
    absence of tests 259
    challenging nature of cases 6–7
    and contributory negligence defence 10
    general principles from case law 263–4
    need for judicial policy choices 260–2
    negligence as 20–1
    and reasonable foreseeability 10
    varying nature of events and circumstances 6–7, 259
    voluntary and deliberate 21–2
intervening criminal conduct 45, 48–9, 70, 74–5, 81–3
intervening events
    plaintiff as author of 33–4
    third party criminal 45
    by third person 34–5
    see also deliberate interventions
intervening force 8–9
intervening gross negligence 125–8
intervening negligent omissions 129–31
intervening omissions 40, 45–6
intervening ordinary negligence 121–5
Ireland
    conduct necessary to exercise legal rights or privileges 228
    Court of Appeal 116
    dangerous chattels and substances 237
    escape from danger 212
    intervening conduct of children 203, 204
    intervening negligent omissions 131
    nineteenth century case 19
    ordinary intervening negligent acts 121, 122
    probability test 98–9
    reasonableness test 66
    scope of risk approach 116
    Supreme Court of 98–9

joint liability 247–8
judges
    use of Latin phrases 7–8
    use of metaphor and descriptive terms 7
judicial policy choices, need for 260–2

kidney donation cases 197–8
knowledge of dangerous situations, plaintiff's 18

last human wrongdoer rule 14–15
    reduced use of 121
last opportunity rule 246
Law Reform (Contributory Negligence) Act 1945 (England) 246–7
legal causation 5–6, 260–1
legal professions, intervening negligence by 185–7
liability of firearms owners 15–16
likelihood
    first English decision based on 22
    suitability of 35–8
Linden, A. 181, 223, 249
Lord Campbell's Act 1843 19

Manitoba Court of Appeal 39–40, 190
maritime incidents 22, 92, 147–54
    heavy weather at sea 138–9
    intervening recklessness 128
    reasonableness test 53–5
    rescue of property 196
McNaghten Rule of criminal responsibility 156, 156n7, 158, 162
medical negligence 169
    Australia 171–4, 174n23
    Canada 174–7
    England 177–81
    United States of America (USA) 170–1
    see also refusal to accept medical treatment
medical rescue 196–8
mental institutions and institutional liability 234
motor vehicle accidents
    contributory negligence 250
    and contributory negligence 250
    intervening gross negligence 126–7
    ordinary intervening negligence acts 121–4
    suicide cases 157–8

National Court of Justice of Papua New Guinea 48, 98
natural phenomena, extraordinary 133–9
negligence
    conduct of third parties 47–8
    intervening 20–1
    of a municipal corporation 46
    see also medical negligence
negligence, intervening ordinary 121–5
negligence causing susceptibility to later harm 219–20
    development of case law 220–4
negligent inspection 232–3
negligent rescue attempts 193–5
New Brunswick Court of Appeal 234
New South Wales, Supreme Court of 191
New South Wales Court of Appeal 45, 64, 85–7, 183, 221, 229–31, 238, 241, 261–2
New Zealand
    Court of Appeal 7, 88, 113–14, 162, 163, 239
    dangerous substances 239
    deliberate interventions 88–9
    foresight test 47–8, 47–9
    hospital negligence 163
    inadequate warnings 240
    infection of injuries 145
    intervening conduct of children 206
    probability test 98
    reasonable foreseeability 32
    scope of risk approach 113–15
    suicide cases 162–3
Nineteenth century
    cases during 14–27
    cases prior to 13–14
normality 59–61
    see also reasonableness test
Nova Scotia Court of Appeal 124
novus actus interveniens 3–4
    as breaking chain of causation 18–19
    challenging nature of cases 6–7
    concurrent wrongdoers context 247–8
    and contributory negligence defence 10
    definition 9–10
    emergence of judicially-developed doctrine 15
    first English case to refer to 24–5
    intervening negligence as 125
    as Latin term 8
    link with remoteness of damage 253–8

unreasonable intervening conduct 19–20
varying nature of events and circumstances 6–7, 259

omissions, intervening 40, 45–6
   inspection 232–3
   medical 177
Ontario Court of Appeal 39, 40, 124, 165, 175

Papua New Guinea
   deliberate interventions 89
   foresight test 48
   probability test 98
passing off actions 231–2
personality changes 75–6
plaintiffs
   as author of intervening event 33–4
   contributory negligence by 245–7, 248–51
   disease contracted due to lowered vitality 142–4
   fraud by 232
   intervening negligence of 123–4
   knowledge of dangerous situation 18
   meritorious conduct of 79
   trespass by 17–18
   unreasonable intervening conduct by 19–20
policy choices, judicial, need for 260–2
prisoners
   institutional liability 233–4
   suicide cases 158–60, 164
probability
   of actions 23
   Australia 97–8
   first English decision based on 22
   and the foresight test 32–9
   Ireland 98–9
   New Zealand 98
   Papua New Guinea 98
   Scotland 92
   suitability of 35–8
   United Kingdom 91–5
   United States of America (USA) 95–6
   use of 91
property, rescue of 195–6
proximate cause formula (USA) 13
publication 235–7

Queensland Supreme Court 109, 238

rainfall, heavy 136–7
rape cases 79
reasonable foreseeability 24
   Australia 43–6
   Canada 39–42
   endorsement of 33
   Europe 48–9
   judicial initiative to dilute 50
   New Zealand 47–9
   plaintiff as author of intervening event 33–4
   rejection of 33–5
   suitability of 35–8, 49–50
   United Kingdom 32–9
   United States of America (USA) 42–3
   use of 31–2
reasonableness test 51
   Australia 62–4
   Canada 65–6
   concerns around 66
   Ireland 66
   maritime collisions 53–5
   rescue cases 54
   United Kingdom 52–9
   United States of America (USA) 61
recklessness. *see* intervening gross negligence
refusal to accept medical treatment 181–3
   contributory negligence 250
remoteness of damage 18–19
   link with *novus actus interveniens* 253–8
rescue cases 189–90
   deliberate intervention 73
   development of case law 190–2
   probability 92–4
   reasonableness test 54
Restatement of the Law of Torts, Second (American Law Institute)
   coincidences 140, 141
   exercise of legal rights or privileges 227
   foresight test 43
   functional capacity of children 208
   intervening gross negligence 126
   intervening negligent omissions 129–30
   interventions by animals 142
   liability for acts performed during insanity 167
   negligence causing susceptibility to later harm 219
   negligent rescue cases 193

normality 59
ordinary/extraordinary negligence 170–1
probability 95
rescue cases 190–1
rescue of property 196
scope of risk approach 115–16
voluntary and deliberate human action 70, 76–7
road accidents and contributory negligence 250
see also motor vehicle accidents

sane-insane dimension of suicide cases 155–68
schools and institutional liability 234
Schutzzweck der Norm 101
scientific causation 5
scope of risk approach
    Australia 107–12
    Canada 112–13
    concerns over 117
    emerging use of 101–2
    Ireland 116
    New Zealand 113–15
    United Kingdom 102–7
Scotland
    probability test 92
    suicide cases 156
self-rescue 55–6, 198, 216
    and contributory negligence 251
several liability 247–8
shootings, accidental
    dangerous chattels and substances 237–8
    intervening conduct of children 203–4
    liability of firearms owners for 15–16
significant influence notion 264–5
slander cases 14–15
spousal desertion after disfiguring/debilitating accident 229
Squib case 13–14, 32, 52, 70, 71, 91, 210
substances, dangerous 238–9
suicide cases
    Australia 160–1
    Canada 164–6
    and contributory negligence 249
    England 155–60
    foresight test in Canada 41–2
    institutional liability 234
    motor vehicle accidents 157–8
    New Zealand 162–3

prisoners 158–60
sane-insane dimension 155–68
United Kingdom 155–60
United States of America (USA) 166–7
superseding cause doctrine 3
    definition 9, 10
    nineteenth century USA cases 25–7
Supreme Court of Canada 39, 40, 65–6, 77, 78, 96–7, 112, 122, 127–8, 185, 196, 205, 208
Supreme Court of Ireland 98–9
Supreme Court of New South Wales 191
Supreme Court of Pennsylvania 122, 207
Supreme Court of Queensland 109
Supreme Court of South Australia 45, 64, 223–4, 239, 250
Supreme Court of Tasmania 145–6
Supreme Court of the USA 82–3, 115–16, 135, 137–8, 204–5
Supreme Court of Victoria 84n102, 109, 159n21, 160, 204
susceptibility to later harm, negligence causing 219–20
    development of case law 220–4

Tasmania 145–6
tests, absence of 6–7, 259
third party intervention 45, 47–9
    criminal 70
    deliberate 69–71

United Kingdom
    conduct necessary to exercise legal rights or privileges 227–8
    contributory negligence of the plaintiff 246
    dangerous chattels and substances 237–9, 238–9
    defamation/publication 235–7
    deliberate human action 71–7
    disease contracted due to lowered vitality 143–4
    escape from danger 210–11, 212–13
    escape from inconvenience 213–15, 216
    extraordinary natural phenomena 135–6, 137
    foresight test 32–9
    infection of injuries 144, 145
    intervening conduct of children 200–3, 205–6
    intervening gross negligence 126–7

intervening negligence as *novus actus interveniens* 125
intervening negligent omissions 129–31, 131
interventions by animals 141–2
last opportunity rule 246
maritime incidents 147–52
medical negligence 177–81
negligence causing susceptibility to later harm 220–1, 222–3
negligent inspection 232–3
negligent rescue attempts 193–4
novus actus interveniens and remoteness of damage 254–7
ordinary intervening negligent acts 122–3
probability test 91–5
reasonableness test 52–9
refusal to accept medical treatment 181, 182–3
rescue cases 191–2
rescue of property 196
scope of risk approach 102–7
suicide cases 155–60
wrongful birth claims 184
United States of America (USA)
contributory negligence 249–50
escape from danger 211
extraordinary natural phenomena 135
foresight test 42–3
intermediate appellate courts 59–61
intervening conduct of children 204–5, 206–7
intervening criminal conduct 81–3
intervening gross negligence 128
intervening negligence case 21
maritime incidents 152–3
medical negligence 170–1
normality approach 59–61
ordinary intervening negligent acts 121, 124
probability test 95–6
proximate cause formula in nineteenth century 13
reasonableness test 61
rescue cases 190–1
rescue of property 195
scope of risk approach 115–16
Sixth Circuit Court of Appeals 124
suicide cases 166–7
superseding cause doctrine 25–7
Supreme Court 82–3, 115–16, 135, 137–8, 204–5
Supreme Court of Pennsylvania 122
wrongful birth claims 183n73
unreasonable intervening conduct 19–20
see also reasonableness test

vandalism, intervening acts of 41
Victorian Court of Appeal 109
voluntariness. *see* deliberate intervention

Wagon Mound cases 10, 33, 36, 253
warnings, inadequate 239–41
Williams, G. 140
workers' compensation cases 144–6, 155–7, 171–2, 177–9, 181, 249
wrongful birth 183–5